Jane Lakeland   1985

THE SCIENCE OF
TRACK AND FIELD
ATHLETICS

HOWARD AND ROSEMARY PAYNE

THE SCIENCE OF
TRACK AND FIELD
ATHLETICS

Foreword by Arthur Gold, CBE
President of the European Athletic Association

PELHAM BOOKS
LONDON

The authors would like to say a special thank you to Glenis Barry, Renate Cleaver, Charles Elliott, Paul Gustafson, Pauline Hill, Frank McDonald, Bill Marlow, Margaret Morby, Andrew Payne, Russell Payne, Roy Posner and Betty Wright for their help with this book.

First published in Great Britain by
Pelham Books Ltd
44 Bedford Square
London WC1B 3DU
1981

British Library Cataloguing in Publication Data

Payne, Howard
    The science of track and field athletics.
    I. Title   II. Payne, Rosemary
    796. 4'2

ISBN 0 7207 1288 2

Printed by Hollen Street Press, Slough
Bound by Dorstel, Harlow

CONTENTS

FOREWORD by Arthur Gold, CBE
President of the European Athletic Association

Athletes and coaches who take thought to add a cubit to their stature have always attracted my special admiration, and in *The Science of Track and Field Athletics* Howard and Rosemary Payne have produced a book that should play its part in providing every thinking athlete and coach with information that will enable him or her to add that extra cubit to their performance.

More than forty years ago the late F.A.M. Webster wrote a book called *WHY (The Science of Athletics)*. Rosemary and Howard now set out to tell you HOW. Both have had exceptionally long and successful careers as athletes —I remember them as sterling performers in the 1963 Great Britain team which defeated Russia at Volgagrad—but in addition to them being fine competitors they have specialist knowledge of science and psychology, on which two pillars modern athletics stands.

It has been my privilege in the past to lead teams in which the Paynes were part of the power house. Now I hope that they, in turn, will lead the reader towards improving his power and using it more effectively and efficiently.

INTRODUCTION

GENERAL

Athletics is an activity in which millions of people throughout the world participate and in which many more millions take an interest through the media. Athletics is directly and indirectly a major industry involving high finance, despite the amateur rules forbidding the athletes themselves from 'securing any material gain from such competition'. It is also a powerful political tool and considered by many nations to be a means of gaining national prestige. At the highest level of participation it forms the centrepiece of the Olympic Games, and at its lowest level it provides countless athletes of all ages with enjoyment of physical exercise and the thrill of competition. For the latter it is a sport in the sense that sport is a pastime, but the higher the level the less it is a sport and the more it is a full-time occupation. However it is in the very nature of competition that an athlete at any level should wish to improve his or her performance.

In the early days—though 'early' is only a relative term in organized athletics, and in this instance refers to a time as recent as the 1930s—many athletes considered that training for a race diminished their energies. After the Second World War, however, an explosion of experimentation took place in athletics training and training methods. Much of it was merely trial and error, but some was also trial and success and gradually a body of knowledge began to accumulate. Attitudes towards the sport changed and created a greater public awareness of the thrills of the competition when men and women contested the basic skills of walking, running, jumping, hurdling and throwing. Nations came off a war footing and national pride was diverted into sport, in which entire populations could identify with a soccer team or an individual in an important Games. Political attitudes began to change with this realization of the power of sport in national prestige. The Soviet Union was the first nation to surprise the rest of the world with its organized backing of sport and sportsmen with which it gained so much success in the 1950s and 1960s. While the Western World puzzled over this new approach to sport, the East Germans learned the lesson quickly and were ready when the rest of the world recognized their nation in the late 1960s. Not only did they encourage the popular events such as men's middle distance, but they also poured resources into the relatively unknown women's athletics events. They appreciated the simple principle that an Olympic medal is an Olympic medal, whether it is for the men's 1,500 metres or the women's shot, while the Western World had (and still has) an active distaste for 'grunting ladies heaving metal weights around'.

Changing attitudes to athletics have encouraged, and continue to encourage, the gathering of knowledge about training, and about the human body and human mind that make up the athletes. Gradually the old ideas and the hit-or-miss methods are being displaced by a more orderly and systematic approach to training and the development of athletes. One of the dictionary definitions of science calls it a body of accumulated knowledge. So the science of track and field athletics is growing steadily and helping athletes not only to avoid the avenues of wasted effort but to take the roads that give maximum results in the time available.

The 'Gap'

Nevertheless, the gathering of this knowledge is still relatively disorganized and most of the scientific work is concentrated in only a few centres—some countries loathe to share their medal-winning knowledge with others. Even of this limited output very little actually finds its way in an intelligible form to the athlete himself. A lot of it never reaches him in any form at all! In recognition of the problem of communication, an important international conference was held a few years ago before the start of a major Games. It was entitled 'Bridging the Gap'—meaning the gap between scientific knowledge and its practical application by the athlete on the track. However, the proceedings of that conference have not been published and only the delegates actually present at each presentation are any the wiser. That conference, typical of many like it, perpetrated the very lack of communication it set out to discuss and resolve.

The Language of Science

The language of the scientist is a special one which is quite unintelligible to most laymen. The symbols, especially, which the scientist tosses around so casually, are meaningless to most athletes and coaches unless they are translated into everyday language. Even more, they need to be translated into a 'language of feeling' which the athlete can work for when performing his skill at high speed. To tell a high jumper to increase the angular momentum of his free swinging leg by so many units at take-off is to invite a blank stare, but he will understand if he is told to swing the leg a little faster and higher while trying to keep it straight at the knee. The scientist must be patient in explaining his results to coaches, and they in turn must be able to communicate the essentials of this information to the athletes. The scientist, by the very nature of his calling, has to be thorough and investigate the minute details of his project—but not all of these will benefit the athlete directly.

In the reverse direction, feedback from coach to scientist should ensure that the scientist does not waste his time in pursuing research that will not be of practical use. The athlete and coach, therefore, also have a responsibility in ensuring that the scientist knows about the problems that concern them.

The so-called 'gap' is really a problem, then, of two-way communication. Ideally the person who undertakes the research should be a 'sports scientist', of that new breed who themselves understand the needs of athletes. The 'sports doctor', for example, is better able to realize that an injured athlete must weigh up the advantage of resting his injury against the disadvantage of losing condition because of lack of training, and he will prescribe treatment to hasten recovery, which the average general practitioner would not even consider.

Explanation or Prediction

Much of the scientific analysis carried out on athletes and their events serves only to explain existing techniques, and very little prediction or innovation is suggested by the scientists. This is partly due to the fact that many coaches and some athletes have been, and are, experimental scientists in their own amateurish ways, forever looking for the secrets of success, sometimes deliberately trying a new technique and sometimes stumbling on a method that leads to better performance. The fibreglass pole was the result of deliberation, the Fosbury Flop came about because Dick Fosbury could not perfect the straddle-type high jump, and his 'dangerous' bar clearance attempts coincided with the introduction of raised-up foam landing areas.

Quite often the 'scientific' discoveries of coaches and athletes are foiled by sport administrators, even if for good reasons. The discus-type turn and delivery of the javelin produced world record distances by the average-to-good javelin-thrower in the 1950s, but this had to be disallowed by new rules to ensure the safety of other people inside the stadium. Similarly the simple solution to the angular momentum problem of the long jump take-off that suggested a front somersault in flight was banned by the authorities, who worried about the safety of the long jumpers themselves.

Experimentation in Athletics

In studying the physical world the scientist can merely observe and record what he sees, or he can experiment, interfering with the process he is studying and noting the effect it has. Better still, he can move into the laboratory where he can vary one condition at a time and record the effect while keeping the other conditions constant. His work becomes difficult when it is not possible to control the other variables, or when moving into the laboratory changes the environment so much that there is no correlation with the process when it was 'natural'. For example the sports physiologist has always to be on his guard against assuming too much from his laboratory results and expecting that they will necessarily apply to the athlete on the track. The classic example of an apparently similar movement producing different results in the laboratory is that of treadmill running, which has aspects which do not correlate with those of track running. The process of simply moving the athlete into a controlled environment without other competitors means that the most essential condition of athletics has been removed—the competition. 'Competing' against machines and measuring devices is not quite the same as having another human being pounding behind you as you both sprint for the finishing line. Controlling the variables in an experiment with an athlete should not also mean removing the variables altogether. The variable conditions should still be there, but should be kept as constant as possible. The trouble with the human being in a sport like track and field athletics is that the number of variables is very large and it is virtually impossible to control all of them. The physical educationist will turn to statistical methods to assist him in drawing his conclusions, but the coach and the athlete are not too much concerned with what applies to an average population, even if it is an elite population—they are working to make the athlete unique, so that he will be a champion. Art can be said to be an area of human activity in which the number of variables has become very large and the number of possibilities for manifestation have become infinite. If this is so, we can well understand why coaching has been described as an art. However, the artist must have knowledge of the media in which he works, he must have knowledge of the techniques established in his art, and he must choose the subject that is going to produce a satisfactory end result. The coach similarly must have knowledge of the athletic skill he is coaching and he must have knowledge of the probable results of his use of various training methods. He too must be able to judge how a particular novice is likely to progress and, if it is a champion he wants, he must choose his athlete carefully.

Applying the Results of Research
Although the number of variables in athletic activities is large, scientific study can at least resolve the likely outcome of a particular change in conditions. For example, even though there is still much to be learned, high altitude training for distance runners has been shown by scientific investigation to have a beneficial effect on runners' performances when they return to sea level. On the other hand it has been much more difficult to establish how much long, steady distance running a middle distance athlete should undertake in relation to his faster track sessions. Many champions have included a great deal of long, steady distance in their training and been convinced that it was the reason for their successes, whereas others have been just as success-ful doing most of their work on the track with interval training, in which relatively short runs at high intensity, interspersed by short rests, are carried out. The calm scientific resolution of this question of how much of each type of training to include is clouded by the subjective preference by most runners for the more enjoyable long steady distance work. For many this is the moti-vation, whereas for the very reason that it is more enjoyable some will turn to interval training in the belief that an athlete must suffer in order to improve! The 'scientific' coach will look at it more logically and, even though he is unable to allocate exact proportions of training, he will advocate some long, steady distance and some interval training, probably varying the amounts according to the needs of the individual athlete and the time of year. The coach will recognize, too, that it is wise to vary the training schedule to aid in the motivation of the athlete, and he may even prescribe methods of train-ing which will have little to do with the event in terms of physical benefit in

order to gain a psychological one. In doing this the coach is employing one scientific discipline for a while at the expense of another.

Even within one area there may be similar conflict. The very large number of variables accompanying the athlete in his event sometimes leads to the paradoxical situation in which one sound scientific principle directly opposes another just as sound scientific principle. For example, there are biomechanical reasons for driving the hips into the delivery action of a throw, but there are also biomechancial reasons for driving the hips in the opposite direction to the throw. In this particular example the other technical requirements come down in favour of the first alternative in discus and shot, whereas the second is preferable in the javelin delivery.

The Neutrality of the Scientist

Athletes should also understand that, although the scientist does have a code of ethics in relation to his human 'guinea pigs' during his experiments, he does not judge the morals of the eventual outcome of the knowledge he produces. He deals with the efficiency of the human machine, and, as long as he ensures that the subject is placed in no medical danger, he does not dwell on the question of whether it is right or wrong that an athlete should gain an advantage in competition, when for example, he experiments with the so-called 'blood-doping' of a subject.

Even something as controversial as drug-taking is considered in some countries to be within the legitimate experimental scope of the physiologist. But there are also many grey areas of experimental work in sport, and science would be poorer without this type of work, even though it may be argued that athletics is better without the results. The electric stimulation of muscles to improve strength is one such area now being researched in many laboratories throughout the world. Like 'blood-doping', if it proves successful through improved athletic performance it will be difficult to legislate against. The scientist seeks knowledge, but the administrators and coaches must decide whether the results of his research may be used within the sport. The moralists have to be sensible in their treatment of the scientist. Their thinking was muddled in the early days of the steroid problem, which did much to slow down their arrival at an effective solution—they condemned steroid usage on the grounds of medical risk, but at the same time they also prevented the scientific experiments which would have established whether there were, indeed, any such dangers. Their argument should have been based on the unfair advantages to be gained by drug-takers rather than on unsubstantiated scientific reasons.

Of course the above discussion assumes that the scientist is remote from the sport, and the disadvantages of this have already been pointed out. The new 'sports scientist' is very much involved, and it is not so easy for him to maintain his scientific detachment. Thus the scientific observer in sport has the dilemma of needing to be involved and yet remain detached at the same time. In this book, although we are very much steeped in athletics, we have tried to maintain an unbiased approach as far as possible. The sheer quantity of material covered and the number of disciplines called upon mean not only that we cannot claim to be experts in every area, but also that we cannot provide answers to some of the coaches' questions such as 'How much of this?' and 'How much of that?', 'Which is the best method?', etc.

The coach throughout his coaching career, and the athlete throughout his years of training and competition, must maintain an open mind and be receptive to new knowledge and ideas. They should both aim at a little scientific detachment in some aspects of their sport, while at the same time retaining that supreme confidence of the top athlete, typified here by Dwight Stones, speaking when he held the world high jump record:

'I know the high jump inside out. I've studied everything: mechanics, theory, techniques, training methods, the rules, everything. I can take the event apart and put it together again. This is my job. I have to know it. In fact I know more about it than anyone living. After all, who else knows what it's like to go over a bar set at 7 ft 7¼ ins? Only I know the feeling.'

RISING STANDARDS

A glance at world record lists over the years confirms the obvious fact that standards of performances in all events are rising. In order to quantify the rate at which performance in general is increasing while at the same time eliminating the erratic nature of world records, which, after all, tend to be freak performances at the time they are made, the graphs that follow have been prepared for certain selected events.

The graphs in Figs A and B represent the achievements of the tenth best performers in 10,000 metres and hammer in the world and British ranking lists in each year since 1950. These particular places in the lists have been chosen because they are conveniently available in many athletics publications and they do tend to eliminate the freak performances which would distort averages. Scatter diagrams might have pleased the purists, but joining the points with lines makes for clarity. Like all statistics the graphs sometimes show beautifully what you want them to show, but usually they stubbornly give a straight line when you expect a curve and vice versa! However these graphs do show a steady improvement in performance. Since 1950 tremendous strides have been taken in training methods, coaching, attitudes, equipment and facilities. More people are involved in sport and, because of improved diets since the Second World War, athletes are bigger and stronger now than they were in the 1950s. The illegality of drug assistance results in a veil of secrecy which prevents an accurate assessment of the effect of drugs as a factor in the increased performances over the years.

10,000 Metres
The 10,000 metres has been chosen because the middle distance races are too often run tactically, rather than as time trials, and from 400 metres downwards the variations are too small.

It is presumed that not many long distance runners are tempted to take drugs and their improvement should be 'normal' in spite of the few who might have tried 'blood-doping'. But even here there may be complications, which affect the results, caused by high altitude training and the recent emergence of athletes born and bred at high altitude.

The world graph shows a remarkably steady improvement in performance (the line of best fit would be nearly straight). The old favourite theory that performances in general tend to peak during Olympic years seems to have been upheld in 1960, 1964, 1968 and 1972 but not in the rest. The British line parallels the world's, but there are even fewer Olympic peaks.

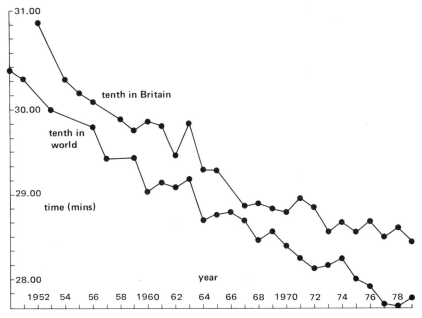

Fig. A. 10,000 metres

Hammer

The hammer event has been subjected to enormous improvements since 1950, the line of the tenth ranking men having risen over 21 metres in 30 years—approximately 38 per cent. Though it is not mechanically correct to make such a comparision with a running event (see Chapter 3), in the same period the 10,000 metre standards improved by a little over 9 per cent.

The difference between the world and the British performances has averaged a disappointing 12 metres or so, but there is only a slight divergence of the two curves showing that the British hammer-throwers are not falling further away from world standards. There are small peaks in the world curve which coincide with Olympic years.

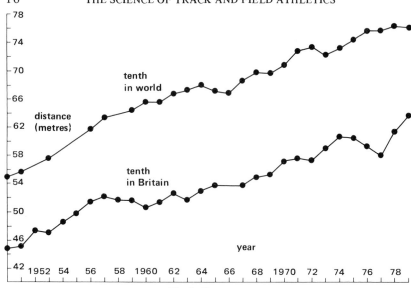

Fig. B. Hammer.

High Jump

The high jump graph (Fig. C) reveals interesting trends. Throughout the period the best men in the world have mastered the difficult skills of the straddle and some continue to do so. However, further down the scale of performances the Fosbury Flop, being an easier skill, has had a large impact which began in 1968, the year that Dick Fosbury won the Olympic title. The British men had been stagnating and drifting further away from world standards until then, but ever since have been converging towards those standards.

The British women have had a better tradition in this event and have tended to parallel the world's women, though the curves show how the Fosbury Flop has benefited women high jumpers generally, to the extent that women straddlers are now the exception.

Pole Vault

The pole vault (Fig. D) shows the twentieth and fiftieth in addition to the tenth best performer of each year. The close paralleling of the curves from the world ranking lists was a feature also of the other event graphs in this section, though the twentieth and fiftieth best are only included in the pole vault. As well as the sharp Olympic year peaks there are very significant increases in the slopes of the world curves from 1961, which was the start of the fibreglass vaulting pole revolution.

The differences between the curves from the British ranking lists are much greater, revealing a rapid drop away from the best pole vaulters, training seriously, to those around the fiftieth position who, although keen club athletes, will put pole vaulting lower down their activity priorities. It is also noticeable that the fibreglass pole took progressively longer to filter through

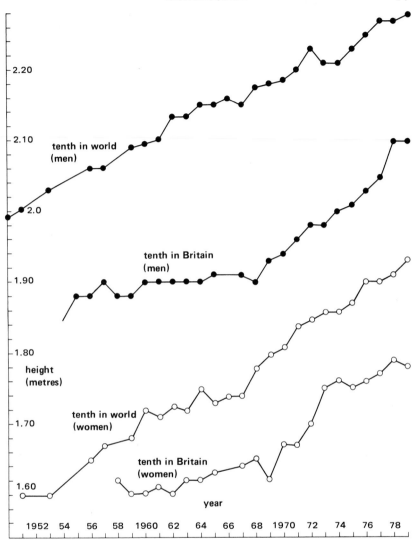

Fig. C. High jump.

to British standards, which is understandable in terms of both availability and
the increased cost of equipment at the time.

Shot and Discus
These two event graphs (Figs E and F) are presented because logically these
events, having a large strength content, should reveal the possible effects of
steroid-taking. Surprisingly there is an absence of slope increase in the men's
curves, and indeed there is a decline in the British men's curves in the later

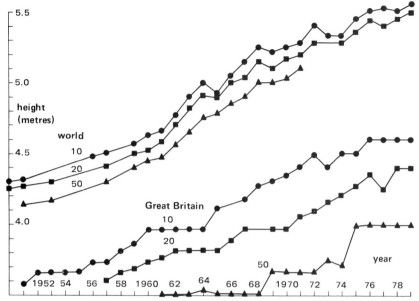

Fig. D. Pole vault. Tenth, twentieth and fiftieth best performer in each year.

years. However there are definite increases in the slopes of the world's women's curves in both events, starting about 1968. It can be argued that more resources have been made available and attitudes have changed towards these 'unfeminine' events, but this can be countered by the fact that the women in these echelons are almost entirely from Eastern Europe, where resources and attitudes were favourable even before 1968. There is also the argument that in terms of these events women stand to benefit much more than men from taking steroids, since the male physiology includes naturally occurring anabolizing hormones. Although it is not suggested that all top women throwers take drugs, there have been several instances of athletes being suspended after official drug tests have proved positive, so it is probable that steroids are a factor in rising standards.

Comparison of Men's and Women's Performances

A slightly more reliable method of comparing men's and women's athletic performances involves obtaining a ratio by dividing the smaller distance, height or time by the larger (Figs G and H). Objections are raised to even this method of comparision, but it is simple, easy to understand and does indicate certain trends, so some events are treated here without apology! The curves for the shot and discus emphasize even more the tremendous improvements in women's performances since 1968. The fact that the men's and women's implements are of different specifications does not affect the conclusions.

However, it is evident that women are drawing steadily closer to men even in events where the conditions are the same, e.g. the high jump, long jump, 400 metres and 1,500 metres. There has been a particularly rapid increase in

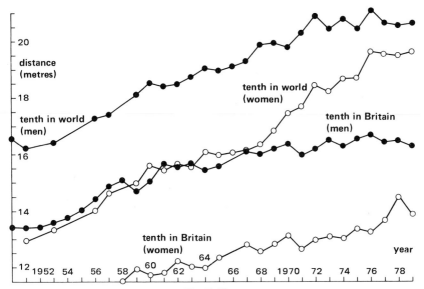

Fig. E. Shot.

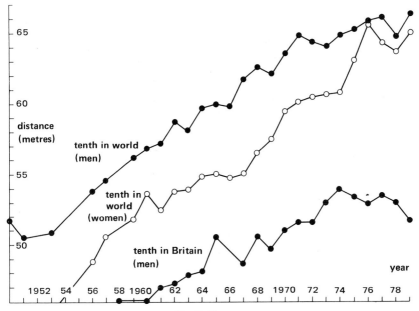

Fig. F. Discus.

the slope of the latter event's curve, but this is because it has only been recognized as an official event for women since the mid-1960s. It should be noted that because implement specifications vary, and because jump and throw performances depend on the square of the 'release' velocity (see Chapter 3) in each case, it is only valid to compare like events. For instance in 1979 women were closer to men in the 1,500 metres than in the 400 metres, but one could not make similar inferences from the curves when comparing the 1,500 metres with the high jump.

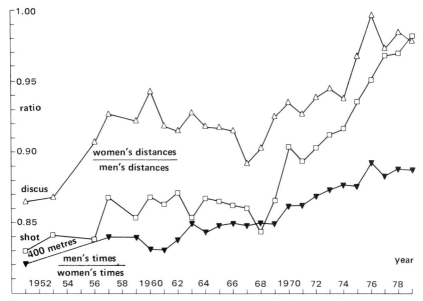

Fig. G. Comparison of men's and women's performances (tenth in world).

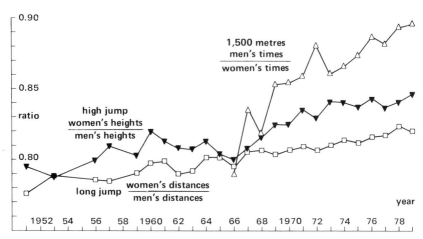

Fig. H. Comparison of men's and women's performances (tenth in world).

ABOUT THIS BOOK

In this book we have tried to present the scientific bases of track and field athletics in what we hope will be an easily understandable text for the so-called intelligent layman. We have aimed to progress systematically through the material, but inevitably some disjointedness will become apparent, for athletics is not one sport but many, with many differing requirements. Some sections are longer than others, but then the scientific approach is more applicable in certain areas than in others, and an exhaustive treatment of every aspect has not been possible. For example, although mention of training for some events has been made in Part III it is not the purpose of this book to be a training manual and therefore we have not included an exhaustive discussion of training for each event. The rules and specifications have also been included only in so far as they affect the scientific aspects of events, and readers are advised to consult the official International Amateur Athletic Federation Handbook for details.

Because athletics is almost in the category of being all things to all men (and all women), the captions to the picture sequences have been deliberately kept to the minimum. Athletes and coaches can then look for the body positions and movements that are of interest to them.

The material is presented in as objective a manner as possible, including many different points of view where controversy reigns. The authors are dogmatic about one thing only—that fixed ideas, closed minds and dogmatism have no place in athletics!

REFERENCE

STONES, D., Interview in *Athletics Weekly* 30:41 1976.

Part I

BASIC CONCEPTS

1

ANATOMY

The skeleton was shaped by man's decision, more than a million years ago, to stand erect. It is superbly poised and organized so that he can run, jump, and balance on his small feet. The skeleton supports the body and to this bony, architectural framework are attached the ligaments and muscles that enable physical activity to take place. The anatomist must consider form and structure with reference to *function*, for anatomy is the science of the *living* body. Bones are designed beautifully for their tasks and none appears redundant, except perhaps the coccyx, or man's vestigial tail. So precise is the relationship between various bones and body height that anthropological detectives with one dried bone as a clue can closely estimate the owner's height.

The skeletal muscles make movement possible. They are subject to command, while the internal muscles of the heart and viscera work without our voluntary control. The body has an incredible range of movement and though we cannot quite look directly behind us or touch our left knee with our left toes, the trained gymnast shows how adaptable our skeleton and musculature can be.

SKELETON OR BONY FRAMEWORK

Although bones can break, they are so strong that they can withstand tremendous force. If they do break, then the bone material shows an extraordinary capacity to heal itself. Bones are also extremely light, e.g. in a 70 kg person only about 13 kg represents bone weight.

There are two main kinds of bone found in the skeleton: *compact* bone which is hard and dense and forms the surface layer of the bones to make them rigid, and a softer substance known as *cancellous* bone which forms a honeycomb structure under the hard outer layers. In the interstices of this bone is the marrow, which among other functions provides materials for repairing fractures.

The surface of every bone is covered by a strong membrane known as the *periosteum*. It is richly supplied with blood vessels through which the bone receives much of its blood supply—therefore it too plays an important role in the repair of injuries.

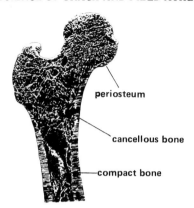

Fig. 1.1 Longitudinal section of a bone.

Ligaments are strong bands of tough white fibres which hold bony structures together, particularly at the joints. Ligaments have little elasticity but they can be stretched.

Types of Bone

Long, heavy bone forms the cylinder-shaped shafts of the limbs with expanded ends covered in cartilage. The cartilage, or gristle, is firm but elastic and can be compressed with considerable force—therefore it is found in joints where rigidity and strength combined with elasticity are needed. The femur is a long, heavy bone specially built to bear weight, and it has a large surface at each end for strong joints.

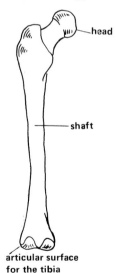

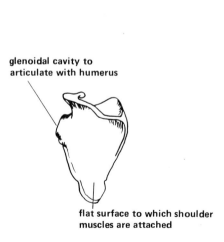

Fig. 1.2. Femur.

Fig. 1.3. Example of a flat bone — the left scapula.

Flat bones are thin plates providing broad surfaces for muscle attachment, e.g. the shoulder bone or scapula.

Long thin bone, e.g. the rib, provides a movable framework.

Small, compact bones are found in the ankle and wrist, for strength and flexibility.

Vertebrae

The vertebral column forms the 'backbone' and is made up of 33 small bones called vertebrae. They are arranged in four curved regions:

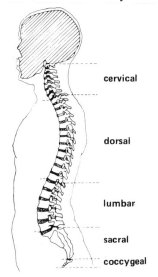

cervical

dorsal

lumbar

sacral

coccygeal

Fig. 1.4. Vertebral column.

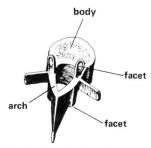

body

facet

arch

facet

Fig. 1.5. A typical vertebra.

1. Cervical (neck), which is convex forward.
2. Thoracic or dorsal, which is concave forward.
3. Lumbar (lower back), which is convex forward.
4. Sacral and coccygeal, which is concave forward.

The vertebrae of the sacrum are fused to form a single rigid structure which acts as the posterior part of the pelvis. The coccyx is continuous with the lower part of the sacrum.

A typical vertebra is composed of (i) a body which is a mass of cancellous bone with the upper and lower surfaces flat and the front and sides rounded, (ii) an arch of bone which projects to give protection to the spinal cord which passes between it and the body, and (iii) bony facets which project upwards and downwards to articulate with the corresponding facets on the vertebrae above and below.

The shape, size and structure of the vertebrae vary according to their position in the vertebral column—the cervical vertebrae, for instance, are thin and light and the lumbar bones thicker and heavier. The cervical vertebrae are shaped to allow a great degree of rotation, enabling us to turn our heads and obtain a wide range of vision. The dorsal vertebrae make joints with the *ribs*, and these, together with the *sternum* (breastbone) form the *thorax*, or thoracic cavity.

The vertebrae are placed upon each other to form a tube, the *neural canal*, which contains the spinal cord. Between the vertebrae are *discs* of fibrous cartilage acting as shock absorbers and making the whole backbone elastic to allow bending movements. The cartilage is pale in colour and firm, and though it can resist considerable compression it is of low tensile strength and can be cut quite easily.

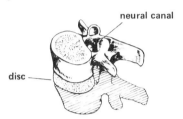

Fig. 1.6. A lumbar vertebra.

The coach and athlete should remind themselves continually of the complex and fragile nature of the vertebral column, especially when training with heavy weights. It is certainly not like a steel girder which can bear huge forces in any direction. Forces which are put on the 'backbone' should be directed along its length as far as possible, and even then should not be large enough to damage the discs.

There are 24 *ribs*, with 12 on each side, forming pairs. Each rib is attached at the back to the body of the dorsal vertebra and, except for the lower two pairs, at the front of the chest to the sternum by their costal cartilages. The ribs are long and curved and form, in barrel-stave fashion, a cage-like structure which is flexible to allow for breathing.

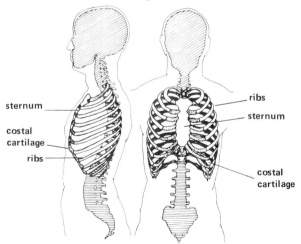

Figs 1.7 (left) and 1.8 (right). Bones of the thorax.

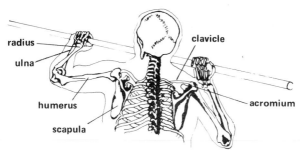

Fig. 1.9. Shoulder girdle.

Shoulder Girdle and Upper Limbs

The shoulder girdle provides a strong mobile anchorage from which the upper limbs are attached to the trunk. It is structured in such a way that very complex movements can be made. The *clavicle* is attached at its inner end to the sternum and the outer end articulates with the *acromium,* that part of the *scapula* which overhangs the shoulder. Fractures of this 'collar bone' are very common, caused by falling on the outstretched arm or on the shoulder.

The *humerus* is the long bone of the upper arm. The head articulates with the scapula to form the shoulder joint, and the lower end articulates with the *ulna* to form the elbow joint.

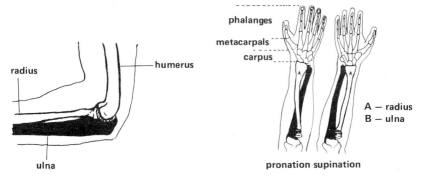

Fig. 1.10. Left elbow joint.   Fig. 1.11. Right forearm and hand.

The shoulder joint is remarkable for its flexibility, which is maintained by ligaments rather than bony structures. It is therefore very susceptible to sprains. The elbow is a smoothly operating hinge between the fitted bone endings of the upper and lower arm. Man's most versatile tools are his arms, which are highly flexible extensions which allow him to reach out, grasp things and manipulate them. The superb jointing allows them to twist, turn and bend.

Hand and Wrist

The *carpus* consists of eight small, pebble-like bones closely fitted together in two rows, making the wrist flexible yet firm. The *metacarpals* form a frame for the palm and support the thumbs. The *phalanges* are the bones of the fingers and thumbs.

Pelvic Girdle

The pelvis is a solid base through which weight can be transmitted to the lower limbs from the upper body, and also provides attachment for the powerful muscles of the legs and lower back. When we are sitting, the body weight is carried on two arches of bone extending below the flaring wings of the pelvis.

The human body solves problems of design and construction that are familiar to the architect and the engineer. For example, great demands are made on the joint between the hip and the thigh—it must be firm enough to support the body weight, and yet flexible enough to allow leg mobility. Nature's effective solution is the ball and socket joint.

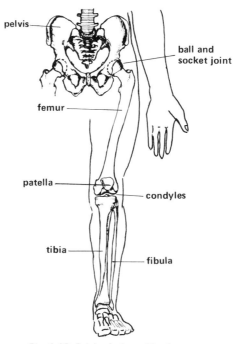

pelvis

ball and socket joint

femur

patella

condyles

tibia

fibula

Fig. 1.12. Pelvic girdle and leg bones.

Bones of the Leg

The thigh bone, or *femur,* is the longest and strongest bone of the body. It can withstand pressure of 160 k/cm² (2 tons per square inch), and even if it is damaged the living bone can shift its stress lines and form new ones where needed. The lower end of the shaft of the femur widens out to form two large articular surfaces or *condyles,* which articulate with the upper end of the tibia to form the knee joint.

The knee cap or *patella* is situated in front of the knee joint in the tendon of the muscles which extend over the knee. Its function is to improve leverage by its pulley-like action as it glides in the grooves between the smooth surfaces of the condyles.

The *tibia* is the shinbone. Its upper surface is plateau-like with two articular surfaces to correspond with the condyles of the femur. The shaft is straight and tapering and triangular in cross-section. The lower end of the shaft forms part of the ankle joint.

The *fibula* is long and thin and does not transmit weight, but it supplies a framework for muscular attachment and acts as a protection for certain important blood vessels.

Foot

The general structure of the foot is similar to that of the hand. The *tarsus* contains seven short bones forming the ankle, one fewer than the wrist, but the large heel bone is possibly two fused together. The *arch* consists of the five metatarsal bones and the *toe* bones are called phalanges.

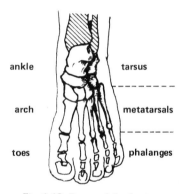

ankle   tarsus

arch   metatarsals

toes   phalanges

Fig. 1.13. Bones of the foot.

The foot is constructed in the form of arches which are held together by ligaments and supported by muscles—therefore they are strong and flexible, but very great strains are put on the feet, particularly during strenuous exercise such as jumping and hurdling. The inner portion of the longitudinal arch, the instep, is high, while the outer portion rests on the ground. If the arch becomes flattened due to muscular weakness the foot is deprived of its normal spring and the gait is flat-footed. There is also a series of transverse arches from one side of the foot to the other.

ARTICULAR SYSTEM OR JOINTS

As the song goes: the 'hip bone is connected to the thigh bone, and the thigh bone is connected to the knee bone, and so on . . ..' Where the bones connect or meet *joints* are formed, of which there are three main types.

1. *Immovable joints.* No movement takes place between the bones. They

may be united by cartilage, e.g. the ribs to the sternum, or they are fused, e.g. the plates of the skull.

2. *Slightly movable joints.* The opposed bony surfaces are united by ligaments or have a fibrous cartilage pad in between, e.g. the bodies of adjacent vertebrae.

3. *Movable joints.* The general structure of such a joint is illustrated diagrammatically in Fig. 1.14 and is made up as follows. The *articular cartilage* covers the surface of the part of the bone that enters the joint. The *capsule,* consisting of strong, fibrous tissue, encloses the 'joint cavity' and parts of the capsule may be thickened to form definite bands of ligament which give support in various directions. Their position and strength will depend on the joint's function, e.g. the mobile shoulder joint has fewer than the hip joint, which is less mobile but bears greater weight. The capsule is lined with the *synovial membrane* which secretes an oily, milky fluid which lubricates the joint. There are also blood vessels, lymph vessels and nerves supplying the joints.

There are different types of movable joints:

1. *Ball and socket.* The rounded head of the movable bone forms a ball which fits into the socket, e.g. the humerus into the scapula and the femur into the pelvis (Fig. 1.12).

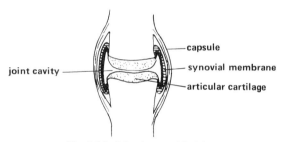

Fig. 1.14. A freely movable joint.

2. *Gliding joint.* This allows a small amount of movement only e.g. between the flat surfaces of the vertebrae (Fig. 1.6).

3. *Hinge joint.* This allows movement only in one plane, e.g. the elbow and joints of the fingers and toes (Fig. 1.10).

4. *Pivot joint.* This allows rotation, e.g. between the cervical vertebrae when the head is turned and between the radius and the ulna which allows the radius to rotate round the ulna when the palm is turned downwards (Fig. 1.11).

5. *Condyloid joint.* This articulation allows movement in all directions but not rotation, e.g. the wrist (Fig. 1.11).

Movement of the Vertebral Column

The slightly movable joints between the bodies of the vertebrae are supported by very strong ligaments. The space between the arches is filled by an unusually elastic ligament which allows free forward movement. The movements

of the vertebral column are: (i) flexion—bending forward, (ii) extension—
bending backward, (iii) lateral flexion, and (iv) rotation. The movements of
the dorsal region, however, are limited in order to reduce interference with
breathing.

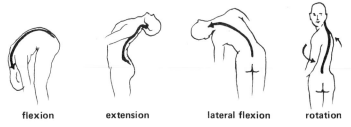

| flexion | extension | lateral flexion | rotation |

Fig. 1.15. Movement of the vertebral column.

Thorax

When breathing in, the ribs, costal cartilage and sternum allow the chest wall
to move upwards and outwards, and on breathing out the reverse movement
takes place. *Inspiration* enlarges the circumference of the thorax. *Expiration*
decreases the circumference.

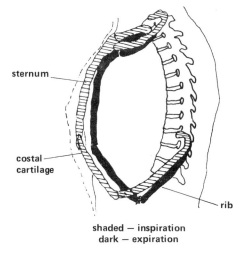

shaded — inspiration
dark — expiration

Fig. 1.16. Breathing — movement of the thorax.

Shoulder Girdle

The joint between the sternum and the clavicle is a freely movable gliding
joint, as is the joint between the outer end of the clavicle and the scapula.
This allows great range of movement and the shoulder can be rotated forwards
and backwards, and the whole shoulder girdle can be elevated (shrugged) or
depressed. Both these joints need to be supported by strong ligaments (Fig.
1.9).

The shoulder joint is structurally very weak and depends greatly on the surrounding muscles. The ball and socket type of joint allows the forward elevation of the arms (flexion), extension in a backward swing, the abduction of the arms away from the body and the adduction of the arms across the body. It also allows external rotation of the upper arm and the opposite movement of internal rotation, e.g. when the forearm is placed across the small of the back. Both external and internal rotation are shoulder movements, since no rotation occurs at the elbow even though it may appear so.

Elbow
The elbow joint is a hinge joint which allows only bending (flexion) and straightening (extension) (Fig. 1.10).

Wrist
The wrist joint can move forwards (palmar flexion) and backwards (dorsi-flexion). The condyloid articulation also allows movement to both sides. Force transmitted through the wrist joint is first taken by the lower end of the radius. Injury at this point is very common as the result of a fall, and the resulting break is known as a Colles fracture after the nineteenth-century Irish surgeon who first described it.

Hip
The hip joint is a ball and socket articulation which allows a wide range of movements—flexion, extension, abduction, adduction, external and internal rotation. A well trained ballerina or gymnast would show the full range. Dislocation of the hip occurs only when great violence is applied, e.g. the impact against the knees in a car crash, which would drive back the head of the femur. The joint is surrounded by very strong ligaments—indeed the ones in front of the hip joint are the strongest in the body.

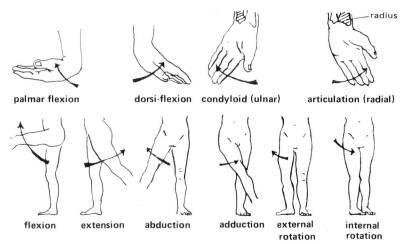

| palmar flexion | dorsi-flexion | condyloid (ulnar) | articulation (radial) |

| flexion | extension | abduction | adduction | external rotation | internal rotation |

Fig. 1.17. Waist and hip movements.

Knee

The knee is a hinge joint in a very loose capsule. There are ligaments at each side and diagonally across the middle of the joint to prevent the femur from slipping forward or back over the tibia. There is a very strong tendon over the front of the knee from the quadriceps muscle which extends the knee, and the patella is fixed in this tendon. The two longest bones in the body impose great leverage on the knee; therefore it is one of the least secure joints. Great care should be taken of the knee joint when training with heavy weights in squats. Those who habitually try for maximum lifts in this exercise usually end up with chronic knee trouble. The joint surfaces are not close-fitting and considerable movement is allowed, but the strong ligaments surrounding the joint means that dislocation occurs only as the result of extreme violence.

Synovitis (water on the knee) occurs commonly in the knee because it is very exposed to minor stresses and strains, and the large synovial membrane is near the surface. The condition is caused by the secretion of an excessive amount of synovial fluid when injury occurs.

The cartilage is frequently damaged by violent twisting movements when the full body weight is on the joint. When landing heavily, flexing the knees can help to dissipate the shock, though trouble is sometimes caused to the knee joint by imbalance between the quadriceps and the hamstrings.

Ankle

The ankle joint is a hinge joint with strong ligaments at both sides and smaller ones at front and back. The ligaments can be torn by twisting the ankle and sometimes their strength is so great that they can actually tear off a piece of bone.

Function of the Limbs

In lower forms of vertebrate life, like lizards and crocodiles, all four limbs are used for support and propulsion. Certain forms started to lift the fore legs and balance on the back legs, and the fore limbs became useful for gathering and manipulating. Man finally adopted a fully erect posture with a wide field of vision. The fore limbs were very light and mobile while the hind limbs became stronger and less mobile. The wrist became specialized to allow mobility of the carpus and delicate movements of the fingers, while the ankle became adapted for weight-bearing, being a very stable joint allowing dorsi-flexion and planar flexion to assist locomotion.

The skeleton is an arrangement of levers, all moved by the muscles. The range and type of movement depends on the joints, the length of the levers and the nature of the muscles acting on these levers.

THE MUSCULAR SYSTEM

The muscles which produce movement of the skeleton are under voluntary control and are called *striped* or *voluntary* muscles. Other involuntary muscles work to maintain heartbeat and to keep the internal organs and viscera operating efficiently without our even thinking or knowing about it. The voluntary muscles, the ones we are interested in, are made up of many thousands of muscle fibres, each sheathed in delicate connective tissue. The fibres are gathered in small bundles which are further gathered into bigger bundles, and so on into bigger bundles, all in their wrappings of connective tissues. These bundles lie parallel to one another and the connective tissue forms a strong framework which can attach itself straight to the bone, or forms tendons which can attach themselves to the bone. Generally the fibres are attached at the end of the muscle nearest the trunk, the stable *origin,* while the tendon forming a more mobile *insertion* is attached at the end away from the trunk. Tendons make it possible for the muscles to act from a distance, e.g. the tendon from the forearm muscles bends the fingers. This leaves the fingers free to be mobile and the muscle mass is nearer to its souce of blood supply. The gathering of a muscle into a tendon also means that greater force can be concentrated in a small area.

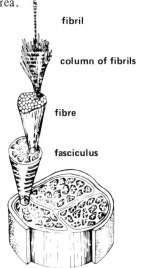

fibril

column of fibrils

fibre

fasciculus

Fig. 1.18. Section through a muscle, to show its structure.

The body's 600-odd muscles are the cables whose pull on the bones makes motion possible. Muscles work in pairs, one to produce movement in a given direction and the other to produce movement in the opposite direction. This is obvious in the arms and legs where large shafts of bone are moved, but muscles also move the rib cage when one is breathing and shift the face into a smile or a frown. Basically the movement in a joint is the result of differences in tension between the appropriate opposing pair of muscles. The contractions of the flexors, e.g. of the knee, bend this hinge joint, and the extensors contract to pull the leg straight again. Muscles are teamed—every one on the right has one on the left, for every flexor there is an extensor. The muscles move by contraction, the precise nature of which is still slightly uncertain. The brain sends signals to the muscle fibres through the central nervous system, chemical changes occur which produce mechanical energy, and the muscles shorten. A concentric contraction occurs when the points of origin and insertion draw towards one another, returning to length again after the contraction passes. A static (isometric) contraction occurs if the muscle length remains the same, e.g. in maintaining the posture of the body when standing still. A third type of contraction, eccentric, occurs when the muscle lengthens against a greater load even while trying to contract. Different lever systems are in action in the body, some more efficient than others.

Muscles require oxygen and food to produce energy for the work they perform—therefore they have a liberal blood supply to carry the nutrients. Partly because of this exceptionally rich blood supply, muscle is the most infection-free of all the body's tissues. The most common ailments among athletes are over-use, and 'Charley Horse' bruising which is the result of a blow or an over-forceful stretch. (Charley Horse is a lame old nag!)

Co-ordination of movements is effected by the nervous system and each muscle has its own nerve supply. Muscle is never completely at rest, but in a state of 'tone', ready to respond, with some impulses always passing through. When a muscle is stimulated to contract, *successive* impulses pass to it so that there is not a single twitch but a sustained contraction or tetanus. (Raeburn).

It is remarkable that bone and muscle give us so little trouble—a machine after a few years of 'athletic' treatment would become obsolescent!

Like the bones, the skeletal muscles range in size and shape to suit the particular functions they perform. Some, less than one inch long, will raise an eyebrow while in contrast there is the diaphragm, the great dome-shaped muscle at the base of the thoracic cavity which is the principal muscle of respiration.

We shall look briefly at some of the main muscles of the body. It is not possible to survey every muscle group, but we can look at the principal ones concerned in the main athletic movements.

Muscles of the Neck and Spine

The *sternomastoids* pass obliquely across each side of the neck. Contraction of one draws the head to that side and rotates it to face the opposite shoulder. The *scaleni* bend the neck forward or back when acting together. They can also act as accessory muscles of respiration. When a runner finishes a race with his head back it is usually because he is making full use of these muscles for respiration. The long muscles of the head and back are like straps holding the head erect on the spine. The long muscles or *sacrospinalis* are powerful extensors of the spine. One of the most important, but difficult, things to do during effort is to keep the head balanced on a relaxed neck. The weight of the head is great relative to the rest of the body and it is essential in any activity requiring balance to have the head aligned correctly, otherwise the rest of the body has to try and compensate. In photographs of very good athletes it is noticeable that they keep their neck muscles relaxed and maintain good posture by balancing their head on the spinal column.

Muscles of the Thorax

The *intercostal muscles* lie between the ribs. Their main action is to pull the ribs together.

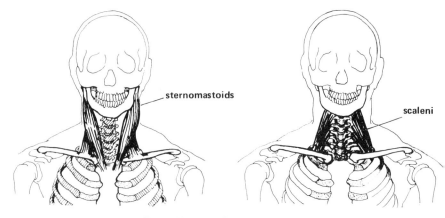

Figs 1.19 and 1.20. The neck muscles.

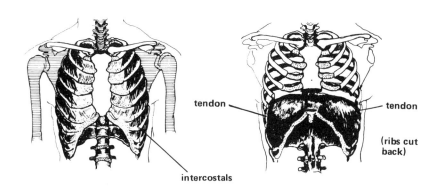

Fig. 1.21. The rib muscles.   Fig. 1.22. Diaphragm.

The *diaphragm* is a vast, dome-shaped muscle separating the thoracic cavity from the abdominal cavity. The middle of the dome is a sheet of strong tendon. As the diaphragm is the chief muscle of respiration it is very important to the athlete, particularly to the middle and long distance runner.

The lungs and heart are in direct contact with the upper surface of the diaphragm, and the abdominal organs including the liver and stomach lie directly beneath.

In normal inspiration the diaphragm draws down, expanding the lungs above and pushing down the abdominal contents. The lower ribs move slightly forward, upwards and outwards, increasing the diameter of the lower chest. The thoracic walls recoil, the abdominal muscles contract and expiration results.

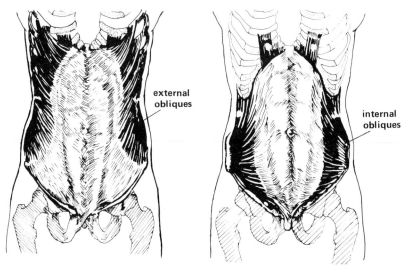

Figs 1.23 and 1.24. Abdominal muscles (oblique).

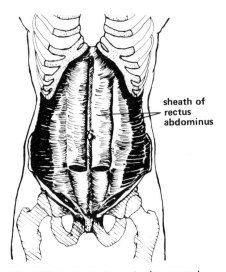

Fig. 1.25. Abdominal muscles (transverse).

Muscles of the Abdomen

The abdominal wall consists of pairs of broad, sheet-like muscles, the *external* and *internal obliques* and the vertical pillar-like *rectus abdominus*. The fibres of these flat muscles are arranged in criss-cross fashion, forming a very strong three-ply layer. They support the spine and allow many types of movements in many directions. The two rectus abdominus muscles act as a support for the abdominal contents. Coughing, defaecating, and straining in any way increase the pressure on them—later in life they cannot stand the strain and the 'corporation' develops. These muscles do not act alone but work in conjunction with the posterior abdominal wall and the muscles of the floor of the pelvis. All muscles work in closely co-ordinated teams and the beautifully synchronized movements of the body controlled by the nervous system are among the wonders of nature. Practically every movement in athletics depends on the efficient working of the abdominal muscles.

Muscles Connecting to the Upper Limbs

Important muscles connect the vertebrae to the upper limbs. These are first, the *trapezius*—the broad, flat muscles of the upper back which have their origins in the upper vertebrae and insert into the outer end of the clavicle and the spine of the scapula. Their main action is to elevate or depress the shoulders.

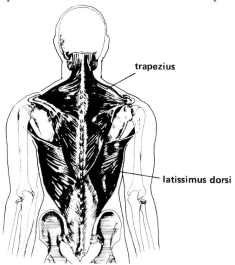

trapezius

latissimus dorsi

Fig. 1.26. Muscles of the back.

The *latissimus dorsi* are the broadest muscles of the back, stretching from the lumbar and dorsal vertebrae to the armpit where the fibres twist over and attach themselves to the humerus. The main action of these muscles is to bring the arm from an abducted position to the side of the body, or to pull the body up to the arm.

The *pectoralis major* are the large muscles of the chest, stretching from the sternum to the armpit where the attachment is just in front of that of the latissimus dorsi. The chief action is adduction—drawing the arms across the chest. The 'lats', and 'pecs', are important climbing muscles and are well used by pole vaulters.

The *serratus anterior* covers most of the side of the chest wall. This is the chief pushing and punching muscle and is important in shot putting and pole vaulting.

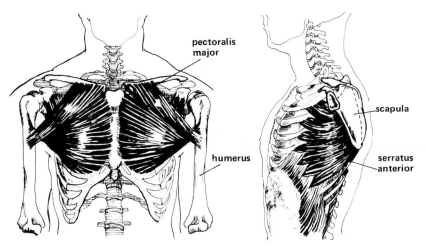

Fig. 1.27. Chest muscles ('pecs').   **Fig. 1.28. The serratus.**

Muscles of the Shoulder Girdle

Deltoid (shaped like the Greek letter Δ or delta)—the fibres converge into a single tendon which inserts into the humerus about half-way down the shaft. Its main action is to abduct the arm from the side of the body to the horizontal.

Muscles of the Upper Arm

The *anterior biceps* lies on the front of the upper arm. This two-headed muscle is the supinator of the forearm and a flexor of the elbow joint. The chief flexor of the elbow is the *brachialis* which lies over the lower end of the humerus and the front of the elbow joint.

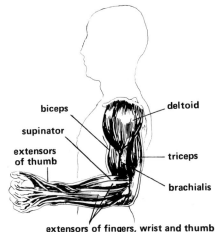

Fig. 1.29. Arm muscles.

The *posterior triceps* is the three-headed muscle at the back of the humerus. Its main action is to extend the elbow and assist in the adduction of the upper arm.

Muscles of the Forearm and Hand

The *flexor* group and the *extensor* group are the muscles of the forearm. The long flexors, lying mainly on the ulnar side of the forearm, are used for gripping and for wrist flexion. The short muscles of the hand are used for the finer, precise movements. The extensor group lie mainly on the radial side of the forearm. They extend the fingers and thumb and assist in the extension of the wrist. The *rotators* roll the lower part of the radius round the ulna and turn the hand palm down, and the *supinator* assists the biceps to turn the hand palm upwards. The hand contains superficial muscles at the base of the thumb and little finger and deep muscles between the metacarpal bones and the tendons. The thumb muscles are among the most important in the whole upper limb, because they enable the opposition of fingers and thumb.

The muscles of the upper limb, including the hand, are of the greatest importance for all throwing events. Hammer-throwers and discus-throwers often have pulls in the shoulder muscles, and javelin-throwers have problems in the elbow joint. Shot putters frequently damage the wrist joint and the muscles of the hand.

Muscles of the Pelvis

The *psoas* is the long muscle situated at the back of the abdomen. It crosses over the rim of the pelvis into the upper part of the thigh. Along with the *iliacus* its action is to flex the thigh and it helps to maintain erect posture.

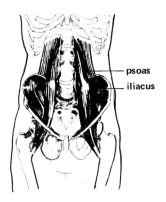

Fig. 1.30. The deep abdominal muscles.

The *gluteus maximus* is the very large and powerful muscle which gives the buttock its rounded shape. It acts to extend the hip joint and is also important in maintaining erect posture. It is the chief muscle of forward propulsion and runners usually have well developed gluteus maximi.

The *gluteus medius* and *minimus,* situated in front of the gluteus maximus, tilt the pelvis and raise the opposite limb from the ground, an action important in walking and running. If these muscles are affected the walk becomes a waddle, since the whole trunk then has to be bent to tilt the pelvis.

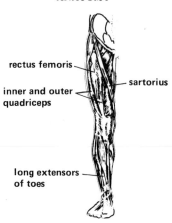

Fig. 1.31. Anterior muscles of the leg.

Muscles of the Thigh

Anterior Group—the *quadriceps* or four-headed muscle is large and powerful and occupies most of the front of the thigh. All four heads converge into a single tendon which envelopes the patella and inserts into the front of the tibia. The origin is from the front and sides of the shaft of the femur, while the *rectus femoris,* the straight muscle of the thigh, arises from the ilium.

The quadriceps is the most important muscle of posture and also acts to extend the leg. The rectus femoris assists in flexing the thigh at the hip joint. It is important to have strong quadriceps if the knee ligaments are injured, because the power of the quadriceps can control the knee joint.

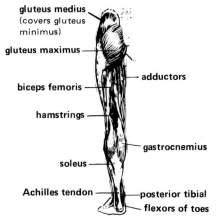

Fig. 1.32. Posterior muscles of the leg.

The *sartorius* (cross-legged tailor's muscle) is the longest voluntary muscle in the body. It flexes the thigh and adducts it as well as rotating it.

Posterior Group—the *biceps femoris* is a two-headed muscle which occupies the outer portion of the back of the thigh. It inserts into the upper end of the fibula by strong tendons commonly known as *hamstrings*. It is a powerful flexor of the knee joint and a very important muscle in sprinting.

The internal group of *adductors* form a sheet of three muscles on the inside of the thigh. Their action is the adduction of the thigh on the pelvis, important, for example, in allowing the hammer-thrower to turn tightly.

Muscles of the Lower Leg

Anterior group. The *long extensors* of the toes become tendinous above the ankle, and across the foot they are enclosed in lubricated tendon sheets. Their action is to dorsiflect the foot and help to support the arches.

Posterior group. The *long flexors* lie on the posterior surfaces of the tibia and fibula and pass under the foot. Their action is the plantar flexion of the foot. The *posterior tibial* passes round the inside of the ankle and inserts into every bone of the tarsus, except the talus. This broad insertion means that it is the main support of the longitudinal arch of the foot.

The *gastrocnemius,* shaped like the 'belly of a frog', is the calf muscle, which can be seen so clearly when anyone stands on their toes. The *soleus* or 'sole fish'-shaped muscle lies under the gastrocnemius and only its outer edges can be seen. The tendons of both muscles blend to form the strongest and thickest tendon of the body, the *Achilles tendon.* The actions of these calf muscles are to raise the body on its toes and to provide spring to the gait. These are the main jumping muscles.

Muscles of the Foot

The small muscles of the foot are covered by a strong tendinous sheet which acts as the tie beam of the arch by pulling on the two pillars of the foot and preventing flattening. Flat feet will not be accompanied by pain if the small muscles are strong enough e.g. in a ballet dancer, but if the muscles are weak and the joints stiff they become painful since all the weight is thrown on the ligaments which inflame and adhere.

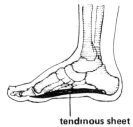

tendinous sheet

Fig. 1.33. Longitudinal arch of the foot.

A muscle which carries out a voluntary movement is called the *agonist* and the muscle which 'opposes' the movement is known as the *antagonist.* All the muscle groups of the body are co-ordinated in this way, e.g. when the elbow is flexed the biceps are agonist and the triceps are antagonist. Muscles which perform actions to help other muscles are known as *synergists,* e.g. the muscles of the wrist holding firm while the fingers operate on a delicate fixed task.

Fig. 1.34. Anatomy in action!

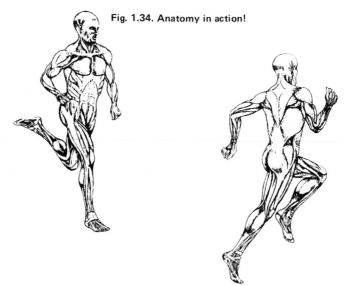

Fig. 1.35. Co-ordination of the surface muscles in an athlete.

The voluntary muscles, as stated earlier, are formed of bundles of muscle fibres which respond to impulses from the central nervous system. The activity of the muscle is determined by the total numbers of impulses per unit of time, and the sum of the impulses is reflected in the state of contraction of the muscle.

Actual movements are carried out by the locomotor system of bones, joints and muscles, but in addition to the outgoing nerve impulses which cause the muscles to contract there is a continuous flow of information inwards to the nervous system. Under stress the heart beats faster, the blood races, the breathing alters and one is aware that other systems of the body are operating. Let us now look more closely at those physiological systems which are distinct yet inextricably linked to the locomotor system when any athletic activity is performed.

REFERENCES

McLINTIC, J.R., *Basic Anatomy and Physiology of the Human Body.* Wiley, 1975.
NOURSE, A.E., *The Body,* Time Life International. Life Science Library, 1965.
RAEBURN, J.K., and RAEBURN, H.A., *Anatomy, Physiology and Hygiene.* Cox & Wyman, 1969.
ROYAL AIR FORCE, *Principles of Anatomy and Physiology for P.T. Instructors in the R.A.F.* HMSO, 1959 (3rd ed.).

2

PHYSIOLOGY

THE CIRCULATORY SYSTEM—HEART AND BLOOD

The human body is like an automated chemical plant with day and night activity. The blood, rightly called 'life blood', circulates continuously, bearing food and oxygen to the cells and carrying waste products away. Blood is the only fluid tissue and every cell is an island which could not exist without the surrounding blood and lymph. It is only three centuries ago that medicine realized that it was the same blood going round, some 4,700–5,700 litres of it pumped every day. Galen had thought that new blood was continuously manufactured from our intake of food and air, but Harvey realized that the veins always moved blood towards the heart and the arteries away from the heart. He demonstrated this with a simple experiment—he pressed blood upwards from the vein section and placed his fingers as in Fig. 2.1. If he released the left (to the reader) finger, blood flowed into the section, but if he lifted the right finger first, blood did not run backwards to fill it. It would have been impossible to produce the quantity of blood that the heart was pumping—therefore he reached the logical conclusion that it was the same blood circulating in this cardiovascular system. An extremely powerful pump is needed to keep up the pressure of the flow so that the blood reaches the further extremities of the limbs. Indeed, a double network is maintained, with the oxygen-rich blood flowing from the heart to exchange oxygen for carbon dioxide in the capillaries at the extremes of the network, and the return system carrying the waste products, particularly carbon dioxide, back to the heart and lungs for reoxygenation.

Fig. 2.1. One-way veins.

The blood from the upper part of the body returns by gravity, but the movement upwards is caused by muscular contraction against the walls of the veins and the closing of valves to keep the blood from flowing back down to pool at the feet. The unsightly blue bulges of overfilled veins are the 'varicose veins' that we see in people who do standing jobs or who have inherited poor circulation in which the valves in the veins are not working efficiently.

The *heart* is mainly made up of muscle fibres and this very strong cardiac muscle pumps away for the whole of one's lifetime, day and night, with exercise demanding an increased output. Within the muscle walls of the heart are four hollow chambers: a right and left receiving chamber or atrium, and a right and left pumping chamber or ventricle. To get from one side of the heart to the other the blood must go the long way round, through the body. The circulation is endless, but if we start with the oxygen-rich blood in the left atrium it is pumped by the left ventricle through the aorta, the main artery, to the rest of the body through the network of large arteries, to smaller arteries, to the ever-decreasing arterioles and finally to the tiny capillaries. In yielding up oxygen and taking in waste, the blood changes from bright red to a dull red. (The red colouring is caused by the presence of haemoglobin, an oxygen-carrying substance, in the blood.) It then starts on its way back to the heart where it is received in the right atrium. It is pumped by the right ventricle through the pulmonary artery to the lungs, from where it returns bright red and freshly oxygenated to the left atrium to start the cycle again.

The general circuit of the body is known as the *systemic circulation,* while the route to and from the lungs is known as the *pulmonary circulation.*

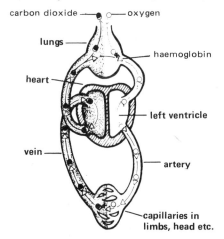

Fig. 2.2. Schematic diagram of the circulation of the blood.

The systemic circulation is further divided into sub-areas which aid the functions of particular organs, e.g. the renal (to the kidneys), the hepatic (to the liver), the cerebral (to the brain), and the coronary (to the heart itself).

The double pumping activity of the heart continues without our conscious awareness. A small specialized area of tissue called the pacemaker in the right atrium produces bursts of electrical activity which initiate the beats with alternating waves of contraction and relaxation. Each contraction forces a quantity of blood through the heart valves into the systemic circulation and the extra pressure is felt as a wave or *pulse* through the large arteries. It can be felt in any of the arteries where they cross a bone, though the radial artery of the wrist is the normal place, because it is easy of access being so near the surface. No pulse can be felt in the veins, as the pressure has expended itself in the capillaries. The opening and closing of the valves of the heart can be heard through a stethoscope or simply by placing one's ear on the chest wall.

The difference between the pressure in veins and that in arteries can be seen in a bad cut. The blood from an artery spurts out and the pumping action is obvious, whereas blood from capillaries and veins flows more slowly and evenly.

Blood pressure is taken by binding a rubber bag round the upper arm and pumping it with air until the pulse at the wrist disappears. At this point the pressure in the bag equals the pressure in the artery of the arm and can be read off on a scale.

Blood pressure rises during exercise and falls during sleep. It also rises due to age or with the hardening and narrowing of the arteries which increases the resistance to the circulation. This necessitaties an increase in pressure to maintain the circulation, hence the term 'high blood pressure'.

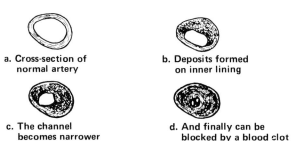

a. Cross-section of
normal artery

b. Deposits formed
on inner lining

c. The channel
becomes narrower

d. And finally can be
blocked by a blood clot

Fig. 2.3. Progressive narrowing of coronary artery.

During exercise or emergency (and to some bodies the only exercise is in an emergency!) the heart has to step up its pumping action to supply the increased requirements of the body. Only a limited blood volume is available to supply all the tissues of the body, but since not all the tissues are working together at maximum rate it is possible for the body to meet specific metabolic demands. During vigorous exercise the muscles receive almost 90 per cent of the blood supply, and because it is drastically reduced to other areas it is not a good idea to exercise immediately after a large meal, for the blood required by the digestive system will be diverted. The heart is stimulated to beat faster and increase the flow, and also to increase the volume pumped by each contraction. The heart of the conditioned athlete beats more slowly but more efficiently than that of the untrained person. The important factor is the *cardiac output,* which is the stroke volume times the frequency of the heart beat.

Exercise strengthens the heart and increases the drive of the blood through the muscles. Training produces an efficient increase in stroke volume and the greater output of blood can be maintained at a reduced pulse rate—e.g. the average pulse rate of a resting adult is about 70 beats per minute, but the trained athlete's can be below 50 and there are cases of it being as low as 30 for the resting trained heart.

Where regular training demands are put on the heart the muscles thicken and the chambers enlarge. There are myths of athletes straining their hearts through extreme exertion, but a sound heart cannot be injured by physical activity. Only those with an already damaged heart need have any fears, and enough exercise early enough, and consistently maintained, is a good preventive of heart disease (Cooper). Overloading the heart in training is very different from pathological overload. The stress is not continuous and it is in the rests between sessions that the body adapts and compensates before the next controlled demands are made.

Blood has four main components. About 55 per cent of it is fluid *plasma,* which is mainly water but also contains vital nutriments—fats, glucose, amino-acids and proteins as well as hormones. Plasma plays a crucial part in maintaining the body's chemical balance, water content and temperature at a safe level.

The remaining 45 per cent of the blood is made up of three kinds of cells: *Red cells,* shaped like tiny flattened discs, have the vital job of conveying oxygen from the lungs and distributing it through the body. One cubic millimetre of blood contains 5 million red cells in a man and 4½ million in a woman. The red colour comes from the haemoglobin content which combines with the oxygen and holds it in transit. A shortage of haemoglobin produces the condition known as anaemia. The red cells have only a limited lifespan because they suffer considerable wear and tear and lack nuclei, but they are continuously being replaced from the bone marrow.

White cells are not so numerous as the red cells, being in a ratio of 1:700, but they can mobilize for action against the invasion of bacteria. The corpuscles can attach themselves to and absorb an invading bacillus in minutes. An increase in the white count can give early indications of infection.

Platelets are cells which have the function of assisting the blood to clot when there is leakage.

There is another set of channels associated with the blood vessels which carries *lymph.* This watery fluid is the 'bridge' across which pass oxygen, nutriments and wastes between the capillaries and the body cells. The liquid in a blister is lymph.

Blood is the great transport system of the body. It ferries the products of digestion from the intestines to the liver where it picks up sugar to power the muscles and amino-acids to repair the tissues. Some relatively small organs such as the kidneys receive large supplies of blood. The kidneys' primary function is regulating and filtering, and to maintain the filter system blood flow must be high and constant. The skin comes a close second—the primary function of the high blood flow to the skin is to regulate body temperature.

Muscles take most of the blood supply during exercise—the increase in flow is proportional to the increase in oxygen uptake of the working muscles. The pumping action of the skeletal muscles is also effective in increasing the flow. When one has been standing for a long time one may feel faint because the venous blood is flowing only very slowly back to the heart, but movement causes the muscles to improve the venous blood flow, and the faintness passes. The blood also carries complex coded chemical messages from the glands to the brain.

THE RESPIRATORY SYSTEM

The respiratory system consists of the *nasal passage*, the *pharynx*, *larynx*, *trachea* and the *bronchial tubes* into the *lungs*.

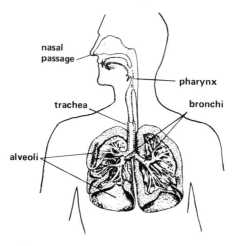

Fig. 2.4. Respiratory system.

The heart and lungs control and balance the oxygen which must be taken into the body, and carbon dioxide which must be expelled. Air passes through the nostrils where it is filtered and warmed by the mucous membrane, thence to the pharynx, down the trachea and through the large and small bronchial tubes into the lungs. The bronchi divide into smaller and smaller branches which open into tiny air sacs called *alveoli* in the lungs.

Occupying most of the thoracic cavity are the two lungs, which are shaped like inverted cones with their bases resting on the diaphragm. The right lung is divided into three lobes and the left into two. The bronchi, blood vessels, lymphatic vessels and the nerves enter the lungs on their inner sides, forming their roots. A *pulmonary artery* containing venous, deoxygenated blood enters each lung and divides up into tiny branches to form a capillary network which finds its way into every air sac and partition between the alveoli. The thin capillary wall and the alveolar wall cohere into a layer which allows the exchange of gases between the air sacs and the blood.

The lungs are paired organs and we can survive on one (like the kidneys). They weigh only about a kilogram and yet they have sufficient surface area because the membranes fold over and over on themselves—if they were spread out they would cover the area of half a singles tennis court!

The lungs are soft and spongy and the alveoli are moist, as oxygen must be dissolved before it can enter the bloodstream. The oxygen molecules are taken up by the haemoglobin in the blood and are swept along to the cells where they unite with the body's fuels to produce energy. The quantity of oxygen taken in depends on the bodily activity, and can range in the average adult from 250 cc per minute when sleeping to 5 litres per minute when running. The carbon dioxide exchanges at the same time and the oxygen and the carbon dioxide pass each other like passengers boarding and leaving a transport system, with the carbon dioxide following the same path out as the oxygen used to come in.

It is the level of carbon dioxide in the bloodstream which regulates the respiratory centre in the brain. We can decide on our own breathing to a certain extent, but the involuntary system takes over, alerted by the carbon dioxide level, when there is any stress or threat of danger. Normally the system works so smoothly that we are not even aware of it, though the common cold can obstruct breathing, and bronchitis, asthma and pneumonia are respiratory diseases which also prevent comfortable and adequate exchange.

Mechanism of Respiration

As the domed diaphragm contracts, the ribs lift upwards and outwards and the volume of the thoracic cavity is increased. The lungs expand with the inspired air which comes in because of the reduced pressure in the cavity. As the thorax returns to its original size the diaphragm moves upwards and the pressure on the lungs causes the air to be expelled. The *vital capacity* of an individual is the maximum amount of air that can be expired after a maximum inspiration, and can be determined by measuring with a device called a spirometer. The vital capacity gives an indication of the ability to respond to the additional oxygen requirements of the body during exercise. The average is 3.5 litres in normal health, but it can be increased with exercise to more than 5 litres. A high vital capacity gives an indication of potential, but a large one does not necessarily make a champion.

As well as supplying oxygen to the muscles, respiration keeps the acid/base balance of the blood constant. It is a very efficient system which can respond to the different demands that changes in bodily activity make, indeed often before work starts there is an anticipatory increase in breathing. Nervousness may cause shallow breathing which is very inefficient, but training can bring about well-defined changes in the mechanisms of respiration. In the untrained the diaphragm moves little, but if the muscles are trained the volume of air intake is increased because of the increase in lung surface made available in the enlarged thoracic cavity. As well as deepening the respiration, the actual rate of breathing is increased by training and there is a quicker return to normal after exertion. Rate of breathing is automatically adjusted by the controlling respiratory centre in the medulla oblongata when the level of carbon dioxide rises. A rise in carbon dioxide of only 4 per cent doubles the rate of breathing. During exercise the air increase may go up tenfold, and as the rate of respiration increases the heart rate increases also to promote the blood flow. Exercising at high altitude has a dramatic effect on breathing. At an altitude of 3,000 metres the atmosphere has only three-quarters of the density it has at sea level, therefore the partial pressure of the oxygen is correspondingly reduced, and the rate of inspiration has to be increased to obtain the same amount of oxygen. In extreme conditions of exertion and/or altitude there may be an insufficient supply of oxygen to the brain, which causes the individual to act as if slightly drunk. More seriously if the brain is deprived of oxygen for longer than three or four minutes, irreparable damage may be done.

In races of 100 metres or less breathing may be temporarily suspended, though most runners prefer one inhalation. The event can be completed, however, without the necessity for more oxygen, and it is after the race that the sprinters breathe heavily to restore the balance upset during the race. Under these conditions, and also during the final sprint in endurance events, there is insufficient oxygen available and *anaerobic* processes operate. Continuation of work depends on the body's tolerance to the lactic acid which forms in the muscles and the feeling of fatigue as the 'oxygen debt' builds up. The ability of the human body to carry on work temporarily without adequate oxygen is a great safety factor in emergency and also enables great sporting feats to be achieved. In an event which lasts only a short time the debt can be repaid afterwards, but in a long-lasting event the debt has to be paid as we go along. Exercise that is within the body's ability to utilize atmospheric oxygen is termed *aerobic*, i.e. sufficient oxygen is inhaled to oxidize the carbohydrate sources of energy completely to carbon dioxide and water.

There is thus a 'steady state' during moderate exercise where the intake and expenditure are balanced. The athlete can go on when short of oxygen, but efficiency is greater during the aerobic phase. The anaerobic phase should not be entered too early in a race, but if it is saved for the end the athlete can afford to be more reckless (like the sprinter) because afterwards the body can 'recharge' with high oxygen consumption. Oxygen debt is much lower from intermittent work because of the recovery phases.

Oxygen uptake depends on the capacity of the body to absorb, transport, deliver and utilize oxygen. One can measure uptake using direct methods in the laboratory, or indirect ones in the form of running tests, step tests, etc.– e.g. Cooper's aerobic 12-minute run with a table of standards for comparison.

THE ALIMENTARY SYSTEM

The alimentary system deals with the ingestion and digestion of food, its absorption into the blood, and the excretion of waste. Before food can be utilized by the body it has to be converted into soluble, diffusible substances that can pass through the walls of the small intestines and blood vessels into the blood to be conveyed round the body. This preparation of the food for absorption is termed digestion and takes place in the alimentary canal. This canal is a long, muscular tube from the mouth to the anus, which, if its coils and folds were straightened out, would measure about 30 metres in an adult.

The system is divided as follows:

Mouth: The tongue, teeth and salivary glands prepare the food before it goes into the stomach. Saliva has a slight digestive action but its main purpose is to lubricate the food and make it easier for chewing and swallowing. Saliva

Fig. 2.5. Alimentary system in relation to the rest of the body.

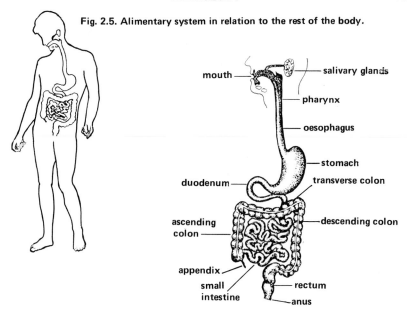

mouth

salivary glands

pharynx

oesophagus

stomach

duodenum

transverse colon

ascending colon

descending colon

appendix

small intestine

rectum

anus

Fig. 2.6. Alimentary system in detail.

flows at the sight, smell, or even thought of food, and a second flow occurs when food is actually in the mouth.

Gullet: To prevent food going into the respiratory system the epiglottis closes over the air passage and the muscular action of the oesophogus carries the balls of food down into the stomach.

Stomach: The stomach is the widest part of the alimentary tract, forming a bag below the diaphragm and the heart. It varies according to the amount of its contents. (An adult's stomach can hold 2 litres of food or deflate like a balloon.) On reaching the stomach the food is thoroughly mixed with the gastric juices and enzymes produced from the glands in the inner mucous lining of the stomach. The gastric juices, which are strongly acid, start the digestion of proteins and also destroy any germs in the food. About half an hour after the food is swallowed small quantities of semi-liquid chyme (as the food is now known) pass into the alkaline juices and enzyme bombardment of the duodenum and small intestine. Food takes about two hours to pass through the small intestine's 6 metres of coils where, as well as being subjected to alkaline juices, bile and pancreatic juices also act on the fats and starch in the food. Absorption through the walls of the small intestine passes fat into the lymph, while amino-acids, glucose and fructose pass into the blood-stream.

Large intestine: Undigested food passes from the small to the large intestine, and here most of the water is absorbed leaving the more solid faeces to be held in the rectum until expelled by defaecation.

Movement of the food through the alimentary canal is started by the voluntary act of swallowing, but after entering the gullet the involuntary muscles contract and squeeze it onwards to the stomach and intestines.

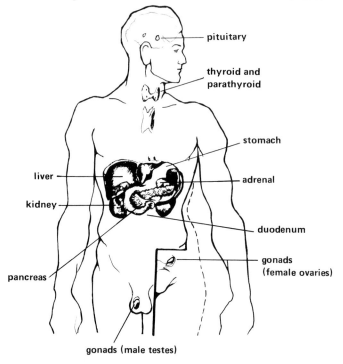

pituitary

thyroid and
parathyroid

stomach

liver

adrenal

kidney

duodenum

gonads
(female ovaries)

pancreas

gonads (male testes)

Fig. 2.7. Organs of metabolism and endocrine glands.

METABOLISM

Liver and pancreas: Foodstuffs are absorbed through the walls of the small intestine into capillaries which join to form the hepatic portal vein which takes the blood to the liver. In the liver glucose and fructose are converted into glycogen which is stored in the liver cells as well as in the muscles. Some glucose remains in the blood, and as the blood circulates the tissues which require energy are continually removing the sugar. When the blood sugar level goes down the liver responds by converting some of its stored glycogen to glucose. When glycogen reserves are exhausted the liver converts fat for use. A see-saw effect keeps the sugar at the correct level in the bloodstream. If the blood sugar level is low hunger is induced in the brain and the eating of food again leads to the conversion of the foodstuffs to glycogen for storage in the liver. The pancreas manufactures insulin which facilitates the absorption of glucose. (Where there is a lack of insulin, as in diabetes, the glucose is not absorbed and the blood sugar level becomes too high.) At times of particular stress the glands produce adrenalin, which stimulates the liver to produce more glucose.

Another function of the liver is to convert waste products into urea which is passed to the kidneys. The liver in fact acts as a general detoxifier of the body. It also acts as a store for iron and it secretes bile which is stored in the gall bladder for use in digestive processes in the intestine.

The pancreas produces pancreatic juices which are used in the duodenum, and it secretes insulin directly into the blood.

When the blood concentration of sugar goes down it causes a feeling of tiredness known as hypoglaecemia which can be relieved by taking glucose.

The digestive system works without our conscious intervention but it can be heavily influenced by the reactions induced by emotions such as fear, anxiety, anger, insecurity and general tension. When the athlete has a dry mouth and that feeling in the pit of the stomach caused by tension, the gastric secretions are being affected. When we are angry the juices are very active and food is digested more quickly, but when we are sad or fearful the stomach lining becomes bloodless and pale. Emotional reactions cause the stomach to produce acid which can cause heartburn and eventually ulcers.

WASTE DISPOSAL—EXCRETORY SYSTEM

The waste products of tissue activity are excreted through
1. the lungs, as carbon dioxide and water vapour
2. the skin, as salt and water in the form of sweat
3. the kidneys, as urine containing nitrogenous waste and unwanted mineral salts.

Indigestible food, e.g. cellulose, is excreted through the anus. (The bile pigment from the liver, from the haemoglobin of worn-out red cells, is excreted in the faeces and gives them their characteristic colour.)

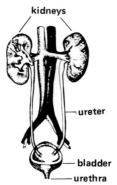

kidneys

ureter

bladder

urethra   Fig. 2.8. Kidneys.

The collection of urine is continuous and it passes down to the bladder situated in the pelvis where it is collected and emptied from time to time through the urethra. The two kidneys (they are so important that we need a pair, though we *can* function on one), which are surrounded by a mass of fat, lie in the posterior part of the abdomen on either side of the vertebral column. They act as filters, but not merely passive ones because much energy and oxygen are used in forming urine. As much as 100 litres of liquid which the body cannot afford to lose are filtered every day through 80 km of filtering tunnels, so a great amount of fluid is reabsorbed into the bloodstream. The kidneys control the level of salts in the blood plasma and they also balance the levels of water and acids. On a hot day, when one has been active without much liquid intake, the urine passed will be highly coloured but low in salt. On the other hand on a cold day, when one has drunk a few pints of liquid, the urine will be dilute and passed in large quantities.

THE NERVOUS SYSTEM

The nervous system is the 'wiring' of the body which gathers information and directs all our activities. Tiny electrical signals are passed through the network which carries the sensations to the brain and there the information is perceived as having meaning and importance or not. There are 160,000 km of nerve fibres in the human body.

The central nervous system (CNS) includes the brain and spinal cord, protected by the skull and vertebrae respectively. The afferent (incoming) nerves carry impulses bringing information about pressure, pain, touch, body position and so on, with particularly detailed and important sensations from the ears, eyes, nose and mouth. The receptors for pain, temperature and touch are in the skin, and the nerves running from the tendons and joints give information regarding the position of the limbs. Ears and eyes obtain evidence from beyond the body limits, monitoring our relationship with the surrounding environment, selecting from the welter of stimulus information available the cues that are important for the task in hand.

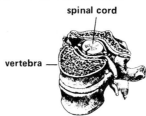

spinal cord

vertebra

Fig. 2.9. The spinal cord, well protected by the vertebrae.

These nervous impulses come through the peripheral nerves, up the spinal cord and into the sensory areas of the brain, where the cerebral cortex receives the incoming messages, analyses them and initiates responses which are translated through the efferent (outgoing) pathways to the muscles, causing the required actions.

The motor actions that are concerned in athletics activity are under this voluntary control, and the learning of skill is largely a development and co-ordination of the CNS to effect certain movements easily and rapidly. It is the CNS that reacts to the environment and co-ordinates our mental and physical activities, with the messages into and out from the brain taking only fractions of seconds. It is estimated that nerve impulses move through the 'wiring' at up to 90 metres per second, so reactions are almost immediate. There are certain actions at the reflex level which do not even impinge on consciousness, e.g. the quadriceps tap where the reflex arc does not go beyond the spinal cord and the cerebellum. Our posture is maintained without our thinking of it and this control is achieved largely by the cerebellum, or little brain, which acts as the co-ordinator of our muscular activity.

The CNS is kept very busy monitoring and analysing our conscious and voluntary activity. It is a system, however, which thrives on stimulation and where there is too low a level of sensory input it does not function efficiently. As the famous deprivation studies at McGill University show, the human body does not react happily to isolation, an equable temperature, or a comfortable limbo where there is neither sound, nor touch, nor sight to stimulate the system. Boredom, loss of concentration, even loss of contact with reality starts to occur. The CNS has an appetite for sensations which needs to be fed.

While the CNS is looking after voluntary activity the autonomic or involuntary system works steadily away monitoring our internal bodily functions. The sympathetic part of the system is geared for reaction to fright or fear and sets the body up in preparation for stress responses without any conscious decision being made. The parasympathetic part of the system quietly looks after our digestion and bladder functioning and all the myriad tasks of keeping our complex internal organs working smoothly. Because it is so efficient we normally do not even know it is functioning. Only in the case of malfunction due to disease or injury is our conscious awareness brought to bear on it.

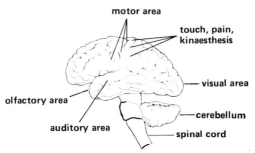

Fig. 2.10. Primary sensory and motor areas of the cerebral cortex.

The Brain

The sensory areas of the brain receive information while the motor areas initiate any physical response. The motor area is a large one located in both hemispheres of the brain, with the area on the right side of the brain mainly responsible for controlling muscular movement on the left side of the body, and vice versa. The tongue and the hands have particularly large areas available.

The association areas of the cerebrum are used for reasoning, memory, thinking and cognitive activities. The brain of each individual perceives and builds up a picture of the world for that individual—a personal and idiosyncratic view according to the experience of the perceiver in his active interaction with his particular environment.

Balance: Inside the ampulla of the semi-circular canals inside the ears are sensory cells. The fluid or endolymph in the canals moves as the body moves

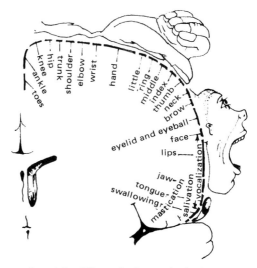

Fig. 2.11. Representation of the different body muscles in the motor cortex of the cerebrum.

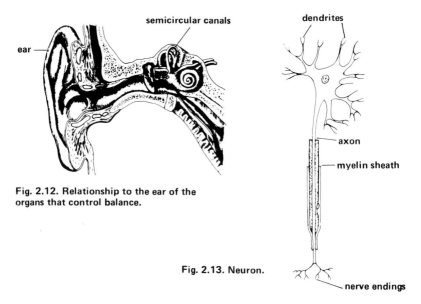

Fig. 2.12. Relationship to the ear of the organs that control balance.

Fig. 2.13. Neuron.

and stimulates the cells in three planes, indicating all directions of body movement even when the eyes are closed or the body is in free fall.

Individuals may have well-developed muscles but without good neuromuscular control they will not be able to co-ordinate the use of these muscles efficiently. The basic unit of the nervous system is the *neuron*, which is the nerve cell responsible for conducting nerve impulses to and from other parts of the body. *Dendrites* receive impulses and the *axon* passes on information to other dendrites and finally end organs such as muscles. The gap between the axon of one neuron and the dendrites of another is the *synapse,* and some authorities believe that the increase in skill developed with practice may be produced by the more efficient crossing of synaptic junctions, so that the pathways to the muscles are improved.

Motor neurons are those efferent neurons which terminate directly in muscles to supply particular muscle fibres. A *motor unit* is a motor neuron plus the fibres it innervates. Tension of the muscle depends on the number of motor units that can be synchronized, hence the intense concentration necessary in athletes preparing for maximum explosion (Edington and Edgerton).

Emotional excitement produces high levels of electrical activity in the CNS, with many motor neurons near the threshold of activation. Great muscular tensions are obtained, and indeed the stress of competition frequently causes an overshoot of the force required for the movement (Edington and Edgerton).

In the CNS there is an awareness of the external environment and the internal situation with reference to joint angles, muscle tension, muscle length, etc. The CNS receives the sensory feedback and modulates the motor activity, while the autonomic nervous system adjusts secretions to keep everything chemically in balance when the stress of exercise is induced. The stimulus for activity and its fluent co-ordination is orchestrated by the CNS.

ENDOCRINE SYSTEM

The endocrine system also helps to co-ordinate the physiological functioning of the organism (Fig. 2.7). Hormones are transported by the bloodstream, therefore the reactions to stress are not quite so rapid as in the nervous system, but the effects are more long-lasting and generalized.

The *pituitary gland* is situated at the base of the brain. This important gland, known as the 'master gland', controls the release of hormones in conjunction with the hypothalamus. The hormones secreted influence the growth of bone, muscle, kidneys, liver etc. The posterior pituitary influences muscle contraction, blood pressure and blood sugar levels.

The *thyroid* is situated in the neck, with two lobes on either side of the trachea. It secretes thyroxin which influences the metabolic rate—thus, for example, an over-active thyroid leads to fast pulse and excitability. The *parathyroid* controls the calcium content in the blood.

The medulla of the suprarenal glands, situated at the upper end of the kidneys, secrete the hormone *adrenalin.* Adrenalin stimulates the nervous system by increasing the heart rate, causing the liver to produce extra glycogen, and the walls of the blood vessels to contract to raise the blood pressure, and affecting the water and salt balance of the body. In addition the pancreas produces insulin, the ovaries produce oestrogen, the corpus luteum secretes progesterone and the testes produce testosterone—all hormones which have an effect on development and function.

Emotional stimuli can elicit endocrine reactions, with perceived stress as important as actual stress. The system will respond at different stages of the exercise process, and in anticipation of activity the individual's response can range from complete unconcern to being sick with nerves and anxiety. The release of hormones increases the heart rate, the sweat glands activate themselves and the blood pressure rises.

The endocrine system is largely under the control of the nervous system, and as a result emotions can readily alter hormonal secretions during exercise. The hormonal response is related to the relative degree of stress that exercise places upon the body, and the more stressful the activity the more severe the hormonal response. However the degree of stress on a well-trained individual will be less than the stress imposed on a non-trained person doing the identical task (Edington and Edgerton).

The initial stages of exercise elicit great endocrine response as the body moves from a resting state to the exercising condition. Then, during prolonged exercise, the body attempts to find a new steady state and it may try shifting energy sources or attempting a more acute stage of response. When the stage of exhaustion is reached adrenal or pituitary depletion may occur, but it seems that the endocrine system is not the limiting factor, since post-exercise levels of hormones are still high until the recovery phase is complete.

The heart and its vessels, circulation, respiration and digestion all contribute to the body's response during exercise. These are the energy support systems which respond to the demands made by training, competition and stress. The efficiency of these systems, the CNS and glands is vital to the athlete, and their complex interaction is a miracle of organization which comes into play whenever the human organism functions and athletes make demands on themselves.

REFERENCES

ASTRAND, P., and RODAHL, K., *Text Book of Work Physiology.* McGraw-Hill, 1977.
COOPER, K.H., *The New Aerobics.* Bantam, 1970.
EDINGTON, D.W., and EDGERTON, V.R., *The Biology of Physical Activity.* Houghton Mifflin, 1976.
HEALY, C., *Methods of Fitness.* Kaye & Ward, 1973.
HOCKEY, R.V., *Physical Fitness.* C.V. Mosby, 1973.
KARPOVICH, P.V. and SINNING, W.E., *Physiology of Muscular Activity.* W.B. Saunders, 1971.
SAGE, G.H., *Introduction to Motor Behaviour — a Neuropsychological Approach.* Addison-Wesley, 1971.

3

MECHANICS

A sprinter exerts *force* against his blocks in his start, *accelerates* over the first part of the race and finishes at a certain *velocity*. The shot putter exerts force on the shot as he moves across the circle, accelerating it up to a high final release *speed* directed at a certain optimum *angle*. Mechanics is the branch of physics concerned with force and movement, and since athletics is very much concerned with these, an understanding of mechanical principles is invaluable for coach and athlete. There are a few words and concepts in mechanics which seem strange and new to the uninitiated. In fact almost everyone can understand the basic principles involved by realizing that mechanics is like learning a language—except that it is a very easy language to learn because there are only about fifty new words. And it is possible to get a very long way in the study of mechanics without any mathematical knowledge.

'Mechanics' is a general name for the study of forces and everything to do with forces; 'biomechanics' is concerned with human and other animal forces,

Fig. 3.1. Only in comics can we actually see a force!

and there are one or two other words like 'kinesiology' which mean very nearly the same thing.

It is interesting to stop for a moment and ask oneself: 'What is a force?' It is such a familar word, and yet it is rather difficult to define it better than being a pull or a push, because you can't see a force—you can only see the results of a force.

NEWTON'S FIRST LAW OF MOTION

It was Isaac Newton who first stated clearly the principles of motion. He pointed out the obvious, but very important, law of nature that nothing can move unless it experiences a force. This he extended in saying that nothing can change its state of motion unless an external force acts—which is not quite so obvious, since for example a shot launched by a shot putter very quickly comes to rest without help from anyone, until we take into account the ever-present forces of gravity and friction. This first law of motion states the simple fact that an athlete is not going to produce or change motion in his own body or in an external object such as a discus, unless he can 'evoke' a force or two.

Strictly speaking we should refer to an 'unbalanced force' or 'nett force' when considering a change in rest or change in movement of a body, since more than one force may be acting on it at the same time and it is possible that these may cancel each other out.

MOTION

When we talk about the motion of an object we usually imply that it has a certain speed—that is it moves through equal distances in equal time intervals. If we want to specify a speed in a particular direction we use the word *velocity*. Velocity is a *vector* quantity since it has magnitude and direction (see p. 62).

Imagine a race between a runner and a shot putter of twice the runner's size. Although they may be sprinting along neck and neck there seems to be more 'something-or-other' about the shot putter's motion. The physicist calls this *momentum* and defines it as mass multiplied by velocity—although the shot putter is moving at the same velocity as the runner, his larger mass gives him a greater momentum.

MASS

Like many of the terms already mentioned, mass is not a new word to us, but it may be useful to define it nevertheless. It is a measure of the quantity of matter in a body. We shall come back to it later.

Centre of mass of a body is an imaginary point where all the mass can be considered to be concentrated (Fig. 3.2).

ACCELERATION

Whenever an object starts to move from rest, or whenever it changes its velocity, it must *accelerate* (increase its velocity) or *decelerate* (decrease its velocity). So the definition of acceleration is that it is the rate of change of velocity. If the change of velocity is very rapid, as with a sprint start, the acceleration is large, and, by contrast, the acceleration of a marathon runner at the gun is relatively smaller.

NEWTON'S SECOND LAW OF MOTION

With the definitions of the terms used so far it is now possible to understand Newton's Second Law of Motion, which states that the rate of change of momentum of an object is proportional to the impressed force on that object. Since in our examples the mass doesn't change, we can alter this statement to say that 'the mass multiplied by the rate of change of velocity is proportional to the force', or, because of our definition of acceleration, 'the mass multiplied by the acceleration is proportional to the force'.

Newton's Second Law states:

$$F = k \left(\frac{mv_2 - mv_1}{t} \right)$$ where   F is the impressed force

k is a constant

m is the mass of the object

$$\text{or} \quad F = km \left(\frac{v_2 - v_1}{t} \right)$$ v_2 is the final velocity

v_1 is the initial velocity

and   t is the total time of application of the force

$$\text{and since} \quad \frac{v_2 - v_1}{t} = a$$

$$F = k\,m\,a$$ where a is acceleration

A very useful concept is that of *impulse,* or force multiplied by time:

$$Ft = km\,(v_2 - v_1)$$

It will be shown later that the final release velocity of the shot is most important for a good distance to be achieved. Newton's Second Law makes it clear that a larger force will make the shot go further; or a lighter shot will go further if the same force is applied; or the same shot will go further if the same force is applied over a longer time. It can now be seen that mass is a measure of the inertia of a body, i.e. its reluctance to change its state of rest or motion.

This is all highly simplified because in actual fact forces rarely stay constant, and for example in shot putting the force on the shot is changing all the time as the athlete goes through his complicated movements. However the principles are still true and just require the application of slightly more complicated mathematics in the analysis. The O'Brien style of shot putting is an excellent example of mechanics aiding sport, for this technique allows the longer application of body forces to the shot than the sideways-on style which was used before the 1950s.

NEWTON'S THIRD LAW OF MOTION

Newton's Third Law is also very simple, and states that if a force is exerted on an object an equal and opposite force must act on another body. The shot putter experiences the same force backwards on his hand as he himself exerts on the shot. Normally this is transmitted through his body to the ground, but if his feet have left the ground before the shot has been given the final push with the arm his whole body will receive the same force as this arm push and experience a backwards acceleration. The runner drives downwards and backwards in the propulsive phase of his stride, and the earth pushes upwards and forwards on his body. The earth, being so large in comparison to the runner, experiences an infinitesimal acceleration in the opposite direction. Runners training on beaches will know how difficult it is to apply force to the loose sand. It is amusing to see beginners attempt the hitch-kick in long jumping even when they are given springboards or trampettes to help them stay a long time in the air. Running in the air with no resistance to the backward drive of the leg is a very different sensation from running on an athletic track, and the novice long jumper in flight will waggle his legs in the strangest manner!

Newton's Third Law has many implications for the athlete, especially when airborne—for example the hurdler when crossing a hurdle will find that a movement in one part of his body may have an unexpected reaction in another part of his body if he is not well trained (see Figs 21.1 and 21.2).

ADDING FORCES AND OTHER VECTORS

Frequently two or more forces act on a body at once, and the total effect has to be determined by summing the forces to obtain the one imaginary resultant force which produces the movement. In sprint starting the contribution from each leg must be taken into account in the final movement. However, force is a vector quantity in which the direction of the line of action is as important as the actual size of the force. A vector is a physical quantity which has magnitude and direction and can be represented by a straight line drawn to scale. Vectors are usually drawn with arrows showing the direction. The arrowed vectors in Fig. 3.2 represent the forces evoked by each foot at this particular moment in the sprint start, and they have been drawn to scale so that their lengths indicate the size of the forces and their directions show the appropriate angles to the horizontal. Vectors in the same direction can be added simply by adding the magnitudes, but usually they are not in the same direction and the parallelogram or triangle methods of addition have to be used.

athlete's centre of mass

Fig. 3.2. Forces evoked during a sprint start.

force vectors (lengths of lines proportional to magnitude)

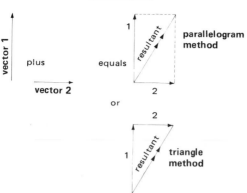

Fig. 3.3. Addition of vectors.

Fig. 3.4. A biomechanical investigation of the sprint start, using instrumented starting blocks.

TYPES OF FORCE

Forces of interest to us in athletics are:

Muscle forces
By means of a complex timing of muscle contractions in his body the athlete is able to exert forces to be able to walk, run, jump, hurdle and throw. How-

ever he is also subject to the external forces of friction, air resistance and gravity.

Friction forces

Two surfaces in contact experience the force of friction if there is any tendency for them to move relative to each other, and friction will always oppose this motion. It is fortunate that this is so, otherwise our feet would just slip out from under us when we tried to walk or run.

Friction increases as the forces tending to cause relative motion between the surface increase. Eventually however a point is reached when slipping occurs, and this limit depends on the nature of the surfaces which hold them together. A light grip on a smooth vaulting pole will slip much easier than will a tight grip, and 'friction' tape wound on the pole will create an even more secure grip. Similarly a sprint start on a cinder track by an athlete wearing ordinary flat shoes is a disastrous endeavour, even though it is possible to run quite fast under these conditions. In the sprint start the forces tending to move the foot in relation to the track are great, and because of the body lean the proportion of body weight directly over the feet is small. The situation is changed completely if the nature of the surface of the foot is changed by wearing spiked shoes.

Aerodynamic Forces

Air resistance experienced when running is connected with the frictional forces caused by the viscosity of the air. Unfortunately athletes cannot do much about this unless they are runners in the events at 800 metres and upwards, where they can try to run in the lee of the leaders. Only the discus-thrower and sometimes the javelin-thrower benefit from winds blowing against them.

Gravity

The force of gravity acts on all bodies, and if they are free to fall it accelerates them all at the same 9.8 m per second every second (this value changes slightly depending on the locality, and actual motion is affected by air resistance). Gravity is an ever-present force, which tends to modify the motion of athletes and their implements.

TYPES OF MOTION

Linear

Newton's laws, as we have stated them, apply to motion in a straight line— linear motion. However, because it is difficult to nullify the effect of friction and gravity, and because of the structure of the human body, true linear motion is rare in sport. Sprinters run down the track in a fairly straight line, but this is only apparent, since their mass centres are moving up and down and their limbs are moving in angular motion about their joints. Linear motion is the consequence of the resultant line of action of forces acting through the centre of mass of a body.

Curvilinear

Even when the motion in athletics tends to be linear, other forces act to pull the body or implement off-line, e.g. the shot starts off in a straight line at the instant of release, but gravity, which has been opposed until then by the body forces, immediately causes the shot to be accelerated in the vertical direction back to the ground—the resulting trajectory being a curvilinear one produced by the compounding of the motion at release and that caused by gravity.

Angular

When the line of the resultant force acting on a body does not pass through the centre of mass, angular motion and linear motion are caused. The discus-thrower directs the forces he applies to the discus slightly off-centre, so that it leaves his hand with spin as well as forward linear motion. This has a gyro-scopic effect like a spinning top which tends to stabilize the discus in flight. Sometimes angular motion is an embarrassment in athletics and has to be slowed down or even reversed. For example, the long jumper generally gains forward rotation from the eccentric, or off-centre, forces of the take-off, and he can either slow this down by means of the 'hang' technique or he can counteract it by using a hitch-kick (see p. 308).

In angular motion there is a centre line, or axis, about which the body rotates—a hurdle, when hit hard, will topple over by rotating about the end in contact with the ground. Similarly in falling over with a rigid body from the standing position, one rotates about the feet, since they are restricted by friction and the ground. Once in flight however, if angular motion is present, the athlete rotates about his centre of mass (note that this statement is true only for the athlete in his own frame of reference—to an external observer the athlete appears to rotate about an 'instantaneous' centre which is continually changing).

We measure distance travelled in linear motion, but in angular motion we have to refer to the *angle* traced out by the body as it rotates about its axis. The angle moved through in unit time is the *angular velocity* and the rate at which angular velocity changes is the *angular acceleration*. This similarity to linear motion can be taken even further if we replace mass, or inertia, with the concept of rotational inertia, or *moment of inertia* as it is called, which defines the reluctance of a body to start rotation, or to change once it has started. This quantity is dependent not only on the total mass, but also on the way in which the mass is distributed about the axis. A long jumper in the 'hang' position in flight has a larger moment of inertia about a horizontal axis though his centre of mass because he stretches his body segments away from his centre of mass, but in the 'sail' position, where he jack-knifes at the waist, he brings his legs and arms in towards his centre of mass, resulting in a smaller moment of inertia.

Linear momentum, it will be remembered, was defined as mass multiplied by velocity. The analogy in angular motion is *angular momentum* and is defined as moment of inertia multiplied by angular velocity. Just as linear momentum gives us more information about linear motion, so angular momentum is a much more precise measure than the descriptive term 'angular motion'.

We have one more important analogy to make before applying Newton's laws of motion to angular movement. In order to produce rotation a force must act in a direction which does not pass through the axis of rotation. Here we talk about the *moment of force*, which is defined as the force multiplied by the perpendicular distance from the axis to the line of the force.

The first very important principle to arise from Newton's laws of motion applied to angular movement is that the angular momentum of a body remains unchanged unless an external moment of force acts. While in contact with the ground, e.g. during the high jump take-off, the athlete can evoke a moment of force which will produce rotation, but once in flight he has nothing to push against, and his angular momentum must therefore remain the same until he lands. A springboard diver appears to be changing his rotation in mid-air when he performs a multiple somersault, but in fact his angular momentum remains constant all the time he is in flight. Because angular momentum is determined by both angular velocity (the rate of spin) and the moment of inertia (dependent upon the body posture in the air) the diver can speed up his spin by going into a tuck position, and he can later slow down the spin by opening out for the entry into the water. All the while his angular momentum will have a constant value.

Transfer of Angular Momentum
The human body, being so flexible and mobile, can transfer its angular momentum from the whole body to a part, or parts, of the body in flight. The actions of a long jumper have been mentioned already, and now the reasons for these actions become clear—at the take-off the jumper tends to gain some forward rotation which can make his landing inefficient in that he doesn't get his feet out in front of his body and so loses some distance. By adjusting his take-off he may be able to jump with no rotation at all, but then the take-off would be inefficient and he would still lose distance. He can therefore either (a) slow down his rate of rotation by ensuring a large moment of inertia with a hang position, or (b) take up the rotation by 'running in the air' with a hitch-kick action, which is in effect a transfer of the angular momentum from the whole of his body to the legs and arms.

If the forward rotation of the legs and arms is such that their combined angular momentum is greater than the angular momentum of the whole body at the instant flight begins, then there will actually be a slight backward rotation of the whole body since the total angular momentum in flight can only be that which is developed during the take-off.

The long jumper, in taking up unwanted body rotation in his legs, is transferring angular momentum from the whole to a part. But the reverse—transferring angular momentum from a part to the whole—is a mechanical principle used in many athletic techniques. For example the straddle high jumper's free leg swing, in addition to providing a reaction force to help lift him in the air, also helps him to rotate into a horizontal position for clearing the bar. During the take-off angular momentum is built up in the free swinging leg, and as flight begins this angular momentum is transferred to the whole body. Sometimes the biomechanics of the body cause unwanted rotations and compensating movements have to made. The eccentric thrust of the legs in ordinary running has to be counteracted by swinging the arms—one arm being swung upwards and forwards as the leg on the same side drives downwards and backwards—otherwise rotation about a vertical axis through the body would result. The arm action becomes even more pronounced in running over a hurdle, since the forces tending to produce rotation are even larger in the hurdle take-off.

Newton's Second Law equation may be written as follows for rotational motion.

$$Fd = \frac{Iw_2 - Iw_1}{t}$$

where   F is the force
         d is the perpendicular distance between the line
           of the force and the axis of rotation
         I is the moment of inertia
         w_1 is the initial angular velocity
         w_2 is the final angular velocity
and   t is the time during which the moment of force,
           Fd, acts

Generally the initial angular velocity w_1 is zero and the equation may be written:

$$Fdt = Iw_2$$

A hammer-thrower strives for great turning speed about a near-vertical axis, so it is clear from the above equation that he can achieve this by exerting a large moment of force for as long a time as possible, i.e. by extending the duration of the double contact phase.

The same equation shows that a bent leg (less moment of inertia) can be brought through quicker than a straight one (large moment of inertia) in the swing phase in running.

CONCLUSION

The treatment in this chapter has been deliberately kept as simple as possible, but the mechanics of the human body with its multi-segmented construction are rather more complex. For example even in an activity as apparently simple as running, the various segments of the athlete's body are rotating in various directions, some even in opposite directions. In many activities, e.g. high jumping, the mechanical analysis is even more difficult because movement takes place in three dimensions. When applying mechanical principles, the coach should aim to look for the overall effect rather than scrutinize the movement of a single limb. He should also be aware that because of the complexity of the human body it is sometimes possible for two sound mechanical principles to be in opposition to one another—for example there is a good mechanical reason for forcing the hips backwards in a throw but there is also a good mechanical reason for forcing them forwards into the delivery. The coach may have to decide which mechanical principle will give the better overall result. Similarly he may have to weigh up mechanical reasons for a particular action against conflicting physiological or tactical considerations. A simple example is that of running on the toes—efficient mechanically over short distances, but too demanding in terms of fatigue over long distances.

The coach must also be aware that patterns of movement in an athlete have been learned over a period of time and are the result of complex neurophysiological processes in which timing of muscle contractions is critical. To change a pattern may also mean upsetting the timing and the flow of the movement, and a decrease in performance can actually result from an attempt to make an action more mechanically efficient. It is therefore essential that promising athletes are in the charge of a good coach as soon as possible in their careers.

On the other hand the application of mechanics in athletics (Fig. 3.4) is becoming more and more important as the returns from physiological training become less. Biomechanics researchers such as Ariel are already using computer modelling to suggest more efficient movements in athletics.

REFERENCE

ARIEL, G. 'Computerized Biochemical Analysis of Track and Field Athletics', *Track and Field Quarterly Review*: 72:2. 1972.

4
PSYCHOLOGY, CHILD DEVELOPMENT AND SOCIOLOGY

Psychology and sociology are young sciences. Psychology has only been established as a separate discipline from philosophy since just before the turn of the century, and sociology is even younger. They are sciences because they try to employ the techniques of observation and experimentation that are the trademarks of the natural sciences but, as the subject for study is the behaviour of men and women in all its complexity, it is difficult to establish clear-cut laws. Psychology is the study of behaviour, though 'psyche-logos' means literally 'discourse on the soul' in the more romantic Greek version of the activity.

What the social scientist observes are the outward manifestations of man's behaviour, and 'behaviour' with the broad meaning that encompasses everything that a person says, does, or expresses in any way. The outward signs are the evidence, but from this inferences are made regarding thought processes, feelings and internal functioning . . . what goes on inside the 'black box'. There is a famous school of psychology known as the Behaviourists, who are particularly devoted to the scientific approach—introspection, intuition and any conclusions not based on strictly controlled experimental procedures are denied. Early work in psychology was often anecdotal—the description of an unusual individual case which led to interesting speculation on the human condition. Freud, perhaps the best-known name in psychology, based his brilliant and imaginative analysis of human personality on a small number of middle-class Viennese hysteric patients—hence the unwillingness of many empirical psychologists to accept his work. His terms have become part of the language, however, and though not all of his ideas are accepted, many of his intuitive leaps are still the best explanations we have of certain behaviours.

Introspection, describing how one felt when undergoing certain experiences, was a favoured technique, but after rejection by the Behaviourists some interest in the reportage of individual experience is returning today. The humanistic and ideographic outlooks of writers like Allport and Maslow are gaining in recognition, and we are all curious to know how top athletes 'felt' in crucial competitions—this is often the first question the press ask. Much modern personality study is based on self-report and interest is again being shown in the contents of the 'black box'.

Do top-class athletes actually see, hear and sense sporting situations differently from ordinary mortals? Do they perceive in a particularly acute way that facilitates their performance?

Perception was studied carefully and methodically by the Gestalt school in Germany at the beginning of the century and conclusions were drawn which suggest that much of our perceptual organization is innate as opposed to learned. A great deal of time and energy in psychology has been taken up over nature—nurture arguments and many disagreements still exist, many of them generating more heat than light. In the field of intellectual functioning the fashions have swung between the predetermined view of the believers in the omnipotence of heredity and those who consider experience is everything. Watson said, 'Give me a child and I will make of him anything you will', whereas many thinkers still believe that 'You cannot make a silk purse out of a sow's ear', and after all 'Blood will out.' The evidence is conflicting, but the ethologists have shown that what appears to be instinctive behaviour in birds, like pecking and nest-building, is learned. On the other hand problems like ulcers and schizophrenia are strongly influenced by heredity. The answers are difficult to disentangle because as soon as an individual is conceived the environment starts to operate—are children good athletes because their parents were good athletes and passed on the right genes, or is it the family setting of participation and encouragement that is provided?

The stance of the social scientist must always be a neutral one—it is his brief to observe and record but not to pass judgment. It is difficult to be completely objective, since the observer always carries his prejudices, interests and perceptual idiosyncrasies with him, but he can be self-aware and replications can be attempted. Cross-cultural studies are particularly difficult because the student of any other society is a product of his own society and will view with the background, concepts and understanding that his own education and experience have given him. Though conclusions must be guarded, techniques go on developing and even a few seeds from the study of other cultures and systems may blossom into fascinating comparisons with our own. Other cultures are not necessarily in other countries—within our own society there are subcultures whose manners and morals are largely unknown and misunderstood by those outside such social groups and within the familarity of their own.

The sports psychologist is an up-and-coming member of the fraternity which already includes industrial, occupational, clinical, educational, social and developmental psychologists and many others. The sports psychologist is interested in certain areas of overlap with other specialists—occupational psychology where professionalism is involved, clinical psychology where there is mental breakdown or extreme emotional problems, and there is a broad sharing of topic areas with educational psychology, which is concerned with principles of learning and motivation, and individual differences in personality and development. The coach is an educator where pedagogy is his applied field of psychology. Studies in sports psychology have been initiated in the main by those interested in physical education who wish to improve the quantity and quality of sports involvement. PE specialists and teachers have sometimes been accused of destroying tentative participation of the not-so-good in competitive and embarrassing school sports programmes, but these teachers also represent the group who strive most to develop our athletes of the future.

When a superb athlete is seen in action the questions that are often asked are, 'What programme got him to this stage of excellence?' 'How did he begin?' 'What were the earlier experiences that laid the foundations for the record-breaking performance?' In studies of human functioning the psychologist is always forced back in time to the earliest childhood experiences, the parents, the home, the family, the neighbourhood and the particular features that make up that individual's environment, from the most obvious physical and material conditions, to the most subtle establishment of attitudes and values, and delicate emotional and personal reactions. Let us spend a little time now on more aspects of children's development which are particularly relevant to motor progress.

CHILD DEVELOPMENT

The child's first interactions with the mother are physical—kicking before birth, and sucking, crying, touching and orienting after birth. Crying, though eventually having an emotional basis, is at first a physical demonstration of excitement; kicking and moving and wriggling show levels of physiological arousal; and the orienting reponse—attending to visual, auditory or tactile stimuli by turning towards the source and following the mother's gaze, is a perceptual motor response. The intellectual efforts of the infant are, in terms of movements, integrating what is seen and heard and kinaesthetically felt. The eyes follow toys that are moved, hands and feet are 'discovered' through movement and its recognition and repetition. The physical senses are the avenues through which the environmental stimuli impinge upon the child and at first it may be William James' 'booming, buzzing confusion', but such chaotic sensations become organized, selected, distinguished and made meaningful perceptions as a result of the child's continuous interaction with the world. Constant repeated features, both objects and people, become stable and recognizable, and the perceptual constancies of shape, size, colour and texture are formed. The child can only master this complex process if he is given the opportunity to do so, if he is in what the developmental psychologists call a 'stimulating environment' in which there are variety and change as well as comfort and stability and security. The child is not the 'tabula rasa' waiting to be written on, but an action-packed bundle of senses, feelings, co-ordinations, chemistry, neurology, physiology, anatomy and curiosity— getting to grips with novel surroundings.

The famous child psychologist Jean Piaget was originally a biologist interested in the interaction of plants and animals with their environment. He noted that development towards maturation depended on how hostile or supportive the conditions were in which growth was taking place. He brought to developmental psychology this interactionist view of maturational stages and applied it to stages of thinking through which children progressed. The first two years of life he termed the sensori-motor stage, in which the child's thinking is through action. Concepts of space and distance are discovered through movement in such space, and concepts of cause and effect are initiated through action and its result. Properties of objects are discovered through handling them and investigating them in a physically active manner. The mental and the physical are inextricably interwoven and our thinking processes are movement based.

Developmental Age

The course of physical development has been well observed and documented by writers like Gesell and Tanner. The pattern of development is similar for all children—big movements before delicate ones, crawling before walking before running and so on. Different children move through the stages more quickly than others and progress can be encouraged by interested adults giving opportunity for play and skill development. Tanner has introduced the term 'developmental age' which is related to physiological maturity rather than chronological age and is estimated generally through the study of the bones and teeth. The concept of developmental age has more relevance to physical skill development than that of the birthday age, though the latter is always used in organized sport.

Critical Stages

There is another important developmental concept and that is the idea of 'critical stages'—these are stages of development lasting for limited periods of time when it is crucially important for the organism to undergo, or not undergo, particular experiences. A well-known example is that of rubella (German measles) contracted by the mother during the first three months of pregnancy —sensory defects of blindness and deafness can result in the child—but it is only during that critical stage of development that the damage is done. In the animal world it is vital for the 'following behaviour' of an emerging gosling from the egg that the most important moving object in the environment during the first hours of life is mother goose. Konrad Lorenz discovered that goslings could imprint on a toy goose, a model duck, a cardboard box and even himself or any other individual who happened to be present at the 'critical stage' for imprinting. Though imprinting is most easily observed by ethologists, it is becoming evident that similar imprinting occurs in human development. The discussion is really part of the nature—nurture debate. Behavioural patterns which are innate are triggered off by certain environmental stimuli. Such experiences in early life persist, and the lack of them leaves an unfillable gap, which can exist in intellectual, emotional, physical or social terms. Unless, for example, young children interact consistently and regularly with an attentive and positive mother figure, the critical stage for the development of loving human relationships may be affected (Bowlby 1953, 1969). If children do not have the opportunity to develop speech and language of an elaborate nature during their early years, it is very difficult to compensate for the loss later (Bernstein). It is also suggested that appropriate masculine and feminine behaviour may be the result of imprinting (Cratty). Although there is little definitive evidence, it is certainly recognized that there are particularly appropriate times in development for acquiring physical skills. 'Learning' to swim, skate, ski, etc. is very much easier in childhood than in adulthood, and though tension and self-consciousness in the adult play a large part in his difficulties, the ease with which children 'pick things up', particularly those activities involving the whole body in balance, suggests that it is more than an emotional and social difference, rather it is a 'critical stage'.

Perceptual Skill

Perceptual experience is also closely tied to maturation and development, with the eye and brain developing in response to various visual stimuli. After cataract operations formerly blind persons have to 'learn to see' or rather 'perceive' the objects in their environment, even though their eyes are now functioning adequately. It is impossible for a human being to take in all the incoming sensory information available for processing—the human information-processing channels just cannot cope with such overload. In order to function efficiently the growing child and the emerging adult have to select those elements of the information which are important, and reject others which are redundant. What we eventually attend to is a product of our learning and experience, and the more skilled we become in certain aspects of work or play the better our selection and attention-giving. Postulating evidence from throwing and catching, Cratty believes that children develop perceptual ability and the motor competence catches up. But good early movement experience is a feature of the childhood of many talented athletes.

Children's Games

As childhood progresses opportunity arises for independent action, when a range of complex motor skills emerges. Jumping, hopping, climbing etc. are all practised repeatedly in the games played by children in street and playground. Girls and boys are equally lively, though sex differences begin to show in the girls' skipping and ball routines and the boys' more physical contact games. It appears that children's games are not quite so popular or widespread as they used to be, as described by the Opies. Unsafe streets, lack of play space and too much television may be destroying a valuable heritage for children.

There are several theories of organismic development in which the physical, emotional, intellectual and social elements are seen as interacting. Certainly some measure of positive correlation is found between physical and mental abilities, but it is strongest at the lower end of the scales where motor impairment and intellectual inadequacy often coincide. The development of physical abilities is important emotionally and socially, and able children are generally healthy and well adjusted. Opportunities for social success are available through physical prowess, particularly for boys in our society, and prestige and popularity can be gained. This is particularly true in adolescence when physically growth spurts take place and physiologically there are sex and hormonal changes. Girls reach maturity some 18 months before boys, but boys eventually surge ahead in size, strength and fitness. General improvement occurs in reaction time, co-ordination, balance and fitness but, except in special cases, girls reach a plateau at 13 or 14 while boys go on improving until 18 and beyond, depending on opportunity and interest. Why some girls and boys continue to be involved in athletics while others drop out will be an important part of the discussion of motivation and social and personality factors in later chapters.

Play

In the introduction some comments were made on play but it is such a pervasive topic in a text of this nature that it will continue to crop up. The 'playful' element is important in motivation, since an enjoyable playful activity will tend to be repeated. Play involves thought, language and creative endeavour and therefore contributes to intellectual development, and in return intellectual development will allow more complex and highly structured forms of play. Play involves exploration, experiment and discovery, which are essential ingredients in the learning process where practice and repetition refine perceptual and motor skills.

Social skills are also developed in the co-operation and competition of the play situation, and friends are made and lost in the group activities in which children discover who are the followers, who are the experts, and who the also-rans. The whole emotional range can be explored in play and some theorists believe that one of the most important functions of play is its therapeutic one by which frightening and unpleasant situations can be played through and made more acceptable. Dramatic play depends on imitating. Role-play, self-expression and the successes desired in reality may be achieved in fantasy.

The type of play the child can handle depends on age and levels of conceptual and social development. Individual play comes first, then playing in parallel though not actually together. Competition follows and it is a fascinating thought that children compete before they can co-operate. Truly co-operative play—sharing, taking turns and submerging self for the good of the team—requires quite advanced social and intellectual development. Rules are a necessary part of the play situation and the complexity of the rules will determine the appropriate play activities for the children involved. Middle childhood is very concerned over fairness and equality and devices are used to even the odds in picking sides and choosing teams. The play boundaries are accepted, however, and although taken seriously at the time, even young children know it is not 'for real'.

Games are also culturally dependent—the style of game will be influenced by geography, whether the child lives near the sea, near water, on low ground or in mountains, in warm or cold or temperate climates. Even the seasons change the games. Each culture also passes on through its game forms the value systems of importance within it—be it predominantly competitive, co-operative, or concerned with achievement or obedience. Our athletic competitiveness is culturally instilled, as we shall see in Chapter 10.

EMOTIONS AND MOTIVATION

The psychologist, particularly the personality theorist, is fascinated by the emotional make-up and development of the individual. Though the raw materials of temperament appear to be inherited (Birch, Thomas and Chess), the individual's reaction to stress, his anxiety levels particularly in relation to competition, the ways he copes with fears, anger and aggression are of vital interest to the coach and social observer. The words 'emotion' and 'motivation' have the same root—being 'moved' in some way, and the positive and negative effect of certain situations and people have important influences on behaviour. The emotional basis to wants and needs can be the deciding factor that influences decisions about sports involvement. When the sport has a positive emotional tone for the participant, participation and effort will be maintained.

Another link between motivation and emotion is that between anxiety and fear of failure. Great effort will be made to avoid failure and even a moderate degree of anxiety will induce effort and often optimum performance. It is a delicate balance, however, and anxiety that is too strong will cause a breakdown in performance, and fear that is too great will make the individual withdraw from the situation rather than face possible failure. The knowledge of successful results is, according to Ogilvie, the strongest form of motivation, and having success is an emotionally toned position—the joy of achievement is sought, to be repeated. Motivation is perhaps the most intriguing topic in psychology. As inquisitive human beings, we always want to know why individuals choose and persist in certain activities. Why do athletes get involved in painful and time-consuming training? 'Never again' says the marathon runner at the end of 26 miles 385 yards—but another time and another race finds him running to exhaustion again. Is it for money, for trips, for celebrity headlines? When asked, athletes themselves give such a variety of answers that one is forced to accept that motivation is very personal, that it is dependent on the individual's background of success and/or failure, on personality factors and on the social motives that may drive him on to further success. An attempt will be made to analyse the theoretical and practical aspects of motivation in Chapter 11, but the great coach Fred Wilt says very simply that 'good athletes want to succeed and they do something positive about it!'

COACHING

Motivation is a key factor in learning and teaching, and in Chapter 12 attention is focused on the role of the coach and teacher in the development of athletic excellence. Though teaching is sometimes called an art rather than a science there are certain principles of instruction which are useful to the 'artist' in pedagogy. The coach is important as a personality and as an inspiration to his athletes, as well as being a source of expertise in a variety of events. The coach needs to be able to call on and understand the range of sciences that are relevant to his field and he must be able to translate technical jargon into a comprehensible form that the athlete can use and apply. As an educator the coach must be familiar with the principles of learning, the effects of repetition and practice, the spacing of such practice to acquire skill and fitness and the fostering of positive attitudes to the sport. This is no mean task. A good coach is rare and in Britain we are guilty of giving too little importance and status to the coach—the man or woman behind the scenes without whom most athletes would be pale shadows of themselves as competitors.

LEARNING

The whole area of learning is one of the most researched in sports psychology. There are so many variables in any learning situation—material or task to be learned, the learner, and the methods being employed by the instructor—that many qualifications have to be made when making statements of principle. The introduction to Chapter 6 will take a closer look at what is known about learning and the ways of acquiring the expertise required by a top athlete.

SOCIALIZATION

All human development and learning takes place against a social background. We are social beings through our dependent childhood, and we remain social beings even when apparently autonomous adults. The process by which we become members of our society is termed 'socialization', and in that process the individual acquires the language, customs, manners, values, attitudes, behaviour and thinking that are part of the sub-culture of which he is becoming a member. A complex system of rewards and punishments operates to ensure that acceptable behaviour is repeated and that unacceptable behaviour is not. 'That's naughty!' 'That's not what we do!' 'That's not for little girls!' 'Clever boy!' 'Fancy doing that at his age!' and so on. Complex sex-typing occurs and often the socializers are unaware of what they are instilling because the process is so subtle and so much part of the social fabric of everyday life. Sex differences and the special problems of women athletes will be discussed in Chapter 15. Women are different in anatomy and physiology—that's obvious—but there are differences in motivation and social expectations that are perhaps not so evident until given a closer, objective, look.

AGE

Expectations according to age operate as well as expectations according to sex, and the athlete is usually expected to be 'over the hill' by the time he is thirty-plus. An interesting development is currently taking place of 'veteran' or 'masters' athletics for the over-forties, in which the standards are so high in many events that we must revise our ideas on age-related performances. Social attitudes are again important and people drop out of a sport less often for physical reasons than because of increased responsibilities and the distraction of other aspects of the mature individual's lifestyle. Medical advice and the increase of hypokinetic disease is bringing older men and women back to physical involvement—but the benefits that accrue to the active older person are way beyond the physical increase in their vital capacity and the reduction of their fat layers! Chapter 14 will examine the effects of physical activity in relation to age.

SOCIAL FACTORS

Athletics is a social phenomenon. Competition is against others; co-operation is with others; the presence of an audience has its effect; the need to do well for one's coach or one's team has its effect; the social class and the community we belong to—all have their influence on our participation. The attitudes to sport that we build up are acquired socially, often during our schooldays, and whether we tend towards conformity or deviance in our behaviour then could influence the sport we take up or ridicule. The 'ethos' of involvement is part of the value system operating in our social milieu, and whether we spend our cash on spikes or fashion shoes is not only a matter of economics but also the priorities we have established and the aspirations we entertain.

The problem of leisure and how to use it is frequently said to be one of our most important social questions of the not-so-distant future. As more leisure time becomes available, with reduced working hours and more labour-saving devices, do people, particularly the younger members of society, have the resources, the interests, the abilities and the sense to make creative and valuable use of their leisure time? Recreation is defined as the activity to build up our energies again, to alleviate boredom, to 'play' and to re-create ourselves mentally, physically and spiritually.

Athletics today has an occupational and business element involving pro-fessional administrators, coaches and athletes. Sports equipment businesses back up athletes' performances, and the top firms are all keen to get the most successful athletes wearing their shoes and track suits. Athletics facilities, such as the new synthetic tracks and elaborate jumping and throwing equip-ment, are extremely expensive. Spectators form an important part of the competitive scene—supporters have their group loyalties and political affinities. Every sport needs an administration and though in Britain this has traditionally been in the hands of devoted amateurs the present trend is towards some form of professional administration, since the tasks are becoming too great for even the most hard-working amateurs to handle. International fixtures, coaching schemes and facilities require large sums of money, and sponsorship involves great financial responsibility. In the background political questions are always looming—government interference in sport, for instance, and issues like professionalism or shamateurism, apartheid and drugs have caused ripples of disturbance that have become big enough waves to upset Olympic partici-pation. The news reporters are ready to get their teeth into controversial issues and a whole sporting press and literature has grown up round sport. All these are social issues which influence individual athletes, sometimes personally and sometimes indirectly. The effects of the social environment will be looked at in more detail in Chapter 10, which describes the differences between nations with regard to the organization of competitive athletics.

In Eastern Europe sport has a high social and political value. Writing of East Germany, Erbach, says that sport 'develops character, utilizes spare time in a sensible way and gives pleasure and joy and teaches people to adopt an optimistic attitude to life'. In Soviet Russia 'sport is for prestige, pride and satisfaction with a programme of heroic proportions' (Dunning). Sport has its rewards in the western world too, though these are felt to be more personal ones. Correlation of sporting ability and intellectual performance is positive, so the athletically proficient child is generally better adjusted than the less proficient one. Similar correlations are found at college and university levels. Self-esteem is built up by being good at an activity that is admired socially. The 'self' concept, which is accumulated from social responses and appraisals which the individual experiences, is enhanced by being 'good at sport'. 'Self' concept is an important element of the personality and there are interesting relationships between personality and performance.

PERSONALITY

Are personality differences the cause or the result of involvement in sport? Kroll suggests that perhaps an individual has a certain set of personality factors that motivate his involvement, but that only those with certain traits will persist long enough to become successful. Ogilvie suggests that those who continue in tough competitive programmes are those who are 'pretty well put together emotionally' anyway. The rich get richer, and the others drop out.

The present state of personality and performance research makes it almost impossible to find total order in the findings. Much remains contradictory but the instruments for research are imperfect and there are problems in defining personality and establishing agreed theoretical positions. Personality research is an interesting, though somewhat frustrating, topic, in the social sciences, with some theorists considering personality to be the centre of the discipline since it embraces everything that goes to make up a person and 'how he characteristically behaves' (Heim). Human individuality may refuse to be pigeon-holed and Allport thinks we are each so idiosyncratic that no personality types exist. In Chapter 13 an attempt will be made to look at the present state of personality research and the findings in relation to athletics.

The main topic areas of psychology and sociology that are relevant to the science of athletics have now been touched on, but scientific knowledge must be applied. In Part II some of the concepts introduced in this chapter will be elaborated and the knowledge available will be applied to the practical task of being an athlete.

REFERENCES

ALDERMAN, R.B., *Psychology of Sporting Behaviour.* W.B. Saunders, 1974.

ALLPORT, G.W., *Pattern and Growth in Personality.* Holt, Rinehart and Winston, 1963.

ARNOLD, P., *Education, Physical Education and Personality Development.* Heinemann, 1968.

BERNSTEIN, B., *Class, Codes and Control.* Routledge & Kegan Paul, Vol. 1, 1971.

BIRCH, THOMAS and CHESS, 'The Origin of Personality', *Scientific American,* August 1970.

BOWLBY, J., *Child Care and the Growth of Love.* Pelican, 1953.

BOWLBY, J., *Attachment and Loss,* Hogarth Press, 1969.

CRATTY, B.J., *Psychomotor Behaviour in Education and Sport.* Chas. C. Thomas, Springfield, Illinois, 1974.

DUNNING, Eric (ed.), *The Sociology of Sport,* Cass and Co. Ltd, New Sociology Library No. 2, 1971.

GESELL, A.L. and ILG, F.L. *Child Development.* Harper, 1949.

GLANVILLE, B., 'The Olympics: What Makes a Team', *New Society,* 10 October 1968.

GLASSER, R., *Leisure.* Macmillan, 1970.

HEIM, A.H., *Intelligence and Personality.* Pelican, 1970.

LOY, J.W., and KENYON, G.S., *Sport, Culture and Society.* Macmillan, 1969.

MASLOW, A.H., *Motivation and Personality.* Harper and Row, 1954.

OGILVIE, B., and TUTKO, T.A., *Problem Athletes and How to Handle Them.* Pelham, 1966.

OPIE, I. and P., *The Lore and Language of Schoolchildren.* Oxford University Press, 1959. *Games of Street and Playground.* Clarendon, 1969.

PARSONS, T., and BALES, R.F. (eds), *Family, Socialisation and Interaction — Process.* The Free Press, 1965.

TANNER, J.M., *Education and Physical Growth.* Unibooks, Hodder and Stoughton, 1978.

WILT, F., and BOSEN, K., *Motivation and Coaching Psychology.* Track and Field News Press, 1971.

5

RESEARCH METHODS

INTRODUCTION

The expression 'the science of athletics' suggests that the study of athletics can be supported by scientific methods. The sciences include the physical sciences, the biological sciences, the social sciences and the science of measurement. Science is factual and based on quantifiable data. It exists to establish causes or causal connections between events and it bases its results on experimental procedures and the collection of empirical data. The mere expression of opinion is inadmissible, unless inferred from evidence, and results are preferable to notions and guesses. An essential of sports research is that it is applied. Rather than starting from theory and making applications, the tendency in sport is to move pragmatically from a problem situation to finding solutions objectively and with neutral evidence to seek to influence practice.

Certain aspects of athletics are easily quantifiable and the stopwatch and the measuring tape are difficult to argue with—indeed in recent years instrumentation has become increasingly more sophisticated and accurate. The results of a performance can be clearly evaluated, but the means of attaining such results involve many complex variables. Two athletes can clear a high jump bar at 2 metres—for one it may be a superb performance within the limits of his physique and ability, while for the other it might be quite an ordinary feat and technically not all that sound. In one respect, therefore, athletics is quantifiable and in another it is not, since human beings are never totally analyzable and to cope with their behaviour and influence may be as much an art as a science.

The problem of research involving individual performers is the quantity and complexity of the variables in any given situation. One difficulty can be the problem in terms that can be clarified and utilized. Is the problem worth investigating? Is it possible to investigate? Research is seen by Burroughs, for example, as a cyclic activity: locating the problem, untangling the variables, formulating hypotheses, appealing to experiment, generalizing from the experiment and then back to locating a new problem. Certainly research in any field must be planned, systematic and objective. Only those variables that *can* be identified and measured are included, even though in a dynamic and stressful situation these might not necessarily be the most important. In top levels of competition, where the performers are so close as to be barely distinguishable, non-scientific terms like 'luck' or 'heart' or 'character' are used for the differences between winners and losers. Some rare individuals exist who on paper are unlikely to win, but who can do so on the day. Perhaps the interest shown in the biographies and autobiographies of top athletes is an attempt to follow qualitative approaches rather than merely quantitative studies. The social sciences generally are witnessing a shift to the acceptance of more idiosyncratic and descriptive work which gives opportunities for insight and illumination that may be partly generalizable rather than producing clear-cut, scientifically acceptable data (Parlett and Hamilton 1972).

Another general problem in research is the lack of results getting through to coaches and administrators. Very often technical reports are neither read nor understood by the people working with up-and-coming talent. Much research is carried out in separate academic institutions in different countries, and though there may be some pooling of knowledge at conferences it is not always clearly applicable to the club coach with a group of middle-distance athletes or a schoolteacher with thirty children for a games lesson. Often the conclusions of research projects are wrapped in qualifications and statistics and so many athletes still 'follow their noses', or their coach's. More is already known in theory than we apply in practice.

There must be adequate resources in terms of money and trained manpower to organize effective sports research. There must be appropriate structures for the dissemination of information; there must be career structures for researchers, and as more money is spent on development it must have sound research foundations (Taylor 1973). A sympathetic political, social and educational climate is also essential, and policy-makers must see research as making a valuable contribution.

We are making some important assumptions—that excellence in sport is desirable, that research and development are worthwhile, and that the application of such knowledge should be used to improve performance even at economic and personal cost. We will return later to a fuller discussion of 'Why people play' (Ellis 1972), and why people want to play better and better, but we must be aware of our objectives when using research and measurement techniques. These are to get our athletes running faster, jumping higher and throwing further than anyone else! If these objectives are agreed, then let us proceed . . . .

Measurement and evaluation are essential elements of athletics. In few other competitive sports is so much determined by measuring instruments or is evaluation so precise. Meticulous training diaries are kept by most athletes and coaches, with every repetition run and every pound lifted carefully and systematically recorded. Objective recording produces clear information and the athlete can not only 'feel' his progress but can see the evidence on paper in front of him. It provides a means of evaluating the training programme with a view to improving results, and continued evaluation is an essential element in the training scheme.

ANATOMY AND PHYSIOLOGY

Physics, chemistry and biology are basic sciences underlying the study of anatomy, physiology and human biology. All the resources of accumulated knowledge and techniques employed by the science of medicine and its sub-divisions are now being used by specialists in sports medicine and sports injuries. We still lag behind in this field in the west but Eastern Europe, particularly East Germany, has recognized the importance of this area of research and development.

Anthropometry

Historically, anthropometric measures of the human body were the first attempts at scientific sports investigation. In the 1860s Cromwell produced developmental progress charts and in 1878 Dr Sargent at Harvard published a manual of physical measurements of outstanding college athletes. Kretschmer in *Physique and Character* in 1925 further developed this interest in body types by his work on asthenic (thin), athletic (muscular) and pyknic (fat) categories, thus influencing Sheldon who developed somatotyping, a scientific procedure which describes the morphology, or form, of the human body in a quantitative manner (Sheldon and Stevens). The physique of the Olympic athlete still attracts attention (Tanner) and analyses continue to be made of the appropriateness of certain physiques for certain events in the athletics programme. An Olympic Village is the place to find the extremes of physical development from 7-ft tall, thin, basketball players to 5-ft 'square' weight-lifters, with everything else in between—it is perhaps the decathletes who have the best-balanced physiques.

Anthropometry has standardized its techniques and the tools used over the years, and the developmental growth of the human being from childhood through adolescence and adulthood, for example, has been charted in detail.

Tests of Physical Fitness

Experts disagree over the definition of 'physical fitness', but most fitness tests include measures of muscular strength, muscular endurance, power, agility, flexibility and cardiovascular condition. Several tests including these and other items have been constructed and standardized in the United States, though British norms are now being developed (Campbell and Tucker). For example the Basic Fitness Tests developed by Fleishman include items like pull-ups, leg lifts, shuttle runs, hand-grips, jumps and a balance test.

Strength

As far back as 1910 J.H. Kellog introduced a dynamometer which recorded grip strength in lbs pull. Increasingly ingenious and refined instruments are now available in the form of tensiometers and dynamometers to measure back and leg strength as well as hand-grip. These are isometric instruments which measure with no movement of the resistance or the joints involved.

Isotonic strength tests included repetitions of pull-ups, dips, sit-ups, push-ups, etc. with the weight of the body acting as a resistance for the muscle groups to work against. Maximum repetitions of pull-ups and dips which are really muscular endurance tests (with modifications for females) are included for example in the Rogers PFI first developed in 1925. Clarke Harrison has now refined a test with precise measures of strength in thirty-nine joint movements, so there are progressively specialized measures being developed.

The 'strength set' of isotonic weight lifting, comprising the squat, the dead lift, and the bench press, can be used with the maximum poundages lifted, giving an index of strength. A certain amount of skill is involved in these exercises, but not to such a degree as in the Olympic lifts, and certainly the one maximum effort gives an indication of strength apart from muscular endurance.

Fig. 5.1. Examples of exercises used in tests. Left, push-ups, and right, modified 'chins' for women.

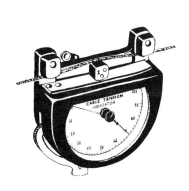

Fig. 5.2. Cable tensiometer used by Harrison.

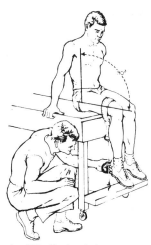

Fig. 5.3. Strength of hip flexion being measured with Harrison's cable tensiometer.

Power

This is defined as the rate of doing work (or force × velocity) and tests include standing jumps, shot put etc., where not only strength is involved but also speed of movement. The best-known test of power, first developed by D.A. Sargent back in 1897, is the Sargent Jump or Vertical Jump. It has been found that systematic weight training can improve power (Chui) and that speed is more significantly related to power than is strength (Wilkin). It would appear that power is an important indicator of potential for athletics. Adamson and Whitney have criticized the use of the word 'power' in connection with the Vertical Jump. They argue that the test is rather a measure of impulse (or force × time).

Agility

This is the physical ability that enables an individual to change his body positions and direction rapidly and precisely. The squat thrust or burpee (it was devised by R.H. Burpee) is the most commonly used test of this ability; dodging runs of various kinds round obstacles are also used.

Balance

Various tests of balance are used, including balance on one leg, with eyes closed, and on narrow wooden supports both crossways and lengthways. Well-illustrated examples of these tests can be found in a variety of recent publications, e.g. Baumgarten and Jackson, Campbell and Tucker etc.

Reaction Times

These have been studied systematically, using various techniques from response to flashing lights, to measuring how quickly a dropping scaled rule can be trapped between the hands. Reaction-time measurement has been the cause of much controversy and the subject is complex. In 1934 it was established that the optimum period of time for the performer's response between a preparatory auditory command and the signal to go was in the range 1.4—1.6 seconds (Nakamura), and this was confirmed by later work in the 1950s.

Flexibility

Flexibility or the range of movement about a joint, is measured in terms of how far the back can be hyperextended, how far the shoulder can be rotated, how far the ankle can be flexed etc., since flexibility is specific to the joint involved. Very general statements therefore cannot be made save that girls tend to be more flexible than boys and flexibility tends to decrease during adult years. However it has been established that flexibility can be improved by stretching exercises, particularly of the static stretching type (De Vries). Leighton has developed an instrument for measuring the flexibility of thirty joint movements, so in accord with other advances in measuring techniques increasing refinement is occurring in this sphere too.

Cardiovascular Condition

The general cardiovascular condition is the ability of the circulatory and the respiratory system to adjust to and recover from the effect of exercise. Using bicycle ergometers and treadmills, specific work can be undertaken and measurements of oxygen uptake (the amount consumed per kilogram of body weight per minute), pulse rate and blood pressure can be taken accurately. Gas analysis equipment can determine the ability to consume oxygen during exhaustive work, and the rate and amplitude of respiration can indicate the vital capacity.

The well-known Harvard step test, in which the athlete is required to step up on to and down from a bench for a set time, is frequently used as an estimate of cardiovascular endurance, with great importance given to the pulse-recovery rate after exercise. The publicity surrounding the publication of Cooper's book on aerobics has also familiarized many with the 12-minute run/walk test, where the distance covered in the 12-minute period is considered a good indicator of cardiovascular fitness (Cooper).

Also in the laboratory blood tests can be taken to establish, for example, haemoglobin levels, and any falls during intense training can be noted and acted on since the red blood cells are vital for oxygen transportation. The discovery of athletes (particularly females) who are anaemic is surprisingly common.

The electrocardiograph can be used to monitor the functions of the heart and assist the laboratory worker to determine the tolerance for exercise and to detect any weaknesses or health problems.

BIOMECHANICS

The science of biomechanics is rapidly becoming established for the objective measurement of movements and forces involved in athletics. For example, measurements from ciné film and the use of force platforms provide data for the analysis of the actions of athletes. Faults can be detected and comparisons can be made with data from the same actions of top-class athletes, so that suggestions can be given concerning points of technique which, hopefully, will lead to improved performance.

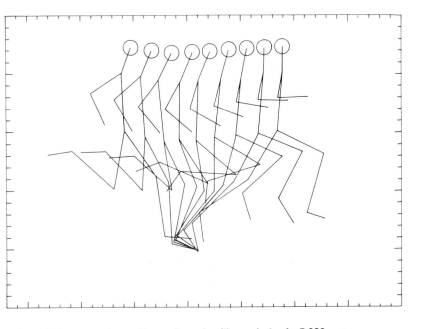

Fig. 5.4. Computer-drawn diagram from cine-film analysis of a 5,000 metre runner.

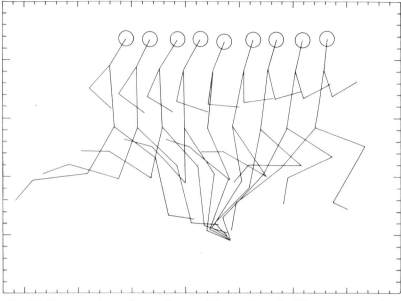

Fig. 5.5. Computer-drawn diagram from cine-film analysis of a 400 metre runner who runs on his toes.

Fig. 5.6. Each of the thrower's feet is on a separate force platform which registers the pattern of the forces on the recorder at the left of the picture.

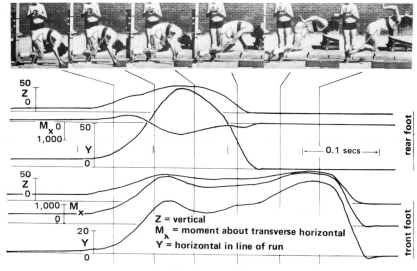

Fig. 5.7. Sprint start forces.

PSYCHOLOGY

Experimental psychologists are very interested in learning—that mysterious process which 'causes a more or less permanent change in behaviour that is not attributable to maturation'. Under controlled conditions the researcher manipulates the variables until consistent and 'reliable' results are obtained—or not obtained, which may be just as important. The acquisition of complex motor skills, the transfer effects of some forms of training, and the phenomenon of 'attention' receive scrutiny.

The behaviour of the individual in stress situations, particularly the psychologically frightening effects of top-class competition with the presence of spectators and TV cameras, is an elusive and difficult area to study but some workers are attempting to seek causes of individual differences in response to such pressures and to find ways of alleviating such stress. Many different methods of personality assessment have been developed, ranging from projective tests based on Freudian theory to paper and pencil self-report forms. Again test constructors have been careful to standardize their instruments, even though no absolute values can exist in such a field.

SOCIAL BEHAVIOUR

Athletics is never carried on alone—even if the training session is a lonely one there is always a competition or a selection involving others and performance is before an audience. It is an essential feature of athletic performance to be compared with others—therefore it is a social activity and sociologists and social psychologists are interested in sport as an expression of cultural and group behaviour.

RESEARCH DESIGN

The *nomothetic* approach seeks to explain human behaviour from theories and laws which apply to large numbers of people and situations, so the focus is on group similarities. The contrasting but complementary approach to research is to employ an *ideographic* viewpoint, which is concerned with individuals and individual events with the focus on idiosyncratic elements.

Whichever general perspective is adopted, the first step is to formulate a problem, a researchable problem with hypotheses formulated against the background of existing knowledge. Richard Nelson maintains that the coach must be the one to pose the problems, and the researcher must try to solve them. As the coach has contact with the athlete, the researcher himself can keep a low profile.

The background of existing knowledge is established by a survey of the available literature.

Library Research

This involves discovering all the relevant information available in printed texts, theses and research abstracts. Has work been done in the area? How was it done? Is it repeatable with more sophisticated technology? With a larger or a different sample? Some researchers go no further than a survey and co-ordination of all the existing material, since some problems cannot be researched empirically.

Historical Research

In many respects this is a form of literature search, though emphasis would be on original documents and source material. Careful relationships would be made with the historical period in which the researcher is interested, and on past influence on present practice. For example, the type and amount of sport involvement of females at different periods in different cultures can be studied in this way.

After the literature search the problem can often be refined and the most appropriate research approach decided upon. The method chosen may be experimentation, or interviewing, or a survey, or a case study, or a combination of several of these. Standardized testing may be employed, or the main method might be observation. If each of these methods is looked at quickly in turn the possible types of information obtainable and the relative strengths and weaknesses may be assessed.

Experiment

This method is closest to that of the scientist working in the laboratory. Conditions can be imposed so that variables can be controlled and many replications made. It may be as simple as having a pre-test group which is then subjected to certain training and then tested again, or two matched groups may be used, only one of which has the special treatment, and then their performances can be compared. Where only one variable is to be controlled, for example two groups doing a similar programme of weight training, one receiving a drug treatment and the other group a placebo, then the results of the drug on training can be determined. There are limits to what one can do ethically, but this method is conducive to economy and precision. It is a very useful method because 'much important theoretical work takes place in experiments because more realistic materials are too complex to get a simple picture' (Simon).

Observation

Data can also be collected by observation where the situation is not suitable for questions or measurements. The disadvantage of observation is that it is very slow and tends to be subjective. The observer has to wait for things to happen and must not interfere in the process that is being observed or the results will be distorted. Using trained observers who will give very clear statements of exactly what is being observed, schedules and categories can be devised to help structure the vast amount of possible material. The samples would tend to be very small but it is sometimes the only method available for fluid situations, e.g. the observation of a sports programme in another country.

Questioning

A partly structured situation can be set up by using an *interview*. The interviewer can have a list of questions available but is free to follow up any interesting sidelines that might emerge in the 'steered' conversation with the subject. The personality and skill of the interviewer is important in establishing rapport with the interviewee, and if the interviewer knows the topic area well he can pick up important points to use in later interviews or for structuring into an actual questionnaire.

The *questionnaire* is an impersonal version of an interview. The printed and posted questionnaire is an apparently quick and easy method for collecting information from a widely spread population. If the material is fairly straightforward and simple enough to frame comprehensible questions, and if the respondents are able and willing to provide the answers, the questionnaire is a useful social research tool.

The disadvantage of a mailed questionnaire is the non-response—40—60 per cent at best is the usual return and the sample tends to become a biased one. It is difficult to ensure that the respondents to either interview or printed questions are telling the truth, though reliability can be looked at in terms of internal consistency and it is sometimes obvious if someone is faking. Factual information can be conveniently gathered in this way and with the aid of the computer many thousands of responses and relationships between responses can be analyzed. The researcher will only get out what he puts in in terms of the questions asked—and there is always the danger that one is not asking the right questions!

Surveys or Field Studies

These are conducted to establish the nature of existing conditions and the researcher starts with observations of what has already occurred. A variety of instruments may be used including interview, tests and questionnaires, and the scale may range from a few cases to a national census. The time orientation may be to the past or the present, with a cross-sectional study gleaning a vast amount of data from a large number at the same time, and a longitudinal study collecting information from a necessarily smaller number over a period of time.

The advantages of a survey are that the setting is the 'real world' with no interference, the samples may be large and the range of material obtained very wide. The disadvantages are lack of control and the fact that the variables cannot be manipulated. There are dangers of triviality too, in that the sample population must have the relevant information and be ready and willing to supply it.

The smallest scale of survey would be of a few cases which could be examined in much greater detail. Such *case studies* need careful observation and collection of materials which might include tapes, films, letters and diaries. It provides an opportunity to study rare or unusual cases, and though it is a narrow viewpoint it can be intensive and qualitative. Though it may take a long time in practical terms, a longitudinal case study could be important in establishing critical periods when certain major events or developments occurred. The disadvantage, of course, is that it is dangerous to generalize from individual cases and even experienced researchers may introduce unknown subjective bias. Autobiographies and biographies of famous athletes would fall into this category.

Tests

Standardized tests may be used in case studies and in survey work. A wide range is available, though some of them are restricted to experts in the field. Standardized tests, as the name suggests, are administered and scored according to very specific instructions. It is important that the tests are objective, with answers or performances that will be scored in identical fashion whoever is the tester. The objectivity of scoring and the standard procedures make the tests high in reliability as measuring instruments. The validity of the tests lies in the claim that they measure what they claim to measure, concurrently in that they correlate highly with current performance, and predictively in that they are indicative of future performance. The best-known tests are those of verbal reasoning and of different school attainments, but tests of physical abilities of the type mentioned earlier in the chapter are also structured in this way.

Inventories may also be used to estimate *attitudes*, in that they gather observations about the behaviour of individuals by asking for responses to statements expressing some attitude on a scale along the agree/don't know/ disagree continuum. Such attitudes towards success, failure, competition, events, coaches etc. can be used in establishing a system of values and behavioural dispositions which could be important relative to athletic participation.

EVALUATION

The evaluation of the data obtained and of the programmes studied is the vital last stage. After statistical analysis of the data what inferences can be made? What effective changes can be introduced? What objective information have we obtained of interest to the athlete and coach? What can be applied?

REFERENCES

ADAMSON, A.T., and WHITNEY, R.J., 'Critical Appraisal of Jumping as a Measure of Human Power', *Medicine and Sport 6, Biomechanics II*. Karger, 1971.

BAUMGARTEN, T.A.., and JACKSON, A.S., *Measurement for Evaluation in Physical Education*. Houghton Mifflin, 1975.

BROOKE, J.D., and WHITING, H.T.A. (eds), *Human Movement — a Field of Study*. Henry Kimpton, 1973.

BURROUGHS, G. E. R., *Design and Analysis in Education Research*. University of Birmingham School of Education, 1971.

CAMPBELL, W.R., and TUCKER, N.M., *An Introduction to Tests and Measurements in Physical Education*. G. Bell and Sons, 1967.

CHUI, E.F., 'Effects of systematic weight training on athletic power', *Research Quarterly 21,* 188—194. October 1950.

COOPER, K.H., *The New Aerobics*. Bantam, 1970.

DE VRIES, H.A., 'Evaluation of static stretching procedures for the improvement of flexibility', *Research Quarterly*. May 1962.

ELLIS, M.J., *Why People Play*. Prentice Hall, 1972.

FLEISHMAN, E.A., *The Structure and Measurement of Physical Fitness*. Prentice Hall, 1964.

HARRISON, C.H., *Application of Measurement to Health and Physical Education*. Prentice Hall, 1967.

NAKAMURA, H., 'Experimental Study of Reaction Time of the Start in Running a Race', *Research Quarterly Supplement* 5 : 33—45. March 1934.

NELSON, R.C., 'Practical Approaches to Research', *Track and Field Quarterly Review*. Winter 1975.

PARLETT and HAMILTON, *Evaluation as Illumination, Occasional Paper 9*. Centre for Research in Educational Sciences. 1972.

SHELDON, W.H., and STEVENS, S.S., *A Psychology of Constitutional Differences*. Harper, 1942.

SIMON, J.L., *Basic Research Methods in the Social Sciences*. Random House, 1970.

TANNER, J.M., *The Physique of the Olympic Athlete*. Allen and Unwin, 1964.

TAYLOR, W. (ed.), *Research Perspectives in Education*. Routledge & Kegan Paul, 1973.

WILKIN, B.M., 'The Effect of Weight Training on Speed of Movement', *Research Quarterly 23* : 361—369. October 1952.

Part II

FACTORS AFFECTING PERFORMANCE

6

TRAINING

'There are no shortcuts to the top. Training, training and more training, along with your ability and will, it will take seven years.'

Martti Vainio
(1978 European 10,000 metres champion)

INTRODUCTION

What is training? All athletes rush off to do it each day, but what exactly happens? When one asks athletes why they train, they are sure to say that it enables them to compete at a higher level, and that the training prepares them for their events by getting them fit and strong and by improving their skills. But what does this all mean?

It is difficult to define fitness as it depends on age, sex, occupation and previous experience. It also depends too on what one is considering fitness *for*—in short-duration activities it can be strength and co-ordination that are most important, while in longer-term events endurance and stamina are at a premium. In the past, when life depended on hunting and gathering, good physical condition was essential for survival. Before the days of mechanization the human body was the machine used in labouring, and in some societies today this is still true. Where legs are used instead of wheels, the conditioning for speed and stamina obtained is well demonstrated by great African runners from rural backgrounds who have been running since childhood. In more settled and sedentary times the promotion of fitness has to be deliberately sought through training procedures.

Training is a systematic process of repetitive, progressive exercise or work involving learning and acclimatization. (Klafs and Arnheim)

Training is the net summation of adaptations induced by regular exercise [and] exercise results in a tissue state that enables the body to tolerate more effectively subsequent stresses of a similar nature. (Edington and Edgerton)

The process of stressing the sportsman and his adaptation to these stresses is called sports training, and it is the means by which sports performance is improved. (Thomas)

Specific training effects will depend on the individual, the type of exercise or stress, and the previous levels of training of that individual. Various systems of the body can be stressed and adapted according to the type of work carried out, and each event and each athlete will have different needs and objectives to be met in training, hence the need for individual schedules, though these are based on general principles.

The *muscular system* can be trained to adapt to sub-maximal work by increasing the utilization of oxygen and stored glycogen. Greater proportions of muscle can be trained to take part in the oxidative processes during endurance activities.

The muscular system can also be increased in its capacity to exert contractile force, and heavy resistance work can produce hypertrophic effects and increases in strength.

The *cardiovascular system* can be adapted to increase oxygen transport and to increase its ability to deliver oxygen to specific muscle fibres.

The *respiratory system* can be improved in its ability to extract oxygen from the atmosphere and to facilitate gas exchange for aerobic activity.

The *nervous system* can be trained to pattern responses and to integrate and co-ordinate skilled activity. Central nervous system adaptation can also be effected by raising the pain threshold, e.g. in endurance training, and new levels of tolerance to pain and distress can be developed.

The *endocrine system* can increase its ability to communicate responses to stress, and the *metabolism* alters in response to the demands of exercise.

Generally the principles of training operate in terms of gradually increasing stress—a form of loading where increasing controlled demands are made on the body which gradually increases its ability to adapt and respond to such stresses, whether they are in terms of strength, endurance, skill or the response to the competitive pressures of the athlete's chosen event. (It applies to other sports than athletics, too, and Neil Wilson describes how Eddie Chapman improved the badminton play of Gillian Gilks, who was already very good, by putting her through a fitness training routine which made sure that 'no one could live with her' as he put it. The skill was there, but stamina, strength, flexibility and relaxation techniques were added, which improved her skill and made her performance more devastating.)

The principle of overload holds in that the body adapts to increased demands made on it and the rate of adaptation will be related to the *intensity* of the sessions and the *specificity* of the programme. *Repetition* is essential for muscular efficiency, be it low reps against high resistance for strength gain, or high reps against low resistance for endurance. The athlete and coach must always have a goal in training, and the exercise tasks must be specific to that goal. Athletes need speed, strength, endurance, flexibility and skill but different events demand different levels of each, so training must be geared to the event, the athlete and his developmental stage. Response to training is individual and unique, but all athletes need to be motivated (see Chapter 11), for where there is interest and effort and variety, the desired effect of progress and improvement in performance will come.

Even allowing that response to stress is individual, some general factors in training for different ends can be examined.

SPEED

This is the capacity to perform successive movements at a fast rate. It is difficult to analyze athletic speed in scientific terms. Is it the reaction time in the laboratory? Is it the general speed of movement, the time taken to move the limbs rather than the time taken to respond to stimuli? Is it the rate of motion of the whole body? Is it the ability to accelerate?

Early experimental work was mainly done on reaction time and it was found that boys tend to have faster reaction times than girls, that reaction time improves up to the teens, that athletes have faster reaction times than non-athletes, and that sprinters have faster reaction times than long-distance runners (Karpovich). The pre-motor *reaction time* is that elapsing between a stimulus and the initiation of the response by the contractile mechanisms (Clarke). *Movement time* is the time taken in the act of moving the limbs — and these times are not necessarily the same. Cratty notes that an intense stimulus produced a quicker reaction time, and also that a 'set' to respond is important in influencing the speed of reaction. The brain has to send messages to all the body systems to initiate action, and practice in making such responses—to the starter's gun, for example—will cause changes in the central nervous system rather than in the muscles themselves. Speed is perhaps the most difficult of the basic training essentials to tackle in terms of training advice because it is the element which appears to be least susceptible to change. As Sharkey says, 'Reaction time is a function of the nervous system and pathways cannot actually be accelerated, only awareness can be improved which will facilitate the movement.' The speed of reaction is affected by the state of the body and muscles, though no matter how stressed and practised the reactions are, a drop in temperature, for example, can reduce speed of reaction by half.

Movement speed is more important to athletics than simple reaction time. Speed is important in so many events apart from the obvious sprints against the clock. Speed of approach in jumping is vital and so is speed of execution of movements in the air. The distances attained in the throws are influenced more by speed of delivery than by any other single factor. The ability of athletes to go through complex movements at speed is crucial. If it is so important is it trainable?

It is essential that practice is done at speed, at the rate of performance required in the contest (Singer). As skill and strength are developed, speed will emerge. It is difficult, however, indeed counter-productive, to attempt to perform skilled acts at speed before one is capable, but where accuracy and balance and strength are attained then speed is one of the results. Sharkey also maintains that movement time can be improved with a weight training programme involving the related muscles. This tends to be very task-specific, however.

As Klafs and Arnheim note, in speed activities there is an expenditure of energy for only a brief time. Sprints, jumps and throws are anaerobic and allow oxygen debt to be built up which can be paid back during recovery. In a stress-type event lasting only seconds, the heart rate goes up and sends increasing oxygen to the muscles—in readiness for the recovery demands (Clarke).

One of the most interesting physiological discoveries of recent years has been that of 'slow twitch' and 'fast twitch' muscle fibres. They are identifiable in that they differ in colour under the microscope with the white fibres (fast twitch) predominant in those who perform speed activities of short duration and the red fibres (slow twitch) predominant in those who perform sustained activities. It would appear that there is little change in fibre make-up as a result of training and that the presence of 'white' or 'red' is mainly genetically determined (Edington and Edgerton). In all activities no one type of motor unit is used exclusively and everyone has in their musculature a variety of slow and fast twitch fibres, e.g. the soleus contains more slow twitch fibres and so fatigues more slowly than the gastrocnemius which contains more fast twitch fibres (Edington and Edgerton). The legs of weight lifters and sprinters can have up to 80 per cent fast twitch, while the legs of distance runners and the arms of distance swimmers have only 20—25 per cent fast twitch fibres. It would seem that sprinters really are born rather than made, but of course speed can be improved—and the fast interval training at both over and under distance is an essential part of the sprinter's programme. The throwers get faster and are able to accelerate better as increasing skill and co-ordination and strength permit. Indeed it is impossible to talk about speed in isolation and we must now look at agility, co-ordination and flexibility.

AGILITY

Agility is the ability to shift direction with balance and accuracy. Speed is required but so also is the smooth integration of movements in a co-ordinated pattern. Accuracy of movement requires body control and good timing, and is largely the result of skill training which will be discussed presently. De Vries notes that co-ordination depends on feedback of information concerning what the muscles are doing. This proprioception can be of two types, (i) kinaesthetic feedback from the receptors in the muscles, tendons and joints, and (ii) vestibular feedback from the receptors in the non-auditory labyrinths of the inner ear. The ability to pick up and understand this feedback is again partly innately determined but also the result of training and practice.

FLEXIBILITY

This will also encourage speed of running, turning or jumping because the range of movements at the joints is increased. Skills can also be developed where there is sufficient flexibility to allow the desired movements without restriction.

Flexibility varies according to age with young children more flexible than adults, and females more flexible than males. Young female Olympic gymnasts are evidence of this. Active individuals keep more flexible than inactive ones, as the connective tissue round the joints shortens and loses elasticity when in the shortened positions of inactivity. Flexibility can be improved greatly by a well-structured regular programme of stretching exercises. It is better, of course, that flexibility is not lost after childhood, but even fairly rigid adults

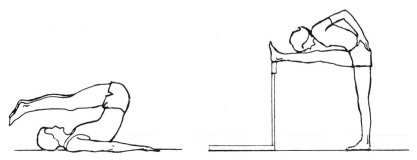

Fig. 6.1. Examples of flexibility exercises.

can improve the range of movement in their joints—the popularity of yoga classes gives some support to the satisfaction obtained from steady and controlled stretching.

The limits of flexibility are controlled by the bone structure and the soft tissue of the joints. These impose limits, but the latter can be improved particularly by static stretching programmes rather than ballistic exercises where bobbing and bouncing often damage the ligaments and tendons rather than stretching them.

The athlete/coach must analyze his event and establish *optimum* flexibility for improved performance. *Maximum* flexibility could be undesirable, since *too* great a range could actually slow down certain movements. Specificity of training again applies, so that sprinters might concentrate on hamstrings, hurdlers might concentrate on hip suppleness, javelin throwers would develop shoulder range and floppers would concentrate on back flexibility. The style used in any event would have to be adapted to existing mobility levels.

Generally flexibility is a component in all-over fitness and, as Klafs and Arnheim state, 'There is better performance and less injury if one is flexible.' Flexibility exercises should be a part of warming up, with a range of stretching of the main joints of the whole body.

It is also important when building up muscle bulk that flexibility is maintained. It is a favourite myth that in weight training the body will become 'muscle bound', but fortunately this does not appear to be true and many weight training exercises actually increase flexibility. However it is wise to maintain and develop mobility deliberately when doing weights and to include regular static stretching in one's general and specific preparation.

STRENGTH

Impossible records go on being broken, partly because of increased participation, partly because of specialization and coaching, and partly because of nutrition and technology, but one of the most important factors is the increase of strength through weight training (O'Shea). An athlete's level of strength affects so many other factors of performance. Speed is increased by strength, and endurance also requires a strength basis from which to work. Skills can be executed more efficiently when athletes have sufficient strength to perform the tasks set. According to Hooks strength is the key to success in modern athletics.

The acquisition of fitness requires the development of muscular strength and endurance, but the term power is perhaps the most important concept for the athlete as it involves the application of strength at speed. As with all other factors influencing performance it is the utilization of the strength that is important, since only dynamic strength is really useful.

Strength is developed using the overload principle so that weight training is progressive against increasing resistances. Strength is particularly developed by few repetitions against strong resistance, whereas muscular endurance is developed by frequent repetitions against light resistance. The body adapts— weight trainers sometimes use the term SAID which stands for Specific Adaptation to Imposed Demands.

There are three main types of muscle tissue: the smooth voluntary muscles forming the walls of vessels, the cardiac muscles of the heart, and the striated skeletal muscles that are under voluntary control. It is the last group that are of importance in strength training. The muscles are arranged in opposing and antagonistic groups, as explained in Chapter 1, and the light and dark bands of the fibrils within the fibres give the striped appearance and the name. Each muscle fibre contracts maximally or not at all, so there is an 'all or nothing' principle operating, and the magnitude of the force exerted depends on the number of fibres employed and the number of motor units recruited. When one stimulus is followed closely by another they summate. Increasing strength depends partly on supplying nerve impulses of sufficient intensity to recruit the maximum number of muscle fibres (Clarke). Performance is affected by other factors, of course, when the whole body is considered—for example the length of the levers employed, the time and range over which the force is exerted, the physiological state of the tissues, and the efficiency of the energy supply all contribute.

At the muscular level concentric contractions occur when the muscle shortens against a load within its capabilities, and eccentric contractions when the muscle fibres lengthen because the load is too great or because the load is being lowered under control. Various types of resistance training are as follows:

Isometric
Isometric training is static—no object is moved and the muscles do not shorten but hold steady in contraction. This can be done by pressing against a wall or other immovable object, and holding the contraction. Certain stresses induced by isometrics must be noted, e.g. cardiac output doubles, though the venous return of blood to the heart is limited.

Isotonic
Isotonic training is more dynamic and the fibres do shorten and lengthen according to the tasks set. Gains are specific to the angle and range of motion at which the resistance is met in training. The pumping action of the muscles in the more familiar isotonic training helps to avoid stress building up in the

heart. Muscle speed can also be altered in isotonic according to the loading of the weights handled. The heavier the weight, the slower the action, and vice versa.

Isokinetic
Isokinetic training uses the range of motion that can be employed in free isotonic exercises, but the speed of movement is kept constant by mechanical devices.

Fig. 6.2. Weight training with a barbell.

Training appears to increase the number of myofibrils though there is no agreement on this. What is more likely is an increase in the cross-section of the fibres composing the muscles (Klafs and Arnheim). The response to training also includes enhanced protein synthesis, particularly for muscle shortening and tension. As strength increases, the velocity of shortening increases, as does the maximum tension capacity. The connective tissue also strengthens as well as the muscles themselves. An obvious result of training is hypertrophy, an increase in size which is generally an indication of increase in strength. Body builders develop enlarged muscles mainly by very specific exercises using high repetitions, 'pumping up' the required muscle groups. Body builders are very strong, but their intentions are different from that of the weight trainer working for improvement in other events.

The mechanisms for gains in strength are not absolutely clear—they may be neurological changes as much as changes in muscle quality. Trained muscle contains higher amounts of glycogen, and the darkening hue shows the increase in myoglobin which creates favourable conditions for obtaining oxygen, but it is also important that training helps to overcome the inhibitory impulses in the cerebal cortex. As Karpovich states, there is a great psychological effect in knowing that one is stronger when competing, and though the excitement of competition may decrease skill it tends on the other hand to increase strength.

Weight training is really very old—the principle of progressive overload was initiated by Milo in 540 BC when he trained for the Olympic Games by lifting a young calf on his shoulders every day until it grew to be a 400 kg heifer. Today we have a much more efficient and tightly controlled method of strength training available using bars and weighted discs. The feats of strong men in the past gained show business and circus fame, but weights as a means of improving athletics skills was probably first used for the 1936 Olympics by the German team.

Today some form of weight training is a must for all athletes. This is obvious for the throws, but all athletics events are power events to some degree. One of the greatest advantages of weight training is its adaptability and flexibility to meet whatever need is required, and the athlete can actually measure progress either by being able to handle higher poundages or by achieving increased repetitions with the same poundages. One danger is that sometimes athletes get so involved in weight training that they tend to rely on strength too much and forget about skill, flexibility and endurance!

Some Terms Used

A predetermined number of repetitions of an exercise is a *set*. A *schedule* will include a number of sets of each exercise selected.

Poundages may be increased from one set of repetitions to the next. Berger, for example, found three sets of six repetitions a good balanced routine for strength gain, e.g. 6 x 50 kg, 6 x 60 kg, 6 x 70 kg. As weights get heavier the number of repetitions may be decreased until the lifter can do just one. This method of training is known as the Pyramid System, e.g.

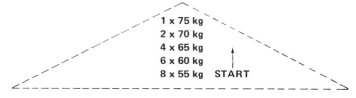

This enables one to discover maximum poundages and it is easy to retest oneself every month to check one's progress.

Instead of just the one maximum lift Carl Johnson, the national coach, advocates several e.g. in the above example the apex would be 1 x 75 kg x 3 sets. Exercises can be selected to suit the different muscle groups that are important in each event.

In a much publicized study Müller maintained that one daily isometric contraction was sufficient to induce strength gains—which sounded very encouraging for the lazy athlete until it was realized that these were postoperative hospital patients who were improving, and not athletes! However, in any state of health, to develop muscles one has to use them and strength has to be maintained. Weight training used to be considered a winter activity but now it is done all year round. It is interesting that strength gained in youth before growth ceases appears to be maintained whereas adult gain is more easily lost (Morehouse and Miller). How frequently should training sessions be carried out? Hettinger found that a session every second day led to an 80 per cent increase in strength, though again it must be remembered that progress depends greatly on existing levels of development. The duration of a session can be from half an hour to two hours, according to experience and capability though in a study by Karpovich it was found that during a weight training session lasting two hours the actual time spent lifting the weights was six minutes!

It is important when weight training to obey simple safety rules. Collars must be secure, footing must be secure, the back should be kept straight, spotters should be available and the build-up should be gradual.

CIRCUIT TRAINING

One method of combining a variety of exercises to help produce strength plus endurance is circuit training. Morgan and Adamson, when working with youngsters, found that a series of quick performance exercises in rotation led to significant gains in strength and fitness. The principle is simple: a series of exercise points, say 8–12, is set out in a hall, gym or outdoors. The exercises should be varied so that arms, shoulders, back, legs etc. are all used. There should be several exercises for the development of stamina, such as step-ups and shuttle runs, in which the continuous nature of the activity ensures cardio-respiratory exercise. There should be a range of resistance exercises using actual weights, and also those using one's own body weight, e.g. chins, dips, rope climb etc. Some exercises for flexibility should be included, e.g. stretching, bending and twisting. All these are to be performed in quick succession in a 'circuit' and gradually the athlete will build up to be able to perform several circuits, generally three, against the clock. The number of times each exercise is repeated can be increased as the athlete improves, and a further target is to reduce the time taken.

Circuits can be performed in a limited space in a fairly short time. The setup promotes competition against oneself with measurable individual progression and it requires little supervision once the circuit is established and the exercises learned. The whole body is used in a variety of ways and exercises can be introduced which are specifically useful for different events, or, more commonly, it can be part of a conditioning programme. It is not so useful for skill but it does give a basis for skill acquisition. Circuits develop cardio-respiratory efficiency and endurance with the minimum of boredom and the maximum of range and effectiveness.

ENDURANCE

Endurance is the capacity of the body to undergo prolonged activity. Its need is most obvious in longer-distance events in which the onset of fatigue occurs and the body is unable to maintain sufficient oxygen uptake or waste disposal to maintain a balanced state as described in Chapter 2.

Endurance fitness gradually improves through childhood up to the early teens mainly because of the regular play activities of children and school based physical education and sports activities. After 13 girls tend to deteriorate, though boys generally continue to improve until their late teens. This is largely the result of social influences, and our sedentary modern life encourages a diminution in cardio-respiratory activity as we get older.

In anaerobic activity oxygen debt is built up which is paid back during recovery, but the energy for sustained exercise must come from aerobic metabolism, where the rate of oxygen intake and utilization and removal of waste products are crucial limiting factors. Muscular contraction can be inaugurated as soon as it receives the stimulus and it can continue for a short time at maximal effort or for a longer time at sub-maximal effort. A level is reached where oxygen income and energy expenditure are balanced.

Where activity is highly sustained for less than 30 seconds the limit is in the work capacity of the muscles. When activity is sustained for one to three minutes there is oxygen debt and lactic acid concentration build up. Beyond three to four minutes the respiratory and circulatory systems are stressed for oxygen. In longer events where a steady state balance is maintained between oxygen uptake and use, the glycogen stores in the muscles are reduced until exhaustion.

Even when there is not sufficient oxygen and lactic acid is produced, exercise can continue according to the tolerance of the body (Clarke). Fatigue may be as much psychological as physiological before a state of physiological exhaustion is reached. The tolerance to the pain and discomfort of the accumulation of waste products is one of the important adaptations to stress developed through training. More work can be done before the production of the carbon dioxide, lactic acid, and heat becomes unpleasant, and there is greater tolerance once production does occur (Corrigan and Morton).

Frequent repetitions against light resistance improves the *quality* of muscle contraction, not the size, as in high-resistance work. The trained muscle contains larger amounts of fuel and conditions improve for oxygen utilization and the removal of wastes—the development of endurance is largely a problem of improving transport within the system.

It is advantageous to have large quantities of red fibres (slow twitch) since they contain myoglobin which stores oxygen and they are therefore better equipped for endurance work.

ENDURANCE TRAINING EFFECTS

Up to 75 times more oxygen is used during exercise than when resting. The oxygen has to be obtained from the air by breathing and it is then carried to the working muscles by the blood. It is necessary, then, that both breathing *and* the circulation of the blood are improved—hence the importance of the cardio-respiratory system.

Respiration
Exercise and training improve the efficiency of breathing in that more air can be taken in by an increase in the rate and depth of pulmonary ventilation. An endurance athlete can handle up to 200 litres of air per minute compared with the average person's maximum of 100 litres. Not only is the trained athlete able to breathe more deeply but he is able to extract more oxygen from the air he does take in. A high oxygen consumption (VO_2) can be achieved with a reduction in the *rate* of breathing but an increase in the *volume*. The respiratory system becomes altogether more efficient, with the intake of oxygen across the lung membranes increasing from 250 cc per minute at rest to 4,000 cc per minute during effort.

The presence of increased myoglobin in the blood enables greater quantities of oxygen to be delivered and an efficient circulation carries away the waste and reduces the build-up of heat. (75 per cent of the body energy is dissipated in heat.) As the muscles are trained the capillaries increase and more blood and fuel can reach the muscles. Fuel and oxygen produce adenosine triphosphate (ATP). ATP is used to produce energy, and the by-products are returned to the circulatory system to be excreted or reconverted by the liver. There are over 20 enzymes related to oxygen utilization which respond to endurance training, so the training effects from endurance work are largely chemical in nature.

Cardiac Output
Endurance training develops the muscles of the heart as other muscle is developed, and the heart of the marathon runner is actually bigger and stronger and has greater capacity than the heart of a similar-sized inactive man. Training reduces the heart rate by improving the efficiency of stroke volume so that the same work can be done at a lower pulse rate. Heart rate and stroke volume can increase from processing 5 litres of blood per minute to 40 litres per minute.

In order to transport 4 litres of oxygen from the lungs to the muscles, 34 litres of blood are required. The blood therefore needs to be circulated more rapidly with the co-ordination of many physiological factors, hence protracted exercise can only be maintained at sub-maximal levels as in the steady state— but the sub-maximal level of work for the trained athlete is much higher than that of the untrained, and yet the heart rate of the trained man is lower.

Heart rate is increased by the transmission of nervous impulses, and before exercise the rate can increase in preparation for exertion and stress (Clarke). Even in an event lasting a few seconds the heart rate responds in preparation for recovery. It is important for *all* athletes therefore to improve their cardiac functioning. A training effect on the heart is achieved if work is done for as little as 20 minutes three or four times per week, which keeps pulse at about 60 per cent of the difference between the resting and maximum heart rate. Cooper reckons that 150 beats per minute is sufficient to have a training effect—of course, as the levels of the athlete's condition rise, more needs to be done to incur improvement.

Another training effect is that the return of the heart beat to normal occurs more rapidly after exercise than it does before adaptation occurs. The shortening of recovery periods enables more quality work to be done if using an interval training programme.

METHODS OF ENDURANCE TRAINING

This topic is treated in detail in Chapter 18. In summary the main methods of improving endurance are:

1. Continuous slow running. LSD = 'Long *Slow* Distance'.

2. Continuous running at a faster pace, but maintaining a steady state. LSD = 'Long *Steady* Distance' is the more usual meaning.

3. Interval training where high intensity work is done for shorter distances than the event, interspersed with a recovery phase of walking or jogging.

4. Fartlek is a form of 'speed play' where there is a variety of the above. The variations in pace are made according to the terrain and according to the inclination and ability of the athlete.

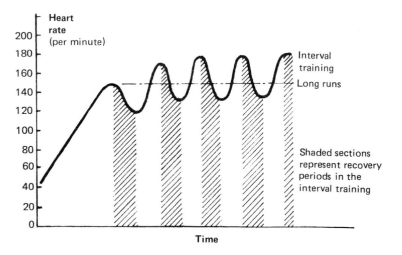

Fig. 6.3. Effects of different training methods on heart rate. (From Thomas.)

Shephard maintains that:

(a) continuous work puts the heart and circulation under stress.

(b) interval work with short bursts near maximum effort produces lactate locally which is oxidized during the recovery phases.

(c) prolonged interval work with intense activity for up to two minutes incurs maximum oxygen debt.

(d) circuit training also improves oxygen uptake.

He considers that interval work is the most effective at improving oxygen uptake, though this is not fully proven and is still a topic of much controversy.

The heart can function more safely if given some type of warm-up and beneficial effects can also be had from warming down to prevent venous pooling of blood when exercise is completed. (See Chapter 16).

Fatigue

Fatigue is important in endurance training and one of the main aims of training is to reduce feelings of fatigue. Specific fatigue occurs as the result of specific exercise but it is difficult to define what fatigue really is. It is the inability to meet demands made (Edington and Edgerton), but Hooks considers that it may be the loss of ability to transmit nerve impulses from the brain to the muscles.

Training is limited by a range of factors—by heredity, by the physique, by early experience of movement, and by the environment in which it takes place. Much is known but there is still much to be discovered about the effects of different patterns of work on different individuals. One of the mistakes made, particularly by endurance athletes, is to train rather than to compete —the best is not saved for the contest. Adequate rest is a vital part of the conditioning process.

SKILL

After the basic concepts involved in the science of athletics have been identified, the necessary next stage is to see how these basic concepts are dynamically put into use in the athletics situation. Every individual has a certain anatomy, physiology and nervous system but how he or she comes to use them will be dependent on the learning experiences each has undergone.

The skills and abilities that are used in competition have been acquired over a long learning period and competing itself is a learned way of behaving (Whiting).

There are many learning theories in existence—perhaps as many ideas exist on how learning takes place as there are things to be learned! The same term is used for the acquiring of the simplest movement to the display of the most complex levels of intellectual and physical functioning. Learning is a covert activity—it is something that only the learner can do. No matter how talented the teacher, the learner must still be active in the learning process, be it physical skills or mental strategies, or a combination of both. The teacher can only set up a situation in which learning will, hopefully, take place.

What is seen by the outside world is the performance, the evidence of the learning having taken place, so judgements on learning are always made in retrospect. Definitions are often not helpful, but learning is described as 'a relatively permanent change in behaviour which is the result of experience'. (Stones). Skill learning is described by Cratty as 'stable performance changes due to practice'. This contrasts with the behaviour found among lower animals, who do much that is pre-programmed or instinctive. Human functioning has its instinctive roots also, but the skills of the athletics arena require the artificial control and discipline of human rules and circumscribed events.

Motor skills are very specific, although underlying them are general basic physical abilities like speed, strength and agility, plus motivational and behavioural supports (Cratty). It is impossible to separate physical skills from perceptual and mental activity, since the skilled person is able to select accurately from the environment those cues that are relevant and important to his performance. The skilled performer 'obtains the maximum of information from the minimum of cues' (Singer).

How do we recognize skilled performance? First, we observe the appearance of ease and confidence and simplicity in the movements. With the minimum of energy expenditure and the greatest economy of movement the actions are completed with certainty and consistency. In an open situation like a game in which decisions have to be made, much of the skill lies in the ability to anticipate and make decisions relative to what other competitors are doing and what the environment is demanding. This is obvious in games and in direct confrontations with opponents, as in wrestling and boxing. It is also present in athletics, though often in a more subtle form, since the tactics of a race are not so obvious as the placing of the ball in tennis or the shuttle in badminton. The runner in the long distance race needs to be able to read his opposition as clearly as a football player does his marker, and the winner in a tactical race has usually been able to dominate and dictate pace and tactics to his opposition. Vital decisions are made about when to inject pace and when to play a waiting game. Even in field events, where individual turns are taken to perform a well-rehearsed, relatively closed skill, there is an openness to the situation which means that decisions have to be made relative to wind and weather and ground conditions and opponents. No thrower or jumper should made his attempt without paying attention to the particular environmental conditions prevailing, and adjusting to the situation.

How are skills acquired? Practice seems an obvious answer but the quality rather than the quantity is important. Repetition must never be blind and each attempt needs modification in terms of feedback from previous performance (Welford). The learner progresses from visual information and verbal instruction to the 'feel' of the correct movement.

No skill is ever completely new, as one transfers elements from previous learning and utilizes principles gained from experience of movement in general. Good early movement experience is of great advantage in later skill learning (Rarick). As practice continues an integration and a reduction of errors takes place, to reach co-ordinated levels that will withstand the stress of competition. Overlearning is necessary for retention under conditions different from, and more stressful than, the practice situation. It is good to train as near as possible to competitive conditions, including distractions and unusual timing and waiting, as the competitive period approaches. In the beginning stages of the season the athlete can modify and build new feelings, but newly learned movements are liable to break down in stress situations and old patterns or poorly integrated ones emerge. 'He didn't look like himself at all in competition.' Training helps to groove an almost automated response and encourages a confident psychological 'set' to the competition.

In skill training transfer is essential and transfer occurs only where there are identical elements in the skill already learned and the one to be learned (Cratty). Performance in a skill event needs good coaching. At first the coach gives verbal instruction and provides models to imitate, but eventually the performer has to understand proprioceptive cues from within, because in the competition he is on his own (Dickenson).

As the skill learning continues the sensitivity of the learner changes. What were at first disjointed and insecure 'sequences of emergencies' become smoothly co-ordinated chains of responses. To learn a skill requires concentration and an intention to learn which involves attention-giving and ordering of experience. Whiting notes that 'sequential and hierarchical ordering' develops as in cognitive development when the learner attains higher conceptual levels. Metheny notes regretfully that the learning of the gymnasium is ranked below the learning of the classroom but 'mind and brain are used in both and intentional structuring of behaviour is taking place'.

How long should practice be? Knapp says that 'It can be as long as standards are maintained and interest is not lost.' Quality matters more than quantity. Many studies have been made of the relative merits of massed and distributed practice, but the results are inconclusive as it depends on the particular task. Singer notes that practice should be spaced where it is difficult, tiring and uninteresting. Arnold says that in short spells of activity only short rests are needed in between, but in long spells of work long spells of rest are required.

Which should be emphasized—speed or accuracy? Knapp encourages speed from the start, but with the action steady. Do not attempt the fastest possible until you have achieved accuracy. This is again a controversial area in which some conflicting findings exist. Finer motor skills like piano playing and typewriting require slow movements until accuracy is attained and then the subject can speed everything up. Where more gross actions are being rehearsed it is necessary to keep closer to the final speed of performance during rehearsal.

Should skills be broken down and learned in parts or should they be learned as entities? Most authorities agree that whole patterns should be attempted as soon as possible, but sometimes the activity is so complex that it needs to be broken down so that the separate elements can be rehearsed. Fitts and Posner see the need for breakdown where there is complexity, and Sage agrees on part learning where the energy demands are high. If the learner is mature enough and experienced enough to cope, then whole methods are desirable, as eventually the whole sequence of movement is to be organized spatially and temporally. Knapp thinks that mastering parts at a time helps motivation as the learner can see some progress and aim for intermediate targets. A judicious mixture of the two is obviously required and even the experienced athlete in each technique session will gradually build up the pattern of movement, e.g. in the discus, through standing throws, half turns, full turns, slow turns and gradually faster turns. Perfection is never attained in a technical event, so technique learning goes on as long as one feels one can improve.

Practice, according to Holding, is the gradual discarding of inefficient responses. A feature of the learning curves for skill are the plateaux that are reached where for a period of time there appears to be no further improvement and work does not seem to be producing results. After a time there can be quite a leap forward with a rising curve of performance before another plateau is reached. This phenomenon is not clearly understood. It can sometimes be attributed to fatigue or boredom but it is more likely to be a period when more advanced integration is taking place and time is required for the organism to settle to the new improved pattern.

Mental Practice
At certain stages of learning and training mental practice can play a very significant role. It is effective when combined with physical practice, particularly when the learner is at a fairly advanced stage of self-awareness and can feel the movements necessary. Singer found a 15 per cent improvement in the performance of senior athletes in college, when mental rehearsal was used.

Feedback
Feedback of knowledge of results is the information an individual receives as a result of some response. Bilodeau in fact considers that feedback is the most important variable controlling performance and learning. Intrinsic feedback is the natural consequence of the response, whereas augmented feedback includes supplementary information mainly from others. Feedback gives information, motivation and reinforcement.

Age
Is there a best age or stage for learning skills? Munrow believes that we learn to 'work the machine' before we know 'how the machine works', and certainly we go on improving up to and through our teens with boys continuing to improve longer than girls. Recent East German researchers have come to the conclusion that the best ages for learning skills are eight to eleven years for girls and nine to thirteen for boys (Dick). They believe that it is better to obtain co-ordination early, and strength can be built up later while the co-ordination is retained. It is interesting that optimal performance curves for achievement in science and for achievement in sport were very similar in terms of age (Lehman).

To return to our starting point of learning theories, it is necessary to be eclectic and to select what is most useful to the task and learner as many different theories have contributions to make. In skill training performance is reinforced by successful movement outcomes. Connectionism involves frequency, recency and effect with Skinner's 'successive approximations' frequently in evidence. As the skill develops the learner builds a more total Gestalt view of the whole environmental field in which he is operating and he is able to understand and utilize principles in a true learning hierarchy (Gagné). The skilled athlete has gained experience and insight himself because his is a dynamic and purposeful activity. In sport one obviously learns by doing, so long as the doing changes the cognitive structures and facilitates the motor pathways. Motor skills that are well learned are very resistant to being forgotten (Cratty), and complex skills are always integrated at the cortical level as mind and body work together in an integrated partnership.

Fig. 6.4. Long years of hard training go into the perfect delivery of the discus by Wolfgang Schmidt (East Germany).

PERIODIZATION

Long-term training makes good sense. A year-long programme, or even a programme over a period of years with sub-goals *en route*, is a necessity for really top-class performances. The level of skill and condition required necessitates a very long, organized build-up. This planning has been studied and developed, particularly in Eastern Europe, and has been termed 'periodization' by the original presenter, Prof. L.P. Matveyev of the USSR in 1965.

In an elementary way many athletes think in terms of an off-season period, a pre-season period, a competitive season, then rest and the cycle starts again. This basic planning can be very much elaborated into macrocycles—long cycles covering several months, a year, or several years, and microcycles of smaller units within macrocycles when specific amounts of work are done in a developing order, with balance between heavy and light workouts, and between the strength, endurance, technique etc. required.

Matveyev divides the year into three periods:

1. *The preparation period* is the longest phase, of approximately four months, in a single periodization year. The main aim is to increase the adaptation level of the athlete with units of general fitness training and foundation work for particular events. As the phase progresses the competition-specific elements will be increased and the general fitness training decreased.

2. *The competition period* stabilizes performance with the total extent of training decreased, but the intensity and specificity increased. The general components are never eliminated but the balance is adjusted, and with a well-judged progression of competitions and competition-specific training, the major performances should be achieved.

3. *The transition period* can include several weeks of 'active recovery' with leisure pursuits, not complete rest. A full recovery is necessary before the next, higher-key, preparation period begins.

There are many elaborations of the above basic plan, with a double periodization year very popular and effective with many sophisticated coaches and athletes.

Cyclic preparation within the above periods is frequently advised. O'Shea, for example, advocates weight training cycles in a similar year-round programme for athletes. The off-season period is the vital time for strength gain, when total body strength is worked for, with progressive resistance exercises to maximum poundages. The pre-season period is shorter, with an increased emphasis on explosive power. In-season is the time for maintenance of the strength fitness developed during the off-season part of the cycle and the sessions will be shorter and less demanding. The other elements in a complex training programme will also be structured into the macrocycle in this way.

The periodization plan is made with the intention of building up to peak performances in important matches and big games. During the competitive season an athlete may require several peaks—for national championships, for selection trials, for international matches and other big events. It is difficult for western nations to use a periodization system effectively because of their random fixture lists, but the East Germans and the Russians space out their big meetings to suit the cycles or preparation of their athletes.

For the young and developing athlete the system need not be rigid, but for a high-level performer it is necessary to maximize performance at the right time. We well know those few great athletes who seem to be able to 'rise to the big occasion'—people like Viren and Oerter. There are obviously important personal factors at work also in their success, but their preparation tends to be very organized and clearly planned over a long period, with careful picking and choosing of competitions before and after the important ones.

Intensity of workload and duration of units within microcycles within macrocycles has to be scheduled for the individual athlete's requirements. The pattern provides a framework within which 'progression of loading in pursuit of a progression of performance improvement' can be made, and this, as Frank Dick says, 'states the whole purpose of training in a nutshell'.

REST AND RECOVERY

Any training programme should allow adequate *recovery*, either from one training task to another, or from day to day. It is particuarly important after a very exhausting session or a stressful competition. If daily practice is so demanding that sufficient recovery does not take place within 24 hours, the physiological compensations will be inadequate and improvement will not occur.

In interval training a recovery period is necessary before the next run is attempted. A greater volume of work can be covered by breaking the total work into short, intense bouts with rest intervals between. The length of the rest, of course, is determined by the intensity and duration of the work and the state of fitness of the athlete. It is important to remember that the adaptation of the body to increased stress actually takes place *during the periods of recovery* from effort.

Rest need not, indeed should not, be total inactivity, since the concept of 'active rest' is a valuable one. Going for a swim can be active rest for a track and field athlete, or the playing of a ball game for enjoyment and physiological benefit.

Athletes are often surprised that, after an enforced lay-off—perhaps due to a very mild injury or to lack of time or inaccessibility of facilities—when they next compete they do exceptionally well. This would suggest that a longer period of rest than usual before competition may allow for a good build-up of reserves and a true recovery from training stress. The body needs time for compensation for its extreme expenditures of energy, and the wise athlete and coach will recognize that it is the alternating rhythm of stress and recovery that produces adaptation.

Like training, rest is a matter for the individual athlete and the only way to discover what is suitable is to experiment with varying amounts of rest. For a start we suggest:

(a) a one-day rest per week,

(b) three consecutive days' rest every six weeks, and

(c) three weeks' active rest at the end of the competitive season,

to be incorporated into the athlete's training cycles.

REFERENCES

ARNOLD, P., *Education, Physical Education & Personality Development,* Heinemann 1968

BILODEAU, E.A. (Ed.), *Acquisition of Skill.* Academic Press, 1966.

BORGER, R., and SEABORNE, A.E.M., *The Psychology of Learning.* Penguin, 1966.

CLARKE, D.H., *Exercise Physiology.* Prentice Hall, 1975.

COOPER, K.H., *The New Aerobics.* Bantam, 1970.

CORRIGAN, B. and MORTON, A. *Get Fit the Champions Way.* Souvenir Press, 1968.

CRATTY, B.J., *Perceptual and Motor Development in Infants and Children.* Macmillan, New York, 1972.

DICK, F.W., 'Evaluation and Selection of Youth for Track and Field', paper presented at Midlands Sports Conference, University of Birmingham, 1976. 'Training v. Straining', *Athletics Weekly* 23 August 1975.

DICKENSON, J. *A Behavioural Analysis of Sport.* Lepus Books, 1976.

EDINGTON, D.W., and EDGERTON, V.R., *The Biology of Physical Activity.* Houghton Mifflin, 1976.

FITTS, P.M. and POSNER, M.I., *Human Performance.* Brooks/Cole, 1967.

GAGNÉ, R.M., *The conditions of Learning.* Holt, Rinehart and Winston, 1970.

HETTINGER, T., *Physiology of Strength.* Chas C. Thomas, 1961.

HOLDING, D.H., *Principles of Training.* Pergamon, 1965.

HOOKS, G. *Application of Weight Training to Athletics.* Prentice Hall, 1962.

KARPOVICH, P.V., *Physiology of Muscular Activity.* W.B. Saunders & Co., 1965.

KLAFS, C.E. and ARNHEIM, D.D. *Modern Principles of Athletic Training.* C.V. Mosby Co., 1963.

KNAPP, B., *Skill in Sport (The Attainment of Proficiency).* Routledge & Kegan Paul, 1963.

LEHMAN, H.C., *Age and Achievement.* Princeton University Press, 1953.

METHENY, E., *Movement and Meaning.* McGraw Hill, 1968.

MOREHOUSE, L.E., and MILLER, A.T., *Physiology of Exercise.* C.V. Mosby Co., 1971.

MORGAN, R.E., and ADAMSON, G.T., *Circuit Training.* G. Bell & Sons, 1961.

MÜLLER, E.A., and ROHMERT, W., p. 73 in WILMORE, J.H., *Athletic Training and Physical Fitness.* Allyn and Bacon, 1977.

MUNROW, A.D., *Physical Education: a Discussion of Principles.* Bell, 1972.

O'SHEA, J.P., *Scientific Principles and Methods of Strength Fitness* (2nd edn). Addison Wesley, 1976.

RARICK, G.L. (ed.), *Physical Activity: Human Growth and Development.* Academic Press, 1973.

SHARKEY, B.J., *Physiology and Physical Activity.* Harper and Row, 1975.

SHEPHARD, R.J., *Endurance Fitness.* University of Toronto Press, 1969.

SINGER, R.N., *Coaching, Athletics and Psychology.* McGraw Hill, 1972.

SKINNER, B.F., *Science and Human Behaviour.* Macmillan, New York, 1953.

STALLINGS, L.M., *Motor Skills.* Wm C. Brown Co., 1973.

STONES, E., *An Introduction to Educational Psychology,* Methuen 1966.

THOMAS, V., *Science and Sport.* Faber & Faber, 1970.

WELFORD, A.T., *Fundamentals of Skill.* Methuen, 1968.

WHITING, H.T.A., *Concepts in Skill Learning.* Human Movement Series, Lepus Books, 1975.

WILMORE, J.H., *Athletic Training and Physical Fitness.* Allyn & Bacon, 1977.

7

FOOD AND NUTRITION

Food is a subject of interest to all, mainly because we enjoy consuming it and because we believe that 'we are what we eat'. Nutrition gets considerable publicity because of anxiety concerned with obesity and the *mal*nutrition of eating too much of the wrong kinds of food.

Athletes are always keen to find out if there are any factors besides their actual exercise and training programmes which will help them to improve their performances. Food intake has therefore become a subject of much discussion and analysis and indeed there are many myths about 'magic' diets. Some of these myths have been taken from the biographies and autobiographies of successful sportsmen and if a well-known athlete always ate a big steak before competing then a big steak became the touchstone for other athletes who wanted to emulate his performances. If another athlete was on a diet of fruit and nuts then others would try that formula too. In competitive situations, where the margins of success and failure are so fine, anything that may change the body and its functioning, even by a fraction, is at least worth a try.

It was not realized that every body requires different fuel and that a variety of fuels can produce the same result—it all depends on what the athlete needs and wants and, very important, what he *believes* will help him. Diets are as important for the mind as for the body.

GENERAL

Let us first try to establish some general principles about food intake and its effects. Every individual requires a certain intake of nutrients to keep him functioning adequately. The very task of keeping alive even at rest uses up a certain amount of energy, since our internal organs and various physiological systems have to keep functioning. This is the basal metabolic rate or BMR of the individual. Nutritionists have borrowed from physics a scale for measuring energy in calories. A calorie is the amount of heat required to raise the temperature of 1 gm of water by one degree centigrade from $15°C$ to $16°C$. The calorie is a very small unit of energy and the kilocalorie (= 1,000 calories) is a more useful practical unit. However care should be taken with the units in the literature, since very often 'calorie' really means 'kilocalorie'. As the chemist Lavoisier stated: *'la vie est une combustion'*—life is a fire. The oxidation of food is a series of carefully controlled chemical reactions. The production of energy can be to some extent separated from its utilization and energy is stored for use in the form of chemical compounds in the muscles. The food energy taken in is converted by the body very inefficiently into mechanical energy, and much food energy is 'wasted' in heat production, as in any engine. The heat is useful for coping with our environment, but in terms of conversion only about 20 per cent of man's food energy is used for mechanical work. As we work or exercise, different activities will use up different numbers of calories, with the energy expenditure varying according to whether one is walking, jogging, sprinting, swimming or weight training or whatever (see Table 7.1). The energy expenditure will also vary according to the physique of the individual, since it will require more calories to move a large person's mass than a smaller person's. The state of fitness of the individual concerned is also influential, as a fit body will be more economical in its energy use.

The body is always balancing a complex input and output. The food and drink is the input which can be measured approximately in calories, and the output is the exercise activity which can be similarly calculated. Energy

TABLE 7.1. TYPICAL ENERGY EXPENDITURE FOR VARIOUS PHYSICAL ACTIVITIES.

(Adapted from Wilmore, p. 45, and Edington and Edgerton, p. 120.)

ACTIVITY	ENERGY COST (Kcal/min.)
1. Lying at ease	1.5
2. Standing at ease	1.7
3. Canoeing, 2.5 mph/1.12 metres per sec.	3.0
4. Canoeing, 4.0 mph/1.79 metres per sec.	7.0
5. Cycling, 5.5 mph/2.46 metres per sec.	4.5
6. Cycling, 13.1 mph/5.86 metres per sec.	11.1
7. Golf	5.0
8. Tennis	7.1
9. Squash	10.2
10. Wrestling	13.1
11. Swimming crawl stroke, 2.2 ft/sec., 0.98 metres/sec.	12.0
12. Swimming crawl stroke, 5.8 ft/sec., 2.59 metres/sec.	125.0
13. Swimming backstroke, 2.0 ft/sec., 0.89 metres/sec.	10.0
14. Swimming backstroke, 5.0 ft/sec., 2.24 metres/sec.	135.0
15. Swimming breast stroke, 2.5 ft/sec., 1.12 metres/sec.	18.0
16. Swimming breast stroke, 4.0 ft/sec., 1.78 metres/sec.	78.0
17. Skiing, 8.1 mph/3.62 metres per sec.	20.9
18. Long distance running	14.9
19. Running, 11 mph/4.92 metres per sec.	23.6
20. Running, 14.5 mph/6.48 metres per sec.	43.9
21. Running, 16.2 mph/7.24 metres per sec.	62.1
22. Running, 18.6 mph/8.31 metres per sec.	124.0
23. Running, 20.0 mph/8.94 metres per sec.	186.0

expenditure is mainly physical, though there is some burn-up for mental activity, particularly if it is stressful, but it requires less energy than physical activity. The problem of the desk-bound executive eating and drinking too much and not having sufficient exercise is classic in medicine today.

Hormones are the chemical messengers of the body which help to regulate the BMR, and lack of thyroid secretion can send weight up whereas too much can lead to thinness and nervousness. Some bodies are efficient in their fuel use, while other constitutions will burn up fuel quite rapidly, even when doing what to the impartial eye is the same amount of work. BMR is also affected by temperature, inside and outside the body, and by levels of excitement.

Some people appear to eat and eat and never put on weight, and others only need to look at a cream bun to put on another kilogram. It is certainly true that there are body types which are predisposed to leanness (ectomorphy) or plumpness (endomorphy), but one must be careful to check on the actual intake and output of these types—fatter people often look at that cream bun and then eat it, whereas leaner types have a more frugal diet and are easily satisfied by their intake.

Calorific input obviously depends on the quantity of food and drink taken in, but also on the quality and type of food. If one ate equal weights of lettuce leaves and chocolates the calorific intake would be vastly different.

In the developed countries of the world a huge range of foods is available. With the discovery of preserving methods, canning and freezing in particular, and with the rapid transportation of perishable goods, the diet of modern man is wide, with the cuisine of many countries available in the shops and restaurants of most high streets. To have a large variety of foods available does not necessarily mean that we select the best for our consumption. Some interesting experiments have been done with animals and young children, who show a certain 'wisdom of the body' when they are offered a wide selection of foods, cafeteria-style. Their meals might not be what their mothers would have provided, but over a period of days a well-balanced diet was evolved. Unfortunately our artificial foods, particularly sweetened items, have developed in us an addiction for sugar which means that much of our food intake is unnecessarily high in calories. Animals, too, develop a taste for sweetness, and rats rewarded with saccharined water will work hard to solve problems in order to obtain this non-nutritional drink. The body is not wise enough.

Food is necessary for (i) energy, (ii) growth and replacement of tissues, and (iii) essential bodily functions, but the food on the table and in the supermarket comes in a mixed-up multitude of forms, colours and flavours which do not indicate their values. To the scientist these varieties of culinary delights can be analysed into three main groups of carbohydrates, fats and proteins, along with a necessary sprinkling of vitamins and minerals. A 'balanced' diet requires a certain amount from each of the three main categories.

TYPES OF FOOD

Carbohydrates
Carbohydrates are the most abundant source of energy in nature. The starch

in cereals, potatoes, bread and root vegetables is converted to glucose in the body and stored in the liver and muscles as glycogen. Other foods rich in carbohydrates are cakes and biscuits, pastas and puddings, and all forms of alcohol and beer. Foods based on flour and sugar are particularly high in calories. The body finds carbohydrate easier to burn than protein or fat. It is readily convertible to energy and after the ingestion of carbohydrate the level of blood glucose rises within 20 minutes. If there is insufficient storage of glucose, less energy will be available for physical activity. Sugar is an important energy source but it is the only food abounding in calories with no protein, vitamins or minerals. However, glucose is useful for immediate high-energy consumption, hence glucose tablets and varieties of glucose drinks for use during competitions. Assuming that sufficient glucose and fat are available, glucose yields 5,010 calories per litre of oxygen consumed by the individual, and fat 4,650, so glucose uses oxygen slightly more efficiently and economically than fat. This is vital for the endurance runner, who needs to utilize oxygen as economically as possible and so requires a supply of carbohydrate to burn up. As there is only limited carbohydrate storage in the body, loading up prior to exercise is beneficial. A large store acts as a reserve in competition when the blood glucose level drops.

The overshoot diet: a method of carbohydrate supercompensation has been developed by marathon runners. About eight days before the event the athlete runs to near-exhaustion and so depletes the muscles of glycogen. For the next few days he ingests a low-carbohydrate diet to maintain a low store of glycogen in the body with just enough carbohydrate to keep training going. For the last three or four days the athlete drops his levels of training very low and takes in a very high-carbohydrate diet. This achieves an overshoot effect, with the glycogen stores in the muscles increasing above the normal and providing extra reserves for the competition, but this type of diet has to be handled with care because not every athlete's constitution responds favourably to it.

Fats

These are found in cream, oil, butter, cheese, etc. Fats contain two and a quarter times the calories of carbohydrate, therefore they form good energy storage, but fats take longer to digest and the stomach is slower to empty, so one does not feel hungry so quickly after eating fatty food. Fat, then, is a good reserve but as it requires more oxygen for oxidation than carbohydrate it is not such a readily available source of energy. If carbohydrate is not available, fat stores will be used. Sub-maximal exercise releases more fat from adipose tissue into the blood stream than anaerobic work and there is a breakdown of fats by the liver during light work. As fats are non-soluble in water they are used by the body to waterproof membranes. Fat is also useful for thermal insulation and the extra layer of fat on females enables them to withstand cold better than males.

Trained individuals are able to utilize more of the fatty acids during exercise than sedentary people who use carbohydrates more directly. If one wants to lose fat, then exercise has a two-fold beneficial effect, for the exercise uses calories and depletes the fat stores, and as the body becomes more efficient it actually uses up more fats.

Proteins

Many athletes have an obsession for proteins, particularly red meats but there are many other sources of proteins, e.g.

meat				
fish	27 protein grams per 100 gm portion			
poultry				
cheese	6	"	"	"	30 gm portion
eggs	6	"	"	"	1 egg
milk	9	"	"	"	1 cup
peas and beans	6	"	"	"	½ cup

Protein is the basic unit of each cell and it is necessary for growth and tissue repair. Protein is not necessary for immediate energy supply, but it is particularly important during periods of growth and development up to and including adolescence. The muscles, skin and soft tissue are mainly made of protein, but one gram of protein per kilogram of bodyweight per day is sufficient intake for adults. Sharkey maintains that it may even be harmful to exceed two grams per kilogram per day and it is only if the balance of the body is upset by taking anabolic steroids that this level of protein will be utilized.

Protein needs are not increased by general physical activity which uses up fats and carbohydrates, but if no protein was taken there would be some loss of muscle mass. The advocates of high-protein diets are found most frequently in body building, and writers like Ben Weider advise 8.2 grams per day per kilogram of bodyweight, but such a high-protein diet would only be undertaken if a very strenuous weight training programme was maintained by the athlete.

Protein is important as a source of nitrogen and essential amino-acids, so vegetarians need to supplement their intake because they are found predominantly in animal foods.

Vitamins

Small amounts only of vitamins are necessary. They are important, and lack of them can cause deficiency diseases, but the daily diet of most people normally includes sufficient vitamins. Vitamins do not provide energy but they help functions to occur in the body which are energy-supplying.

The body cannot make them and cannot store any excess, therefore any extra intake of vitamins is useless. Indeed too great a vitamin intake can be toxic and do damage by causing ulcers and kidney trouble.

Vitamin A is found in fat, milk, liver, cod liver oil and yellow and green vegetables. Without it the soft lining tissues of the body grow dry and become readily infected. The eyes, the respiratory tract and the urinary tract are particularly susceptible if there is a shortage of Vitamin A. Vitamin A is added to margarine.

The vitamins of the B group are found in some amounts in most foods.

Without enough B_1 there is a danger of heart failure and paralysis. Riboflavin deficiency produces sore and inflamed skin, particularly round the lips and eyes. Pellagra, beri-beri, stomach upsets and rough skin result from nicotin-amide lack, and B_{12} deficiency can cause certain forms of anaemia. Breakfast cereals have small quantities of Vitamin B complex added.

Vitamin C is contained in fresh fruits and vegetables, particularly citrus fruits (except limes). This vitamin is easily lost in cooking, so vegetables should not to be over-boiled. Sailors discovered that scurvy resulted from Vitamin C deficiency, but of more interest to the athlete is the possibility that Vitamin C supplementation results in improved endurance capacity (Wilmore). Large doses of Vitamin C are also recommended to help prevent colds.

Vitamin D is added by law to margarine and is also found in fish oil and eggs. The 'sunshine' vitamin is particularly important for pregnant women and young children whose bones are still developing. Without enough vitamin D the body cannot utilize the calcium in food for bone-making. It is produced from fat under the skin by the action of the ultra-violet rays in sunlight.

Vitamin E. Deficiency of this vitamin produces certain forms of anaemia and causes muscular weakness. There have been many contradictory studies of Vitamin E uptake (wheatgerm), some showing that it helps endurance events while others are inconclusive. Adelle Davis, the famous nutritionist, strongly advocates Vitamin E for a variety of bodily problems, and maintains that Vitamin E aids oxygen utilization and that any athlete, particularly if working at altitude, will benefit from taking Vitamin E.

Salts

The body also needs sodium (found in salt), calcium (in milk and cheese), iodine (in sea foods and iodized salt) and iron (in meat and eggs).

John Yudkin, Professor of Nutrition at London University, lists four groups of foods:

(1) milk and cheese,
(2) meat, fish and eggs,
(3) fruit and vegetables,
(4) butter and margarine,

and suggests that, if something from each of these groups is eaten every day, all the necessary vitamins and minerals will be taken in.

The general conclusion is that if one takes a balanced diet with a variety of fresh food it is not worth paying for supplements that the body cannot use. A medical check-up will soon show if there is any deficiency, e.g. extra iron is often needed by female athletes because of anaemia.

MYTHS

Contrary to popular belief an athlete in training requires no specific diet pro-vided his energy requirements are met. No individual food constituents have been found to have any significant effect on physical performance (Sloan). There appears to be a psychological belief in steak, and athletes, particularly the big field events men, consume huge excesses of meat and eggs. De Vries criticizes the belief in 'miracle' foods like honey and molasses, and notes also that no evidence is available that performance is altered by changing an already sound diet. Skill and conditioning are more important than diet, and after all the same nutrients exist in shin of beef that are in rump steak!

It is interesting that recent studies done by Astrand and others have led to revisions of traditional ideas about protein being an energy-producing food. The ultimate sports diet they conclude is 12 per cent protein, 33 per cent fat, and 55 per cent carbohydrate, for athletes doing very heavy workloads (Hughes).

PRE-EVENT EATING

It is best to eat lightly, well before any activity or competition, since blood will be diverted from the musculature to the stomach for digestion. Fat is slow to digest and stays in the stomach longer than carbohydrate. Steak is probably one of the worst pre-event meals! It is possible to take light foods which require a little digestion and it is better not to eat roughage in case of diarrhoea. If no food is taken for about three hours before activity, the athlete is more likely to avoid gastric disturbance and the stomach volume will be comfortably small. For stamina events it is wise to take plenty of fluids to avoid the dangers of dehydration, and to help regulate body temperature. There is controversy about the use of salt when sweating has been excessive, but salt intake should be regular.

OBESITY

One of the modern problems in the West is that of obesity, which most commonly is the result of excessive intake of calories. Too much rich food is consumed in relation to our very low levels of exercise. Many people have sedentary occupations and we travel by car and by lift instead of using our legs. Obesity is often established early, when children are given high-calorie diets and start bad habits that remain with them into overweight maturity. It is believed that obesity is affected by the nature and number of cells in the adipose tissue as well as the size of these cells, and if obesity starts young then the number of cells is increased. Tables of heights and weights are given in many texts, e.g. tables for 'average' men and women, but the body weight and height do not indicate how the weight is made up—what is fat and what is muscle. Muscle is more dense than fat and exercise can increase muscle weight while actually decreasing the body's dimensions because of fat loss. Measurement of fat is usually done using the skinfold technique, in which special calipers are used to 'pinch' and measure the folds of skin at various points of the body. 'Spot' reducing is not really possible, and if one loses weight it tends to be all over, though most goes from the places where most is accumulated. Diet tables are available for men and women and many publications list them.

To lose weight, both exercise and diet are recommended, but the more important of the two is diet—a suitable reduction in calorific intake while maintaining the same exercise level must result in weight loss. If a reduced intake is accompanied by increased exercise then the debit balance will be even more effectively achieved and the muscle tone and body state will improve. It is often argued that exercise increases appetite, but very vigorous exercise actually produces lactate, which is an appetite-reducer, and the tightening of the stomach muscles can help to reduce feelings of emptiness. A great deal of exercise is necessary to lose even a small amount of body-weight, so it is hopeless to expect to do it by exercise alone. Exercise is better as a preventer of obesity than as a cure. Short-term exercise of less than an hour should not overstimulate the appetite, though being outdoors in chilly weather makes one feel hungry. Often heat and humidity will reduce appetite, but it is also well known that social and environmental factors, rather than physiological need, control appetite.

If food is there one often takes it. A particular danger of Olympic and Commonwealth Games Villages is the wonderful restaurant service and the never-ending supply of food at all hours which tempts one to eat far too much and experiment with foodstuffs to which one is not accustomed—nearly all athletes put on weight in such situations unless they are very strong-willed.

Is there an ideal diet? Perhaps the best thing is to be flexible and adaptable, since after all skill and condition are much more important than food intake as long as one is moderate. When travelling abroad for matches, team members often worry about the 'foreign food', but athletes should not be too conservative about their food and part of the excitement and interest of a foreign trip lies in trying new dishes.

CONCLUSION

The physique and body composition of individuals are largely hereditary and changes in diet will change the body shape only within certain limits, according to skeleton and build. Starving a St Bernard will not produce a greyhound —only a thin St Bernard. One cannot change one's makeup however much one wishes—it is said that inside every fat person is a thin person trying to get out, and indeed physique evokes social and emotional reactions very early in life. Chubby adolescents are not always eating, but they do have much less physical activity than their peers, partly through isolation and rejection and because their poor body image will tend to make them avoid physical activity —a vicious circle (Harris). The sport one takes up may be largely determined by one's physique, and the extremes seen at an Olympic Games show the range of the human body. Within track and field athletics the various events will be suitable for different builds—the decathlete and the heptathlete are probably the most satisfactory all-rounders in performance and physique. One of the attractions of athletics is the variety of opportunity for participation by people of different physiques and temperaments.

REFERENCES

ASTRAND, P.O., and RODAHL, K., *Textbook of Work Physiology*. McGraw Hill, 1977.

BUSS, D., and ROBERTSON, J., *Manual of Nutrition*. HMSO (Ministry of Agriculture, Fisheries and Food), 1976.

DAVIS, A., *Let's Eat Right to Keep Fit*. Unwin Paperbacks, 1971.

HARRIS, D.V., *Involvement in Sport*. Lea and Febiger, Philadelphia, 1973.

SLOAN, A.W., *Physiology for Students and Teachers of Physical Education*. Edward Arnold, 1970.

WILMORE, J.H., *Athletic Training and Physical Fitness*. Allyn and Bacon, 1977.

YUDKIN, J., *This Slimming Business*. Penguin, 1970.

8

DRUGS

The discovery and use of a variety of drugs has proved a mixed blessing. The sufferings of the past have largely been allayed by the controlled medicinal use of drugs to relieve pain and to cure disease. Forms of drug have been in use for centuries—often the effects of healing plants and substances were known long before the processes by which they were achieved were understood. The witch doctor, monk and herbalist had discovered nature's cures long before modern medicine.

Unfortunately interference with bodily functions often brings problems, and overdoses of drugs can act destructively. Addiction problems hit the headlines today but opium addiction has been known for centuries, particularly in the Far East, and the extraordinary effects of drugs like mescalin and LSD have been discovered afresh by young people today though their use has been known by more 'primitive' peoples for a long time. Not quite so drastic as addiction, but nevertheless a problem, is the use of drugs to influence sports performance.

The image of drugs is a mixed one. Pill bottles are for the bedside table of the patient under medical care, though unfortunately they also seem to be in the training programme of many athletes. It has been said, only partly in jest, that the big international competitions of today take place not so much between the athletes of the different nations but between rival biochemists! The International Amateur Athletics Federation rules are clear:

Rule 144

1. Doping is strictly forbidden.
2. Doping is the use by or distribution to an athlete of certain substances which could have the effect of improving artificially the athlete's physical and/or mental condition and so augmenting his athletic performance.

The rule goes on to list various substances and to detail the procedures for testing. Drugs, therefore, have no legal place in sport except for therapeutic purposes when athletes are ill or injured.

STIMULANTS

One of the greatest battles an athlete has to fight is the one against fatigue. It is particularly obvious in the distance runner but sprinters tire also, and long training sessions and competitions for technical events involve this battle against tiring muscles and weary limbs. Any preparation which can delay the effects of fatigue or make one forget one's tiredness is obviously going to be attractive to competitors, and the group of drugs known as stimulants has been used for this purpose in many sports for a long time. Amphetamine, epinephrine and benzedrine mimic the natural release of adrenalin and noradrenalin in stress situations, and feelings of excitement and wakefulness are the result of their stimulation of the central nervous system. The heart rate is increased, the blood pressure goes up, the appetite is suppressed and there is a feeling of 'high' or 'up'—hence the nickname of 'uppers' for these drugs. These feelings can be deceptive of course, and often the athlete 'feels' great but his performance is actually worse than he thinks. One can feel better and do worse.

Nature's signals of fatigue are over-ridden by stimulants, which can be dangerous and in extreme cases even fatal. The body knows when it has had enough, but if the artificial presence interferes with these warning messages the athlete may go beyond the safety margins until collapse occurs from heat exhaustion. If the heart is overstretched, death can occur.

If amphetamines are taken regularly they become addictive and too much in the system is toxic. The effects of stimulants are short-lived, and if the feeling is desirable then not only will they be taken for competition but also for training sessions. Big events incorporate random tests but training is not monitored and those who do not risk the tests in competition may be using the drugs to aid training. A clean sheet when tested does not prove that drugs are not used.

Other stimulants include caffeine, found in tea as well as coffee, and though some extra tea and coffee would not show in tests everyone knows the stimulating effects on the central nervous system (CNS) and the reduction of fatigue —many essays have been written and reports prepared in the small hours aided by numerous strong 'fixes' of coffee! Over-indulgence in caffeine can have bad effects including nervousness and irritability, and over time it encourages ulcers and heart disease since it dilates the coronary blood vessels. Simple motor tasks are improved, isometric strength is raised by 13—14 per cent (Clarke), and laboratory tests show that caffeine raises work output on the bicycle ergometer but that finer motor tasks are impaired (De Vries). Cocaine also masks fatigue and pain and South American Indians are reputed to travel for days without rest, chewing on coca leaves as they go.

TRANQUILLIZERS

Another great problem experienced by athletes, particularly in important competitions, is over-excitement and tension which impair performance. To relieve chronic anxiety many are tempted to use sedatives and tranquillizers. Barbiturates, narcotics, opiates and hallucigens can all induce a feeling of well-being, though again feelings are deceptive and performance may not be improved but actually deteriorate because of lack of concentration and control. Strength diminishes and drowsiness may occur (Edington and Edgerton). It may be necessary to relax after the excitement of competition to encourage sleep, since some athletes, who have not had sleepless nights before, have them *after* big events.

ANALGESICS

Pain-relievers like aspirin and morphine may be prescribed for headaches and feverishness and they often have generally relaxing effects for stiffness and soreness. In terms of dosage, one reaches a difficult point at which a shift takes place from normal medicinal usage to abuse. It is difficult to state when it becomes an aid for performance. Would it have been used anyway, even if there was no competition? On the other hand, athletes who are suffering from colds and nasal blockages are not able to relieve them because of fears of doping control.

Pain-killers can also be dangerous when applied externally to sprains and injuries and injected into painful joints. This practice relieves the symptoms but these signals are important, and injuries may be made worse by camouflaging the pain.

The high motivation of athletes and their coaches explains much of this 'madness' to perform well at all costs. For the sake of competition they do things to their bodies that would never be approved of, or tolerated, in any other situation.

If an athlete is actually ill or suffering from some infectious disease then he will be prescribed antibiotics—if he is ill enough to be undergoing such treatment should he be competing anyway? Again a difficult question to answer if an important competition is threatened by sickness, and if another chance will not arise perhaps for years if this one is missed.

OXYGEN

In 1968 when the Olympics were held in Mexico there was much controversy over the effects of altitude (see Chapter 9). There were a few cases in which collapsing athletes were rushed off the track and oxygen masks placed over their gasping mouths. Obtaining sufficient oxygen is even a problem at sea level in endurance events, and, though oxygen itself is not a drug, the inhalation of oxygen deliberately before, during, or after performance is an *ergogenic aid* (substance to improve performance—Wilmore). Oxygen inhalation before performance apparently helped swimmers in short distance events and the Japanese team used it in the 1932 Olympics. There is a limit to its usefulness, however, as storage in the body is a problem and the effect is lost in less than two minutes. It would be impossible to administer in actual competition, though in the laboratory situation performance on a treadmill has doubled by giving oxygen (Sharkey). Perhaps the most beneficial and legitimate use of oxygen in athletics is that it helps recovery after extreme effort at altitude. The oxygen enables a more rapid resaturation of blood haemoglobin and muscle myoglobin. This would occur at sea level in normal training recovery periods, but for the unacclimatized at altitude it is a useful aid.

BLOOD 'DOPING' OR 'BOOSTING'

This is a fairly recent phenomenon made public mainly due to rumours concerning the fantastic performances of Lasse Viren of Finland in the Montreal Olympics. Sports medicine had discussed the feasibility of the blood boosting process (Ekblom et al., 1972—see Wilmore, p.175) long before, but it really only came to public notice in 1976. It is important to note that nothing was ever proved against Viren and his performances still stand as superb examples of human determination and skilful training procedures.

Here is a simple outline of the technique. A litre of blood is removed from an endurance athlete who continues with his training for another couple of weeks during which time his body compensates for the loss of the red blood cells by producing more. His original red cells are reinfused so that he then has an increased number of cells (all his own production) which boost his blood's oxygen-carrying capacity. Under laboratory conditions a 23 per cent improvement in treadmill work with the VO_2 maximum increased 9 per cent (Ekblom) has been recorded. The interesting point is that, since it is the athlete's own blood being replaced he is not taking any form of illegal drug or artificial aid. It becomes a controversial moral and legal issue.

ANABOLIC STEROIDS

An important and controversial area of drug-taking involves the use of anabolic steroids. The natural steroid testosterone has anabolic properties of protein-building and androgenic effects of masculinization. Male hormones 'naturally' make the male of the species heavier, more muscular and more aggressive than the female. An increase of the effect of male hormone would help any athlete, particularly a female, who wishes to improve in strength, explosiveness and aggression. Artificial steroids do not have such pronounced androgenic effects, hence the name 'anabolic' steroids. If anabolic steroids are taken in conjunction with a high-protein diet and a strength training programme, the effect is to increase the muscle mass of the athlete (hypertrophy). This may be accompanied by an increase in weight, and under certain conditions there is a dramatic increase in muscular strength.

These drugs are used legitimately in medicine to counteract the effects of wasting diseases and to help the elderly to retain protein and build up bodily strength. In this situation the controlled intake is beneficial to the patient, but in the case of an already healthy body a very large intake could have undesirable side-effects. It is very difficult indeed to get genuine evidence concerning the effects of anabolics as, of course, the athlete, coach, doctor and chemist involved are certainly not going to admit to taking or giving a strictly forbidden 'aid'. Side-effects may include liver damage, prostate damage, sterility and the masculinization of females. These effects would appear daunting, but to the ambitious athlete the 'positive' effects are those of increasing strength and explosiveness. If an athlete feels big and powerful, and if he or she is increasing distances and reducing times, it is a thrilling present reward, while the ill-effects are in the distant future, and are perhaps exaggerated anyway. If some of those who have suffered ill-effects could demonstrate them to young people, they might be discouraged from starting.

MISCELLANEOUS

There is a range of substances that would be difficult to define as drugs but which have effects on performance. Alcohol, for example, provides a slight 'warm-up' effect, and a teaspoonful of brandy may settle a nervous athlete though too much has adverse effects on motor co-ordination. Probably more important are the effects of taking alcohol in the social context of late nights in smoky, crowded atmospheres.

Attempts have been made to neutralize lactic acid accumulation by an intake of alkalis—sodium bicarbonate or potassium bicarbonate—but nothing useful has been established so far. There is indeed little to recommend the use of aids unless there is an actual deficiency in the athlete's system, e.g. it is important to have sufficient water and electrolytes if losing sweat rapidly (see Chapter 7). The over-intake of fluids has never been shown to cause problems—though no athlete would be comfortable with too much in his stomach—but the lack of fluids and salt are thought by some to cause cramps and heat exhaustion. Similarly the intake of glucose during events is not considered a drug, but it can be beneficial to performance.

The psychological effects are important, since the use of placebos frequently give the same effects as the drugs themselves. If the athlete *thinks* he is getting something to boost his performance he will feel confident and his performance *will* improve, even if he has taken a few grams of harmless powder.

DETECTION

Stimulants need to be present in the body at the time of the event in order to be useful, and are easily detected from a simple urine sample. Anyone risking taking a stimulant knows that they can be caught.

An important difference from the detection point of view is that steroids need to be taken over several months in order to develop the muscle and strength gain gradually. After an athlete stops taking these drugs his muscles will begin to return to normal (atrophy) but the effects will remain for quite a long time—several weeks, depending on the dose rate of the initial intake and the training programme of the athlete. After a few weeks the drug's strength effect is still there for the competition, but the drug may not be traceable. Reliable test procedures took a long time to develop and even now they are much more complicated and expensive than the tests for stimulants. Proper screening can only be conducted in specific centres, and there are accompanying problems of transport, storage and record-keeping. Sometimes samples get mysteriously lost or damaged in the weeks after big competitions, and it is difficult for those trying to enforce the laws to obtain sufficient co-operation and proof to disqualify.

A number of experiments have been carried out to try to establish the effects of anabolic steroid intake. There appear to be very individual reactions in different subjects, but generally the results have not been impressive. The experiments have not really been successful in demonstrating strengthening effects. One of the difficulties here is that for ethical reasons the experimental dosages have always been small, while the intake of some athletes may be 10 or 20 times the recommended medical dosage, e.g. Fowler in 1965 did not find strength gains. Harvey in 1975 gave dianabol and placebos to students. Those on the drug detected it because of weight gains but there was no appreciable improvement in muscular performance. Johnson and O'Shea did find gains in strength but they did not use placebo controls. However they estimate that as many as 70 per cent of athletes and weight lifters use them.

If effective means of detection and control are established then the record books may need rewriting with 'before', 'during' and 'after' steroid-taking ranking lists! Throwers and lifters are the most criticized for abuse of these drugs, and it is believed that it was the weight lifters in the 1950s who first started using them, when they were being used on cattle to increase their weight before shows. The explosive strength gained from the anabolics is useful for many events besides throwing, and sprinters, jumpers and runners can all gain from such improvements. Nearly all the athletics events have their accompanying training programme and for many their accompanying steroid programme. Several positive cases have been found even at junior levels, and the sanctions now employed against detected culprits will need to be much stronger to discourage further risk-taking. On temporary suspension an athlete will soon be back, but threatened with a ban for life even the wildest athlete might hesitate. The men were accused first, but as has already been suggested, the greatest effect of male hormone intake is on women. Though the incredible improvements in women's events in recent years may be partly influenced by the change of social pressures, much may be also attributable to the intake of pills and injections.

CONCLUSION

To sum up: various systems of the body can be affected by drugs. The CNS and the circulatory system can be stimulated by adrenalin, caffeine, epinephrine, amphetamine etc. and calmed by tranquillizers. The digestive system may be affected by emotional upsets caused by the pressure of competition, which may be counteracted by tranquillizers. The muscular system is affected by hormonal intakes. There is little indication that the respiratory system can be directly improved in function by drugs but some infections may be treated by their medicinal use.

Mental effects are important and as yet not well understood. Warm-ups and rituals have 'ergogenic' effects and some experiments with hypnosis suggest possible increases in performance from a temporary changing of mental attitudes and beliefs. Even when actual foreign substances are used the expectation of effect is important for the athlete. 'Mind over matter' is an important concept in sports performance—one of the main effects of repeated training is to alter the mental reaction and resistance to stress and fatigue as much as the physical reaction.

Whatever the effects, drugs are illegal and immoral. The rules exist to try to ensure fair play and the athletics authorities are not spoilsports to ban them. It is not only the health of the athlete that is at stake but also his conscience and peace of mind. Is it worth winning by cheating? Even if nearly everyone else is cheating too, does that make it excusable? The worst offenders are the coaches and medical men who encourage and permit such abuse. The athlete has to get drugs from somewhere—access should not be allowed. It is important to win in athletics competition but one must not win at any cost, because the cost may be the young athlete's health and honesty and the sport's clean image. As Corrigan and Morton say, 'Don't be a dope!'

REFERENCES

CLARKE, D.H., *Exercise Physiology*. Prentice Hall, 1975.

CORRIGAN, B., and MORTON, A., *Get Fit the Champion's Way*. Souvenir Press, 1968.

DE VRIES, H.A., *Physiology of Exercise for Physical Education and Athletics*. Wm C. Brown, 1974.

EDINGTON, D.W., and EDGERTON, V.R., *The Biology of Physical Activity*. Houghton Mifflin, 1976.

EKBLOM, B., GOLDBERG, A.N., and GAUBRING, B., 'Response to Exercise After Blood Loss and Reinfusion', *Journal of Applied Physiology* 33, 175—80 (1972).

FOWLER, W.H., GARDNER, G.W., and EGSTROM, G.H., 'Effect of anabolic steroid on physical performance in young men', *Journal of Applied Physiology*. 20, 1038—40 (1965).

JOHNSON, L.C., and O'SHEA, J.P., 'Anabolic Steroid: Effects on Strength Development', *Science* 164, 957—59 (1969).

SHARKEY, B.J., *Physiology and Physical Activity*. Harper and Row, 1975.

WILMORE, J.H., *Athletic Training and Physical Fitness*. Allyn and Bacon, 1977.

EFFECTS OF
PHYSICAL ENVIRONMENT

Athletics performance and training are always carried out in a physical setting
—in a certain place, at a certain altitude, at a certain time of year, at a particular time of day, in a given state of weather where certain atmospheric conditions and temperature prevail—and all of these will have an effect on
performance. Internally the athlete is constrained by morphological and biomechanical conditions. His anatomy and physiology, his skeletal levers and
his general physique plus his state of skill and conditioning will all influence
what he can do, but his performance is also constrained by the conditions in
the external physical environment.

Optimum conditions seldom prevail and little account is officially taken of
environmental variables except the rule about records only being allowed in
short races, long jump and triple jump if the following wind is below 2 metres
per second. However the wind can help or hinder in other events too—in the
throws, jumps and distance races. The discus thrower prays for a good
quartering wind from the front/right of the circle, while the hammer throwers
prefer a gentle breeze from behind. The vaulters like a following wind into
the bar, but not too strong, and too strong a wind either way is disliked by
hurdlers because it may make the hurdles difficult to reach or easy to crash
into.

The human body and its organizing intelligence enables a vast range of
adjustments to be made for prevailing conditions, and though athletics skills
are mainly closed ones it is wise to rehearse them in training under a variety
of conditions. Those athletes who always rush indoors at the first spots of rain
will not compete well in a heavy shower. The wind will blow in competitions
as well as in training, so it is worthwhile getting used to it from all directions.
Certain extremes of environment are not so easily coped with, however, and
a period of acclimatization is necessary for competitions at a much higher
altitude, or in a hotter and more humid climate than one is accustomed to.

HEAT

The human body operates efficiently only within a narrow range of temperatures externally, and the internal temperature of the body is maintained at a
steady 98.4°F (36.9°C) by a regulating system in the hypothalamus, an
important part of the human fore-brain. Under resting conditions heat is
gained from the metabolism of foodstuffs, but when exercising the body

produces a great deal of extra heat. The conversion of chemical energy into mechanical energy in the human body is very inefficient with only 20–30 per cent converted to useful work and the remaining energy wasted as heat. When the external temperature is high, maintaining an acceptable body temperature during exercise is very difficult, particularly if the atmosphere is humid.

The body has four methods of heat loss (i) conduction–losing heat directly into a cooler environment, (ii) convection–heat moved away by the movement of air or fluid around the body, (iii) radiation in the infra-red part of the electromagnetic spectrum, and (iv) evaporation–changing the liquid sweat into water vapour. Invisible perspiration is going on nearly all the time. When one is exercising in heat the first three methods are not effective, and, indeed if the external air is very warm and still, with direct sunlight, the body could gain heat rather than lose it. The most important method of heat loss is by evaporation of sweat, as a great deal of heat is absorbed in the process of evaporation. If the air is hot and dry the moisture is taken up easily, but if the air is already heavily saturated then the sweat rolls off but does not evaporate, so less cooling takes place.

To keep the body core temperature down, heat is transported by the blood to the skin. The flushed look of a warm person is explained by the increased blood flow to the peripheral vessels near the surface. The increased flow puts a strain on the cardiac system, which may already be under strain due to the exercise. If the blood is diverted from the working muscles, work capacity is reduced. Where heat cannot be lost, body temperature may rise rapidly and the situation can become quite dangerous.

A great deal of liquid and electrolytes can be lost due to heavy sweating, and if this is not replaced the tissues become dehydrated and heat cramps can occur. When the system starts to break down heat exhaustion occurs, the skin becomes cool and pale and the pulse weak and rapid. The athlete in this condition must be made to rest at once and take in fluid. If this is not done the next stage of heat stroke is very dangerous, with a hot dry skin, high temperature, delirium and even death.

It is advisable to avoid strenuous exercise at a temperature of over 40°C if it is humid. The clothing worn in heat should expose as much of the skin surface as possible, and it should be of a loosely-woven natural fibre, to allow moisture through. Light colours are better than dark ones, since more heat is absorbed by dark clothing.

If athletes have to compete in a warm, humid atmosphere they must acclimatize themselves preferably by a period of time in the actual locality of the event or by creating a similar artificial environment at home for training. (Don Thompson, exercising in his steamy bathroom before going to the Rome Olympics in 1960, had the right idea and it helped him win a gold medal.) Several days in a hot atmosphere will improve the athlete's response, but exercise must be done during that time because exposure alone is not sufficient. It is important to subject the sportsman's body to some stress, and his adaptation to this stress in these conditions is called acclimatization.

The events most affected are the endurance events, so long distance athletes should keep a careful check of their bodyweights to monitor fluid loss. If protein is reduced in the diet, the heat produced by the metabolism will be slightly reduced. It is vitally important to take in plenty of liquid, and hyper-hydration appears to do no harm. The rules about providing refreshments during competition were for many years physiologically very damaging to the athletes. They are now allowed every 5 kilometres in marathons and 50 km walks, but many medical authorities would prefer unlimited feeding stations.

Fit athletes adapt more quickly than unfit ones, but they should also build up the stress gradually. The athlete has to develop new sensory thresholds and tolerance of distress. A lowering of the body temperature also occurs for the same work, and it can do more work before exhaustion. Exercising at 70 or 80 per cent of the workload of training done in cool conditions encourages adaptation. Taylor et al. found that five to eight days were necessary for acclimatization. (Karpovitch)

People who live in the tropics have a greater number of sweat glands, so the surface area for the loss of heat by evaporation is maximized. Their basal metabolic rate is lower and often their build is long and thin rather than stocky. Hot, dry climates do not have such an adverse effect on the athlete as body fluid is so easily lost in the dry air and continuous cooling by evaporation takes place and even a light breeze can temper the effects of heat.

Marathon runners can lose 5–7 lb during a race, even though they are taking in fluid. Since 80 per cent of the body is water a loss of blood volume occurs due to the evaporation. Deliberate weight loss by athletes should be achieved slowly over a long period, so that fat rather than fluid is lost. In the past fluids were withheld during exercise because it was thought that cool drinks would cause stomach cramps. It is now realized that it was unwise to withdraw fluids and that athletes exercising in heat should drink even more than their thirst tells them to. Gisolfi recommends about half a pint at least every 15 minutes (Wilmore).

Temperature variations affect nearly every chemical, biological and physical process (Karpovich). When the body temperature rises only 0.5°C. respiration increases by five or six breaths per minute. Pulmonary ventilation and oxygen consumption are higher in hot and humid atmospheres and lower in hot and dry atmospheres than at room temperature (Karpovich). The heart has to do more work because the blood vessels in the skin are dilated and the discomfort felt in a hot environment is largely due to the increase in the pulse rate. Even when competing at 'normal' temperatures the man or woman who can lose heat efficiently during exercise is at an advantage. Females do not sweat so easily or so profusely as males and therefore have particular difficulty in adjusting to high temperatures.

COLD

At the extremes of climate in the Arctic and in the Tropics man spends much energy merely surviving, whereas in the temperate zones people have more energy left over to produce mechanical work. This has geographic, economic and demographic results, but it is also influential on sport. Rather low temperatures can be tolerated fairly comfortably when exercising, as long as suitable clothing is worn. Several layers of thin material trap air between them which acts as insulation, and yet is it important to let water vapour escape. The extremities are vulnerable, so warm socks and gloves should be worn. A warm covering for the head is advisable because much heat is lost through the scalp.

At rest in cold the metabolic rate increases and the blood supply to the skin surface is cut down as the blood vessels are constricted to conserve heat in the body. The muscles may begin to twitch to produce heat, resulting in the typical shivering and teeth-chattering of a cold day. The skin is rather pale and 'gooseflesh' forms due to the constriction of the capillaries. If the athlete is very active the heat produced at the muscle sites will maintain the required body temperature. When the body temperature rises due to activity clothing should be removed, and when the activity ceases, even temporarily, the layers should be replaced to prevent chilling. Again it is not simply the air temperature that is important, since a still, dry day with little cloud can be quite pleasant for exercise, but if it is windy and wet with low temperatures then body heat is difficult to maintain. A layer of fat is useful, and females tend to be able to withstand cold more readily than heat because of their extra subcutaneous fat.

Acclimatization to cold also develops with repeated exposure to low temperatures. The basal metabolic rate increases and examples are known of elevated metabolism in peoples living at low temperatures, e.g. Eskimoes and the Nepalese. The rounder, stockier, fatter physique is more efficient at conserving heat. Exposure to cold raises the heart rate and increases the cardiac output, just as the shock of a cold bath sends the pulse racing.

Athletics competitions are sometimes held when ice and snow are lying on the ground, e.g. the 'Powderhall' New Year professional sprint in January in Edinburgh, and cross-country runners have to cope with extremes of cold and wet. A certain amount of training for all athletics events has to be carried out outdoors in winter even when conditions are unpleasant.

Shot putters carry out their shots in buckets of hot water to warm them up and avoid chilling their fingers, and throwers in Eastern European countries often have warm areas to toss from but cold ones to go out to and collect their missiles! Runners have to be careful of taking freezing cold air into their lungs. In cold weather the muscle tone is altogether more tense even at rest, whereas in heat the muscles feel loose and even flabby. The body tends to be more readily active in cold to produce heat energy and we also tend to eat more fat and protein to increase our fuel for metabolism.

Again it must be noted that man can adjust to a range of temperatures, but if the body temperature itself changes by more than a few degrees the organism may be destroyed. In a climate like that of Britain it is particularly important to have indoor facilities because of the cool and wet weather, and it would probably be a very worthwhile investment to create more indoor areas. The traditional British expertise in the middle and long distance events is partly explainable by the weather situation, as distance running is one of the events least affected by miserable conditions. Technique work is often impossible but at least one can run. Indoor areas would also be useful in very hot and humid countries where air conditioning could allow training to be carried on more easily than outdoors.

ALTITUDE

A very interesting and controversial discussion area in relation to the effects of environment centres around changes in performance capability due to altitude. When Mexico was chosen for the Olympic Games in 1968 it was stated 'there will be those who will die' because of the change in air conditions at over 2,100 metres above sea level. Much research was stimulated in the 1963–8 period and continued interest has been shown ever since. Birth, living and training at altitude has been proved without a doubt to have beneficial effects for competitors in long distance events. Impressive performances have been achieved by Kenyans and Ethiopians, whose homes are thousands of metres above sea level. The physiology of those born at altitude is different from normal sea level physiology, with heart and lungs functioning more efficiently due to years of living and working in an atmosphere at lower pressure. In addition to living at high altitude, however, many of the Kenyans live a physically demanding open air life.

The greater the altitude, the lower is the atmospheric pressure. At 3,000 metres there is only two-thirds the pressure at sea level. Though the relative concentration of gases is the same, only two-thirds of the oxygen is available. The same amount of oxygen is required for exercise, therefore the ventilation rate of the unacclimatized athlete has to be increased by a third to supply the same amount of oxygen as at sea level. The arterial blood is not fully saturated and the oxygen delivery system is reduced in direct proportion to the decrease in the total pressure, or in inverse proportion to the altitude. The athlete reaches an aerobic threshold at a much lower level of work as an additional volume of air is required to supply a similar number of oxygen molecules. The heart rate therefore goes up to deliver a greater volume of blood to the tissues. Work capacity declines and so does motivation, because the athlete feels so bad with poor performances related to his efforts. Lactic acid levels also rise more readily at lower workloads.

Ron Clarke, the well-known distance runner, said that when he went to the Mexico Olympics he felt fine on the first day but on the second day he felt very tired, his times in training were poor, and he felt palpitations. Interestingly he did say too that he felt as if his muscular system was affected more than his cardio-respiratory one. It could be that he was accustomed to cardio-respiratory stress, but that the lack of oxygen in the muscles so early in the training effort gave him particular discomfort.

The reduced air density is not adverse to the sprints and throws, indeed because of the reduced air resistance there are mild advantages in certain events, but the greater the aerobic component the more the event will be affected. In sprint training it is important to include speed work, but with shorter workouts and longer recovery periods.

Training Effects

By living and training at altitude various effects are noted:

1. Increased pulmonary ventilation.
2. Increased cardiac output.
3. Increased diffusing capacity of the lungs.
4. Increase in number of red cells and haemoglobin levels.
5. Increased vascularity of the tissues.

After a period of acclimatization performance will improve, but it will not reach the performances attained by the same individual at sea level. Controlled research studies are not wholly supportive, but it is theoretically sound that tissue hypoxia (lack of oxygen) initiates a training adaptation. Symptoms of altitude sickness gradually disappear and the work tolerance improves as well as the tolerance to discomfort.

Bruno Balke, the aviation physiologist, believes that high performance in endurance events will only result from a sophisticated programme of altitude training. Every runner in Munich who obtained a gold medal from 1,500 metres upwards had been altitude trained. In 1974 Frederick concluded that 'altitude training must be a basic ingredient of success in modern distance running.' Those who are fortunate to have been born at altitude and who live and train there have great advantages, of course. Living at altitude increases the vascularity of the muscle which provides more space to store the greater blood volume of those who live at altitude. The total circulatory-respiratory system is much superior to that of people living at sea level.

It appears from research that training at an altitude between 2,000 and 2,500 metres promotes the greatest adaptation, and that on return to sea level subjects feel the beneficial effects for about two weeks. It is well established that altitude training is beneficial; what remain to be finally resolved are the best programmes for individuals and the exact timing of the descent from altitude before competition when physiologically one is at one's best. When racing at sea level, those from altitude find it delightfully easy breathing and do not experience the agonizing struggle for breath felt at altitude.

The organism must adapt to any set of conditions that tend to change the normal physiological reactions. The body has remarkable abilities to compensate either wholly or partly to environmental conditions, if given the opportunity.

POLLUTION

Many cities have problems of industrial air pollution and the smog caused by car fumes. Nature provides problem conditions but man also succeeds in creating adverse conditions for himself. In polluted air the cost of breathing is increased because the respiratory channels are blocked. Often the bronchial tubes get irritated by dirt, dust and smoke and the diffusing surfaces of the lungs are affected. One does not need to smoke oneself to suffer the ill effects of smoke from other sources. The fumes of motor cars increase the carbon monoxide in the air, which reduces the oxygen transport capacity of those breathing it. Where athletes are taking vigorous exercise, the increased pulmonary ventilation actually encourages the flow of pollutants into the respiratory passages, so it is not a good idea to do aerobic work in smoggy conditions. In Los Angeles, famous for its smog on certain days, the performance of student athletes was monitored over a period of five years and clear correlations emerged between the smog levels and performance levels—when the smog levels were high performances were low (Edington and Edgerton).

GENERAL

Extreme examples of adaptation to environmental conditions have been given so far, but the athlete must be prepared to adapt to minor changes too—to changes in track surface, circle and run-up surface from one venue to another, and even to changes in conditions from one part of a competition to the next. Between trials the weather can change, with the wind altering one's run-up and a shower changing the surface of the circle.

Experienced and prepared throwers carry with them a variety of shoes with different types of soles to suit different circle surfaces. In the 'fast' circle, which can become glassy in the rain, a rough-soled shoe is worn and for 'slow' rough circles smooth-soled shoes are used. Different lengths of spikes are needed for wet and dry conditions and for different track covers, from grass, through cinders and blaise, to different types of artificial surface.

The huge sports bags carried by athletes may contain an emergency kit, including perhaps another track suit, a wet suit, gloves and hat, extra shorts and vest to change into between preliminaries and finals, resin for the discus thrower's fingers, an old towel to wipe the shot dry, measuring tapes, extra spikes, pins for numbers, spare hammer handles and a glove, bottles of water and glucose preparations, blankets to wrap up in between jumps, sunshades, dark glasses and tanning lotion, everything in fact but the proverbial kitchen sink. It is important to be meticulous about equipment, because anything that makes the athlete feel more secure at the start will help concentration.

Similarly it is important to be flexible, adaptable, and prepared for anything. It is no excuse for the athlete to come from a competition and say, 'I wasn't expecting this or that—such and such put me off—the conditions were bad', etc. Conditions are the same for every competitor.

The physical environment of one's home and training areas can have a great influence on the amount and quality of training done. If an athlete lives close to his coach and near a good track, it will be much easier for him or her to get to the track and get started. If they have a long wait for a bus or a long walk carrying heavy bags, then that much extra effort will be used up just to get going on a session. Time is precious and convenience is time- and energy-saving.

A well-appointed weights room is conducive to efficient and organized weight training sessions. If 20 minutes is spent looking for a certain set of discs or a key is lost and everything is in a muddle then energy will be dissipated on these distractions rather than getting on with the job. Similarly a clean changing room and warm showers encourage tidiness and hygiene. It is not easy to start on a hot and sticky session if one knows there is no shower available at the end!

On the other hand a determined athlete will often make up for a lack of facilities. Hammer throwers frequently lay their own concrete circles in convenient throwing areas when they are not allowed on tracks. Weight training rooms are established in empty attics and garages and we even know one keen lifter who did presses in the dining-room until a heavy bar went through the sideboard. The set-up at home matters a great deal, too, and good food, good sleep and good encouragement are important.

If one lives near the sea, sand dune running and beach running are inviting. At Percy Cerutty's famous training camp/home at Portsea, Australia, good use was made of the local facilities by his protégés, including Herb Elliott. If one lives near hills and woods there should be some attractive runs. The beautiful pinewoods in Scandinavia and Finland, carpeted with soft needles, are perfect for long, easy runs. Even in the city, perhaps a routine of running to work in the morning and home again in the evening can be established. Often local conditions are what one makes of them, though many athletes move job and home in order to find the kind of facilities they want.

'For effective goal accomplishment external elements must be matched by adaptation in the athlete' (Higgins). Sometimes adaptation needs days at altitude or in the sun, but adaptations in other situations have to be more immediate. There is much that is predictable in athletics events, and as the competitor becomes more experienced and familiar with a variety of situations he can regulate his behaviour to suit. Stressing the sportsman and encouraging his adaptation to such stress is all an essential part of training and preparation.

REFERENCES

BALKE, B., 'Variation in Altitude and its Effect on Exercise Performance', in *Exercise Physiology*, ed. H.B. Falls. Academic Press, New York, 1968.

CERUTTY, P., *Be fit or Be Damned!* Pelham, 1967.

CLARKE, R., *The Unforgiving Minute*. Pelham, 1966.

EDINGTON, D.W. and EDGERTON, V.R., *The Biology of Physical Activity*, Houghton Mifflin, 1976.

FREDERICK, E.C., 'Training at Altitude', in *The Complete Runner*. World Publications, Mountain View, California, 1974.

HIGGINS, J.R., *Human Movement, An Integrated Approach*. C.V. Mosby Co., 1977.

KARPOVITCH, P.V., *Physiology of Muscular Activity*. W.B. Saunders & Co., 1965.

WILMORE, J.H., *Athletic Training and Physical Fitness*, Allyn and Bacon, 1977.

10

EFFECTS OF
SOCIAL ENVIRONMENT

Sport is a social phenomenon with a particular set of rules. Every culture has forms of play, and team and individual sports occur in a social setting. The form will be influenced by the climate and terrain of the country and by the values and attitudes of each society towards different sporting activities.

Play is a freely chosen activity without serious compulsion and yet it has strict rules and regulations, uncertain outcomes, time limits and physical boundaries. It is important while it is in progress and yet all participants, even children, know that it is not 'for real' (see interesting discussion by Huizinga). Many elements of sport are aggressive but it is a socially accepted form of expression—as Ashworth says, it is 'civilised violence' (Dunning).

Play is attractive because it is different from work, from the world of reality, and everyone in the game accepts the conditions which detach it from reality. Play can sometimes be more energetic and physically demanding than work, and yet, because it is freely chosen and a contrast from work, it is 'recreative'. Schiller maintains that man is only fully human when he plays (Munrow).

PLAY AND CULTURE

A classification of different types of play is made by Caillois and different societies, and subcultures within societies, support different forms. The four main categories he identifies are (i) competition, (ii) chance, (iii) mimicry, and (iv) vertigo. Athletics falls almost totally into the first category, where there is effort between equals in a controlled situation. Chance would include games like roulette and forms of gambling; mimicry involves drama, dance and spectacle, and vertigo occurs in activities like skiing, diving, and the fairground gadgetry that send one reeling.

Roberts and Sutton-Smith use a threefold classification of sport or games that are mainly strategy, or chance, or physical skill, and they relate sex and social class to the activities generally favoured as a result of child-rearing practices. Strategy is found more in higher-class activities and women often prefer it to physical challenge. Chance is related more to lower-class activities, and often women again. Physical skill is related to higher-class activities, and predominantly males who have been trained in achievement.

There are different combinations of the above, and exceptions can be found to the system, but it is an interesting attempt at classification and there are reminders that sports and games are related to certain societies, often for particular, if not obvious, reasons and the sports change where there are changes in outlook and values, e.g. it may seem strange to our competitive background that the Hopi indians are not interested in competition and in their games try to end up equal! Zurcher and Meadow relate bullfighting in Spain to the hostility felt towards the dominating males in the society, whereas in the United States baseball is more neutral and abstract to suit a more egalitarian society. 'Play reflects the traditions and values and the degree of social control in a given culture' (Dunning).

A child is socialized to accept the attitudes and beliefs of the society in which he grows up. Play is an important means of social learning and the emphasis on competition or co-operation in adult society can be seen in children's games. There are differences, too, in the levels of stress-seeking according to the security levels of the society, and in our own modern western world, where most people know where their next meal is coming from and that their homes and families are safe, there is a need to seek stress in recreative activities. Such stress may be part and parcel of the life of other more precarious societies which are engaged in struggles with others or with the environment. Play is an opportunity for the young to learn about others and about themselves in a social situation. They compare themselves with their peers and establish relative levels of skill and competence; leaders and followers emerge and those who can co-operate and those who can stand alone are identified. Sport is an important means of establishing the habits and attitudes of the peer group and of the parent culture. The family plays a very important part in socializing its members into the sport and physical recreations which are part of the culture of that family's social milieu.

In adolescence sporting prowess becomes very important for young males and deliberately unimportant for most young females! Gradually actual participation decreases but vicarious participation continues with the not-so-young, or the young and not-so-able, by spectating and reacting to sport in the media. Sport is always with us even if we are not direct participants, and our attitudes towards sport will be passed on through the subculture. Our sport has a history.

HISTORICAL INFLUENCES

In Ancient Greece sport has a religious and ritual function and the Games had importance socially as well as athletically. In Roman times there was a shift to theatrical presentations in the arena with play giving away to display (Dunning). In the Middle Ages play and games were for 'holy' days and feast days and the peasants evolved many riotous, energetic team games with the emphasis on the action rather than the rules. In parts of Britain today there are still unorthodox ancient games on certain days of the year, e.g. Jethart Hand Ba', a 'no holds barred' ball game played by the people of Jedburgh.

The aristocra y had the opportunity to develop more personal and individual skills like horse riding, jousting, archery, hawking and swordplay, for which more expensive equipment was needed, and they had the time and expertise to develop skills. There was a need for a physically fit body of men to fight battles, and the skills developed in the leaders were often military in their basis too.

Today's athletics programme has military connections in 'weapon' events like discus, and javelin, and the cannon 'shot' originally thrown by off-duty soldiers. The hammer perhaps originated in country games using sledge hammers and farm implements, though of course racing and leaping have been part of competitive athletics since earliest times.

Moral and ethical influences in society help to determine the local types of sporting activity allowed, e.g. in Britain we consider bull baiting and cock fighting cruel enough to ban, and we disapprove of bullfighting. After the relaxations of the Stuarts the Puritans, for ethical and religious reasons, were anti-play and looked on sporting activities as time-wasting. The way to a physically healthy body and a better mind was through hard work and self-denial. Protestantism emphasized the importance of individual responsibility —everyone had a personal relationship with God and it was up to individuals to make their own way in the world. Hard work has a virtue and play made work for the devil's hands. One attained through effort, ambition and competition. However, many of the qualities of the Protestant ethic are those required by the competitive athlete—the individualism, the effort, the self-responsibility, the self-control and personal striving.

Sport, particularly team games for young men and later young ladies, was considered in the nineteenth century a means of training the young in strength of character as well as of body. Muscular Christianity was a feature of English public schools, and physical educationists were training the soul as well as the body. Codes of honourable conduct were established and it was, and is, supremely important to be a 'good sport', a 'gentlemanly loser' and a polite and modest winner—it was important to play the game both on and off the field, and whether it was 'cricket' or not became a measure of quality in life-style and behaviour.

LEISURE

Today leisure is becoming an important social issue. Hours of work become shorter, physical labour and drudgery are reduced, and both men and women have increasing leisure time. One of the main aims of physical educationists today is to encourage youngsters to use their leisure time wisely. If habits and interests can be developed in youth, happier and healthier adults will be participating rather than being bored and sedentary.

Work for many is repetitive in dead-end jobs that are not rewarding or interesting; therefore it is all the more important for leisure to be a recreative 'escape' from work, with social and personal satisfactions.

Participation in sporting activities is increasing but at the same time great concern is felt over the drop-out from sport in older schoolchildren and after they leave. In school teams and extracurricular activities the academically able children are over-represented—instead of sport being an alternative interest for the not-so-able academically, it tends to be the same boys and girls who are involved in school life both academically and sportswise. The self-image of the weaker student is not enhanced by participation in sport connected with his education, and anti-school attitudes are generalized from classroom learning to everything to do with the school situation. McLelland's motivation to achieve (nAch) which is necessary for achievement in one field is also necessary for achievement in other areas of endeavour. School attitudes and success are largely class tied.

SOCIAL CLASS

Social stratification refers to the division of the population into strata on the basis of inequality in the distribution of social rewards—particularly income, but also social status, life chances, education, skills and so on. These strata are commonly described as classes and in western societies are based on the occupational system, and different occupations (and the families of those who are engaged in such occupations) are ranked in a status system marked off by ways of thinking, acting and feeling which are generally recognizable. Part of the complex attitude system is that towards different sports. Even though the edges are blurring today there are still sports which, through tradition and also through the use of certain facilities and equipment, are restricted to certain social classes. Horse jumping and eventing is for those who can afford to keep and train horses, though horse racing attracts the stable lads who may become top jockeys. Golf used to be an upper-crust game in England, though not so much in Scotland. Rugby was associated with the 'better' schools, particularly public and boarding schools, though in certain districts of Wales and in the Borders it is everybody's game. Soccer, because of the simplicity of play area and equipment, is more 'common' in all senses. Cricket was for 'gentlemen', and fly fishing was for the landowners while the others 'poached'. Lacrosse is more exclusive than hockey for girls, tennis was for the ladies on the lawns of country houses though now a broad cross-section play on public courts. Badminton is popular in British indoors clubs but in Malaysia the kids play in the alleys of slum areas.

Where does athletics fall in the British social spectrum? Bruce Tulloh thinks it is mainly lower middle-class (Mitchell). He considers it an opportunity for those who are not the natural elite of games players and yet who want to participate—he said the only thing he could do because of his lack of size and skill was run. Britain has its Harriers tradition—running is the most inexpensive form of athletics—using roads and fields no matter the weather. The more technical events are more expensive and these have only been developed in recent years. The main participants in full matches were from Oxford and Cambridge and the date of their big match used to determine the rest of the season. Athletics is an unusual sport in that it is individual and even anti-social in many respects as far as training is concerned. It is a sport which commands much attention at international level and yet there are relatively few participants. If it was not for one important phenomenon in Britain the participation would be even less, and that particular feature is our proliferation of local clubs. In the whole of the State of Tennessee there is not even one, yet hundreds are registered in Britain. Most of the talent in the USA is in the universities and colleges, whereas there are very few clubs considering the size of the population and the extraordinary levels of available talent. Ranjit Bhatia reports little club activity in India and a feeling of isolation from competition. Similarly in Africa there are few general clubs and athletes are based in army, business and industrial organizations. The attitudes to competition and physical activity are still very different in rural Africa—it would be worth running miles to find your cows but not for a silver cup! (G. Fenwick, in Mitchell).

AMATEUR VERSUS PROFESSIONAL

Great Britain exported many sports to other countries, in the days of Empire, and the true blue amateur attitudes of then are still predominant. Today more and more sports are becoming influenced by commercialism and cash where the amateur v. professional discussion generates more heat than light. There are several reasons for the increase in professionalism and the gradual demise of the amateur. The obvious one is simply that athletics and other sports have become very expensive as the equipment becomes more and more sophisticated. Every Olympics is the tale of expensive facilities catching up and leaving behind the initial budget plans. As well as this, competition has become much more international, and for teams to meet involves long journeys and expensive travel and accommodation. One match can involve several hundred athletes and officials who have to be looked after. Another pressure is that of rising standards of performance and the prestige attached to international success. In order to attain such phenomenal standards the athletes and their coaches have to invest more and more time and energy in training and preparation. It is becoming more and more difficult to carry on with a career and be a top athlete, and of course, athletes who do try to sustain both get frustrated when they cannot maintain job and sport at the levels they aspire to. Something must suffer—the career ambitions can be jeopardized or one can give up the sport—after all what benefit are a few medals and a name in a record book when there is a home and family to keep and a career to carve out? A possibility is that those who have the potential for athletic achievement make that their career, at least for a time, and earn their living at the same time as they are doing their training. This raises other problems, as professional footballers and tennis and boxing pros have discovered—a few at the top do very, very well while the majority are not by any means making their fortunes. Also a sporting career, by its very nature, tends to be a short one.

Attempts have been made to professionalize athletics, though so far not very successfully. The north of England and lowland Scotland have a long tradition of professional 'games' and sports meetings. The 'peds' compete for cash prizes and the bookies take bets on the handicap races from the Powder-hall Sprint downwards. Australia has had some professional running for many years, and in a Spanish bullring runners have raced for cash. In America in the

1970s a bold attempt was made to put a professional indoor circuit on the boards and a number of very good athletes joined the group. It never truly succeeded, however. One of the problems was that not enough of the top athletes joined, as they were already doing so well financially as amateurs! 'Shamateurism' seems to be on top at present and looks like staying there though serious changes to rules are being prepared by governing bodies, e.g. A.A.A.'s amateur status sub-committee report 1980.

One social view of athletics that relates to all this is that it is part of the entertainment business. Entertainers who attract audiences should get paid for their entertainment value. If the entertainers are commodities and yet not getting their cash value they will become alienated, like other workers who are selling their labour. Athletes are also emotionally subjected to a crowd that can be fickle and a press than can be insensitive. If they are the best in the country and doing their best it is upsetting to be sneered at for losing to some athletically superior nation. The media use athletics for reports, stories, photographs etc. all the year round and the big meets and internationals can be watched by millions of followers on TV. The TV companies make handsome contracts to pay governing bodies but the cash has to be used to finance other not so profitable meetings, coaching schemes, and all the expenses of running an 'amateur' sport.

STATUS OF COACHES

Very differing attitudes are held towards coaches in different countries. Tony Ward says that in the US they are the masters but that in Britain they are the servants and instructors. The coach needs respect, autonomy and financial recognition which will all contribute towards a dignified status. In Eastern Europe the top coaches control their athletes much more firmly and have more administrative and selective power than do coaches in Britain, where they are governing body employees and where the relationship with the athletes is more casual. In the United States coaches at universities are on the faculty, whereas British universities do not employ professional coaches at all and rely on the goodwill of staff appointed to other positions. Coaches in Great Britain lack the professional status they should have to advance the sport.

NATIONALISM

Much of the ritual and drama that were such an important element of the original Olympics still hold their appeal, though the ritual is now based in nationalism rather than religion and magic. The ceremonial makes breathtaking viewing, and, though the flags and uniforms are criticized for encouraging international rivalry, they are most colourful.

It was the intention of de Coubertin when planning the first modern Olympics to promote individual efforts, but politicians spoiled that in Paris in 1900. Individuals cannot compete without representing a country and governments support national teams directly and openly. It has been suggested, to no avail, that all athletes should compete unattached, wearing white vests bearing the Olympic emblem. However in the 1980 Olympics for the first time winners were allowed to opt for the raising of the Olympic flag and the playing of the Olympic hymn to celebrate their victories.

In Eastern Europe political states are unashamedly involved in sport, as is also the case in parts of Africa and in Cuba. Their governments judge that the prestige gained in sporting victories is worth a national investment in preparation by providing facilities and developing expertise and selecting youth early. Finance is used to develop sports medicine, research into training, techniques and sports psychology, with a huge back-up system to support the athlete in the field. East Germany in particular has developed great depth in sports performance over a period of only some 20 years, because it has placed sport high on the list of priorities in the development of the state and the country's attitudes and values have been adjusted to accommodate this social and political viewpoint. The success of national teams has acted as a unifying and identifying force in the creation of a proud new nation. They have proved what can be done in a small country with a moderate population when determined, methodical efforts are made to improve in an area of endeavour which in other countries, particularly in the west, is largely left to chance, personal accident and inclination. The value systems of the countries are shown in their attitudes to sport. Justification for the development of healthy youth was often for military purposes, e.g. Nazism engendered a positive attitude towards physical culture and the beauty of the young athlete's body, but it was misused for military reasons. Other totalitarian regimes use sport as a means of harnessing youth and encouraging courage, initiative, and at the same time obedience and conformity.

Sociologists do not presume to judge whether sport is 'good' or not or whether it is 'good for' individuals or society. Sociology does not promote sport but looks at sport as a particular social phenomenon and at social behaviours that occur in sporting situations (Kenyon).

INVOLVEMENT

Adults who participate in sport usually have a previous positive experience of sport. Early enjoyment and success foster involvement after the compulsory stages at school. Where the family is oriented towards sports activity, the children will be influenced by their parents' positive outlook. The high social approval of physical prowess in young male adolescents encourages participation at this age amongst youngsters. Those who are successful boost their self-image and self-esteem, so it is an aid to personal and social adjustment. The converse is also true of course.

Sillitoe in 1969 reported that the middle class were more involved in active sport than the working class. Working-class spectators predominate at soccer matches but actual identifiable participation is more likely to be middle-class. This can only be partly explained in terms of expense as spectators often spend more than players! Adult participation is often in individual skill activities like golf and squash which have a social setting that does not appeal to working-class involvement. This is particularly important when female participation is concerned. More males than females are involved in sport, but those females who are involved, are largely middle-class in outlook.

Another reason suggested by Frost is that the middle class are more secure in competitive situations whatever the outcome, and through training and experience they are better able to cope with winning and losing.

Participation requires action and activity, taking the initiative and not being passive. The dynamism required is again a middle-class characteristic rather than the more passive working-class position in which people feel more at the mercy of circumstances than do those who feel they can influence events. On the other hand determined and talented youngsters sometimes fight their way up from deprived backgrounds—it is perhaps no accident that boxers often come from the slums. They have had to fight to survive and they go on surviving and climbing up the social scale through their sporting success. Here is another parallel with the entertainment industry, where social mobility is attained through showbiz success no matter how lowly the origins.

The success of the negro athlete can be explained in part in terms of differences in physique and flexibility and as early as five years of age negro children show themselves stronger, faster, and better balanced than their white, Mexican and Chinese counterparts (Bonds, in Rarick). American negro athletes are long-legged, very mobile, very relaxed and with a good strength-to-weight ratio. They excel in the speed events and can explode to record-breaking jumps, thus negro athletes have placed well in the sprints and jumps in Olympic Games.

Class also influences the levels of aggression expressed and the ways of expression that are socially acceptable. Sporting competition is a legitimate and civilized channel of expression, preferable to committing crimes of violence and destroying the property of others. The expression of strength and aggression in females is also socially conditioned, with Eastern Europe allowing and admiring female manual labour and skill much more so than in the west.

The levels of competition encouraged are also largely culturally determined. 'Capitalist' society is individually competitive with the race for jobs and success being won by the strongest. The play and games of children can show the cultural values of their society, for example in western Europe and America the education system encourages trying to be 'the best'. Sports competition is also an important means of socialization. In team games co-operation has to be put into effect in order that the team can compete successfully. In the later years of junior school some true co-operation can be expected and the children themselves are aware of the importance of the peer group and the social setting to which they belong. Social pressures become increasingly strong through adolescence, and the levels of sports participation will be determined by what friends are doing and whether the heroes and the heroines of the young people are pro- or anti-sport. It is at this stage that many young girls drop out because sport is not part of the desirable stereotype at this age in our culture.

EFFECTS OF COURTSHIP AND MARRIAGE

After adolescence the participation of young adults and young marrieds is dependent on the attitudes of friends and spouses. There are many athletic 'widows' who stay home minding the children, washing the tracksuits, and preparing expensive meals at odd times to keep the family athlete in trim. It rarely works the other way and husbands who support their wives in participating have to be unselfish, and are often understanding athletes or coaches themselves. Athletics has lost many talented young people because of conflict between friends and athletics, or marriage and athletics. Even where there is wifely support sometimes the strain of sustaining family life causes premature retirement.

CLUBS AND TEAMS

On the other hand one of the attractions towards club athletics for local youngsters is the social atmosphere of the training night, the club outing, and the feeling of belonging and competing together. Humans are social beings and they have a strong need to belong. It is a relief from boredom, a social recreation, a way of finding identity and being part of a team. Athletics is

Fig. 10.1. The presence of a knowledgeable crowd can help an athlete achieve better performances.

largely individual in the competitive situation, apart from the occasional relay run. You are out there alone when the gun goes, and yet you have your team around you and at local club derbys or exciting league matches where every point counts there can be true team and community spirit. An international team can have the same feeling of spirit. Teams can certainly be influenced by an atmosphere of optimism or pessimism, which can be pervasive. In the Rome Olympics everything went wrong for Arthur Rowe on the first day and the gloom spread, so that others in the British team also did badly; in Tokyo everything went right for Mary Rand on the first day and the optimism spread, with others believing and proving that they could do it too.

AUDIENCE EFFECT

A well-known social effect on performance is the presence of others. The top athletes are those who can respond to this audience effect and bring out the best in themselves when they are performing in front of spectators. Again the similarity with theatrical performance is noted—rising to the audience, inspired performance etc.: the same expressions are used. More crudely, perhaps, good athletes are basically show-offs!

POLITICS

Sport is claimed to transcend barriers of race, creed, class and colour. It cuts across national boundaries and across class boundaries. It is outside and above politics. Some philosophers of sport maintain this and we would like this to be true and in certain situations it is true, but in many instances sport promotes the opposite of this idealized view.

International sport, including athletics, is heavily influenced by political and national pressures for prestige, and the frantic medal-counting of the Olympics encourages this hollow nationalism. International competition can promote tension and conflict rather than reduce it. The political feelings of the participants can be brought into the competition, for example in the Hungary v. Russia water polo match in the 1956 Olympics, the Poland v. Russia volleyball final in the 1976 Olympics, and the US v. Russia 1972 Munich Olympics basketball final.

On the positive side it is a source of contact between countries, so even if their governments do not agree, the men and women on the athletics field can join in the special camaraderie of those who have shared interests. Even where language is different, aspirations and emotions are understood, and there can be true feelings of brotherhood in sport.

REFERENCES

BROWN, R.C., and CRATTY, B.J. (eds.), *New Perspectives of Man in Action*. Prentice Hall, 1969.
CAILLOIS, R., *Man, Play and Games*. 1959.
DUNNING, E. (ed.), *The Sociology of Sport*. Cass, 1971.

HUIZINGA, J., *Homo Ludens*. Paladin, 1970.

KENYON, G.S. (ed.), *Contemporary Psychology of Sport*. The Athletic Institute, 1970.

MITCHELL, B. (ed.), *Today's Athlete*. Pelham, 1970.

MUNROW, A.D., *Physical Education*. Bell, 1972.

RARICK, G.L., *Physical Activity: Human Growth and Development*. Academic Press, 1973.

ROBERTS, J., and SUTTON-SMITH, B., 'Game training and game involvement', *Ethology*, Vol. I, 1962.

SILLITOE, K.K., *Planning for Leisure*. HMSO 1969.

ZURCHER, L.A., and MEADOW A., 'Bullfighter and Baseball' in *The Sociology of Sport*, E. DUNNING. Cass, 1971.

11

MOTIVATION

In an Olympic final there is usually very little physical difference between the competitors. Their past performances may have been so close that it is difficult to predict the winner on the day. They all must have superb physical ability to have progressed this far, but there are other factors which become as important as physique, strength, fitness and technique, and the higher the level of performance the more important the other personal factors become. An essential ingredient in success is a high level of appropriately directed motivation—that drive that keeps the training going, that raises the sights and determines the efforts made.

DIMENSIONS OF MOTIVATION

Motivation is a peculiar abstract phenomenon. It has (i) direction—towards certain goals and away from undesired ends, (ii) a level of arousal on a continuum from disinterest to a passionate, consuming intensity, and (iii) a time element, from a brief passing flirtation to a sustained effort that may last for years and even a lifetime. The champion athlete needs clear goals and a sustained level of intensity that will lead to the successful attainment of such goals.

Motives do not operate in isolation. There are myriads of motives that clash with one another in the same individual at the same time, and it is part of the human condition to be frequently in a state of conflict over priorities and competing claims for attention. Those motives that take precedence will vary according to the age, the experience and the past patterns of satisfaction and disappointment the person has undergone. Man is an active, problem-solving, skill-seeking animal. His astonishing technological and material advances are witness to his seeking for progress. In the sports world 'impossible' records continue to be broken as young men and women take up the challenge of running faster, jumping higher and throwing further than ever before. Fortunately man as a species is never satisfied with the status quo, and though in certain domains we might not be advancing in quite the most desirable directions the intensity and effort are there. Can man's 'needs' and 'drives' be explained?

INSTINCTS

Early attempts to explain motivation, notably by McDougall, emphasize instincts, suggesting that we have innate motives to explain our actions. What goes on inside animals, particularly the lower animals, is programmed to go through a predetermined cycle of actions. The patterns may be complex but they are not modifiable in the face of changing environmental circumstances. The frog that whips out its tongue to catch moving flies would die of starvation if surrounded by dead ones, as it can only respond to movement. As we come up the evolutionary scale, instinct becomes less adequate to explain the increasingly variable patterns of behaviour that are developed by the higher animals. The modern view of man being an exceptionally able learner is more in keeping with observed human adaptability.

Freud's libido—that dark, primitive part of the personality—was described as the reservoir of energy that fuels all our actions, but he postulates two instincts, sex and aggression, that give the energy direction. Social training and the development of the controlling superego, a kind of inner conscience, mean that the sex and aggression are not expressed directly but in socially acceptable forms of behaviour that may be indulged in by the reality-orientated ego. His view of human functioning is rather pessimistic, as man is always seen to be in a state of conflict with himself. Can a Freudian explanation be given for athletics participation? Sex can be expanded to cover all the positive feelings towards others and the satisfaction and necessity of interacting in a positive way with our fellows which is an important part of participation, but the affiliation motive as described later in this chapter may be a more acceptable explanation.

AGGRESSION

Aggression is certainly a driving force behind many of our sporting activities. Some writers believe aggression to be one of man's strongest emotions, that emerges in our destructive behaviour and ever-repeated wars, hostility and violence. Violence always appears to be present in our society and, though different occasions may give apparent justifications for aggressive action, the underlying force is waiting just beneath the surface to find opportunities for its emergence. Those who most support this view are the ethologists—Lorenz, Morris, Ardrey—who state that animals and men are concerned with territory, possession, using weapons and asserting themselves in domination. Many of the games we play, even as children, are concerned with territory and boundaries, using some sort of weapon and winning and losing through displays of speed, strength and power. Goodhart and Chataway did call sport 'war without weapons'—if wars are inevitable then it is indeed desirable to have them fought on the sportsfield rather than the battlefield. The language is interchangeable, however, and sports literature is full of warlike and aggressive expressions—'attack' and 'defence', 'zones of territory to be guarded', 'the enemy', 'fighting one's way through', 'victory' and 'defeat', etc.

Harold Abrahams said that human beings crave violent and competitive exercise. Aggression is frequently cited as a desirable and necessary part of the top athlete's personality, and yet aggression is also considered to be a negative and destructive force. Harris has defined assertiveness, dominance and positive action as 'good' aggression, and violent, destructive, and injurious behaviour as 'bad' aggression. It is essential for athletes to be able to *control* their aggression and direct it towards the event rather than towards their opponents personally.

Anthropological studies (Mead, Whiting) have revealed very great differences in the levels of aggression tolerated by certain societies and demonstrated in their child-rearing practices. Aggression and its expression appear culturally learned whatever the innate component, with groups like the Hopi and Zuni tribes 'trained' for peace and the Zulus 'trained' for war. Animal experimentation (Scott), shows quite striking differences in the behaviour of rats and mice according to their social conditioning during upbringing. If aggression is not demonstrated or encouraged it does not emerge. A passive inhibition (see Chapter 6) operates. Harris and others suggest that sport may be one of the most satisfactory means for teaching emotional control as opportunities are given for handling different emotions, and restraint and hostility can be trained for within the boundaries of the games situation. Restraint is unfortunately not a feature of many of our modern team games — both rugby and soccer show high levels of physical aggression and injury. Athletics has little opportunity for physical attack on an opponent, but there is an increase in the pushing, shoving, tripping and spiking in track events that are not run in lanes. Athletes can be over-motivated, and, in the effort to win, the ethics and even the rules of the game can be forgotten.

DRIVE THEORY AND PRIMARY NEEDS

Do human beings have certain needs—for action, for exercise, for success? The theory of needs and the drives exhibited which give the forceful movement towards the satisfaction of these needs is the main theoretical emphasis of Clark Hull. In a very orderly and scientific way he created laboratory situations in which a state of need was induced in the subject and the behaviour resulting from this state of deprivation, its intensity and direction, was calculated to indicate the drive operating to meet the needs. The easiest deprivations to create are needs for food and water and sleep, and to avoid pain and discomfort, and it is these physiological needs which are vital for survival that are of primary importance. If such needs exist then the organism's effort and energies are directed towards trying to restore the balance, to maintaining the homeostasis of the human system. Those people like Aborigines and Eskimos who live in tough natural surroundings have to spend a great part of their time and energy in keeping fed and in protecting themselves against the harsh extremes of climate. In more sheltered circumstances it is quite rare for men and women to be so insecure that they do not know where the next meal is coming from or whether nature is going to strike. In times of war or famine there will be a change of priorities, but when we are materially secure we have other needs and motives—even to the extent of not eating when we are hungry when slimming is more important. Borger and Seaborne extend the view of the homeostatic system beyond the physical by postulating that there is an actual and intended state of the individual and the system will be active until the difference is eliminated. This broadening of the concept of homeostasis has interesting possibilities in considering ambitions and the aiming towards goals.

EXPLORATION AND CURIOSITY

From studies of children it is clear that they act on their environment in additional ways to making demands for nurture. Even an infant shows exploratory behaviour as it investigates objects and finds out about the world. Chapter 5 discussed a stimulating environment and psychologists are emphasizing more and more the curiosity and exploration that human beings show. It may be particularly obvious in childhood when there is so much novelty to investigate, but it continues all through life. Man is seeking, he investigates, he wants to find out how things work, to discover new things. The homeostatic model is not very satisfactory here as the more one is curious and exploratory the more one wishes to continue such behaviour. In certain people this joy of discovering the new never dies and these people are usually lively and interesting as well as being interested. Some athletes can continue training and competing at a high level for many years. Part of the continuing enthusiasm is the result of experimenting with new techniques and ideas, of discovering new training methods, and of inventing novel exercises. There is always something fresh to be discovered about themselves, their bodies and their event.

COMPETENCE

R. R. White postulates a motivational theory of competence-seeking. We wish to master our environment and show ourselves competent in the handling of objects, situations and people. We strive and show a determination to make sense of things for the sheer satisfaction of proving to ourselves and to others that we are capable and independent. Determined athletes, particularly those doing technique work, will often persevere with a movement until they get it right simply because they hate not being able to master it. It is through such effectance motivation that self-esteem and self-image are built up positively.

Joseph McVicar Hunt also views discovery and gaining mastery as important motivational factors in human development. He particularly emphasizes the discrepancy between the tasks that the environment sets and the resources one has to meet such demands. When the inner abilities, either mental or physical, fall just short of the environment's tasks then a motivational situation exists. He calls this 'the problem of the match'—if the tasks are too easy there is no challenge, and life is rather boring and lacking in interest. When the tasks are overwhelmingly difficult then what is the point in trying? Put the high jump bar up a centimetre and it's worth having a try, put it up a metre and it's ridiculous. If the discrepancy is correct for the individual concerned then the problem of the match is solved.

Youngsters with great natural ability for athletics often do not continue in the sport because too easy early success does not encourage the type of application required of a true athlete. On the other hand the 'also ran' may find the gap between his performance and the winner's a motivation to greater involvement in the sport.

Though not obviously a basic physiological need, it would appear necessary for normal human functioning to have an optimal level of stimulation impinging upon the organism, so to the list of primary needs or drives can be added the curiosity and exploration that maintain arousal levels.

PLAY

Desmond Morris emphasizes the exploring and experimenting done by human beings and cites play as a means of carrying out this necessary experimentation. Ellis considers the main function of play to be maintaining arousal level, and competence-seeking. The organism stimulates itself by involving itself in play—and this could certainly be an important reason for sports involvement. When teenagers were asked by one of the authors why they participated in athletics, one of the most common replies was that it was 'for the excitement'—it was stimulating to compete and it caused a little *frisson* that made the heart beat faster. Even if the anticipation of competition can often be quite unpleasant and cause troubled sleep, the athlete still wants to subject himself to the experience again because of the stimulating arousal level—every competition is an opportunity to find out more about oneself.

If childhood experiences of competence-seeking are successful, the individual will continue to seek testing situations in adulthood. As skill improves and self-esteem and confidence are gained, the young man or woman will continue to foster that skill and mastery. Unfortunately the opposite is also the case, and children who lack experience of mastery in childhood do not seek to repeat unpleasing experiences in adulthood. Early-maturing boys have an advantage in that they have opportunities to develop such esteem by growing bigger and stronger and forging ahead physically compared with their slower-maturing fellows. Lack of positive success leads to avoidance (Kagan).

LEVELS OF ASPIRATION

Aspiration levels determine motivation levels—how hard you try depends on how far you want to go. Those who realistically aim high and have considered ambitions are those who direct their energies positively and make the effort to succeed. In schools it has been found that those who do well tend to raise their sights slightly for the next attempt, be it in academic work or in games, but those who do badly are often unrealistic in their next estimates and find it difficult to establish sensible goals. In order that goals can be set and aspiration levels established it is necessary, of course, for the subjects to have knowledge of results, as it is impossible to make judgments about the future if you do not know how you are doing in the present. In athletics it is generally fairly clear how one is performing, though during training plateaux or when changing technique or when working out a long-term aim it is useful to have someone of experience to help set targets. Often the diffident need someone to up their sights for them—after all, someone has got to win the Olympic medals of the future, so a fair number of athletes need to aim for them. Parental levels of aspiration get passed on and important figures like teacher or coach influence goal-setting. What matters is what one thinks one *can* do.

ACHIEVEMENT MOTIVATION

Parental demands and patterns of success or failure influence an important human need, that for achievement. We have now moved away from the primary needs for survival to more advanced and subtle social needs. As we are social beings it is important to us to make a success of our social living, and we are motivated by many secondary needs and drives which are acquired as we become members of our society. Murray has listed many social motives including need for achievement, or nAch, which varies greatly from individual to individual. This nAch is very important in athletics participation which is so competitive and where comparisons are so obvious. It appears from research studies that parents who set quite difficult tasks for their children but are not too critical of their efforts encourage high nAch. Where easier tasks are set but there is greater criticism, lower nAch results. Demands are made but in an atmosphere of affection and support. In most societies, including our own, boys are given higher achievement training than girls, and it is no coincidence that males tend to be more competitive and striving than females. Those with high nAch can compensate for lesser ability by their application and determination. They are highly motivated from within and though they may enjoy social approval and prestige if successful, they also make demands on themselves because they want to do well to satisfy themselves. The models offered to the young also influence levels of aspiration and where adults, particularly 'significant others', are seen as strivers then such striving is imitated. Families and sub-cultures show definite patterns of encouraging achievement or otherwise.

Those who possess high nAch apply it to all their endeavours. In a study by Ryan, students who did academically better than their entrance grades would have suggested also did well in sport and showed nAch as a general trait. This is also true of many good athletes who are not satisfied with second best off the sports field—everything is turned into a competition and they try hard not to let themselves down in any situation.

AFFILIATION

The motive to affiliate is another of the important social motives. This is the need to have positive relationships with other human beings, to belong, to be liked, to be accepted by others as a valuable human being. Athletics is social in that it is always carried on in the presence of others, and to belong to a team is usually a prerequisite to holding matches and competitions. Group identity is indicated by uniforms and badges, points are counted together and medals for teams are tallied. Most athletes soon discover, however, that track and field athletics is really an individual sport when competing one at a time to jump or throw and when alone on the track against the others. The feeling of aloneness can be almost frightening, even in a crowded stadium. One of the few events in which a 'team' does operate is in a relay race, and it is no accident that individuals frequently run their fastest times in relays—it is something special to be running to another waiting member desperate to be off.

Performance in front of an audience is stimulating, particularly for endurance and strength events, though shaky technique can deteriorate. Runners who feel like dropping on their feet go on because they are being observed and in a team—the energy comes from 'somewhere'—the term used to describe this phenomenon is 'social facilitation'. Athletics training is easier and more enjoyable when done with others, particularly if it involves rather drab repetitions of running or weight lifting. Having someone else to do it with helps, and even on a cold, wet evening an athlete turns up because he knows the others will, and he doesn't want to let them down. Certain technical events do not benefit from a crowd, but a few passionate field events devotees can go on for hours in that camaraderie of the circles.

INTRINSIC MOTIVATION

Often youngsters take up athletics for the social life, for leisure in the company of other people of the same age with similar interests. Roger Bannister wrote that he used to run as a relief from study, but what was at first just a change of activity gave him an opportunity to liberate his potential in another field. He said he had a feeling of beauty and power when running that was beyond racing laps of the track. Rod Dixon in a recent interview said something similar—that when he was running through the beautiful countryside of his native New Zealand with the sun shining through the trees it just felt marvellous, and tartan tracks and stadiums could be a million miles away. Running had become a pleasure in itself.

PRESTIGE AND STATUS

Seeking prestige and status are other strong social motives since they involve having others think well of one. To be recognized as being successful, to be able to do something well that others cannot do, is an exceedingly strong drive in many athletes. Repeatedly, when asked why they participate in such a tough game, athletes reply: 'I want to show that I can do something well . . . to be really good at something . . . to be the best.' This is not really pride or a desire to show off, but an intrinsic pursuit of excellence which is demonstrated by mastery of the body in a difficult physical and mental task. Perhaps that is why mountaineers attempt difficult climbs, because they want to do something that no one else has done—and even if few others were interested or understood, *they* would know and that would be the most important fact.

McClelland in his study "The Achievement Motive" found that some societies promote nAch more than others, and that in those cultural groups the sports are usually individual and competitive. Western society is achievement-oriented, though often such achievement is measured in terms of material success. It is certainly difficult for us to understand games which nobody wants to win, or in which the object is to end up all equal rather than have winners and losers (Caillois). Achievement and success-seeking are traditionally masculine attributes. In McLelland's classic text there was little said about females because they just did not fit in well to any kind of pattern similar to the men. This social pressure against girls having or showing too much ambition, or showing aggression, or being openly competitive is a great handicap to females in sport. This somewhat confusing and disturbing state of ambivalence in female athletes—wanting to win and yet not wanting to win—will be looked at in Chapter 14.

FUNCTIONAL AUTONOMY

Allport maintains that some activities, though originally for extrinsic reasons, become functionally autonomous; for example a business man may strive to pull off a deal to keep his business from collapsing and to keep a roof over his head, but the true entrepreneur goes on trying to pull off bigger and better coups long past the stage of needing to do it financially and after reasons for primary survival have gone. The motivation is now independent of this need and so becomes functionally autonomous. There are many cases of individuals being advised to take up sport to help them get over some illness or childhood handicap, e.g. Johnny Weissmuller after being advised to do some swimming as a sickly child became an Olympic free-style champion and a famous Tarzan on films. Wilma Rudolph, the American sprinter who was so successful in the Rome Olympics, had polio as a child and had to fight to overcome threatened paralysis. As they get involved in the activity and become good at it the original health-promoting reason is left behind and they go on to achieve a physical condition beyond the normal state of medical health and strength—new motivations take over. Often those who do regular training feel so bad when they miss the exercise that they *have* to get some activity going—it is almost like an addiction. Perhaps we come to a primary need again— the body feels in need of the level of exercise to which it has become accustomed. Training goes on for ever! There is a biological need for exercise but athletes go beyond that and 'play with their hearts in it' (Harris). It is very rare for us to reach our physical limits and the limits we impose tend to be psychological. Often the most difficult part is to believe that the task is possible, that the record can be broken.

MASLOW'S HIERARCHY

There is a confusion of ideas in relation to motivation, but a very satisfying attempt has been made by an American humanistic psychologist, Abraham Maslow, to integrate a variety of views on motivation into a hierarchical system, as follows:

At the base of the pyramid are those needs which have to be met for human beings to survive—the primary needs mentioned earlier—and they include the need for physical movement and activity. When these basic needs are satisfied the next level of the hierarchy includes the needs for stability, security and freedom from fear. This level is also basic in that if one is not in the desirable state of having such needs met then one is not free to move further up the hierarchy. This is close to the animal level where life itself is always at risk and, where there is no safe haven, there is little human development beyond maintaining safety.

Level three, a need for love and affection, is very important for satisfactory human development. The recently researched deprivation studies have proved how important it is for the human infant to develop loving bonds with the caring adults in his environment. It is crucial for future emotional and social development that a child experiences security, not only in the physical sense, but in emotional terms also. Erikson notes that it is important to develop trust in the world, and, to allow that to occur, the mother and the family must be consistent, reliable, affectionate and loving. It is only from such a secure base that the individual can risk making emotional and social sorties into the environment. The child who has not developed such relationships may be impaired for all future occasions on which trust and affection are offered and received. Such children tend to become rejecting parents whose own offspring will be deprived of the affection they cannot give. Human beings need to belong and to feel that, whatever happens, somebody cares. Our modern world of isolated urban living and stressful conditions can prove too much for the emotionally insecure person who needs human contact. Erikson notes that human beings also need to develop autonomy and the individual most likely to develop such independence is the one with the secure emotional base. Fearfulness and lack of confidence are poor ingredients to bring to the next level of the hierarchy.

At this level are the needs for esteem, for prestige, for status, for self-respect and self-confidence. Such needs are met by achievement, mastery and competence—familiar words in our discussion so far. Through satisfying 'performances' in physical, intellectual, social and emotional terms an acceptable self-picture is built up. The recognition and respect received from others helps to build up one's self-esteem. Those who do not succeed in developing a positive self-picture lose their confidence and think of themselves as failing. Needs for achievement and recognition are possibly two of the most important motives for competing in athletics.

What is at the top of the pyramid? The state that Maslow calls 'self-actualization', when one enjoys 'peak experiences'. These are experiences when everything seems to be just right for the individual, and he or she does everything beautifully; everything feels perfect and a sense of joy and wonder is perceived. Most people will seldom, if ever, have a peak experience. For most they are rare, but to be treasured and striven for over and over again because the joy is so perfect. It is the feeling that one has done something as well as one possibly can and even better than one dared to hope—a feeling that one has been involved in a valuable and unusual experience almost on a different plane of existence for a while. Such feelings are worth working, and trying, and dreaming and sacrificing for. This is self-fulfilment, the joy in realizing one's potential, be it in art, in one's career, in one's hobby, or in one's sport. Such experiences are personal and individual and may not even be recognized by others. For an athlete a world record in an Olympic final against tough opposition should be the ultimate—but there are peak experiences at lower levels too, for individuals of lesser talents. After struggling with badly timed throws an athlete may click one day and have the co-ordinated easy throw that goes metres further than ever before—such a thrill that it will bring him back to the circle again and again until the next good one.

Maslow's hierarchy is not perfect, for it could be argued that stages in the hierarchy can be missed, and that someone lacking in the comforts and security will compensate by becoming successful. However, it is quite a useful way of describing and clarifying the needs we do have, and Maslow's concept of self-actualization has much to offer to the motivational study of the superior athlete.

EMOTIONS AND MOTIVATION

Pleasure and joy are words that can be used to describe some of our athletic experiences. The feeling of joy may be too precious to try to analyze but it is certainly an emotional state. Our emotions move us as our motives do, and we are affected by our emotional state, and the ones associated with sport are not always pleasant since in competitive situations a great deal of anxiety is often generated. Why? Anxiety is usually caused by vague fears, and in competition the greatest fear is that one will fail. We are afraid of letting ourselves, and everyone else, down, and we allow pre-competition tension to take over. If the competitor's past experience has tended to result in failure rather than success, the increasing anxiety over the possibility of failure may even lead to withdrawal from the situation altogether. It is a defensive reaction, as failing may be too hard to bear. Athletics is so individual that one is always aware of one's success or failure and it does not get lost in an overall team performance as it might do in a games situation. Over-tension and over-anxiety contribute to poor performances and help to create failure, the very fear of which caused trouble in the first place—a vicious circle. Sometimes repeatedly putting the individual into competitive situations eventually accustoms him to such trials and he starts to improve as he learns to control anxiety and resulting tension —but sometimes he just gives up the sport as he is so disappointed at performing below his capabilities.

It is important motivationally, however, for some anxiety to remain. If there is little or no caring, if the outcome has not got great importance to the individual or his status then the performance can be careless and carried out at less than maximum effort. An interesting relationship has been worked out between anxiety levels and performance, the Yerkes-Dodson Law, which states that 'optimum motivation levels decrease with increasing task difficulty'. If a task is simple and very well rehearsed, increasing the anxiety levels will tend to improve performance. If the task is complex, under-rehearsed and needs

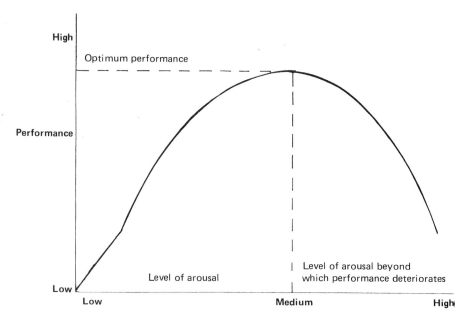

Fig. 11.1. The Yerkes-Dodson Law.

fine judgment and co-ordination, breakdown will occur at a lower level of anxiety, and just being a little too tense is enough to upset performance. As Knapp says simply, 'If the drive is too great the skill breaks down.' It is important for the athlete and his coach to find his optimal levels—just to be 'nicely nervous'—some individuals will need toning down, while others will need building up for the competition because they do not get excited enough to give that edge to their performance. Anxiety certainly centres attention on the task in hand and experienced competitors do not get rid of the anxiety but learn to control it.

STRESS-SEEKING

Competition does cause stress, and the sweating, the pounding heart and the increased muscle tension all show this—yet athletes keep subjecting themselves to it. Stress-seeking is suggested as yet another reason for involvement, and sport offers a legitimate opportunity for stressful experiences. Pleasure and pain are very close and fear and joy have the same source. Certain sports like motor racing and downhill skiing have a big element of physical danger in them and yet it is the very flirting with danger that gives the competitors an extra thrill. Human beings seek excitement and the uncertainty of outcome in any competitive situation gives it a motivational kick. Bernards has coined the term 'eustress' for the type of stress that is thrilling and exhilarating, and it is this eustress that competitors seek. Younger members of the community have more spare energy available than is needed for day-to-day living. Unfortunately their energy is often dissipated in vicarious stress-seeking, since, instead of reducing tensions in participation, they become brawling spectators.

There is an interesting contradiction in that physical activity can act to dissipate tension and unpleasant emotions as well as being a raiser of tensions. A hard session of physical action can be a form of tranquillizer. Sport is an opportunity to handle emotions and the development of a skilful body can help the participants to support a pleasing image of themselves. Layman considers that sports participation promotes emotional health and well-being.

CONCLUSION

When we ask the question, 'Why participate in athletics?', every athlete will have his or her own individual reasons as each finds it meaningful to them in their own way. Perhaps McLelland is correct when he says that motivation is impossible to study because each individual is so different. It is important for the coach to try to find out what acts as incentives, however, and we may have found enough generalizations to try to apply them in Chapter 12 on coaching.

REFERENCES

ALDERMAN, R.B., *Psychology and Sporting Behaviour*. W.B. Saunders, 1974.
ALLPORT, G.W., *Pattern and Growth in Personality*. Holt, Rinehart and Winston, 1963.
BORGER, R., and SEABORNE, A.E.M., *The Psychology of Learning*. Penguin, 1966.
BROADBENT, D.E., *Decision and Stress*. Academic Press, 1971.
CAILLOIS, R., *Man, Play and Games*, 1959.
ELLIS, M.J., *Why People Play*. Prentice Hall, 1972.
ERIKSON, E., *Childhood and Society*. Penguin, 1950.
GOODHART, P., and CHATAWAY, C., *War Without Weapons*. W.H. Allen, 1968.
HARRIS, D.V., *Involvement in Sport*. Lea & Febiger, 1973.
HULL, C.L., *Principles of Behaviour*. Appleton-Century-Crofts, 1943.
HUNT, J. McV., *Intelligence and Experience*. Ronald Press, 1961.
KAGAN, J., *Personality Development*. Harcourt Brace, 1971.
KNAPP, B., *Skill in Sport*. Routledge & Kegan Paul, 1963.
LAYMAN, E.M., 'The Contribution of Play and Sports to Emotional Health' in J.E. Kane (ed.), *Psychological Aspects of Physical Education and Sport*. Routledge, 1972.
LORENZ, K., *On Aggression*. Methuen, 1966.
LOY, J.W., and KENYON, G.S., *Sport, Culture and Society*. Macmillan, 1969.
MCCLELLAND, *The Achieving Society*. Van Nostrand 1961.
MASLOW, A.H., *Motivation and Personality*. Harper and Row, 1954.
MCINTOSH, P., *Sport in Society*. C.A. Watts & Co. Ltd, 1968.
MEAD, M., *Growing up in New Guinea*, Pelican, 1963.
MORRIS, D., *The Naked Ape*. Cape, 1967.
MURRAY, E.J., *Motivation and Emotion*. Prentice Hall, 1964.
NIDEFFER, R.M., *The Inner Athlete* Cromwell, 1976.

RYAN. E.D., 'Perceptual Characteristics of Vigorous People' in 'R.C. Brown and B.J. Cratty (eds.), *New Perspectives of Man in Action*. Prentice Hall, 1969.

SCOTT, J.P., 'Critical Periods in Behavioural Development' *Science* Vol. 138 pp 949–58

VANEK, M., and CRATTY, B.J., *Psychology and the Superior Athlete*. Macmillan, 1970.

WHITE, R.W., 'Motivation Reconsidered: The Concept of Competence' *Psychology Review* 66 pp 297–333.

WHITING, B. (ed.), *Six Cultures: Studies of Child Rearing*. Wiley, 1963.

12

COACHING

One day I would like to be a coach and it is my theory now from observing athletes that there are many different types of persons. I would deal on an individual basis if it works for [an individual] it is right for him. Look at Milburn, Jones, Foster and me and many other hurdlers—they are all different. Each has individual differences. If I agree or disagree with their methods or techniques it really doesn't matter. If it works for them, it is correct.

Willie Davenport
1968 Olympic champion in the 110 metres hurdles.

EXPECTATIONS

The coach is the person who is expected to put all the sciences into practice. The ideal coach has to be knowledgeable about many events, techniques and training methods, up-to-date and yet not a blind follower of fads. He has to be able to translate technical knowledge and research into terms the athletes can use in their training sessions and so bridge the gap between science and application. He must, therefore, be an intelligent, able and involved teacher who can give expert advice on diet, health foods, sleep, kit, equipment, literature, all the rules, other athletes and their performances—everything!

He or she also needs to be very good at handling people, not only athletes at different ages and stages of development but their parents, their teachers, their husbands and wives, their girlfriends and boyfriends, their employers, the press, the public and the sports administrators—everyone!

The coach is expected to make speeches at dinners and conferences, attend meetings, organize courses, run film shows, handle cameras, and gallop round the country finding and cultivating talent — and after all this his or her success has to come through someone else. It is the athlete who gets the records and the medals in the end, and only rarely does the coach get direct praise.

There is a rather nasty saying (possibly attributable to Bernard Shaw) which maintains that those who can, do, and those who cannot, teach—this is frequently wrong as far as coaches are concerned, since many coaches have themselves competed at some level in athletics. Usually they coach their own events, because when they were athletes they developed a knowledge of and interest in the training and techniques related to their events. They were doers and thinkers and they still have to be doers and thinkers and have developed good communication of their ideas. Most coaches keep themselves in good physical shape even though they do not do specialized training any longer. Percy Cerutty, the famous Australian coach, ran many miles every day and was as fanatical about his own fitness training as he was about the training of his athletes.

Cerutty may be an exceptional case but talented coaches have qualities of enthusiasm that make them stimulating and interesting and lively to work with. A good coach 'inspires' his athletes, makes them believe in themselves and that it is all possible and worthwhile. The same qualities that are found in the superior athlete are also found in the top coach (Ogilvie and Tutko) and often they respond to each other because they are 'on the same wavelength'. They are ambitious and striving, they have high achievement motives and seek success through and for their athletes. They have to be competent, tough-minded and emotionally controlled and at the same time very sensitive to people and situations round them. They show qualities of leadership without being totally dominant and, perhaps most important of all, they inspire trust and respect in their athletes. Can such paragons be found? Evolving a good coach is harder than developing an athlete in many ways, because the coach has to be intrinsically motivated. He has to discover his coaching qualities himself and prove them by gaining the enthusiasm and support of athletes.

It is a prime requisite that the coach is a good teacher. After all, his main function is to teach others to do things that they could not do before and to improve the performance of those who come into his care.

THE PROCESS OF EDUCATING

In the process of education there must first be aims and objectives, then some means and methodology and content to enable the learners to attain the aims, and finally assessment at the different stages to check if aims are being attained. The next stage is to review aims and objectives and start the cycle again. We tend to think of training programmes and teaching techniques without asking the important questions—what are we aiming for in the end? What is the training target? What does the athlete and the coach want the athlete to be able to understand and do as a result of the programme? Fred Wilt agrees that the first step a coach must take is to 'help the athlete clearly define his goals'. From our discussion on motivation we know that goal-seeking is a vital incentive but it is important that the goals set are realistic. They must be seen to be possible, if not immediately then in the not too far distant future. It is important to have short-term and longer-term goals, and with the short-term goals deadlines can be set so than an organized plan of action can be established. When the athletes are young or immature and inexperienced the coach will do the goal-setting for them, but when the athlete becomes more experienced he may set his own targets with advice and after consultation. There are great differences in the dependency levels of athletes—some rely very heavily on the coach to think for them, while others prefer to go it alone with only occasional advice. It is going to be more acceptable to both coach and athlete if they can work out a programme together to aim for agreed targets. It is advisable to write down a methodical plan that can be referred to to check progress. Discussion is valuable and interesting but will vanish unless tied to a schedule, and to have the details on paper enables progress to be identified clearly. If an athlete has a schedule in front of him to work through before the night is out, it is much more likely that he will genuinely achieve it—it is surprising how easy it is to become tired and stop when there is no clear instruction to follow. The dogged struggle through the schedule that at first seemed impossible is a short-term aim in itself!

It is easy to say 'set realistic targets', but of course that requires much knowledge, experience and judgment at the correct level of content and ambition for the individuals concerned. Goals that cannot be attained, tasks that are boring, incorrect, unsuited to age or ability, misunderstood, impossible to cover in the time and with the facilities available, or completely antagonistic to the individual's style of functioning, are just a waste of time and certainly a guarantee that that athlete will either seek another coach or give up the sport.

EXPERTISE

Let us next consider the means by which such aims may be attained. What does the coach tell the athlete to do, and how does he tell him? The 'what' is determined by the coach's level of knowledge and expertise—technical knowledge of different events, and the skills and knowledge of training for fitness, strength and endurance, speed and skill. This expertise is built up during the coach's entire athletics life and he must continually augment his knowledge by reading, attending conferences, experimenting, listening to what other coaches and researchers have discovered and being intelligently aware of the content of what he is trying to develop. It is no good teaching the wrong things, no matter how well—he has got to know what he is doing and to be seen to know what he is doing, otherwise those very qualities of respect and trust may be diminished. The coach must be an expert in his field and because that field is now becoming so extensive it is increasingly common to find coaches who are expert in only certain events or groups of events. Research must influence professional practice but this needs the coach as a medium. Many subject areas meet and a variety of knowledge from related fields is required for coaching (Munrow). Coaches have to be able to advise on tactics, on training methods, on techniques and on the latest developments—and coaches range from part-time amateurs to full-time professionals, so when we use the term we are grouping together a wide variety of people.

LEADERSHIP AND POWER

The coach must also have authority and be a leader. Socially, leadership can be divided into three types:

1. Traditional leadership is the type that would be inherited—the boss of an old family firm always being in the family, aristocratic inheritance of titles, etc.

2. The charismatic leader is one who through inspirational personal qualities has acquired followers.

3. The rational-legal leader is the one who is appointed by law, or officially made part of an organizational structure.

The professional coach is appointed, but it helps if he has some charisma. Another division of the basis of leadership is that proposed by Parsons and Bales, 'expressive' or 'instrumental'. Expressive leadership is based on sharing the views of the group, on sharing emotional and social outlooks. The instrumental leader is, on the other hand, task-oriented—part of a producing organization rather than a socially supportive one. The coach is not purely in either of the latter two categories, which makes a delicate balance for him. He must be task-oriented and have the authority to make demands, but at the same time the solidarity and happiness of the team cannot be neglected—he must relate personally and positively to his athletes as more than producers of winning performances.

The basis of power can also vary. It can depend on the ability to give or withhold reward, it can be coercive with the power to punish, it can be based on popularity and personal appeal, it can be legally a position within a hierarchical structure, or it can be based on expertise and special skills that no one else possesses. The coach again cuts across more than one of these bases as he is appointed in a structure if he is a professional man, he may be there because he is popular, but mainly he is in that position because of his special expertise. If he is part of a selection body, then he also has to some degree the power to give or withhold rewards. The behaviour of those subordinate to someone in a position of power will vary according to the grounds on which that power is based. A leader can also be elected by the group, as a team captain usually is, and that again can be based on popularity and/or expertise. If the coach has all the bases—appointed officially, shows great expertise and at the same time is a charismatic personality, then he may have a truly inspirational effect on his team disciples. If authority is imposed in a hierarchy of obedience, like the armed services, with no answering back or questioning, then the coach–athlete relationship is unlikely to be a happy or successful one.

RESPONSIBILITY AND EXAMPLE

Authority also gives responsibility. Is the coach to be held responsible for the performance of the team? Should coaches and managers be hired and fired according to the success of the team? Should good coaching be able to guarantee success? We know this is not true, that winning can never be guaranteed, but correct training should enable success to become possible. If technique, strength and fitness are improved, then the chances of being successful are increased. Both the athlete and the coach must be more confident as a result of the training programme, so preparation and confidence are the bases on which success rests. Any competitive situation always contains an element of uncertainty—the unexpected breakthrough or the unlooked-for accident. Part of the excitement is that even the favourite is at risk from every outsider. The coach—even the greatest—cannot control all the variables, but he can try to prepare his athlete for all possibilities. This flexibility is necessary in both the coach and the athlete—that if circumstances change they can both adapt. If all contingencies of weather, standards, style of opponents etc. are considered, no top athlete should ever be caught by surprise, nor should he see his coach caught by surprise. It is important for the coach to show the attitudes and behaviour that he wishes to see in his athletes, and example-setting can be important. He must be punctual, prepared, cool, calm, collected, clean, tidy and alert and show positive attitudes to others (Singer). Enthusiasm, organization and high standards can only be expected if they are shown.

ETHICAL STANDARDS

It has been assumed from the days of Dr Arnold and public school muscular Christianity that playing sport was an avenue to virtue and improved moral standards. Children became good sports by keeping to the rules and playing fair, so that honesty and integrity on the field transferred to the whole life-style of the player. Unfortunately, at the top in the sports world, winning has become so important that ideas of sportsmanship have gradually died. If one's income and lifestyle, and the status of one's family and friends, can be totally altered by winning then one may try to win at all costs. The rewards given to the Olympic victor make bending the rules tempting, and for those to whom success is almost a matter of life and death taking dangerous drugs and dishonest payments is perhaps worth the risk. The coach must be the guardian of the athlete's integrity and honesty, and yet unfortunately he is sometimes guilty of being the very one to introduce the 'aids' to performance. It is a very difficult balance to maintain, and to win at all costs may ensure failure and dissatisfaction in the end.

METHODS OF INSTRUCTION

In Chapter 6 we tried to establish principles of learning which applied in the variety of cases related to sport. Learning is always done by the learner just as training is done by the athlete—no one else can do it for the pupil—in the end the athlete has to apply what he has learned, using his own body that he has prepared to do the task. The coach's role is to set up conditions for the athlete which are likely to promote the learning required. Instruction or teaching is the promotion of learning, and such instruction has to take account of the tremendous individual differences between athletes. If every athlete responded in the same way to schedules and competition, life would be much easier but much less interesting—indeed coaches would probably become extinct if perfect training methods were discovered to suit everyone.

Difference in age must be catered for, with the young athlete needing more direct teaching and simple instruction. However at the same time age and ability are not necessarily matched and confusion arises when younger performers pick up instructions more readily and are more coachable than older and more intelligent performers. It is a habit to expect age-related standards. In school and college the older and more advanced students in academic work progress through the age levels and only occasionally do younger students actually excel the older ones at their own subject. The exceptions occur in areas like maths, music and sport, and it is a difficult task to cope with—an emotionally and socially immature youngster who is advanced in a particular area, a prodigy in some respects and an ordinary youngster in others.

An athlete brings to the learning situation his general physical abilities, his specific skills, and his particular behavioural dispositions (shy, confident, tenacious, impatient etc.). At any one time he will have different levels of fitness, strength, skill and stamina, and the coach has to try to take account of these as well as the age, sex, background and personality—quite a task. Are there any general principles that can be applied?

TECHNIQUES AND SKILL

It is preferable to start with simple instructions before complex ones. Similarly it is better to build on what the learner already knows and can do, and so proceed from the known to the unknown. It is rare, if not impossible, to be attempting a completely new skill, and the coach must communicate familiar points that can be built up into a new combination or feeling. At first, emphasis will need to be put on perceptual factors, but as the skill improves the athlete can proceed from the verbal and visual to the kinaesthetic.

Many athletics movements, e.g. in throwing and hurdling, do not 'feel natural' at first and so the coach is particularly needed at the early stages to ensure that the learner persists with movements that do not 'feel right'. If bad habits are acquired and consolidated through practice it is much more difficult to try to change the technique. Much time and energy can be saved if the correct fundamentals are established first.

'Fundamentals' are important—a beginner cannot cope with too much information at once. It is better to concentrate on a few simple points than to give great complicated explanations or elaborate on rather obscure personal idiosyncrasies that certain great athletes show. When top athletes in an event are studied on film or video it is noticeable that they are all different in detail. It is important for the coach to establish what it is that the great performers have in common, and try to establish these bases in his charges. There is no perfect way of throwing a hammer or clearing a bar, but there are ways that are particularly suitable for an individual's physique, strength and style of movement. All the top throwers are strong, co-ordinated, able to move fast and yet keep relaxed, but they all have their own styles of using these abilities.

The coach should keep it simple, then, and give positive rather than negative instructions. The word 'don't' should be abolished from the coach's vocabulary just as the word 'can't' should be banished from the athlete's (Singer).

It is inevitable that training involves a great deal of repetition—the skills must be *over*learned. The movements must be so well rehearsed that even if the weather conditions are bad, or the opposition unexpectedly tough, or the athlete feeling very anxious and tense, the skill should not break down. Performance will be made under stress and the preparation must be so thorough that the athlete doesn't 'gag' with stage fright. A certain amount of training must be done under simulated competitive conditions, which duplicate the time, the place, the spacing of jumps or vaults, the distractions and the irritations. If this is not done, practices and competitions are like two different events, and the desired transfer from training ground to stadium will not take place. Motor skills are specific (Cratty), only identical elements transfer, so the relationship of present task to past learning must be clear, and skills must be practised as they will finally be performed (Singer).

FEEDBACK

How can repetition be made interesting? It is important that the athlete wants to learn and intends to learn. What he is doing must be meaningful to him, and he must understand the task and see the relationship of what he is doing to his goal. The coach must ensure that there is progress and that the athlete can have intermediate successes to maintain his interest and motivate further achievement. The athlete needs feedback, which is motivating if it is showing progress, but is also necessary to enable the learner to make adjustments to his movements in practice. The performer always wants to know 'How am I doing?', and the coach is a crucial information-giving agent. It can be argued that an athlete always knows only too well how he or she is doing because there are always stopwatches and measuring tapes and crossbars that stay up or fall down, but it is a great mistake to allow athletes to become too obsessed with performance in terms of the measurable results. That is what counts in competition, but if the athlete strains for optimum performance at top effort every time in training the complex skills and techniques will not be acquired or improved. *How* the distance or height is obtained matters, and sometimes it is necessary to accept reduced results to obtain better-quality performance, which in the end will lead to improvement in results. A coach is vital for this type of triaining, because the athlete who can only see that his old technique can get him further than his new, developing, one is unlikely to change easily unless someone stands over him watching for any sign of return to the old style.

AVOIDING BOREDOM

Skills are not acquired quickly—they often take years to develop and the athlete is usually in too much of a hurry. He wants it right by the next competition. The coach must take time, he must invest in the longer-term future and persuade the athlete to do the same. There are few short cuts in technique acquisition. As every musician knows, practice is necessary even for the experienced expert—and each day must bring its stint of drills and routines since skills need maintaining even after they are acquired. The coach has to establish repetition, drills must be performed and routines must be set up, but the good coach will vary his routines when he sees any danger of boredom. The drills should be lively and fun to do, and if the repetitions are well spaced and well organized then the work doesn't seem so much like work because it has been made enjoyable. The same ends can often be attained by a variety of routes when many methods are used with flexibility (Frost). When athletes play together, having mini-competitions and gamelike activities, they are often building up a background of strength and stamina almost without being aware of it. The drudgery can be eliminated (or very nearly!) and social facilitation helps the work to be done. The coach needs to introduce novelty, variety, change and challenge (Cratty).

Much research has been done on whether practice should be whole or part, massed or specific, and how distributed in time. There is no simple answer to this, and much will depend on the learner and the actual task. A simple guide to length is that enough time must be spent to warm up and practise the skill, but not so much that the skill deteriorates through boredom or overtiredness. If the athlete is highly motivated he can take longer sessions, but he will also need sufficient rests to make a corresponding recovery. It is important for a technique athlete to have enough strength and stamina to last through a technique session without loss of quality. A basic background of physical development is necessary to acquire the desired skills (Singer).

When whole or part learning is examined there is conflicting evidence, but where the task is simple relative to the learner, 'whole' methods are advisable to give the feel of the entire sequence. If the task is very complex in relation to the learner, it is necessary to break the sequence into elements, but as soon as possible the elements should be strung together, since a whole is different from its parts and continuity is essential.

Another problem with skill acquisition is that in the earlier stages the movements must be gone through slowly and in practice sessions the experienced athlete will also start slowly and work up to speed, partly to avoid injury and partly to get the correct actions gradually. When moving slowly the emphasis can be on accuracy, but the event also has to be practised at speed —it is no good only being able to do things slowly when one of the most essential elements is speed. Both have to be maintained.

AIDS TO TEACHING

Demonstrations are useful to show good final action, and to give an idea of standards sought, but demonstrations should not be too far beyond the ability of the observing learners, otherwise it becomes an entertainment rather than a learning situation. Someone tentatively trying to ice skate would not gain from watching the Olympic free skating champion. Though they might enjoy the experience, it would be difficult for them to isolate any useful information applicable to their low levels.

Photographs, photo-sequences, line drawings, films, film loops and video-tapes can also be useful. The flow of a film is preferable to a static photograph, though both ciné and loop need a darkened room and specially set up equipment. Slow motion is useful, though the correct timing should always be shown also. The ability to stop the film or loop at any frame or to go back for required repeats is useful, though the level of the watchers will determine the necessity of the commentary. It is often necessary for a coach with a good 'eye' to pick out the essentials. The great advantage of a video-tape recorder is that the the athletes can actually see themselves immediately after their performance. Waiting for film to be processed creates too long a gap between the doing and the feedback for useful corrections to be made. The VTR equipment can be taken on to the field and the tapes studied on the spot—it can be quite a revelation for the athletes to see what they are doing, particularly when they think they are doing something else!

An interesting modification of the static picture is a special sequence camera which takes a succession of still pictures very rapidly. The sequence of photographs can be studied in a strip form which is very useful for teaching as the flow of the movement can be seen. A demonstration can be captured and processed for teaching purposes.

Another form of information feedback can be acquired by using force platform trace records. This needs specialized equipment and skilled intepretation but it is another means of augmenting information for the coach and athlete by showing them the relationships between movements and the forces exerted at the feet.

The majority of these 'visual aids' give additional information to the coach's verbal reports on what his eye has taken in. Direct instruction is the coach's main tool, and his skill in choosing the correct words to instruct is probably his greatest asset. The experienced athlete can also talk himself through various movements. Mental rehearsal is an important means of practice for the athlete when he thinks through the movements, visualizes and feels situations and actions. This technique of rehearsal has been shown to be useful with the experienced athlete (Singer).

The coach can instruct formally and then leave the athlete to do some independent working out on his own. He then has a chance of becoming independent, self-critical and able to set his own standards. One of the most difficult judgments a coach has to make is when to interject himself and when to absent himself. This will be a function of the athlete's level of ability and temperament, but deciding the opportune moment to come in and the appropriate moment to keep out of the way is a great skill. There is always a danger of *over*coaching.

SPORTS PSYCHOLOGISTS

The Czech sports psychologist Vanek advocates the use of a variety of tests and interviews for team members and advises that a sports psychologist should travel with each international team to gather information and to feed advice to the coach on the handling of the emotional and social aspects of individuals' behaviour.

Ogilvie and Tutko have operated a system of testing and interviewing which could be used by athletes and coaches having problems and they give advice to the coach which he can translate into his training programmes. In their fascinating text, *Problem Athletes and How to Handle Them,* they give case studies of athletes who exhibit a range of characteristic problems. These case studies show the variety of responses and defences that the athletes can try to use to cope with their difficulties, and the observant coach can be made aware of the use of such defence mechanisms and the needs they are trying to meet. Some have strong needs for dependency and crave attention, some are always projecting their failures on to others and trying to blame everyone but themselves, while others withdraw into themselves or show childish regressive behaviours, and the apparently arrogant and confident can often be doing a 'cover up' job. It might be obvious that everyone is afraid of losing but many are actually afraid of winning—because winning puts pressure on them to win again the next time. Coaches can be alert for the symptoms of stress: poor sleep, irritability, tension, and blaming self or others too much. The coach should know the athletes' weaknesses and try to build up their strengths both physically and mentally.

It is important to try to induce the optimum levels of tension for each individual's performance. If the athlete is over-anxious and needs toning down, attempts can be made to reduce the apparent importance of the competition to try to make him more at ease with himself and the situation, and to give the athlete the opportunity to perform before increasing numbers of other people and so desensitize him gradually to audience presence. Some athletes remain too calm and have to be deliberately 'psyched up' to try to get the noradrenalin going and stimulate performance. It is as important for the coach to teach concentration and relaxation as it is to teach the techniques of the sports skills. Relaxation can be considered a skill and be taught (Madders) and it is crucial to be able to concentrate, to be able to eliminate all distractions and, as Al Oerter says, 'to shut out the world'.

The coach has the tool of positive reinforcement to use judiciously, and some well-placed praise from a strict coach is valued (Cratty). One can praise too much so that it becomes meaningless. Blame is very discouraging and negative, but the worst of all is to be ignored.

The approach to coaching that is being advocated here is a holistic one— that one does not teach an event alone, but that one coaches a whole person, with all his individual idiosyncrasies. The teaching has to be related to the physical, social, emotional and intellectual development of the athlete which means that the coach has to take account of the whole personality of the individual. Ogilvie and Tutko note that outstanding coaches intuitively observe, study and apply psychological principles. They are objective in their observations. An examination of the coach's own blind spots will increase the effectiveness of his coaching, and the findings of Ogilvie and Tutko's researches were that coaches generally are not sensitive enough to the uniqueness of each athlete, or of their emotional states. The other tendency is to be over-conservative in relation to new learning and new techniques.

Scott has said that coaches are one of the most authoritarian groups in society, and Cerutty was concerned about the dangers of authoritarian coaches destroying the joy of the athlete in the sport. The coach has to be decisive and capable of making rapid decisions, 'but a traditional stereotyped approach does not seem suitable for an individualised motivational system, and the coaches' expectations can be crucial in depressing the potential of athletes not identifying with the stereotype' (Hendry).

REFERENCES

BOSEN, K. and WILT, F., *Motivation and Coaching Psychology*. Book Division of Track and Field News, 1971.
CERUTTY, P., *Be Fit or Be Damned!* Pelham, 1967.
CRATTY, B.J., *Psychology and Physical Activity*. Prentice Hall, 1968.

DICKENSON, J., *A Behavioural Analysis of Sport*. Lepus Books, 1976.

FROST, R.B., *Psychological Concepts Applied to Physical Education and Coaching*. Addison-Wesley, 1971.

HENDRY, L. B., 'Coaching Stereotype', *Readings in Sports Psychology*, ed. H.T.A. Whiting. Henry Kimpton, 1972.

MADDERS, J., 'Relaxation as a Skill' *British Journal of Physical Education* Vol. 7 No. 3 May—June 1976.

MUNROW, A.D., *Physical Education*. Bell, 1972.

OGILVIE, B., and TUTKO, T.A., *Problem Athletes and How to Handle Them*. Pelham, 1966.

SINGER, R.N., *Coaching, Athletics and Psychology*. McGraw-Hill, 1972.

VANEK, M. and CRATTY, B.J., *Psychology and the Superior Athlete*. Macmillan, 1970.

13

PERSONALITY
AND EMOTIONS

... if you can learn to face up to your strengths and your weaknesses and work on them, sport is one very good avenue for self-expression, self-awareness and personal growth.

David Hemery
1968 Olympic 400 metres hurdles champion

DEFINITION

Personality is a widely used term in ordinary conversation. We talk of 'personalities of stage and screen', we talk of people having 'lots of personality', or we describe more colourless individuals as having 'no personality'. When social scientists use the term to describe the habitual behaviour and general disposition of the individual concerned they recognize the fact that everyone has personality, though different individuals may be more or less excitable, or calm, or aggressive, or anxious or whatever, than others. We do not have more or less personality than others—we just each have our own, whatever the type.

All human beings are amateur personality psychologists. Each individual perceives others, makes judgments about what kind of people they are, and tries to act in social situations on the basis of this person perception, even if this response is not articulated. Some people are much better and more subtle judges than others. A good coach may often be an acute assessor of his athletes' personality, and sensitive to their particular states of mind and emotional reactions.

Personality is a cover-all term, and a working definition is 'how we characteristically behave'. People make assumptions that an individual's actions have sufficient consistency to say that the behaviour is characteristic and therefore to some extent predictable, and that the way individuals behave can be compared using dimensions that allow differences to be assessed. When we ask 'Who is he?' we get answers in terms of age, occupation, education, background, religion, interests etc., but 'What kind of person is he?' is a different matter, and seeking that kind of information is what the personality theorist is interested in.

THE ORIGINS OF PERSONALITY

When the sources of personality are sought there are many differences in outlook and little opportunity to prove one's theories. It is fairly easy to quantify athletic performance but difficult to find good theories and tests to identify personality characteristics. The argument between those who believe that personality is acquired in our social and cultural environment, and those who believe that we are as we are born is a familiar one. As Watson is reputed to have said, 'Give me the child and I will make the man for you.' Other theorists emphasize our inherited qualities, including the emotional dispositions, temperament, physiology and body chemistry that underlie all our reactions. Jung even believed that our personality is dependent on our archetypal racial inheritance from our ancient forebears. There is a New World optimistic belief in the almost unlimited flexibility of the human being, a belief that encourages self-help by positive thinking to change ourselves into the kind of people we want to be. In contrast the European-based Old World view is somewhat fatalistic and oppressive in emphasizing the deep, unconscious, unchangeable elements in the psyche. Freud believed that the main factors in the personality were established in early childhood with the individual's resolutions of experience at the different stages of psychosexual development determining the adult to come.

PERSONALITY TYPING

Approaches
There are two main approaches to the analysis of personality, the type approach and the trait approach. One famous typology is the introvert/extrovert classifications attributed originally to Jung, but other methods of personality typing exist, including even ancient astrology which classifies people according to their birthdays and the signs of the Zodiac—Taureans, Leos, Cancers etc. are all reputed to have their particular personality characteristics.

Body Types
Physical appearance is obviously important and we all know the myths about red-haired people being quick-tempered, fat people being jolly, people with high foreheads being intelligent and so on. These impressions are generalized and influenced by the so-called 'halo' effect in which our perception of other factors is influenced, to the extent that we see what we want and expect to see, and usually act on our subjective impressions.

Some of the oldest theories were based in physical and physiological terms when the dominance of the four humours (bile, phlegm, blood and spleen) was thought to influence the individual's general state. We still use terms like phlegmatic and sanguine to describe certain features of personality.

Another influential and physically-based theory is that of Sheldon and Stevens, whose research on physique is the basis of 'somatotyping'. Three main body types are described and each individual falls somewhere into the pattern between endomorph, mesomorph and ectomorph. Certain personality characteristics are associated with each of these types. The extreme endomorph is the chubby, round, roly-poly figure and he is typically jolly, likes food and comfort, does not waste energy, is not quick or explosive in style or manner, etc. The mesomorph is square and muscular. He is strong, sturdy, dominant, aggressive, a leader, interested in physical activity and, of course,

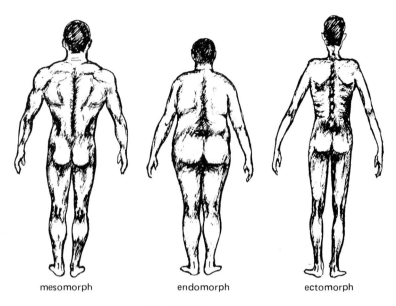

mesomorph   endomorph   ectomorph

Fig. 13.1. Somatotypes.

he is likely to be good at sport because of his build and strength. Our ectomorph is lean and weedy, probably wears glasses and enjoys quiet non-physical
pursuits. He is often on his own and seems to prefer it that way.

   These are almost caricatures because they represent extremes. Occasionally
the extreme versions are found, but most people are combinations of the types,
perhaps with a leaning towards one of the descriptions. High correlations are
claimed by Sheldon et al. between the emotional and personality factors and
the body types, and we can probably think of people who do fit into the
categories. An important consideration is that the physique encourages certain
interests and behaviours and we have expectations about how people should
behave. This stereotyping starts to operate very early and children who are
early-developing, sturdy mesomorphs gain confidence in physical activity.
They have the energy and ability that encourage other children and their
teachers to give them responsibilities and make them leaders. The slow and
awkward endomorphs may resort to being the class clown because they cannot
play other roles. British and American society is unkind to 'fatties' of all ages
and these unfortunates may retreat to over-eating and under-exercising, which
further exaggerates their physique. A lanky person may stoop to give the
impression of being a weedy swot and it is always amazing how ready we are
to play the roles assigned to us. Socially we maintain our stereotype so that
certain emotions and behaviours come to be related to body types, encouraging the theory of physical typologies to be at least to some extent accurate.
As Hopkins says: '. . . the child conforms to expectations . . .' Coaches and PE

teachers hold expectations of pupils, and since they are often of mesomorphic build themselves it may be difficult for them to understand children who are very different. Because of this, potential athletes may be lost or ignored. For example the heavy, slow boy may be useless at cross-country running but may have good potential for hammer throwing.

Body Image

From everyday experience each individual develops concepts as to how his body looks and functions. This process operates gradually and we acquire a very subtle set of attitudes to, and feelings about, our own bodies. Females are particular sensitive about their appearance but males too consider their body image important. One evaluates one's body in terms of its efficiency in movement, and movement itself sharpens the body image. When one feels satisfaction with, and in, the body, emotional and personal security and satisfaction will accompany it. People are reluctant to participate in athletics if they feel that the appearance and function of their bodies are inadequate. Those with positive self-evaluations will experience a cumulative increase in self-perceived value as fitness and skill develop. It is important for the coach to encourage the athlete to have a good, positive, body image.

Self Concept

The next stage is that of the self concept, a whole concept of the self of which the body is part. Individuals develop this core round which the personality is organized and we all have views, feelings and ideas about ourselves and what kind of people we are. We have several 'selves'—for example the *social* self, which is the self as perceived by others in social situations, the *ideal* self—the kind of person we would like to be, and the *perceived* self—as we think we are. The discrepancy between the person we would like to be and the person we think we are is a measure of our adjustment. The greater the difference, the greater the emotional and personal dissatisfaction, but the closer we are to matching these images the happier and more content we are likely to be. This self concept is very important in the development of self-esteem, and attitudes to sport and competition will depend on our perceptions of ourselves in relation to sports involvement. A good athlete will rely on his or her own body for ego-support, since showing mastery of the body is a way of demonstrating excellence so that one's self-esteem and confidence are supported (Ward). Athletes score higher than non-athletes on body image and psychological well-being. Because they feel happier with their bodies they are generally happier about other elements in their lives. We often talk of the mind's effect on the body, but the body also has effects on the mind (Harris —somatopsychic theory).

Traits

It can be argued that people are too complicated to be pigeon-holed neatly into types and that such unique mixtures are involved in personality that what we must seek to identify are certain traits. A trait is a relatively permanent behavioural reaction tendency, a sub-division of the personality, a cluster of responses typical of that individual in certain situations. Each individual possesses a unique blend of such traits. When seeking to establish how many traits it might be possible to possess, Cattell found more than 18,000 words in the dictionary descriptive of personality. He reduced these to related groupings, the 16 Personality Factors (16 PF) that now form the basis of one of our most frequently used personality inventories. By analyzing the answers to a variety of carefully planned questions a profile of the subject can be built up. Eysenck uses a similar reduction technique but comes to the conclusion that the essential dimensions are introversion/extraversion and neuroticism/stability. This method of classification fits in quite well with the old views on the four humours, and with Sheldon's views on body type since the scores correlate well with physique and even the types of illnesses to which they are prone. Both Eysenck and Cattell reject speculative views and armchair theorizing as done by Jung, Freud and others—they concentrate on empirical evidence and measurement. The imaginative views of the tense battles going on in the Freudian unconscious are not for them. It is interesting, however, that no

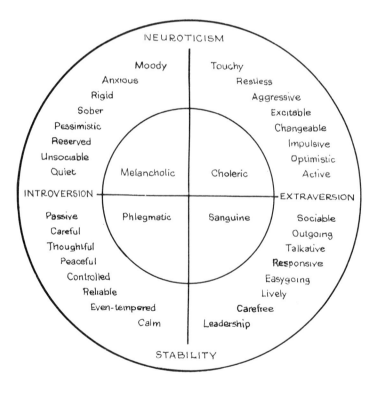

Fig. 13.2. Classification of personality. (According to Eysenck).

matter how much psychoanalytic theory is criticized in detail, the ideas are still of great value and the terms are part of our language.

Other Views

One of the current trends emphasizes certain areas of human behaviour rather than attempting a complex total view, e.g. McClelland emphasized motivation as the mainspring of behaviour, and detailed studies have been carried out on aspects of the personality such as Intelligence, Creativity and the Learning Styles discussed earlier. Self concept, self-actualization, and self-direction by decision-making are the most important elements for writers like Kelly and Rogers and Maslow. Another way of distinguishing individuals is by their mode of perceiving—how they see the world and take in information about their environment. There are differences in the speed of movement preferred, preferences over the use of space, and differences in the ability to attend to detail and make quick judgments about perceptual information. Though these may be described as personal factors rather than personality factors they influence the behaviour of the individuals in the broadest sense and in the field of sport. Witkin uses the terms Field Dependent and Field Independent to classify those who find it difficult to isolate themselves and their world view from the physical and social background against which they are working, and the latter who can isolate themselves and their problems and judgments. The Field Independent are therefore better at closed skills, and very aware of their own bodies. They can also cut out external influences more efficiently and do not allow intrusions on their concentration. An example of a closed skill is the shot put action which remains almost the same no matter the circumstances or the opponent and it is very important for the putter to cut out the external environment and to concentrate.

EMOTIONS

An important component of personality is the individual's emotional disposition. 'Temperament' is the term generally used to indicate the raw emotional materials of the personality which have a physiological basis. Babies only a few days old exhibit consistent patterns of excitability and calmness, the duration and strength of arousal varies and the thresholds of pain, frustration and pleasure are all individual and consistent (Birch, Thomas and Chess). Our body chemistry is the basis of our arousal patterns and we all know the signs given by the athlete of anxiety, elation, relaxation and/or tension. The speeding heart beat and the muscular tension associated with anxiety states in competitive situations can be detrimental to superior performances.

Anxiety

When we are anxious, say in the lead-up to a big competition, we tend to complain about small things, to be very narrow in our thinking and to find concentration difficult. A little anxiety is helpful, but a lot of anxiety is harmful, according to the Yerkes-Dodson law. The level of anxiety in an individual at a given time depends on the general disposition, which is the individual's normal state, and the particular situational anxiety which is related to present events. Such anxiety is biologically based and our bodies are geared for 'flight or fight' with increased chemical secretions. It has been found that the linear build is more stress-prone than the muscular one, but that the muscular types have higher secretions of noradrenalin, the 'aggressive excitement' hormone. How can a very tense athlete try to cope with over-anxiety? Railo wisely suggests that the more automized a technique is the more tension tolerance there is—where the skill is 'in the groove' it is less likely to break down. Deliberate attempts can also be made to control the anxiety by using a variety of techniques based on relaxation. Manning says that good athletes are the ones who have learned to manage their own anxiety levels. Just as self-awareness can make one anxious, so insights into the cause of our anxiety can help us set about desensitizing ourselves to the situation. The idea of desensitizing is based on associative learning, in which by deliberately exposing ourselves to stressful situations that can be kept under control we become accustomed to stress and learn to cope with it.

Athletics participation is definitely an emotional as well as a physical undertaking, and the stresses may show, particularly at certain stages in our careers—when moving from lower school to senior school, senior school to college or club etc. ('Am I still better than the others?' 'I made the school team but can I make the club team?' 'Can I make the district team, the national team, etc.?') These stages are motivating but also stress-inducing if one finds difficulty at any level.

Ego Defences

When under any form of threat we find ways of defending our egos. This concept is Freudian in basis, and in Freud's analysis of personality into the threefold Id, Ego and Superego the reality-oriented Ego is always having to defend itself from the excesses of the selfish and primitive Id and the strictures of the value-laden, conscience-like Superego. Certain athletes protect themselves by being very aggressive, others by being withdrawn, while some are actually afraid of success because of the pressure and responsibility that success brings. Some fascinating case studies of athletes and their problems have been undertaken by the American researchers Ogilvie and Tutko, who used questionnaires and individual interviews to find out family and social background and personal reactions to situations. They did not presume to advise athletes directly but used what they discovered to advise and inform the coaches of these athletes, who could then use the findings in the practical situation. Their research emphasizes the individuality of each athlete, and the personal and situational problems and experience that each has had are similarly unique. Coaches can be made aware of the problems of their athletes, and particularly their modes of defence which may be hiding their real anxieties.

We are familiar with the athlete who frequently gets injured, who seems so injury-prone that he is always at the physiotherapist and spends more time on the sidelines than competing. The injuries may be real or imaginary, but certain athletes do seek extra attention and do it by being injured. The approach that some individuals use in competition and training is conducive to self-hurt—every movement is overdone, warning pain is ignored, and violent and badly co-ordinated efforts are made which result in genuine injuries. Aggression is even turned inwards against the self.

Augmenters and Reducers

There are, as ever, individual differences—we talk of reckless youth, and cautious females. Interesting differences have been found in the ways individuals perceive and tolerate pain (Ryan). 'Reducers' have a high threshold of pain sensitivity and are able to reduce the intensity of their perception—those involved in contact sports, in which physical pressure and pain are experienced, tend to be reducers. They are often also extrovert, mesomorphic, and seek change and excitement. In contrast, the 'augmenters' have low pain thresholds, they avoid physical contact, are satisfied with less excitement and movement and are more introvert in personality. These are the participants in individual sports who are very sensitive to incoming perceptual information from the outside world. If our ordinary lives do not provide us with optimum levels of stimulation we try to reduce or augment to satisfy our individual types.

This is reminiscent of the theoretical position upheld by Eysenck, who emphasizes the physiological bases for the main personality dimensions of introversion/extroversion and neuroticism. The extrovert dampens down much of the incoming stimulation at the sub-cortical level and allows much less to go through to the cortical level. A very stimulating external environment is therefore necessary to keep sufficient stimuli penetrating to satisfy his needs. The introvert on the other hand permits a high level of stimulation to pass to his higher centres and there is little inhibition of incoming stimuli. The identical environment will have very different internal effects on the different personality types. This underlies our whole concept of the typical extrovert who is sociable and excitement-seeking and easily bored, compared with the introvert who likes things to be quiet, can concentrate longer, and who is generally less outgoing.

PERSONALITY ASSESSMENT

How are personality assessments made? We talk confidently of types and traits, and behave as if methods of measurement existed that actually quantified such subtle concepts. There are as many methods of assessment as there are theories of personality, and the method will be related to the views held (Hall and Lindzey have found about 120 views!). We have already considered the 'common sense' everyday ways of assessing people, using the clues of appearance and speech and manner that we can all observe.

An organized way of using interpersonal perception is in the interview which is a loosely structured way of seeing how individuals react in a situation and how they answer questions, giving the interviewer an opportunity to observe a range of responses. It is not a reliable method but it is popular, partly because it is easy to set up and partly because we all think we can find out all we want to know by interviewing. The reliability of the interview increases if the qualities sought are very clearly identifiable, but the results will often tell us as much about the interviewer as the interviewee!

Gordon Allport emphasizes the importance of what he terms 'Expressive Movement'. His view is idiosyncratic in that he does not believe that pigeon-holing is possible, but he does believe that we give ourselves away with every gesture, the way we talk, the way we write, our speech, etc. Our styles are completely personal, and informative.

Observations can be conducted in natural situations where the observer is a participating member of the group. The changing room, the training field etc. are natural settings where samples of behaviour can be noted according to rating scales used by trained observers. The subject can rate herself or himself, of course, and the most commonly used instruments for personality assessment are questionnaires, inventories of questions which the subjects choose to answer in their own way, as honestly or as accurately as they can. It is sometimes suggested that we do not know ourselves well enough to answer, and if we did we would not be honest enough to do so! There are forms of 'lie scales' built into many inventories and they help to detect ridiculous or inconsistent answering.

Other sources of evidence can come from personal documents—diaries, letters, autobiographies, and other self-expressive methods. The books written by top athletes are often very popular, one of the reasons being that the readers hope that they can find in them some of the clues to success that they may be able to use in their own efforts. A view supported by psychoanalytic theorists is that we only betray ourselves when we are not being questioned directly, and when we are not aware that we are being assessed in any way. The techniques of self-projection include the interpretation of pictures, stories, even ink blots (the famous Rorschach), where concentration on unstructured and ambiguous stimuli encourages us, without realizing it, to release information about ourselves. Our dreams and slips of the tongue are similarly considered more revealing to the Freudian theorist than the answers we give to direct questions, since we are always ready to camouflage our true feelings. Acute coaches and team managers will be on the look-out for give-away signs from their athletes and it is certainly true that we ourselves may not be aware of the root causes of our problems and need to be brought to face them by indirect means. Family and parental relationships are important, as are early experiences in childhood, and frequently athletes are unwilling or even unable to identify the causes of their anxieties and insecurities. The ego is vulnerable, and nowhere more so than on the athletics field.

Most of the research conducted on the relationships between sports performance and personality has used inventories, and though the method is criticized it would be unwise to ignore the results of the research. Certain common patterns emerge and differences can be found between participants and non-participants, team games players as compared with individual sports, males compared with females and so on. Many studies have been carried out and though there are some contradictions the general trends are as follows when comparing athletes with non-athletes: Athletes are more outgoing and socially confident, they are aggressive, dominant, have higher social adjustment, greater tolerance of pain, and are less impulsive than non-athletes. They are also interested in prestige and social status, and have high masculine interests as compared with feminine interests (Cooper). Ogilvie also found that college athletes were basically emotionally healthy, extrovert, tough-minded, assertive, could endure stress and were orderly and organized. Singer found, when studying younger sportsmen, e.g. Little League players in US baseball, that even the youngsters showed greater stability and adjustment than the non-participants. Similarly Ogilvie found that young girl swimmers improved in confidence, emotional control and outgoingness with the competitive experience. This allays anxieties about involving youngsters but we must always remember that it is only those who are stable and well emotionally adjusted that are likely to get deeply involved and stay involved at this level.

Hendrey undertook a study in Aberdeen of those who continued into middle age with athletics participation, and found that they tended to be independent, middle-class males, more stable, field-independent and extrovert than non-participants. Non-athletes tend to show higher levels of dependency than do athletes who seek social approval and have higher levels of aspiration. Ryan found that those who tried hard and were over-achievers in one situation tried hard in other situations. Competitiveness and effort-making were general aspects of their behaviour.

INDIVIDUAL SPORTS COMPARED WITH TEAM EVENTS

Athletics is predominantly an individual sport, even though it has teams, but only in relays is anything found like the team feelings of other sports and games. Differences exist between those who participate in team games rather than individual sports, with the individual sportsmen tending to be higher in dominance, adventurousness and radicalism than the team members. Individual sportsmen are also less extroverted and more sensitive. This is also found in women participants—team members are more steady, practical, dependable, emotionally disciplined, and realistic than the individual athletes who, like the men, are more dominant, aggressive, adventurous and self-sufficient than the team groups (Peterson, Weber and Trousdale). Malumphy found that female team members tended to have quite high anxiety levels, particularly in relation to their feminine image, whereas the individual athletes were more confident of their image and their femininity. Kane found that female participants were more like each other than men from different sports, but there were very clear differences between women who were involved in sport and those who were not.

SUPERIOR ATHLETES

Within the group of participants there are those who appear to be particularly successful for personal reasons as well as physical reasons. Do top-class athletes possess definite features? Singer found that there were no great differences between the ordinary and the top-class athlete, but Ogilvie and Tutko found that the superior athletes were higher in nAch, could resist the stress of competition, and were very self-confident and self-assertive. 'I had something that many others had not: I was brimming with eagerness,' (Martti Vainio, 1978 European 10,000 metres champion). They are in many ways similar to the not-so-good athletes, but stronger in certain personality factors. Those who emerge at the top tend to be less outgoing and more sensitive. As they progress through their competitive crises they become more subjective and analytic and more introverted in style to cope with the pressures.

CAN PERSONALITY ASSESSMENT BE USED FOR PREDICTION?

Is it possible for a schoolteacher or a coach to pick his potentially good athletes on personal and emotional characteristics as well as physique and physical ability? It is really related to the basic argument as to whether athletics participation produces certain characteristics in athletes, or do those with certain characteristics get involved in athletics? Are athletes a special breed that develop because of their involvement, or do certain personalities survive while others are eliminated so that certain types are left who were of that nature in the first place? We do not have a clear answer.

We are not yet really confident enough to be able to predict future performance. Even if we were able to test for future champions would our society and our outlook on sport allow us to operate such a system? Too much is left to chance at present, but we must be aware of our aims when our knowledge grows and our techniques of prediction improve.

We are ready to invest huge sums of money in material and technical improvements for our sport. Energy is spent in inventing new equipment and developing techniques for events but little attention is paid to athletes as persons and as feeling individuals.

Occasionally top coaches and athletes build up an in-depth understanding of how a particular athlete responds to certain approaches in training and competition. The importance of this relationship and the understanding and judgment developed are often cited by the champion as an important element in his success.

More time, energy and resources should be devoted to developing techniques for assessing, understanding and helping individuals. We need a greater investment in personal caring for athletes. '. . . . . the knowledge and imagination that characterise the true athlete are knowledge of training methods, technique, the circumstances of hard competition and—paradoxically—of his own character.' (Brian Mitchell).

REFERENCES

ALLPORT, G.W., *Pattern and Growth in Personality*. Holt, Rinehart and Winston, 1963.

ARDREY, R., *The Territorial Imperative*. Fontana, 1969.

BANDURA, A., and WALTERS, R.H., *Social Learning and Personality Development*. Holt, Rinehart and Winston, 1968.

BIRCH, THOMAS and CHESS, 'The Origin of Personality', *Scientific American* 1970.

CATTELL, R.B., *The Scientific Analysis of Personality*. Penguin, 1965.

COOPER, L., 'Athletics, Activity and Personality: a review of the literature'. *Research Quarterley* No. 40 pp 17–22.

COUNSILMAN, J. E., *The Science of Swimming*. Pelham Books, 1968.

COUNSILMAN, J. E., *Doc Counsilman on Swimming*. Pelham, 1978.

CRATTY, B.J., *Social Dimensions of Physical Activity*. Prentice Hall, 1967.

DOLLARD, J. and MILLER, N.E., *Personality and Psychotherapy*. McGraw Hill, 1950.

EYSENCK, H.J., *Biological Bases of Personality*. Routledge & Kegan Paul, 1967.

HALL, C.S. and LINDZEY, G., *Theories of Personality*. John Wiley & Sons, 1957.

HARRIS, D.V., *Involvement in Sport*. Lea & Febiger, 1973.

HENDRY, L.B., 'The Coaching Stereotype' in H.T.A. Whiting (ed) *Reading in Sports Psychology*. Henry Kimpton, 1972.

HOPKINS, B., 'Body-Build Stereotypes', *Reading in Sports Psychology*, ed. H.T.A. Whiting. Henry Kimpton, 1972.

KELLY, G.A., *The Psychology of Personal Constructs*. W.W. Norton & Co. Inc. 1955.

LAYMAN, E.M., 'The Contribution of Play and Sports to Emotional Health', *Psychological Aspects of Physical Education and Sport*, ed. J.E. Kane. Routledge, 1972.

LORENZ, K., *On Aggression*. Methuen, 1966.

MALUMPHY, T.M., 'Personality of Women Athletes in Intercollegiate Competition'. *Research Quarterly* 1968, 39, pp. 610–20.

MORRIS, D., *The Naked Ape*. Cape, 1967.

OGILVIE, B.C., 'Psychological Consistencies within the Personality of High-level Competitors' in W.P. Morgan (ed.), *Contemporary Readings in Sports Psychology*. Charles C. Thomas, Springfield Illinois, 1970.

PETERSON, S.L., WEBER, J.C., and TROUSDALE, W.W., 'Personality Traits of Women in Team Sports vs. Individual Sports', *Research Quarterly 1967*, 38, pp. 686–90.

RAILO, W.S., 'Warm Up'. *Track and Field Quarterly Review*, Vol. 77, No. 2, summer 1977.

ROGERS, C., *Client-Centred Therapy*. Houghton Mifflin Co., 1951.

RYAN, E.D., 'Perceptual Characteristics of Vigorous People', *New Perspectives of Man in Action*, ed. R.C. Brown and B.J. Cratty. Prentice Hall, 1969.

SHELDON, W.H., and STEVENS, S.S., *A Psychology of Constitutional Differences*. Harper, 1942.

SINGER, R.N., *Myths and Truths in Sports Psychology*. Harper & Row, 1975.

WARD, T., 'The Role of the Professional' in B. Mitchell (ed) *Today's Athlete*. Pelham, 1970.

WITKIN, H.A., *et al, Psychological Differentiation*. Wiley, 1962.

14

AGE AND PERFORMANCE

The human life span is getting longer. The Romans had an expectation of 22 years, at the turn of the century in Britain 47 years could be expected, and today men can expect to live to 72 and women to 77 if no fatal illness or accident intervenes. Though the total lifetime is lengthened, is the active and vigorous period enlarged or is senescence lengthened? If the latter is the case there is not a great deal to be said for living longer. Old age does not have a positive image in our society and to be old, lacking in vigour, dependent, and without social status and job responsibility is not an attractive prospect. Ageing has been described as 'a gradual loss of the organism's ability to respond to the environment' (Edington and Egerton). The mystery of ageing is still with us, as medicine does not know exactly what causes the deterioration associated with age and it has as yet little or no control over the process. Gerontology was only established in the 1950s in Britain.

There is a moderate correlation between the sizes of animals and their life spans, with the bigger ones living longer—whales and elephants live a long time and, though tortoises are an exception, the smaller ones with a high basal metabolic rate have only a short span. The longer the growing period the slower is the onset of ageing, though our knowledge is limited because gerontology has mainly been studied in man and in the white rat in the laboratory. Each species under good conditions appears to have an optimum span, though generally, in the wild, animals die of injury or from predators rather than from old age. Animals in captivity sometimes have surprisingly long life spans —e.g. a 27-year-old chaffinch, a cat of 27 years, and an elephant of 70. This life span may be under the control of the nervous system, and a form of 'timing device' operates which starts to 'age' the cells after a given period of time. Other theories of ageing suggest that cell replacement just becomes less and less accurate over time, and that instead of exact copies we have poor imitations which gradually add up to the deficiences of ageing. As a cell ages it is continuously dependent on genetic guidelines to provide information for protein synthesis. It is not so much a wearing out process as a poor replacement system after many years (Comfort).

The peak of athletics performance for speed events usually occurs in the early twenties and for technical events in the later twenties. Curves of optimal performance follow a definite rise from childhood into young adulthood, after which there is a progressive decline into old age.

Sports participation and prowess is associated with youth and society expects 30-year-olds to be thinking of retiring. But is it because of physical deterioration that the young middle-aged give up participation, or are there other reasons?

EFFECTS OF AGEING ON THE ATHLETE

What happens physically and physiologically over the years?

Speed and Agility
These are at their best between 17 and 30, according to Olympic results (Karpovich). Speed of reaction slows with age. Wilmore suggests that the conduction velocity of the 'message' along the nerve fibres actually slows down. There is a rapid improvement in co-ordination from childhood into young adulthood, followed by a very gradual decline.

Skill
Where skill has been acquired over a period of time little deterioration is experienced with age, e.g. there are good golfers in their sixties and older. As long as older people are not rushed too much, a high level of skilled performance can be maintained. Though older people are not so quick to learn new skills as are adolescents they have great capacity for concentration. If there is any transfer to be made from previous learning they have a broader range of physical experience to call on.

Strength
This decreases very slowly from maximum scores between 25 and 30 years of age. Even at 60 years there is as little as a 10—20 per cent loss in strength, particularly if the subject remains active (De Vries). The strength loss in females is more rapid and their trainability for strength also decreases more quickly than it does for males. Over 40 years there is a tendency to lose muscle mass, which may fit in with the protein synthesis ageing theory (Hettinger). It is advisable to avoid isometric training because of the dangers of increased blood pressure, but isotonic training can continue beneficially, particularly as weights can be adjusted and be as gradual and progressive as the individual needs and wants.

The Cardiovascular System
If regularly exercised, it keeps in good condition and marathons are run by 50- and 60-year-olds; much older athletes can hardly be distinguished from younger competitors in situations where sub-maximal work is being carried out. However the blood pressure rises when making efforts to pump blood through arteries and veins that are reduced in cross-section by cholesterol deposits caused by bad diet habits and lack of exercise over long periods (De Vries). Simonsen found a 29 per cent reduction in blood flow in the 40—50-year-old group as compared with the 10—29-year-old group. The maximum heart rate also decreases with age.

Table 14.1. Heart rate as a function of age. (After D.H. Clarke.)

Age	Max.
25	200
30	194
35	188
40	182
45	176
50	171
55	165
60	159
65	153

Pulmonary Functions

The gradual loss of elasticity in the lung tissues and in the chest wall increase the effort involved in breathing, causing the vital capacity gradually to reduce even though the total lung capacity changes little.

Physical Working Capacity

On average this reaches a maximum at 17½ years of age and by the time a man is 75 years it is at half that level. Unfortunately few longitudinal studies are available and much will depend on both the early habits of exercise and involvement acquired in youth and how active the individual remains through

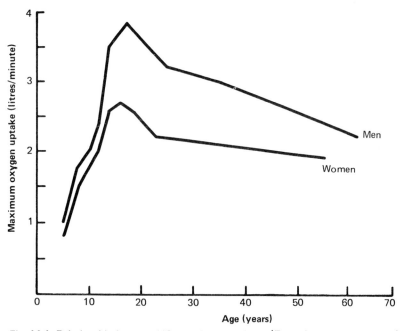

Fig. 14.1. Relationship between VO$_2$ maximum and age. (From Astrand and Rodahl.)

his thirties and forties upwards. One longitudinal study (De Vries) showed a big decline in running on a treadmill by a subject tested regularly between 41 and 66 years. The subject had gained 16½ lb in weight over that period, however, which made comparisons of work performance difficult.

Weight Gain

This is one of the greatest problems of retirement from sport. People who took part in organized PE and games at school, and who have opportunity for activity in college and club, tend to reduce their exercise levels drastically in their late twenties onwards. Often the food intake remains the same and the alcohol intake often goes up, so there is loss of muscle tissue and increase in fat. Nature does not make this inevitable and examples of lean and healthy elderly men and women show that is it our unfortunate living habits that accelerate our physical deterioration.

In controlled situations it has been established that a restricted calorific intake lengthens the life span of laboratory animals. In converse, excessive weight leads to killing cardio-vascular disease. A man, as well as a laboratory rat, is as old as his arteries, and we must remember that the basal metabolic rate reduces by 3 per cent each decade from three years of age until the eighties.

EXERCISE AND AGEING

When studying animals in the laboratory, it is clear that physically active animals live longer than their inactive fellows. There is no clear evidence in humans that exercise actually aids longevity, but it is clear that physical activity keeps the organism livelier and fitter and in better condition for many more years before any ageing sets in. Ageing is not a sudden, dramatic occurrence, but a gradual process extending over several decades, and this process can be delayed by sensible and regular physical activity.

Rats in the laboratory do not smoke or have career and money problems, as human beings do. Much of the human drop-away in physical activity is the result of other commitments and worries. It is a great mistake to relegate physical exercise to such an unimportant level that everything else takes precedence, but this is the pattern that is established in school where PE is given less and less importance as higher classes are reached. This is where important attitudes to physical activity are built up and it is sad that they are often so negative.

Percy Cerutty—who was either eccentric or very sensible, depending on how you look on his crusade for fitness—criticized our modern living and particularly our diet and lack of fresh air and exercise. He advised against too much meat, milk, starch and sugar, and advocated fresh fruit and vegetables as the mainstay of a healthy food intake. In his sixties and seventies he would lead his athletes, including the Olympic gold medallist Herb Elliott, on beach runs up steep sand dunes and in strenuous weights programmes. He considered that most men look after their cars better than their own bodies.

Bromley, in *The Psychology of Human Ageing*, gives us a sobering thought

—we spend a quarter of our lives growing up and three-quarters of our life growing old. Chronological age is only a very rough indication of any individual's capacities, and anyone who keeps mentally, physically and socially active will keep his capacities at full working strength. Disuse slows down the body and also the brain, so that the older person's confidence and self-esteem start to drop.

Social attitude to age, and not just old age, but any age, is important. It is noticeable in the British press that everyone's age gets mentioned—in a court case, in a gossip column, in a political report, in a sports article the participants frequently have their ages in brackets after their names. Age determines legally when we may vote, when we may marry, when we are criminally responsible, when we are obliged to fight for our country, when we must enter and leave school and so on . . . and the ages do not always seem to synchronize sensibly! But obsession with age means that we are often self-conscious about our ages, and the current cult of youth makes those past the first flush embarrassed about it. Women are traditionally teased about never wanting to give away their ages, but men are just as keen to conceal theirs. Athletes are also conscious of age at both ends of the scale because age determines the groupings for competition in the teens, and the expectations of change in size and strength over a few years are related to the weights of the different throwing implements used at different ages. When competing, youngsters always ask about their opponents' age and use even a few months' difference as an excuse for superiority or defeat.

Successful sportsmen and women seem to be getting younger in many fields, particularly swimming, gymnastics, figure skating and tennis. World-beaters emerge in the teens and veterans are 'over the top' at 20. Athletics does not find its talent blossoming so young, but some trends are downwards in the ages of Olympic champions and competitiors. When athletes in their late twenties and early thirties have not 'made it' they feel it is not worth trying any more, and motivation vanishes as they start to believe that they are too old.

The social pressure against training and participation are strong. It is bad enough for a young athlete to be shouted after in the street or teased about the time they are 'wasting' at the club, but for someone a bit older it can be too embarrassing to bear. It may be a form of jealousy, but other mature people often resent anyone but youngsters training and competing. Perhaps it makes them feel guilty and embarrassed about their own lack of fitness.

Several events in recent years have helped to change this view, fortunately. When President Kennedy started the jogging campaign in the USA it caught on. Tests on US children showed that they were poorer in terms of fitness than their European and Asian counterparts, and more and more men in their forties and fifties were dying of heart disease brought on by lack of fitness.

There has been much publicity about middle-aged fitness in the press, which has raised quite a lot of interest, and books on aerobics have become very popular. If one sees an obviously not-so-fit runner out trotting round the track, the chances are that he or she is doing the '12-minute' test or trying to build up a few points for the weekly target score (Cooper)!

It is difficult to define fitness, just as it is difficult to define health . . . is the latter absence of disease? There is no one who is fit in all respects—the person who is fit to be a jockey is not fit to be a heavyweight boxer (Karpovich). Physical exercise of the right type and degree improves health and by health we imply all the physiological processes discussed in Part I. The main banner upheld by the jogging campaigners and the 'sport for all' enthusiasts is health, but the by-products of improved fitness are even more difficult to define.

The exercise and the 'feeling better' can occur without involvement in competitive athletics, but often those who have been involved in competition find that on retiring one of the things they miss most is the excitement of competition—that extra kick of adrenalin in anticipation of testing oneself. There is a certain amount of stress in competition but human beings seek stress to stimulate them and that does not stop just because one is 35 or over.

The middle-aged, even the strong and fit middle-aged, are not really in a position directly to challenge younger people at the peak of their form. Some physiological deterioration takes place, as we have already discussed, and there is also an increased danger of injury which may take much longer to recover from than in younger days. Mature athletes therefore want to stretch themselves but against people of their own age and standard, hence the development of age-related competitions. In the United States it is called Masters Athletics and in Europe Veterans Athletics. There are organized five-year groupings for all events, i.e. 35—39 years (women only), 40—44 years, 45—49 years, 50—54 years etc., so the races are run and records made in competition with one's peers. There are now World Masters Championships, European Veterans Championships and National Championships in a wide range of events. Some of the performances are astonishingly good, or they may be astonishing only as long as we go on believing that good performances are only for the youngsters. Though many of the competitors are ex-athletes, ex-Olympians at that, some only started in their forties and fifties and discovered new interests and thrills of competition that they had never experienced in their youth.

Whether or not very young children should be involved in competitive situations is a much-discussed topic. The children themselves do not seem to suffer too much, even if they lose most of their childhood in training time. Some parents get very emotionally involved and it means more to them than to the children whether the youngsters win or lose. It is bad to live through someone else, and it would be better for the parents to get on to the track and compete themselves.

CONCLUSION

Attitude and interest are more important than chronological age. The human body is a marvellous machine which will respond with high-quality performance if it is given the right kind of treatment. Not everything is on the side of youth. What the young have in physiological terms may be compensated for by experience, ingenuity and dedication. Energy is often wasted by youngsters but the older competitor can conserve and utilize his efforts to his greatest advantage. Athletics is not all guile and gamesmanship but it can help a grea deal in the mastery of many situations. In any case, if a good programme c training is maintained and intelligence and technical ability are applied, th older athlete does compete on more than equal terms. The body deteriorate mainly because we expect it to and allow it to. If we can change our attitude towards involvement then age-related levels of participation and performanc will alter too.

REFERENCES

ASTRAND, P.O., and RODAHL, *K., Textbook of Work Physiology*. McGraw Hill, 197C (Fig. 14.1 also from this source)

BROMLEY, D.B., *The Psychology of Human Aging*. Penguin, 1974.

COMFORT, A., *The Process of Aging*. Weidenfeld and Nicolson, 1965.

COOPER, K.H., *The New Aerobics*. Bantam, 1970.

DE VRIES, H.A., *Physiology of Exercise*. Staples Press, 1967.

EDINGTON, D.W. and EDGERTON, V.R., *The Biology of Physical Activity*. Houghto Mifflin, 1976.

HETTINGER, T., Physiology of *Strength*. Chas C. Thomas, 1961.

KARPOVICH, P.V., *Physiology of Muscular Activity*. W.B. Saunders & Co., 1965.

LAWTHER, J.D., *The Learning of Physical Skills*. Prentice Hall 1968.

LAWTHER, J.D., *Sports Psychology*. Prentice Hall, 1972.

WILMORE, J.H., *Athletic Training and Physical fitness*. Allyn and Bacon, 1977.

15

WOMEN IN ATHLETICS

Historically, competitive sports have been a male prerogative, but female participation in athletics has progressed a long way in the last half-century. Athletics events for women were first introduced in the 1928 Olympics—previously even de Coubertin had considered it was the woman's role to 'crown the winner with garlands'!

Many of the attitudes of the past were built on the assumption that women were physiologically inadequate compared with men. It was also believed that females were not suited emotionally or socially to strenuous and competitive physical activity and that such participation would encourage masculine characteristics. All these assumptions have been shown to be without foundation, and reference has already been made in earlier chapters to factors influencing potential female athletes.

Simultaneously with the increase in the importance of sport and leisure time activities there has been increasing discussion of the role of women in our society with a movement towards greater emancipation and freedom of choice. The male stereotype is compatible with sport in our culture but the female has to try to resolve the problem of being competitive and filling the traditional feminine role of passivity and dependence.

If a woman does well in sport she may be told she 'plays like a man', but what a criticism of a man it is to be told he is 'fussing about like a woman'! The sex tests at important competitions are made to ensure that all female competitors *are* female, implying that if a woman is *that* good she may be a man!

Becoming involved in sport is generally the result of participation and/or encouragement by family and friends. Middle-class females are slightly more likely to be involved than working-class ones and it is particularly important for women to have the support and positive encouragement of 'significant others', and all the more effective if they are male. Unfortunately it is often females who are harder on other females when it comes to critical comments about 'she men', having muscles, and being 'unfeminine'.

Countries which exhibit more equal attitudes to mesomorphic women and displays of female strength have greater and superior participation of women, especially in the power events. There is for example a difference in social attitude in Eastern Europe to women's work activities, which is reflected in a difference in attitude to sporting prowess (Munrow). Western cultures tend to encourage females to avoid participation unless the sport has a feminine image or aesthetic appeal, such as gymnastics and figure skating.

In schools both boys and girls tend to lose interest in adolescence, but the greatest loss is among teenage girls. A young man can gain a certain status as a sportsman and it increases his popularity and self-confidence. Girls may become embarrassed by sporting success and it is even harder to attain, since at this stage in their physical and physiological development their performances may actually deteriorate because of weight gain and the development of secondary sex characteristics. Biology and society conspire to reduce female commitment. Today the emphasis of the advertising media on the female body as a sexual object for a man can clash with the girl's concept of her body as an instrument to be used efficiently in sport.

The main agent for introducing the young to physical activity is the school, but unfortunately physical education does not appear to be very successful in fostering positive attitudes towards female involvement. The tendency away from direct skill teaching towards a freer exploratory style of gym and dance may encourage expression in some girls, but may leave others without a repertoire of skills to use with confidence outside the school situation. It is interesting, however, that in a recent Schools Council study of secondary school physical education, women physical education teachers gave more emphasis to 'motor skills' than men physical education teachers, who emphasized 'preparation for leisure'.

Studies have shown that adult males spent 11 per cent of their leisure time in active recreation while women only devoted 4 per cent of theirs to it. Females certainly have to overcome more restraints to participate, especially when they are married and have children. Convenient provision of facilities is necessary before they can participate, since many females have greater handicaps to overcome before they can get themselves free to take part.

PHYSIOLOGY

The population split into male and female is a very important psychological, as well as physical and physiological, division. Some authorities argue that we have a kind of sexual neutrality at birth and that each infant is socialized into being male or female. Hutt argues strongly against this view and maintains that the brain even of a new-born child is influenced by the secretion of male hormones. There are certainly clearly identifiable physiological differences. Females are generally smaller, weaker and lighter than males except during the pubertal spurt when for a short time girls grow faster because of their earlier maturity. They have narrower shoulders, shorter arms and wider hips and they do not have such a good strength-to-weight ratio as males. Strength in females is trainable but not to such an extent as in males and there is much less build-up of muscle. Males have the advantage of greater leverage and longer limb length which gives them a longer stride pattern in running and a greater radius when throwing. The more rugged physical structure of the male is better suited to strenuous activity. It is important to remember, of course, that though the averages for the sexes may be different, there is tremendous overlap and the better women are superior to the poorer men.

Blood
Females have lower haemoglobin counts and the pulse rate is some seven or eight beats faster. This means that they are not so efficient at oxygenating working muscles. Girls are not infrequently anaemic, partly due to the regular blood loss, and top female endurance athletes need regular medical checks with blood tests. In the trained male the oxygen uptake is some 20–25 per cent better than in the trained female.

Fat
Males are more mesomorphic while females are more endomorphic, with a fairly generous extra layer of fat. The extra layer is useful for coping with low temperatures and fat stores may be used in long stamina events, but the excess of fat to muscle is not useful athletically.

Temperature Control
Females have greater difficulty in controlling heat loss since they do not sweat so easily as men, and heat is less efficiently lost by the flow of blood to the skin. There is some truth in the saying that 'men perspire but ladies just glow', but sometimes it is more comfortable to perspire!

Flexibility
Females are more flexible and are good on balance and stability. Increased flexibility is generally advantageous, though too much flexibility without strength can be a problem for girls and women in certain events.

Injuries
If they have sufficient conditioning women are no more susceptible to injury than men. They tend to suffer from overstrain rather than explosive tears and they frequently go on longer before complaining and seeking treatment. It is interesting that women are more resistant to disease than men and that female babies are born with fewer defects of sight and hearing than male infants, who tend to be more extreme in their abnormalities.

Cycles
Regular menstruation occurs in females but responses to it are very individual (Dalton). Certainly premenstrual tension exists, and, though it may not exert great influence on performance physically, irritability is usually present, and the female may be more easily stressed.

Exercise during pregnancy is advantageous as long as common sense prevails, and indeed the fitness and good body condition gained from athletics will actually help in labour and childbirth.

Development
Girls are often just as strong and fast until puberty, but then boys go on improving their strength and speed because of the increase of male hormones,

which causes growth and development of physique that leads to improved performance, even with little training. The female athlete is more likely to be mesomorphic in physique because that is the body type that will enable more effective physical performance. But training will not make females look like males for all the anxiety that youngsters may feel! Male characteristics do not develop as the result of athletics—indeed girls often improve their female body image through training, by becoming healthier and firmer and better co-ordinated.

Drugs

Females have much more to gain than males from taking male hormone drugs and anabolic steroids—levels of strength and aggression have much more room for increase in the female, and the results of such drug abuse are very effective.

SOCIAL ENVIRONMENT AND PERSONALITY

Male superiority in strength, speed, visual perception and spatial orientation led in the past to a division of labour, but the changes in today's pattern of living and improvements in birth control mean that women are no longer confined to home and child-rearing for long periods.

Males are more adventurous and independent, and any display of early independence is encouraged, whereas girls are more affected by social approval and disapproval so that any adventurous or aggressive behaviour is discouraged as not being ladylike. It is considered all right for girls to be tomboys when they are very young, but they soon get the message as they get older that tomboyish behaviour is not the best way to gain approval and admiration.

It is an important need of all people to have self-esteem, and for the young female to maintain an acceptable self-image in sport she needs the approval of family or boyfriend or husband. She needs to be able to resist the pressures of the media and adverse social comment as well as do all the necessary work and training. Potentially good female athletes frequently give up because their boyfriends disapprove. Like men, they experience conflict over time, fitting in training with work, with exams, coping with injuries, poor facilities, plus the social pressures. Athletes need to compartmentalize their lives and that ability tends to be a male rather than a female attribute—men seem to be better able to separate their work and their home life, their worries and their joys and sorrows.

When the personalities of women who compete in individual sports are compared with those who participate in team games there is a tendency for individual activities, like athletics, to have more dominant, aggressive and adventurous participants. They are more independent, but more introverted and self-absorbed than participants in team sports (Peterson et al.). Malumphy found similarly that individual sportswomen were more adventurous and tough-minded than the team sport participants who showed quite high levels of anxiety. There is no evidence to support the contention that women are 'too emotional' to compete (De Vries). Interviews conducted with international women athletes showed that they were as dedicated and committed as men, and were just as willing to make sacrifices and train hard (Payne). It was interesting that in their home background the interviewees had not experienced very biased sex-typing. Their parents had shared authority, and the brothers and sisters in the family had shared household tasks equally. Many of these internationals had married athletes or had athletes as boyfriends. They were ambitious, independent and wanted to prove themselves.

Achievement

Females tend to fear failure but they also fear success. It is common for both sexes to fear failure and, as stated earlier, such a fear is a very strong motivator though it brings a great deal of anxiety. In *Problem athletes and how to handle them* it was noted that some male athletes have this problem of fear of success, but it affects women more, since achievement itself is not considered so important for females, and they tend to lack self-confidence. Girls use achievement as a means of receiving approval from others, while boys are more independent of such external sources of reinforcement (Bardwick).

There are many ways that women can obtain self-actualization, and sport is only suitable for those who have the necessary physical and mental attributes to enable them to participate at a level of competence that will give them satisfaction. It is important that they should be allowed to do this without social threat and that such an avenue of fulfilment is left open to them.

REFERENCES

BARDWICK, J.M., *The Psychology of Women*. Harper & Row, 1971.

DALTON, K., *The Menstrual Cycle*. Penguin, 1969.

DE VRIES, H.A., *Physiology of Exercise for Physical Education and Athletics*. Wm. C. Brown, 1974.

HARRIS, D.V., *Involvement in Sport*. Lea & Febiger, Philadelphia, 1973.

HUTT, C., *Males and Females*. Penguin, 1972.

KANE, J. (ed.), *Psychological Aspects of Physical Education and Sport*. Routledge and Kegan Paul, 1972.

KLAFS, C.E., and LYON, M.J., *The Female Athlete*. C.V. Mosby Co., 1973.

MUNROW, A.D., *Physical Education: a discussion of Principles*. Bell, 1972.

PAYNE, C.R., *An Investigation into Female Participation in Athletics*. Unpublished M.Sc. thesis, Aston University, 1975.

PETERSON, S.L., WEBER, J.C., and TROUSDALE, W.W. 'Personality Traits of Women in Team Sports vs. Individual Sports', *Research Quarterly* 1967, No. 38, pp. 686–90.

16

INJURIES AND THE WARM-UP

Injury, illness and accident are particularly frightening prospects for an athlete. Even a small injury can assume gigantic proportions in an athlete's mind when an important competition is imminent, and the effects of any disability increase as the importance of the event and the prowess of the athlete increase! An illness or strain that is too slight to keep a person off work will be enough to prevent training, and by missing training the athlete loses fitness and so loses confidence and competitiveness. A cold in the nose or a blister on the heel can lose a race, and even a very slightly injured wrist or finger can spoil a throw.

The physical state of a trained individual is very superior to that of an ordinary person. Injuries to a finely tuned body can be minor in ordinary terms but sufficient to drop performance by a fraction, and since selections are made and competitions lost and won by fractions, that 'minor' injury is certainly important. The length of time it will take for recovery matters in relation to the season, but even in the off-peak period the last word an athlete wants to hear from his doctor or physiotherapist is 'Rest'.

A keen athlete is usually quite obsessive about training and about the state of his health. When one uses one's body a great deal and to its extremes, one is sensitive to any change or weakening in condition. Individuals react very differently to any twinges or pain—some battle on and occasionally it does wear off, but generally it does not and the injury may develop into a chronic condition. Females tend to put off seeking attention longer than males, and physiotherapists say that the strains that women develop are often harder to cure since the athletes have carried on past the danger signals. Any pain or discomfort that we feel in our bodies is nature's way of telling us to take it easy because we are overdoing it. Today's training methods talk of 'going through the pain barrier', of continuing even when the athlete is very fatigued, and of ignoring the signals to stop that our bodies send to our contrary and determined brains.

Some athletes, in contrast, become quite neurotic over the slightest imagined disability—they are hypochondriacs who rush, or rather limp, to the massage plinth or the surgery when they have a twinge, who lie awake at night worrying over the possible effects of illness and who just need to hear of, or see, an injured athlete to develop the symptoms.

PREVENTION

Some athletes appear to be able to survive long competitive careers with very little upset due to injury—they may be just lucky but they are are also probably very sensible and careful in their preparation and training. A well-structured, progressive build-up in weights, or in endurance and speed work, will develop the body gradually to take the stresses of all-out effort. These athletes take care of their equipment, and their footwear is of the correct size to prevent blistering. They take note of ground and weather conditions, they handle their equipment with care and they obey all the safety rules for themselves and others. Also they are neither too aggressive nor too timid, since this attack, or the lack of it, can be important in injury proneness. Some athletes are quite suicidal in their strained, uncontrolled efforts, even in training, and the way they throw themselves over a bar or at a hurdle makes one wonder how they survive at all! In contrast an athlete who is too timid, who hangs back at the last stage of the jump or vault or throw may end up hurting himself because of his lack of confidence. Tension is also a major cause of injuries and the competitor who cannot relax, and strains against his tense muscles, may damage his body. Prevention is always better than cure, further injury can be prevented by improving technique and co-ordination—there may be technical faults which are both impairing performance and causing injury, e.g. overstriding often leads to hamstring pulls.

A broad range of injuries is found in athletics and each event has its particular problems and dangers. A preventive programme of well-planned training, a good emotional climate and regular screening by experts in sports medicine reduces injuries to the minimum.

POSTURE

The human body is a marvellous machine but in some respects it is not very efficiently designed. The erect human posture is fairly recent in evolutionary terms, and the multitude of postural defects we suffer would suggest that perhaps the evolutionary process of walking and standing upright is not yet successfully completed. The spine is structured in a long column with one bone upon another, and the heavy weight of the skull is balanced precariously on this unstable, twisting structure. Round backs, hollow backs, rigid backs, shoulders and head too far forward, or too far back, spines bent laterally and so on—these and many other problems stem from poor posture, and posture is largely determined by the alignment of head, neck and spine. Faults often develop in late childhood and early teens, and become so ingrained that anything else feels wrong and we persist with our faulty posture because we have got so used to it. The problem may be exacerbated by poor seating, badly designed work surfaces, ergonomically unsatisfactory machines and just sheer lack of care and concentration as to how we use our own frames. We need 'to re-educate ourselves', as Mathias Alexander advises, and relearn the correct use of our bodies.

On the track the easy runner can be identified even by the non-expert. These runners carry themselves well; everything is aligned beautifully and the carriage is light, balanced and forward on the driving legs—they feel no tensions, exhibit no awkwardness and probably suffer no injuries. Throwers keeping their backsides tucked in, their heads up, shoulders down and spine erect will not hurt themselves and will throw more effortlessly. But it will take a long struggle to develop this style, which can feel peculiar when the body is not accustomed to it. Even in ordinary everyday living the athlete must pay attention to seating, lighting, working heights and methods of lifting and carrying. It is surprising, but common, that people used to the rules and principles of weight training make errors when they leave the training room and forget to use their leg muscles when lifting. The discs of the vertebrae act as cushions and shock absorbers but when the vertebrae are repeatedly stressed they may slip out or even burst at times of too great effort. Squatting can be dangerous for the lower back, particularly if the lifter goes too low. Half-squats are advised, particularly for the beginner or those susceptible to back injury.

INJURY TO MUSCLES

Co-ordination is important in the avoidance of injury, because muscles work in groups under the control of the central nervous system. Muscular action is required to maintain erect posture and Elizabeth Page recommends that re-habilitation should follow the line along which correct posture has been acquired. One muscle in a group is the prime mover, and when it contracts, any muscles situated in opposition to the movement must relax. The antag-onists must actively relax and lengthen. When a muscle contracts it changes its form by shortening and the belly of the muscle bulges. Muscles can tear when violent contraction takes place, and tearing usually occurs at the junc-tion of the muscle fibres with the tendon. A periosteal tear occurs at the insertion of the tendon into the bone (see Chapter 1). This damages the covering of the bone, which interferes with nutrition and healing. Tearing and disruption of the fibres affects the connective tissue and the blood vessels. A tear can cause quite a great deal of bleeding into the surrounding tissue, and the pain of a tear is mainly caused by the pressure built up by the space-occupying haematoma. The most frequent injuries are those where a muscle spans two joints, where flexing and extending take place. Pulls and strains may affect only a few fibres which do not regenerate but are replaced by fibrous tissue.

Treatment
Arrest the internal bleeding by cold applications. Use a pressure bandage, and after two or three days gentle massage and diathermy should enable a full range of movement. It is necessary to keep down the swelling in order to let the physiotherapist get to work on an injury as soon as possible, and the ath-lete can help himself by stopping before the injury goes too far, and if there is swelling, by cooling it to reduce inflammation. Complete rest is not necessary, and unless there is a complete rupture movement around the muscle is desir-able to prevent adhesions and scarring. In any case the parts of the body not

injured can be used to the full.

INJURY TO TENDONS

Tendons are composed of white fibrous tissue connecting muscles to bones. They have very little elasticity but they are extremely strong. Often under stress the muscle or even the bone itself goes before the tendon. Total or partial rupture of tendons may necessitate immobilisation in plaster for six to eight weeks.

Tendonitis, that great bugbear of athletes, is caused by repetitive trauma. Tenderness and swelling occur, so movement needs to be restricted by strapping or by changing the pattern of activity causing the trauma. Tendons moving repeatedly through their sheaths are subject to frictional stress which can cause internal lesions, small tears and even blisters. The vulnerable long tendon running upward from the heel is truly the Achilles heel which is so troublesome to so many athletes. Early treatment consists of raising the heel by using cushioning pads in the shoes and restricting movement, if necessary by using strapping. Rest is required to stop the friction, and after the swelling is reduced the physiotherapist can employ massage and diathermy.

Other tendons that are often troublesome are the adductors of the thigh. Hurdlers and jumpers are usually the victims—they may still be able to walk and even run but pain occurs in the groin when jumping is attempted. This injury needs heat, massage and manipulation.

Tendons themselves do not have any blood vessels in them, and therefore they are immune from inflammation, but the sheaths in which they run can be irritated by overuse. Common examples are found in the hands and wrists of pianists, typists and shot putters.

INJURY TO JOINTS

The junction between two or more bones is separated by cartilage and fibrous tissue. The fibrous capsule surrounding most joints is reinforced by ligaments and synovial membrane is present where movement takes place.

Injuries to joints can be direct or indirect, and either extrinsic or intrinsic — an extrinsic injury is caused by a knock or blow coming from the outside and an intrinsic one involves internal pulling or tearing because of an awkward or violent movement. Injury can affect both contraction and extension when it occurs at a joint. If bleeding occurs, the blood escapes into the tissues and causes swelling and pressure since it cannot escape back to the heart. If adhesions take place, the fibres cannot move easily.

Treatment

First the haemorrhage must be stopped by ice packs, strapping and the elevation of the limb. Some rest followed by a gradual resumption of activity is a useful general principle. Isometric contractions are possible and helpful since no movement is required. Only if the injury is very slight indeed should any attempt be made to run it off—stretching and warming can be helpful, but if the injury is anything more than a slight one it will only make it worse.

INJURY TO BONES

Bone may be hard (compact) or soft (cancellous) and the proportions in any given skeletal unit depend on the function of the unit, which can be protective, supportive or acting as an attachment for muscles. Injuries to bones come in the form of fractures which are simply breaks or cracks. As in soft tissue healing, fractures are repaired by haematoma, which is replaced by soft callus, then hard callus and finally union, when the fracture site has been bridged by bone.

Stress fractures in bones are similar to fatigue fractures in metal. Loss of strength occurs through repeated minor stress.

Fractures should be treated by orthopaedic surgeons according to generally accepted principles, though a special problem of athletes is that of morale (Williams). There are many instances of sporting activity being resumed after very severe fractures have healed, even with artificial insertions. If the injury is less severe the patient must be encouraged to maintain fitness with vigorous supporting activities. Muscle atrophy rapidly follows immobilization in plaster, so it is important to use the limb as normally as possible and to employ static exercises. Progressive resistance exercises have recently become standard practice with physiotherapists.

SPECIFIC BODY AREAS

Let us look more closely at the particular problems that affect different parts of the athlete's anatomy:

Feet

Properly fitting shoes and socks are important. Meticulous hygiene is also required. The toenails should be short and cut straight across to prevent them becoming ingrown. Any infection such as athlete's foot should be treated immediately. Callouses, corns and blisters are usually caused by unsuitable or ill-fitting footwear.

To prevent heel bruising, a heel cup can be used as protection, and attempts to give at the knees when landing can prevent further irritation. Jumpers particularly need heel protection, and should use shoes and cups which prevent lateral displacement. For fallen arches a pad can be used under the arch with firm strapping to hold it in place. Foot strains and spring ligaments are also often caused by the wrong footwear. Hard ground combined with shoe spikes that are too long for it can cause strain, and athletes often wear shoes that are too lightweight and give too little support for going over rough ground. It is a mistake to have a shoe that fits like a glove, since the active foot needs space to work without constriction.

Ankles

Sprains are very common in this joint, and obvious swelling and soreness are generally treated properly from the first. In cases where a sprain is not so clinically obvious the ankle is often neglected and may become chronically sprained through continued use. There is always the danger of loss of balance and support in the ankle area, but protective strapping may be more dangerous than wearing nothing. Sprains need cooling, a pressure bandage, and elevation of the limb. The athlete should keep active but do no weight-bearing activities until he or she can stand on the toes without pain.

Shins
Shin sprains and shin soreness are very common among athletes. They may be caused by a stress fracture but more commonly by intra-muscular tension. All muscles swell after exercise, and if expansion is restricted by surrounding tissues, as in the shin, increase in fluid will increase stress and cause pain. The condition is difficult to treat and where possible it must be prevented by using only a very gradual build-up of training mileage.

Knees
A great variety of injuries can be suffered by the complex knee joint. It is very liable to get bruised because it lacks padding. It is also vulnerable to wrenching and twisting, particularly if the foot is fixed while the rest of the body keeps moving. Tl is happens very frequently to footballers, though athletes, particularly triple jumpers, may also be victims. There are two cartilages in each knee to enable smooth movement between the tibia and the femur. This cartilage can withstand large forces, but if it is torn or loosened the knee jams up. It cannot repair itself since it has no blood supply, and surgical removal may be the only solution.

There are ligaments on the outer sides of the joint to prevent abnormal movement and any violent movement of the knee sideways can damage these ligaments. Any excessive movement of the joint in an abnormal direction causes a sprain. There are many degrees and variety of sprain but the general treatment is to cool it with ice and try to maintain movement. As in other situations it is the bleeding and the pressure of fluid in the injured area that cause the pain, and the first task is to try to prevent or break down this haematoma.

During rehabilitation the limb should be mobilized as soon as possible to maximize the rate and completeness of repair to the ligament. Immobilization for long periods can almost destroy the knee as a moveable joint.

Upper Legs
The femur is the longest and strongest bone in the body. Surrounding it is the quadriceps groups of muscles and the hamstrings. Hamstrings give the most problems in the group because they are long and require good regular stretching to prevent pulls and tightness at the insertions. Sprinters frequently pull their hamstrings and are well advised to follow good warm-up procedures to warm and stretch them before all-out effort.

Treatment is the same as for other pulls and strains, but support is particularly necessary for this group. Hamstring injuries tend to recur and one can feel knotty fibrous thickening in the hamstrings of veteran sprinters.

Hips
The hip is strong and well protected so injuries to it are quite uncommon in

sport. Similarly injuries to the pelvis are very rare, and pain in the buttocks is usually caused by hamstring strains.

Neck and Back
A broad range of injury can be suffered in these areas, from minor muscle strain to complete dislocation with paraplegia. High-level dislocations are very serious and the patient must be carefully moved to hospital. Muscle strains and minor sprains can be treated by local massage and heat application to relax muscle spasm. The most frequent injury to the back is muscle strain, and the most frequent area of lesion is at the lumbosacral joint. Athletes, particularly jumpers and throwers, and weightlifters produce more strained backs than most ball games combined. Ligament sprains of an intact back are rare, but ligaments are susceptible to rotational strains and the weight lifting room is the main danger area.

Errors in technique are frequently responsible for back strains, so field event athletes and those lifting fairly heavy weights must look to their techniques if they have back trouble. Even a short loss of concentration may be enough to lose control in a throw or a lift and the back may suffer. Time should be taken between throws, lifts and jumps to enable maximum concentration to be built up. The principle of treatment for the neck and back are the same, with mobilization for minor injury and immobilization for the major ones (Williams). Heat and massage will reduce haematoma, increase movement and prevent fibrositis. A firm bed is necessary to prevent curving of the back while the athlete is asleep.

Abdominal and Thoracic Areas
Abdominal and thoracic injuries are rare in athletics and are much more likely to occur in sports which involve body contact. Such injuries are also much more common in the unfit people who have poor muscle tone, so the best prevention is gradually acquired fitness.

Shoulders
Dislocation is most common among vaulters and high jumpers who fall awkwardly, but today's good landing areas reduce risk dramatically. It needs reduction back into place as long as there is no fracture—some people who have this trouble recurrently can often push it back themselves!

The main treatment for painful shoulders is exercise, with heat after some rest. Fibrositis is often a problem with shoulder injuries, and massage is needed to break down the 'nodules'.

Arms
Injuries to the arm are nearly always in the elbow, and the most frequent sprain is some form of tennis elbow or javelin thrower's elbow. Such injuries are of the whiplash type where the joint is hyperextended. Expert javelin throwers suffer this olecranon lesion, whereas poorer ones with a 'round arm' throwing style strain the medial ligament. The way to cure the latter is to change technique. See, however, Fig. 16.1.

Hands and Wrists

Injuries to the hands and wrists are often related to particular sports, notably cricket and boxing, but the athletics event in which most hand and wrist trouble occurs is the shot put. Hyperextension sprains of the metacarpophalangeal joints generally occur. By and large the best form of rehabilitation for the sportsman is speedy return to normal use (Williams).

Skin

The skin acts as a protection against minor injury, though it may be damaged by laceration, punctures or infections. It is important to clean lacerations to avoid infection. Punctures, particularly with spikes used on grass, require anti-tetanus injections. Infections can be cut down by controlled hygiene and by not sharing toilet articles.

Small blisters can be covered, but large ones need pricking and keeping sterile until healed. The skin can be dried with surgical spirit.

Sunburn can be painful, particularly on fair-skinned people, and it is best to avoid direct exposure and get accustomed to hot sun gradually. Calamine lotion will sooth burnt skin.

SORENESS AND STIFFNESS

Soreness and stiffness can hardly be termed injuries but sometimes stiffness can be debilitating. It is believed that soreness may be caused by minor tearing. There is also an accumulation of waste products after exercise, which increases pressure in the tissues. If the body is unused to such a level of exercise it will be inefficient in returning the extra blood and dissipating the fluid gathered after exercise. This situation can be largely avoided by building up the exercise level gradually, by warming down after the exercise—even two minutes' jogging can be helpful.

Soreness can also be caused by jerky movements, bouncy stretching exercises, and over-vigorous contractions when the muscle is in a shortened position (De Vries). Ten minutes or so of static stretching is a helpful preventive. It is worthwhile trying to determine exactly which activities seem to be causing the problem, and then modifying them. Proper warm-up may help to prevent soreness too (see below), and holding the affected muscle in the stretch position also gives some relief.

Cases of severe soreness are best treated with radiant heat and massage.

CRAMP

This is an involuntary tightening of the muscles which causes very sharp pain. Several theories exist as to the cause, but it is possibly a local increase in lactic acid, particularly if the weather is cold and the vessels are constricted. Cramp

Overleaf

Fig. 16.1. The breaking of the pole in this particular vault fortunately only resulted in a bruised left forearm, caused when it struck the pole (Fig. 16.1h).

also tends to occur in people with circulatory disorders or varicose conditions, and when overuse of small muscles in tension has taken place. The favourite theory, though not universally accepted, is that it is caused by loss of salt and body chemicals, because when there has been heavy salt loss due to sweating the tendency to cramping increases noticeably. To relieve cramp it is best to stretch the affected muscle in the opposite direction to the tightness.

STITCH

Again there is some uncertainty as to the cause. It occurs in the unfit more than in the fit, and it appears more in those who run over uneven ground than those who work on level terrain, and it definitely appears to be connected with previous food intake. Gassy food in quantity causes painful stretching of the abdominal wall which may pull on ligaments. An athlete who loved beans on toast found that if he cut them out before running his recurring stitch vanished!

GENERAL BODY MAINTENANCE

To maintain the body in a healthy state an athlete needs plenty of sleep, and regularity in eating, working, training and lifestyle. Some sunshine, as little smoking and drinking as possible, some relaxation, particularly before competitions, and an opportunity to build up the system gradually to co-ordinate strength, speed endurance and flexibility are required. Adequate rest periods, such as one day per week and three consecutive days every six weeks, are a vital part of the training programme.

PSYCHOLOGY

Singer and Ogilvie and Tutko suggest that athletes sometimes get themselves injured almost deliberately, though they would be the last to admit it. Injury does provide an escape from difficult situations, however, and the excuse of 'what might have been' if an athlete had been fit is easier to carry than the stress of open competition and losing. Tensions can often bring on injuries which are genuine physical problems though they may have been psychosomatically induced. The important thing for any athletics doctor or physiotherapist is to remember that he is treating a person as much as an injury, and the more that the physiotherapist can understand the particular physical stresses that his event involves, the more effectively he can help his patient.

WARM-UP

There is a great deal of confusion over warming-up. To different individuals warming-up means many different things. Some athletes start more than an hour before the event and go through a very complex, hard routine of jogging, exercises, sprints, technique practice and deliberate periods of overstress and relaxation. To other athletes a few yards' jog and a couple of swings of their arms is overdoing it! It is difficult to obtain conclusive experimental evidence to support one extreme or the other, and generally warm-up is as useful and as important as people think or make it. There is some indication that it should be helpful—Edington and Egerton state: 'Warm-up is a technique to prepare the body for exercise at a competitive rate.' Warm-up increases muscle temperature, activates energy sources within the muscle and alerts the central nervous system. As muscle temperature increases, the time to complete a task reduces and overloading a muscle group prior to performance increases the excitation of the motor units, which carries over to the actual performance (Edington and Edgerton). Performance in a laboratory-controlled vertical jump experiment was found to improve after three minutes' running—and yet there is no conclusive proof that warm-up is necessary. For instance Clarke says: 'There is no definitive statement that can be made in spite of the extensive literature.' Sharkey states that: 'The metabolic implications of warm-up have yet to be fully explained experimentally.' Karpovich writes: 'Neither massage nor warm-up had any beneficial effect on 440yd running or on sprinting on ergocycles.' Karpovich distinguishes between formal warm-up, which involves practising the actual skills to be used, and general warm-up, which includes exercising the large muscles of the body in a general way with exercises and jogging. He is of the opinion that a moderate formal warm-up is beneficial, but he considers that the general warm-up is sometimes overdone.

Corrigan and Morton (1968) compare the body before warm-up to an engine on a cold morning. They think three advantages can be gained from warming-up:

1. Skill factors are rehearsed by actually practising the event. This is not so necessary to the expert but could be very useful to the more inexperienced technical performer—literally getting into the swing of the activity.

2. Physiological factors are affected positively by increasing the internal body temperature, increasing circulation and generally adjusting the body in preparation for effort.

3. Psychological effects are also important, with a reducing of tension encouraged by going through a ritual. One prepares mentally for the event as well as physically. Corrigan and Morton also consider that risk of injury is reduced.

But Williams and Sperryn 'found no relation between lack of warm-up and incidence of muscle injury'!

Evans Robson notes, however, that most muscle tears occur near the beginning and near the end of games, and he considers lack of warm-up the cause for the former and increasing fatigue the cause of the latter. He emphasizes, too, the importance of warming-down.

De Vries is generally a supporter of warm-up and notes that both active and passive warm-up seem to have an effect. Passive, or non-metabolic, warm-up can be carried out through taking hot showers, for instance, to raise the body temperature, but he does note that the inner muscle temperature is what matters, rather than the external temperature. External muscle temperature can be raised in five minutes but internal temperature could take half an hour.

De Vries found when working with sprinters that increasing inner temperature and circulation had a more positive effect than static stretching. Maximum oxygen uptake increases after warm-up, and the increased blood flow through the system is helpful.

The intensity and duration of warm-up depend on the athlete's condition. A well-conditioned athlete can go on improving his preparatory state for at least 30 minutes, but an athlete in poor condition would be tired out by such an extensive programme. Individuals have to develop a routine which is comfortable for them, though to be effective warm-up must be vigorous enough to raise the inner temperature, as previously stated.

One of the problems in undertaking experimental studies of warm-up is that every athlete in the study is treated in the same way, and many individuals require an individual warm-up. There is also a tendency for the experimental studies to involve rather short warm-ups. The subjects' attitude to warm-up is important, and it is difficult to get maximum effort from subjects who have not done their usual warm-up if they believe it is important or if they think they might sustain injury. Even when incentives are given or when the subjects say they are trying, it is difficult to prove experimentally.

Don Franks has carried out a survey of the evidence on warm-up (Morgan) and again there is a certain inconclusiveness. He notes that lack of warm-up does not seem to lead to injury, because in the course of many studies only two injuries have been sustained, and they were both to 100 metre sprinters. His conclusion is that the general level of conditioning of the athlete is more important than the warm-up, and the higher the level of conditioning the more strenuous the warm-up can be. Warm-up is more helpful to older subjects; there do not seem to be any differences according to sex; and generally the acquired attitude to warm-up is important. He concludes: 'Each individual will have to determine the optimal warm-up to suit his own performance.'

The authors of the present book firmly believe that warm-up is beneficial physically and psychologically, and they have noted that almost every high-grade athlete they have seen in action used a positive and demanding warm-up in his or her preparation.

REFERENCES

ALEXANDER, F.M., *Constructive Conscious Control of the Individual.* Methuen, 1923.

CLARKE, D.H., *Exercise Physiology.* Prentice Hall, 1975.

CORRIGAN, B. and MORTON A., *Get Fit the Champions Way.* Souvenir, 1968.

CRATTY, B.J., *Psychology and Physical Activity.* Prentice Hall, 1968.

DE VRIES, H.A., *Physiology of Exercise.* Staples Press, 1967.

EDINGTON, D.W., and EDGERTON, V.R., *The Biology of Physical Activity.* Houghton Mifflin, 1976.

KARPOVICH, P.V., *Physiology of Muscular Activity.* W.B. Saunders, 1965.

LARSON, L.A., and MICHELMAN, H., *International Guide to Fitness and Health.* Crown, 1973.

MADDERS, J., 'Relaxation as a Skill', *British Journal of Physical Education*, Vol. 7, No. 3, May—June 1976.

MORGAN, W.P., (ed.), *Ergogenic Aids and Muscular Performance.* Academic Press, 1972.

OGILVIE, B. and TUTKO, T.A., *Problem Athletes and How to Handle Them.* Pelham, 1966.

PAGE, E.M., *Athletic Injuries and Their Treatment*. Arco, 1962.
ROBSON, EVANS, in J.G.P. Williams and P.N. Sperryn (eds.), *Sports Medicine*. Edward
    Arnold, 1976.
SHARKEY, B.J., *Physiology and Physical Activity*. Harper and Row, 1975.
SINGER, R.N., *Myths and Truths in Sports Psychology*. Harper and Row, 1975.
WILLIAMS, J.G.P., *Medical Aspects of Sport and Physical Fitness*. Pergamon Press, 1965.
WILLIAMS, J.G.P., and SPERRYN, P.N. (eds), *Sports Medicine*. Edward Arnold, 1976.

Part III

THE EVENTS

17

SPRINTS

GENERAL

Running is the most natural of athletics movements. Children run as part of their play and practically every game requires reserves of stamina and the ability to run fast. Every track event has running as its essence, sometimes alone, sometimes with a team, and sometimes between obstacles. Every field event, perhaps even including the hammer, requires a sprinter's speed, and it is not unusual, for example, for top shot putters to be able to hold their own against sprinters over short distances. Every training and conditioning programme contains an element of running, and tests of fitness or physical ability always include running for speed.

There is no doubt that speed is the most essential element in the short distances of 100, 200 and 400 metres, but the 800 and 1,500 metres now also require very fast basic speed, and the tactical races from 1,500 metres upwards are frequently won in a last few hundred metres' sprint for the tape. Even marathon races have developed into sprints down the home straight to resolve the first three or four places.

What is sprinting exactly? It is defined by Ward and Watts as 'running at, or close to, maximum speed'. It is frequently said that sprinters are born and not made, and although research indicates that this is true, as Mike Agostini says: '. . . an average sprinter can become top class with the right training and competition.' Certainly there is no one physique which is dominant in sprinting, and the elite include all builds from lightly built wiry runners, through short stocky powerhouses and tall rangy striders, to the big muscular strength athletes. Techniques vary—lighter men appear to float over the track, while muscular types power their way to the tape—but all runners have in common fast natural movements with rapid leg cadence. Textbooks on sprinting always point out that sprinting speed is a function of the product of stride length and cadence (i.e. number of strides per second), and go on to explain that the cadence, which is dependent on the rate of movement of the legs, can only be marginally improved, but the length of stride can be increased by training.

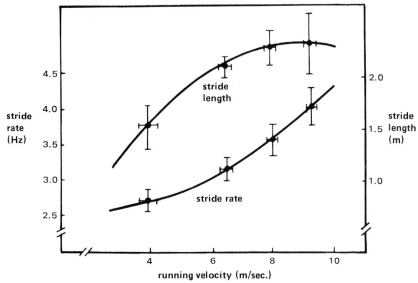

Fig. 17.1. Stride length and stride rate at various running speeds. (After Luhtanen and Komi.)

Table 17.1. Dependence of running speed upon stride length and stride frequency. (After Scholich.)

Distance (metres)	Time	Velocity (m/sec.)	Stride length (metres)	Stride frequency per sec.	No. of steps
100	9.9	10.10	2.25	4.40	44.4
400	43.8	9.10	2.20	4.13	181.8
800	1:43.4	7.72	2.10	3.67	380.9
1,500	3:32.2	7.07	2.00	3.53	750.0
5,000	13:12.9	6.31	1.80	3.50	2,777.7
10,000	27:30.5	6.06	1.75	3.46	5,714.2
marathon	2:08:33.6	5.44	1.60	3.40	26,371.8
20 km walk	1:23:39.8	3.98	1.16	3.46	17,391.3
50 km walk	3:52:44.6	3.58	1.05	3.40	47,619.0

If the same cadence is maintained while the stride length is increased, more ground is covered in the same time. Strength can be more than doubled, and endurance can be developed some 20–50 per cent, but it is unusual for speed to develop more than 10 per cent over years of training. The best sprinters need a genetic combination of good length levers, strength, flexibility and a majority of white, fast twitch fibres in the muscles.

Although strength is needed for sprinting, and performances can be improved by strength training, there is not a simple relationship between strength and speed. Radford notes that it is not only the application of force that is important, but also the time in which it can be applied to the retreating resistance of the track surface going away beneath the sprinter's feet. In order to go faster the athlete must be able to drive his legs backwards faster than the ground is moving away from him. Inevitably there comes a point at which he cannot achieve this, when he is at his maximum speed. This is a simplified explanation of the mechanics of the ground forces, and in reality at maximum speed the picture is complicated by a slight braking, or deceleration, of the sprinter's body as the contact foot lands, followed by an equal drive, or acceleration, as the contact leg extends. Unlike walking, the running action involves a series of take-offs, flights and landings of the athlete's body, and in each stride the landings must blend smoothly into another take-off with as little deceleration as possible. Basmajian has seen the action as analogous to the rolling of a wheel, in which the only parts of the rim existing are the feet.

Because of the critical timing and speed of his muscles the sprinter requires a very rapid recruitment of his forces with a hair trigger excitable motor system. Athletes who do short-term intensive work appear to be able to fire their motor units synchronously (Radford). The flow of a sprinter is a critical combination of selective arousal, activation and relaxation of the muscles, but 1936 Olympic champion Jesse Owens described it as running as if the ground was hot and burning him at every step! Research scientists have some difficulty in elucidating this concept of motor activation and recruitment of high velocity strength, though there now seems to be a correlation between white muscle fibres and sprinting speed. Weight lifters and other athletes who make fast movements also have a large percentage of these rapid twitch fibres.

In the 100 and 200 metres the exercise is within the body's capacity to carry stored oxygen, so the sprinter can afford to be reckless in his energy expenditure. The race is over before the waste products have built up to serious amounts in the muscles, and he knows that he can recover at the end of the race. In the 400 metres the discomfort and reduced efficiency of the muscles can be seen in the last 100 metres when, as Ron Pickering, the well-known television commentator, has remarked, the athlete 'is swimming in a sea of lactic acid'. The biochemistry of fatigue is more complex than this, and still being researched, but the better the preparation and conditioning of the athlete the less is the build-up of waste products and the better is the athlete's tolerance to fatigue pain.

THE SPRINT START

The start is an essential part of the event—a good start takes vital hundredths, or even tenths, of a second from the total time compared with a mediocre start. In a major games, in which athletes are well-matched, the start of a sprint race may decide the result. Although a beginner may be better off with a standing start, and Paul Nash equalled the 100 metres world record in 1968 with this method, most experienced sprinters use a crouch start from blocks. Several world-class sprinters have spurned starting blocks but the author has investigated the athletes' starts from force platforms and shown that the force patterns of the starts without blocks were inferior to starts in which blocks were used. These results were also confirmed by the times, measured photo-electronically, taken by the athletes to sprint various distances (up to 50 metres) down the track. Even world-class sprinters who do not use blocks can improve if they take the time to learn the modified techniques necessary for the transition to starting with blocks. Having said that, it must be emphasized that there are almost as many variations of sprint starting technique and style as there are sprinters. From the sequence in Fig. 17.3 it is immediately evident that sprinters block spacings, and their body positions while in the 'set' are anything but similar. For example, Andrea Lynch (left) has her blocks close together but a long way back from the starting line, whereas Monika Hamann (right) seems to be too cramped with blocks close to the line; Marlies Göhr (second from left) is very low, with a lot of her bodyweight supported on her hands, whereas Hamann has a high hip position and has her weight mostly on her legs; and Göhr and Sonia Lannaman (third from left) have both legs well bent while Lynch's rear leg is almost straight at the knee. Even in this race, with only four athletes, it is clear that the start 'set' is a matter for individual preference. Research in this area indicates that the coach should concentrate on improving the athlete's preferred style rather than attempting to alter it drastically. Fig. 17.2 confirms the point.

Fig. 17.2. A wide range of 'set' positions. The 1976 Olympic champion Haseley Crawford is third from the camera.

Whichever method they use, it is essential that sprinters react quickly to the starting gun and that they get up to top sprinting speed as soon as possible. Although the four athletes in Fig. 17.3 have small individual differences, they share certain common characteristics in their starting techniques. There is a powerful drive of the legs against the blocks, with each leg extending fully before it loses contact. The arms pump in an exaggerated punching action, and the whole body comes out low from the blocks. There is no urgency to assume the more upright position of full-speed sprinting, rather the body is angled so that the emphasis is on a horizontal drive. Blader and one of the authors have researched the starts of elite sprinters and found that:

(a) The reaction of the athlete to the gun is extremely fast, with a pre-motor time (time between gun and first muscle action) of typically 0.09 seconds,

(b) The start of the drives of the legs is almost simultaneous, with delays seldom more than 0.01 seconds,

(c) The better performers have larger rear foot impulses, and

(d) The better performers leave the blocks in a low posture, even to the point of feeling as though they had stumbled out of them.

TOP-SPEED SPRINTING

As the speed increases away from the blocks the sprinter's body gradually becomes more upright and the arm action becomes slightly less exaggerated, but the full extension of the driving leg continues throughout the race.

Although many coaches insist on the characteristic high knee lift, it is the angle between the thighs which is important in this aspect of sprinting, for it ensures that the swing of the free leg evokes optimum reaction force through the support leg and adds to that leg's drive, and prevents premature grounding of the free leg. A large angle at the thighs at the end of the drive is the result of a powerful and complete extension of the driving leg, flexible hip joints and a high, bent-knee action of the free leg, all of which produce the optimum stride length to bring the body in a correctly balanced position for the next leg drive.

'Controlled relaxation' is important if maximum sprinting speeds are to be obtained. This means that the muscles involved in every movement must be fired and then relaxed in correct sequence, that supporting muscles must be optimally toned and that all others should be relaxed. Neck and facial muscles, for example, are good indicators of unnecessary tension—'Smile as you sprint', say Ward and Watts. Agostini feels that the best style is the one where most motion is obtained from least effort.

There is some confusion in the literature on the importance or otherwise of 'running on the toes'. Some writers advise sprinters to 'get up on the toes', others maintain that although the toe makes contact with the ground first on

Overleaf

Fig. 17.3. Four of the world's best women sprinters. Left to right: Andrea Lynch (Great Britain), Marlies Gohr (East Germany), Sonia Lannaman (Great Britain) and Monika Hamann (East Germany).

landing, the heel follows down immediately afterwards. The author has used force platforms and high-speed sequence photography to show that in reality all variations are used between the two extremes of ball-of-foot contact only, and pronounced heel-impact running, and these are related to distance run. Toe, or rather ball-of-foot, running uses a lot of energy and therefore tends not to be used by long distance runners except sometimes in the final sprint. On the other hand many elite sprinters run with some heel contact, which may be due to their inability to extend their ankles in the short time available. The optimum range of distances for ball-of-foot running appears to be 400 and 800 metres, in which rapid leg movements and energy requirements are less restricting. Certainly logical consideration of ball-of-foot running shows its advantages:

(a) Stride length is greater in toe to toe contact than in toe take-off to heel landing,

(b) Heel strike generally produces a sharp impact between heel and ground which provides little or no force for the drive and thus represents a loss of energy.

(c) The energy lost in (b) is stored as elastic stretching of the lower leg muscles and tendons in ball-of-foot running. The force available from an eccentrically contracted muscle is greater than from normal concentric contraction.

However, it should be noted that the above is a simplified view of foot action in running, and that many so-called toe runners actually land the foot on the outside edge of the ball of the foot, and that the movement of the foot while in contact with the ground has many nuances, depending on the nature of the ground surface and the type of shoes worn by the athlete.

THE FINISH

Every textbook emphasizes the importance of running *through* the finish line without any premature slowing down or anticipation of stopping running. Even so, this requires a strong effort of will on the athlete's part, for the finish line represents a powerful psychological barrier, almost like a wall urging the runner to slow down. Training can be adjusted so that the athlete always has to run to a line some 5 metres past the finish line. For this reason the lean-in to the finish line is a controversial technique of use only to the very experienced runner. The lean-in has lost as many races as it has won, because of the critical nature of its timing. Generally athletes anticipate it incorrectly and end up slowing down before the finish, because it inevitably upsets the rhythm of running. Hurdlers, with their superior spatial judgment, are better able to use the lean-in than flat sprinters.

100 METRES

The short distance sprinter is most dependent on his reaction to the gun, the acceleration away from the blocks and maintenance of his top speed right through the tape, because for him hundredths, and perhaps even thousandths, of a second are vital. He must be able to concentrate his whole consciousness into exploding from the blocks at the gun, but is generally not advised to listen for the gun. He must be able to maintain this concentration even through several false starts, and he must be able to cope effectively with both official starters who are trigger-happy and those who hold the runners for an eternity.

Even though sprinters run in lanes and tactics are virtually absent, the presence of other competitors is vital to performance and it is wise to train with others to ensure that over-tension and over-striding do not occur when they are in the lead.

BEND RUNNING

Simple though it seems, not all runners appreciate that it is most important to keep close to the inside limit of the track when running around the bends. It is not so important, but unwise nevertheless, to run wide in the straights. This means that in races run in lanes the athlete should keep close to the inside line of his lane, and in races not run in lanes there is a very strong case, tactics permitting, for him to run close to the kerb. In the short relay it is essential for bend runners to hug the inside of their lane.

Elementary geometry proves the point: the track is made up of two semi-circles stretched out by two straights. Put the two semi-circles in Fig. 17.4

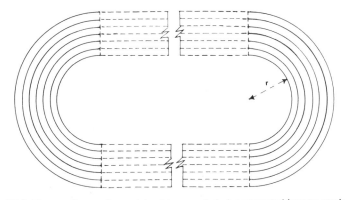

Fig. 17.4. The running track consists of two semi-circles separated by two straights.

together and it can be seen that the athlete has to run a complete circle in each lap. The circumference of a circle is given by $2\pi r$ where π is a constant equal to 3.14 and r is the radius of the circle, which will depend upon which lane is being considered. The distance run around the track in completing one circuit is equal to 6.28 r plus the length of the two straights. If the athlete should run just 25 cm wide around the bends in one lap he will run 6.28 (r + 0.25) plus the length of the straights or an extra 6.28 x 0.25 m, i.e. 1.57 m.

Not many athletes can afford to give away this distance to their rivals on every lap! A 10,000 metre competitor running in the second lane throughout the race runs his distance plus another 176 metres.

Although a runner has to run wide of the inner limit of his lane, this is allowed for because the measurement of total distance run is made 0.3 m from the kerb or 0.2 m from the outer edges of the lines marking the other lanes.

200 METRES

Two hundred metre running may require the speed of the shorter distance sprinter, but by no means all 100 metre sprinters can compete successfully at 200 metres. In addition to the extra distance, there is also a bend that must be negotiated at top speed—it is not a long 100 metres or a short 400 metres, but an event in its own right. In the 100 metres the runner must have strength and speed, but in the 200 metres he also needs control, balance and poise, according to Radford.

The blocks are placed in the outside of the lane, pointing at a tangent to the curve, so that the first few strides are run in a straight line. The actual start is the same as in the 100 metres though the athlete may have other competitors behind or ahead of him in the echelon, which ensures that each runner has the same distance to cover.

Radford describes the 200 metres as consisting of four important phases:

(a) The start and the straight line acceleration to the point where this straight line forms a tangent to the inside of his lane is very similar to the 100 metres start.

(b) The turn for the 200 metre runner presents technical difficulties, since he must continue accelerating and hope to reach top speed while running part of a circle. In order to run in a circle close to the inside line of his lane he must lean into the centre to maintain balance. The right leg has to swing across the body to hold it in to the curve in the left leg support phase. An unbalanced runner or one who tends to carry weight on the right leg will have trouble running a bend well. Runners with strong lateral movements, such as the short stocky 'power' type runners, will find that this style is not effective in the 200 metres bend since the feet need to drive under the body in the line of movement. The smooth flowing stylists are often the 200 metre specialists. On the bend, then, the outside leg and arm must work hard to maintain the lean-in. There is no coasting period in this part of the 200 metres, as used to be advised, and stamina is needed to ensure that the athlete comes out of the bend with top sprinting speed.

(c) Coming out of the turn into the straight requires a change of posture again, so that a central balance is achieved. This is a crucial stage of the race because the style of running has to change. The turn requires a fast cadence, but as the athlete enters the straight the emphasis is on a stronger leg action.

(d) The straight part of the 200 draws on the mental and endurance reserves of the runner, for he must maintain his form and try to lose as little speed as possible as he nears the finish. The danger is in 'tying up' with tense muscles as fatigue sets in.

The 200 metre runner, like the 100 metre athlete, must train for greater speed through high-quality sprinting, paying special attention to particular points of technique during repetition runs. In addition he must train at high speed bend running, and he must work for stamina with full- and over-distance repetitions.

400 METRES

This is a sprint for the well-trained athlete. The distribution of energy has to be carefully controlled because very few can maintain an all-out sprint over the entire distance. It is very important for the 400 metre runner to judge pace and to be able to assess his own ability in relation to the competitors. An evenly paced race will be more economical and effective, for example it is better to run each 200 metres in 25 seconds and 27 seconds than in 23 seconds and 30 seconds. It is the total time that counts, and even if that last example ended with 29 seconds, the rapidly slowing athlete would act as an incentive for other competitors to chase and overtake him. The first 200 metres is generally run faster than the second because of the fatigue in the second, but an even faster time will not necessarily cancel out the slower time recorded in the second half.

A common pattern is to try for a good start and first bend, a comfortable fast stride down the back straight, and a big effort off the last bend while trying to maintain relaxation and speed to the finish. The good 400 metre runner often has a buoyant, relaxed style with a long stride, keeping mainly on the ball of the foot. (See Fig. 17.6.)

Sprinting, then, is a technique that can be learned and improved like any field event. Although very good sprinters are born with advantages, such as a high proportion of fast twitch muscle fibres, they are unlikely to reach anywhere near their full potential without correct training.

REFERENCES

AGOSTINI, M., *Sprinting*. Stanley Paul, 1962.

BASMAJIAN, J.U., 'The Human Bicycle', *Biomechanics VA*, ed. Komi, P.V. University Park Press, Baltimore, 1976.

LUHTANEN, P., and KOMI, P.V., 'Mechanical Factors Influencing Running Speed', *Biomechanics VI-B*, ed. Asmussen, E., and Jorgensen, K. University Park Press, Baltimore, 1978.

PAYNE, A.H., and BLADER, F.B., 'The Mechanics of the Sprint Start'. *Medicine and Sport, 6: Biomechanics II.* Karger 1971.

RADFORD, P. 'The Fastest Feet on Earth' *Sports Review*, August 1976.

SCHOLICH, M. 'East German Study of the Distance Stride', *Track Technique* 74, Winter 1978.

WARD, I., and WATTS, D., *Athletics for Student and Coach*. Pelham, 1967.

WHITEHEAD, N., *Track Athletics*. E.P. Pub. Ltd., 1976.

Overleaf

Fig. 17.5. Don Quarrie (Jamaica), 1976 Olympic 200 metres champion, in a start in which he ran wide around the bend.

Fig. 17.6. Sebastian Coe (Great Britain), world record holder of three middle distance events, getting in some speed work in a 400 metre race.

18

MIDDLE DISTANCE

GENERAL

With the relentless advance in performance in athletics the 800 metre race now attracts athletes who in the past would have been sprinters—however, it still just makes it into the category of middle distance running. Even more controversy has raged about the classification of the 5,000 metres, but it is now almost agreed by top coaches and athletes that this is no more a long distance but rather a middle distance race. The divisions between sprints and middle distance and between middle distance and long distance have become blurred because of the emergence in recent years of the super-athlete who, although specializing in, say, the 1,500 metres, can hold his own against mere mortals in the 200 metres and is a danger to all who consider themselves 10,000 metre specialists. Today's middle distance athlete has both sprinting speed and endurance. His running style is a model of mechanical efficiency, and even in the later stages of a race when fatigue is sapping his strength his skill does not break down.

TECHNIQUE

The essence of good technique lies in the full body extension at the end of the leg drive. In Fig. 18.1 the leg and hip have combined to drive to the limit of the athlete's flexibility, the high bent front leg has produced an angle between the thighs which will allow an enormous stride length without actually causing overstriding, the chest is high and the arms are swinging actively to add their contribution to the drive. Note the extreme bend in the knee of the athlete's swinging leg through the positions shown in Figs 18.1 d, k and r. With the athlete's heel almost touching his buttocks the moment of inertia of this leg about the hip joint is minimal, allowing for speed of movement in the swing forward without too much energy usage. It is the moment of inertia of the recovery leg that is, to a large extent, the biomechanical barrier to increasing size of the distance runner. An athlete may have the necessary speed in his legs and good cardiovascular characteristics, but if his limbs are beyond a certain critical size the moments of force necessary to move them may use too much energy and the athlete will be confined to running lesser distances than his smaller-limbed colleagues.

Sprinters can affort to have idiosyncratic forces and movements which require extra energy expenditure, but as distance increases the energy a runner puts out must go more and more into the horizontal movement along the direction of running. The middle distance races include this transition, in which, for example, some 800 metre athletes run 'high' on the ball of the foot, but only in the final sprint for the tape is this style of running seen in the 5,000 metres.

The muscles of the body must be relaxed, toned or contracted in an exact synchrony which produces a free and fluent movement with no jerking through the cycle of each stride. 'Run fast and relaxed' is advice constantly given to the athlete. Suppleness and mobility are essential for full free movement of the limbs, and this is an area of conditioning which should be given special attention. Stretching exercises of the yoga type should be incorporated in a warm-up and warm-down at each training session.

TRAINING

It is important for the middle distance runner to remember that his is a range of events which benefits from the progressive overload principle of training, i.e. increases in muscular strength and endurance result from an increase in the load or intensity of work performed. Without increase in load the athlete's condition does not adapt beyond the point necessary to meet the demands of the stress existing.

Most coaches and athletes recognize that training for middle distance running is all about endurance. However 'endurance' is a wide term. It has been defined as the ability to withstand fatigue. But fatigue at the end of an 800 metre race and fatigue near the end of a marathon race are caused by quite different biochemical processes. Holman lists three types of endurance required by the middle distance runner:

(a) Aerobic endurance or the capacity to utilize as great a proportion of inspired oxygen as possible.

Overleaf
Fig. 18.1. The Ovett farewell glance. Steve Ovett (Great Britain) ignoring the textbook advice never to look back.
Overleaf
Fig. 18.2. A single stride by Christine Benning (Great Britain) with a perfect blend of relaxation and drive.

(b) Strength endurance or the capacity to maintain the quality of the muscles' contractile forces.

(c) Speed endurance or the faculty for co-ordinating the speed of contraction in the climate of endurance factors.

This assumes that a fairly steady pace is maintained throughout the race, but of course much middle distance racing ends with a fast sprint which varies in distance depending on the tactics of the race. Since the athletes know—like the sprinter—that they can recover and rest once the race is over, they can afford to gamble with their anaerobic reserves in the final stages. In some dawdling 'tactical' races the runner may have to rely very little upon his aerobic endurance, though of course these races are becoming more and more the exception.

Even before exercise physiologists had begun seriously to study endurance, athletes and coaches had experimented with different methods of training. There have been, and still are, fashions and variations in training ideas. Much depends on the coaches who influence great athletes—everyone wants to copy these coaches because they think the secrets have been found at last. For example Arthur Lydiard, the famous New Zealand coach, considered that even 800 metre runners should be able to run marathon distances, so his athletes, including Olympic champion Peter Snell, would go out for very long runs. This was disapproved of by many, except in the pre-season conditioning period. One argument against was that the running technique of the shorter distances was so different from that required in very long distances. Bruce Tulloh agreed with Lydiard in the belief that sheer stamina was vitally important, stating that: 'If you have stamina the speed will look after itself.'

The main rival method of training to the long steady distance (LSD) runs of Lydiard is the interval training started by Emil Zatopek and developed to a fine art by Mihaly Igloi. It consists almost entirely of short (50–1,500 m) bursts of speed or fast running broken by short recovery spells.

Although a few athletes have been highly successful with one or the other of these extremes of training, most athletes reason that if both are good by themselves, a little of each should be better still, and adopt a combination of the two. The real arguments start when coaches talk of the proportions of each to be included in schedules! As Mitchell explains: '. . . our constant search for the significant link between training and racing has persuaded many people that a ratio of energy sources operating when an athlete races a set distance can be matched exactly with a ratio of kinds of training. At the very least this link is unproven.' He himself thinks that: 'The simplest session —steady, prolonged running—is the most important and the most profitable; where effort is made and sustained, almost all that needs to happen will happen'. He goes on to emphasize that 'steady' describes five-minute mile pace for one man and six for another and going on long enough for the runner to know he has been out.

Certainly long steady distance running is enjoyable, and in Chapter 11 it was pointed out that enjoyment of an activity is the best motivation for going on. But there must also be specificity in training, and the middle distance athlete must train on the track, which is where he will make the necessary adaptation to other conditions such as track surface, bend running etc., as well as to his actual running distance.

INTERVAL TRAINING

It is in interval training that the coach with a leaning towards precision comes into his own and all manner of exact formulae have been worked out to produce the super-athlete! However exercise physiologists recommend anything from the use of distances from 50 to 1,500 metres, so even they are not too sure. Astrand and Rodahl consider that 80 per cent of maximum speed run for three to five mintues is the optimum, since this maintains the heart rate at up to 180. Coaches interpret this so that a distance which can be run at a maximum in three minutes is incorporated into an interval sequence of 3 minutes 24 seconds, with a similar recovery period.

Holman, recognizing that speed endurance is of paramount importance for the 800 metres in particular, recommends two kinds of intervals:

1. 'Flat out' runs at 10–20 per cent more than racing distance, so that for 800 metres this means 880–960 metres. For example, 2 x 900 metres in 2 mins 7 secs with 20 minutes' recovery for a 1 minute 48 second 800 metre runner.

2. Intensive intervals at 90 per cent maximum speed for between two-thirds to twice racing distance. For example, two sets of 3 x 600 metres in 90–95 seconds for the 1 minute 48 second runner, with recoveries depending upon the current condition of the athlete.

Thomas emphasizes the principle that the runner covers each distance at a very fast pace, finishing with his body in an anaerobic condition.

In interval training there are four variables which can be manipulated: (i) distance, (ii) speed, (iii) length of rest in between runs, and (iv) the number of repetitions, so that many varieties of overloading can be introduced gradually. Some swimming coaches have controlled their swimmers' intervals by monitoring heart rates. During the effort the heart rate is allowed to rise to about 180 beats per minute, and rest is only allowed until the pulse drops to about 125 beats per minute. Other methods involve different heart rate values.

Athletes on the whole tend to base their intervals on times and pacing. For example, a popular method is to run 200 metre intervals starting and finishing in the middle of a straight of an athletic track, with the coach keeping a close check on times. Recovery is a jog across the centre of the track, with the next fast run beginning as soon as the athlete arrives at the start. Pace judgment is also learned through 400 metre interval runs.

Paarlauf (running in pairs in relay fashion on the track) is useful for a change, for motivation and for learning pace judgment. For example, with each runner putting in 300 metre stints, the athlete recovering jogs 100 metres back down the track to meet his partner.

STRENGTH ENDURANCE

'Strength' is a vague term when used by middle distance runners and coaches.

Sprinting up hills of about 15 degrees incline is usually the type of work recommended for strength endurance. Percy Cerutty conditioned Olympic champion Herb Elliott on sand dunes and weight training. Mitchell talks of the hill-and-sprint as being 'valuable for everybody because it gives sheer toughness, length of stride and a forcefulness needed in competition'. Dellinger uses the phrase 'callousing effect' to mean almost the same, though his use of it includes many types of conditioning.

The weight training programme, if used for strength endurance, should consist of high repetitions of 20 or more per set with suitably light weights. Indoor circuit training, using a wide range of exercises with bodyweight, barbells or dumb-bells, is also considered to produce strength endurance.

Harry Wilson trains his athletes specifically for the changes of pace which are inevitable in competition. For example, part of a training session would be repetition 100 metre sprints in which each 100 metres would be divided into 30 metres fast, 30 metres relaxed and 40 metres fast and/or 30 metres relaxed, 40 metres fast, and 30 metres relaxed. At slightly slower speeds the athlete would use a similar pattern of 50 metres relaxed, 100 metres striding, 50 metres relaxed over 200 metre repetitions. During increases in pace the athlete must concentrate on trying to remain relaxed.

REGULARITY OF TRAINING

Middle and long distance athletes tend to train more frequently than athletes in the other events. Ron Clarke used to run three times a day to notch up his 150 miles per week, and most runners manage to fit in at least two sessions per day. Russian and American research, however, indicates that there is not much to be gained from training more than once per day. Regularity is undoubtedly necessary, but too much overloading of the adaptive mechanisms of the body inevitably leads to injury. As Holman warns, there are other stresses—school, vocation and/or those of a personal nature, for example—which cumulate with the athletic training stresses, so the coach and athlete should be aware of the need for rest to prevent break down.

TRAINING AND COMPETITION

Middle and long distance runners often suffer from a peculiar addiction—running! The coach may find he has to dissuade his runners from going out for yet another run when all the indications point to rest. He will know that the desire to train has become an obsession when they will not rest even before an important race. Although there may be a little truth in the saying: 'Racing often spoils fitness', if the race is a very tough one, perhaps following a series of other tough races, racing can be selective in a way that builds up fitness for some important games. As Mitchell says: 'The problem is to find out how often you can race and still go forward', listing as factors to be considered: the length of the race, the quality of the opposition, the temperament of the athlete and the stage of the training programme.

The period before a big race is as important to the runner as it is to the thrower, jumper, sprinter and hurdler, and he must realize that if training has gone to plan no more fitness will be achieved in the day or two preceding the race. He must use his self-discipline to conserve his physical condition, while preparing mentally to release all his energies when the right time comes. As Martti Vainio, 1978 European 10,000 metres champion said: 'It is a fine art to be able not to run.'

TACTICS

The start is given 'on your marks', and then the gun is fired, after which the athlete should attempt to gain as good a position as possible. Often the first 200 metres is run quite fast in order to achieve good positions, and it may be necessary to shorten the stride for this purpose. The reader is reminded to study the section about bend running (p. 219), since these principles have to be balanced against the tactical advantage of running wide just behind the right shoulder of the athlete in front. The leading runner has the advantage of being able to run on the very inside of the inner lane, and yet he may even have to sacrifice this by moving slightly wide on the bends to discourage attempts at passing. On the other hand the leading runner cannot see what is happening behind him and he must set the pace against the full impact of the air resistance. Trailing runners in the pack always run the risk of being boxed in if they try to minimize distance run by hugging the inside of the track.

When passing, the athlete must be confident and do so with a good burst of speed in order to open up a large gap which will be psychologically deterring as far as a counter-attack is concerned. Once he has committed himself to the final run in, he must not change his mind and hold back, otherwise the others will be on him. Once committed, the athlete must try to drive straight on to the tape.

'What you lose on the swings you gain on the roundabouts' does not hold when running on a windy day or when running alternately fast and slow. The physiological cost of struggling against the wind down one straight is greater than the gains obtained by the easier running with the wind behind on the other straight. Similarly, energy costs rise enormously with running speed, so it is not possible to repay a burst of speed with a similar amount of reduced speed for the same length of time. However, provided the athlete has the ability to keep going on alone, a burst to the front several laps from the finish of a race of 3,000 metres and upwards can be tactically advantageous. In shorter races there is usually not much to be gained from a long run for home like this, since the average speed is so much higher and an increase of speed costs too much effort.

Middle and long distance runners, in addition to knowing the capabilities and condition of their own bodies in relation to the race, should also make an effort to find out all they can about their rivals. Knowing what the opposition

Overleaf

Fig. 18.3. Alberto Juantorena (Cuba), 1976 double Olympic champion, showing full leg extension in a powerful last drive for the finish.

is capable of slightly reduces the number of variables in the race, though no athlete should ever accept with fatalism the fact that his rivals have better performances to their credit.

REFERENCES

COSTILL, D.L., 'What Research Tells the Coach about Distance Running', AAHPER, 1968.

DELLINGER, B., 'A Runner's Philosophy', *Track and Field Quarterly Review*, Vol. 79:3, Fall 1979.

HOLMAN, R., 'The Theory and Practice of Endurance Training', *Track and Field Quarterly Review*, Vol. 79:3, Fall 1979.

MITCHELL, B., 'Total Training', *Athletics Weekly*, Vol. 33:43, 27 October 1979.

THOMAS, V., *Science and Sport*. Faber, 1970.

WILSON, H., *British Coach*. Private Publication.

19

LONG DISTANCE

GENERAL

The reader should first study Chapter 18, on middle distance running, since there is some controversy as to the dividing line between middle and long distance, and much of what was discussed in that chapter will be relevant in this. For our purposes we will say that 5,000 metres is the transition and certainly everything from, and including, 10,000 metres is clearly long distance. Athletes seem to draw a line at 5,000 metres, a distance they will run almost as regularly and often as an 800 metres runner will race his speciality, but they are more wary about fast 10,000 metres races, spacing these out with several weeks in between. Marathon runners restrict themselves to only a few races per season, with intervals of months between. The ultra-long distance involved in the marathon brings with it several new factors—road conditions, gradients, feeding stations, large numbers of competitors, etc.

AEROBIC VERSUS ANAEROBIC

Even though it is difficult to apportion the exact contributions of the aerobic and anaerobic processes in the longer races, certainly the former predominates as the distance increases. However the long distance athlete can no longer rely exclusively on his aerobic ability, since few 10,000 metres races lack a final sprint, and tactics usually involve temporary excursions into the anaerobic demands of surges, lasting sometimes a lap or two. Recovery from surges is particularly difficult, because the athlete cannot stop but has to continue at the more usual pace for the standard of the competition. Marathons involve a third main energy process, or rather the cessation of the other two, if, and when, the runner 'hits the 20 mile wall' and finds that his body is depleted of readily available fuel. If they have not already done so, it is at this stage that the better prepared runners separate out from the other competitors. In the final sprint for the tape—which is becoming more and more frequent with the rising standards of marathon running—the athlete who neglected some anaerobic training may find that coping adequately with the 99.9 per cent demand of the race for aerobic processes was not sufficient to win!

TECHNIQUE

Technique is of utmost importance to the long distance runner, for he cannot afford to waste a scrap of energy on inefficiently directed forces. Idiosyncratic movements may have distinguished the great runners of the past, but we have only to study their times to realize that these movements would only handicap them against present day runners.

The sequence in Fig. 19.1 shows Henry Rono in 1978, the year that he established world records at 3,000 metres steeplechase, 3,000 metres, 5,000 metres and 10,000 metres. Rono is one of the great Kenyan athletes who have emerged in recent years to rewrite the record books and provide evidence that living and training at high altitude (much of East Africa is above 1,500 metres) gives one a blood composition with superior oxygen-carrying capability which helps the athlete to run faster over long distances at sea level.

However Rono's superior running is not just due to the fact that he was born and brought up at altitude—he is also a superb athlete, especially in the economy of effort which is very evident in the sequence of photographs. His head and upper body do not bob about, even though he is so relaxed that his mouth is open. Notice also the relaxed hands and smoothly swinging arms on loose, low shoulders.

It is the long legs with their well-developed muscles that provide the power —but even in the legs there is no wasted effort, since they drive like well-oiled pistons in a machine. There is perhaps not quite so much flexibility and stretch in the hip as is seen in shorter, faster races, but Fig. 19.1b shows that the optimum amount of force is obtained by an almost complete extension in the leg drive. The angle of body lean ensures that the drive goes into a movement which provides maximum horizontal travel with only a little raising of the centre of mass.

The free swinging leg is brought through well bent to reduce its movement of inertia and consequently the effort required. A certain amount of braking is caused by the free leg coming down ahead of the centre of mass, but Rono minimizes this in Figs 19.1c, h and m by not overstriding.

TRAINING

It may seem obvious, but the majority of a long distance runner's training

Overleaf

Fig. 19.1. Henry Rono (Kenya), holder of world records in four events.

schedule should simply be long, stready, distance work. Typical weekly average distances range from 120 to 240 kilometres. Stan Long believes that all runners need a long conditioning period but not at maximum aerobic effort—taking about three months after the rest following the competitive season to build up to 160 kilometres per week. However, as Wieneke warns, there are many studies and generally accepted facts indicating that continual running at slow pace hampers maximum performance. He gives four reasons against long, *slow*, distance running:

1. Improvement in cardiovascular endurance only occurs if the pace raises the pulse above a so-called 'critical' threshold in the region of 135 beats per minute.

2. There is a correlation between stride length and use of arms, so that arm carriage and usage in slow work does not duplicate that used in racing.

3. It has been proposed that fatigue in the leg muscles, rather than pulmonary restrictions, limits performance.

4. Adaptation of the body to improve its condition only occurs when exercise is taken above the ordinary level and the body is stressed.

Wieneke goes on to say that 'jogging, which is what many of our runners are doing, is excellent groundwork for the beginner, but it is hardly an effective training method for an athlete wishing to be highly competitive. The athlete must not be allowed to fall into the trap of a slow, smooth rhythm (which his body seeks)—the no pain, no strain pace.' The long distance runner must constantly strive to increase the tempo of his continuous work.

However, this argument does not mean that the athlete should never run slowly and easily, but rather that he should attempt to reduce the percentage of this type of training, confining it to rest days and to periods of minor aches and injuries.

In his quest for superior fitness the long distance runner must always be certain to put more into his body than he is taking out of it in order to complete the set training task. At the extreme end of overwork lies the prospect of injury and actual loss of condition, but the athlete receives many warning signals from his body before this occurs. On the other hand it is not so obvious to him when his workload is only just over the sensible limit, and he may enter every competition without the edge that makes the difference between success and failure. The solution is to keep a careful diary, and experiment with different workloads until a pattern becomes clear.

Regularity in training is usually no problem for the long distance runner, since he can go out running at almost any spare time and place, requiring only a road or a field. Early morning running before school or work has the compensation of placing an extra stress on the athlete because blood sugar levels are low at these times.

Weight training is a subject of great controversy for the long distance runner and his coach, since it is quite apparent that the exercises are far removed from the demands of long duration running and not at all specific. For every runner who has trained with weights and had success, there is the world beater who is never seen near a weights gymnasium. However this can be countered by pointing out that not all training need be specific to the event.

Even if the training only breaks the normal routine once a week and helps to maintain interest in the programme, it will have served a useful purpose. Weight training can be designed to be of a general strength-conditioning nature, which although not directly specific to the running action can strengthen all the secondary muscles involved which are not usually sufficiently stressed during running to cause improvement.

The coach will need to keep an open mind on weight training and will direct towards it those of his long distance runners who require it.

TACTICS

This topic has been well discussed in Chapter 18. However in long distance the steady pacer must beware the fast finisher who sits on his shoulder until the final run-in. The steady runner without an equivalent fast finish must attempt to put himself far enough ahead of the sprint finishers by either a punishing pace throughout the race or by putting in bursts of speed several laps from the finish. There is nothing more motivating for the trailing runner than to see his rival a few strides in front of him, but also nothing more demoralizing than for his rival to be 20 metres or more in front.

This writer believes that most top-class middle and long distance runners have an obsession always to finish a race, and sometimes play over-safe in holding back reserve energy for the rescue operation of jogging in. A more reckless attitude which resists being dropped by the accelerating leaders may result in total collapse and withdrawal from the race, but on the other hand the leaders will generally be suffering as much, and all may not be lost if contact is maintained. At this stage of possible surrender it is vital to have prepared adequately for the race. The energy used up in that last-minute training session may have been the crucial factor!

REFERENCES

LONG, S., 'Training for Middle Distance', *Athletic Asia,* Vol. 10:2, September 1980.
WIENEKE, G., 'The Continuum Theory in Over-distance Training', *Track and Field Quarterly Review*, Vol. 79:3, Fall 1979.

20

STEEPLECHASE

GENERAL

The 3,000 metre steeplechase, an event for men only, is a branch of middle distance running that also demands the ability to hurdle, for 28 hurdle jumps and seven water jumps are included in the race. The exact distance of each lap is not specified in the rules since the water jump position depends on whether it is inside or outside the normal track, but there is a run-in distance from the start to the beginning of the first lap, then seven laps, each including four hurdle jumps and one water jump. With its heavy wooden hurdles that do not tip over when struck by the athlete as do those used in the other athletics hurdle races, the steeplechase is a race for the brave and determined man. He also needs to be a very fit and able hurdler with a good tactical brain to keep out of trouble in a crowded field of jostling runners.

As Wiger points out, judging and 'feeling' the distance to the hurdle is very important. The distance between hurdles is too large, and the race too long, for the runner to be able to make a fixed number of strides between the barriers as in the other hurdles events, so the steeplechaser must have good spatial judgment in order to make very small adjustments to his running strides a long way from each hurdle, so that clearance can be made without losing speed and with minimum energy loss.

TECHNIQUE

Each hurdle is 0.914 metres high and 3.96 metres wide and competitors must pass over each one without trailing their legs to the sides.

The water jump hurdle is a similar size, but firmly fixed into the ground in front of the water, which is 3.66 metres in length and width. The bottom is 0.7 metres in front of the hurdle and slopes up to ground level at the far end. Competitors must go over or through the water.

The hurdles are therefore low enough to hurdle in the usual manner, but do not allow for errors which cause the athlete to collide with them. Also, a water jump hurdle taken with the usual hurdling action would mean the first step afterwards being taken off balance in about 0.5 metres of water!

The cross-section of the top bar of the hurdles is 127 mm square and the rules allow for the athlete to place a foot on each hurdle and on the hurdle at the water jump.

Coyne has calculated the following:

Time-lag for hurdles = 0.4 seconds x 28 hurdles =   11.2 seconds
Time-lag for water jumps = 1.1 seconds x 7 jumps =   7.7 seconds
Total 18.9 seconds

Assuming an average time differential between 3,000 metres steeplechase and 3,000 metres flat of 35 seconds, this gives a time-lag due to the fatigue of clearing the obstacles of 16.1 seconds. Perfection of technique not only reduces the mechanical time-lag but also the fatigue time-lag.

Hurdle Technique (not Water Jump)

Many steeplechasers use a modification of normal hurdling technique and clear the barriers without putting a foot on the top of the hurdle, which would inevitably lose vital fractions of a second. The modified clearance is similar to a normal dynamic hurdling action except that it involves a higher and safer position over the hurdle. The foot-on method is used by some of the world's best—the steeplechaser tries to make the contact time short by keeping a low centre of mass over the hurdle and using the contact leg to drive him forward off the hurdle when his body is clear.

It is best if the steeplechaser can clear the hurdle completely with a sound technique, using either right or left as the leading leg, and it pays to learn to use either leg early on in the steeplechaser's career. If this is not possible the athlete can lead with his preferred leg when his stride permits and can use the foot-on method with his non-preferred leg if his stride does not permit a normal complete clearance.

Popov prefers complete clearances early in a race, but conservation of energy in the later stages with the foot-on method.

Technique over the Water Jump

The water jump is a formidable obstacle with both its hurdle and trough of water to clear, especially when the athlete is tired and running in a bunch of other competitors. The athlete has to put his leading foot on top of the hurdle and must drive hard with this leg in order to clear most of the water. The

Overleaf

Fig. 20.1. Dennis Coates (Great Britain) at the water jump.

usual compromise between his fatigue and the energy necessary to keep his feet dry is for him to drive only hard enough to carry him to a landing with one foot in the water, while the other swings forward to the track.

A check mark on the side of the track to indicate the start of the acceleration into the hurdle may sound a useful idea, but is likely to prove impractical in the bunching that occurs and will not be the same from lap to lap as fatigue increases. The steeplechaser has really to learn to get a visual spatial 'fix' on the jump as he approaches it, so that he can confidently and positively accelerate up to it with only a minimum change of stride length. Fig. 20.1 shows that the athlete leans slightly back as he comes into the take-off for the water jump. This lean back assists the jump, in which the athlete's centre of mass has to be raised higher than in a normal hurdle action without a step-on. However, there is still the lean into the hurdle during the take-off, though it is not so pronounced. He places the middle of his leading foot on the edge of the hurdle, keeping the knee of this leg well bent. Elliot prefers the athlete to place the ball of his foot on the hurdle to prevent any possibility of slipping. The knee of the leg on the hurdle stays bent to keep the body in a low crouched position as it comes up over the top of the hurdle. Raising the centre of mass any higher than necessary is a waste of energy and increases the impact on landing. The athlete therefore pivots low over the hurdle as his support foot rolls over the top surface. When the main body weight passes the hurdle the support leg drives against the hurdle, propelling the steeplechaser in a low trajectory across the water. The trailing leg is important for balance and for ensuring smooth resumption of running—it should be brought through with a high bent knee lift. The style of the athlete shown is slightly faulty in this respect, for although he has a high bent knee it comes through to the front rather too soon, so that he lands in a slightly awkward position which affects his recovery out of the water. The pronounced swing through of the trailing leg as in normal hurdling is desirable, but needs good leg strength.

TRAINING

The reader should study Chapters 18 and 19 since the principles outlined there are relevant also to steeplechase training. Much of the mechanics and technique of hurdling in the event is similar to normal hurdling, and Chapter 21 should be referred to as well. The successful 3,000 metre steeplechaser must train for the speed and endurance of a 3,000 metre/5,000 metre runner, for the hurdling ability of a 400 metre hurdler, for the ability to surge like a 1,500 metre runner, and for the leg strength of a cross country expert. It should be noted that always hurdling and practising the water jump when fresh, although of benefit to the first lap or two of an actual race, will not accustom the athlete to the demands of the event later in a race when he feels fatigue. So it is useful to include the barriers in some of the larger distance interval work on the track. Winter cross country with plenty of gates and fences also disciplines the athlete to negotiating obstacles when he is tired. Maintaining of good technique throughout the race is essential, so in addition to watching for an unacceptable change in stride pattern to the hurdle or jump, the coach should be aware of fatigue-induced technique errors.

Specific training for changes in pace is necessary because the steeplechaser needs the ability to slow down and surge to avoid trouble in a race.

COMPETITION

The fact that the world record for the steeplechase has been regularly broken in the past decade by middle distance athletes more used to running on the flat indicates that the event is far from well developed. The reputation it has for attracting middle and long distance flat runners who have not 'made it' lives on, because really fast men can be successful even with poor barrier technique and little specific training. Part of the reason, though, may be that the trained steeplechaser becomes inhibited by the obstacles, which, combined with an obsession to finish the race, allows the self-preservation instinct to prevail. This may be felt at a subconscious level and we are not suggesting cowardice!

Although there are disadvantages for the front runner, who has to set the pace and meet the full force of air resistance, these are outweighed in steeple-chasing by the fact that the leading man has a clear sighting and run at every barrier and keeps free of the jostling and jockeying for position of the rest of the pack.

REFERENCES

COYNE, W.N., 'Notes on Steeplechasing' *Coaching Newsletter* No. 8. 1958.

ELLIOT, C., (British Coach). Private communication.

POPOV, T., '3000m Steeplechase Hurdle Clearance', *Track and Field Quarterly Review*, 79:3, 1979.

WIGER, E., 'The 3000m Steeplechase', *Proc. 10th European Track and Field Coaches' Conference*, Edinburgh, 1979.

21

HURDLES

Hay describes hurdling as a specialized form of running in which some strides (one in four for 110 metres and women's 100 metres, and one in approximately 15 for 400 metres, excluding the run-in to the first hurdle and the run from the last hurdle to the finish line) are exaggerated to allow the athlete to negotiate the ten hurdles in his path.

Table 21.1. Hurdling specifications.

Event	Hurdle Height cm	Distance of start to first hurdle m	Distance between hurdles m	Distance of last hurdle to finish m
Women's				
100m hurdles	84	13	8.5	10.5
400m hurdles	76	45	35	40
Men's				
110m hurdles	106.7	13.72	9.14	14.02
400m hurdles	91.4	45	35	40

GENERAL TECHNIQUE

The object of any hurdle race is, of course, to get from the start to the finish as quickly as possible and today this means, even in 400 metre hurdling, that the race is a sprint, with hurdles that must be crossed with as little interference as possible in the sprinting efficiency. Horizontal speed is the essence in running to, over and between the hurdles. Time must not be wasted in raising the centre of mass of the athlete's body any higher than is necessary for him or her to clear the hurdle safely. Jumping over the hurdle checks the forward momentum and interrupts the sprinting action, so the clearance must be a running step-over movement by the leading leg combined with a late sideways swing of the rear leg. The angle between the thighs must be large during the first part of the flight and this, with the sideways swing of the rear leg during the second part, requires great mobility of the hip joint. If, because of lack of hip flexibility, the trailing leg has to swing through under the body in a movement similar to a normal running action, the body has to be raised much higher to clear the hurdle.

Dyson reports that, in comparison with their flat times, elite high hurdlers need no more than about two seconds to clear ten barriers—an average of 0.2 second per hurdle. He also points out that, theoretically, the high points of the path of the centre of mass should be directly above the hurdles, but in practice they have to be slightly higher and in front of the hurdles because the athlete needs time and space to raise his leading leg. Take-off and landing distances from each hurdle depend upon the approach speed, the speed of the leading leg action, the height of the athlete, the height of the hurdle and the skill and economy of the clearance.

If the hurdler maintained his normal sprinting upper body posture as he went over a hurdle he would have to raise his centre of mass higher than if he had leaned forward. But, worse still, he would land awkwardly because the angular momentum of the leading leg in swinging up to clear the hurdle would be transferred to the whole body in flight, tending to rotate him backwards. Indeed, this is a difficult phase to coach in the beginner, who must be encouraged to 'lean in to the hurdle' in a posture which he may consider is exaggerated. This forward lean at take-off and dipping of the upper body over the leading leg in flight cancels out the backward angular momentum of the leading leg swing, ensures that the centre of mass remains as low as possible in flight, and allows the athlete to land with the correct forward lean to enable him to continue sprinting. Davenport gave his own 110 metres hurdles impressions as: 'You don't go up and over the hurdle, you come down over the hurdle. You are high on your toes like a ballet dancer and you step down over the hurdle.' The leading leg should remain in one vertical plane throughout, especially during the take-off, so that twisting forces are minimized.

As the front foot clears the hurdle, the so-called 'leg-pivot' of the leading leg down towards the ground must begin so that the foot snaps down quickly and lands only slightly ahead of the centre of mass with maximum backward speed relative to the hips. A delayed rear leg action helps the leading leg-pivot. The rear leg must be brought around the side of the athlete so that the heel is level with the knee, which remains bent as it swings round to a position high in front of the athlete, who is then able to stretch out that leg in a stride which is as near to the normal sprinting stride as possible.

In a hurdle take-off the eccentric thrust of the take-off leg is even greater than in running and must be countered by even greater upper body movements. In order that the trunk does not have to twist away from the square position to the running direction, the arm on the side of the driving leg must be driven forward towards the leading foot in an exaggerated fashion which involves a free forward movement of that shoulder as well. Some athletes push both arms forward in a 'double-arm action', but Dyson considers this is contrary to efficient body mechanics.

As the athlete starts the leading leg-pivot down towards the ground he experiences the full effects of Newton's third law of motion, since every movement produces a reaction in another part of the body, and, if he is lacking in flexibility and/or co-ordination, he will land off-balance. It has been pointed out before that a correct take-off will help ensure a good landing, but the mid-air movements of the body are also important. The rotation down to the ground of the leading leg in the sagittal plane about the transverse horizontal axis produces an upward and backward rotation of the upper body. A correct lean at take-off will have ensured that this backward rotation is not an embarrassment on landing. The sideways swing of the trailing leg to the front similarly has to be countered by an opposite rotation of the upper body.

Fig. 21.1. The downswing of the leading leg produces a backward rotation of the trunk.

Fig. 21.2. The forward swing of the trailing leg produces an opposite rotation in the upper body.

This can be minimized by a good dipped body position which maintains a large moment of inertia of the upper body about the vertical axis and most, if not all, of the counter-rotation can be take up by a vigorous arm swing, though this need not be the wild flurry seen in beginners.

THE HURDLER'S PHYSIQUE

Although the tall hurdler—and leg length is the important criterion here—has the advantage of a higher centre of mass than in shorter athletes, he also has the disadvantage of a longer, heavier leading leg whose larger moment of inertia sometimes results in a sluggish rise over the hurdle, and demands a take-off from further back, with a consequent higher lift of the centre of mass. The tall hurdler finds it easier to fit in the stride pattern of the 110 metres and 100 metres, but very tall, fast and long striding athletes can find that the spacing of the hurdles is too close. The short hurdler, on the other hand, may have to overstride to reach the hurdles. A difference in style is apparent—the tall, fast athlete must work at take off for a bent knee in the leading leg which is forced up quickly to the chest, whereas the short athlete can stretch out with a straight leading leg. The 1968 Olympic champion Willie Davenport recommended a slightly bent leading leg which stays unlocked even on landing, though he himself tended to straighten his knee once it had passed over the hurdle.

The 110 metres and 100 metres hurdles are perhaps the most demanding of all the athletics events on the physical attributes of the athlete, because the spacings between the hurdles are such that stride patterns have to be very nearly the same for all competitors. Certainly one sees very few short men at the starting lines of top-class 110 metres hurdles events. The rigidity of the stride and the demands of clearing the high hurdles ensure that this is not an event for the casual athlete. Indeed Marlow considers that the true champion 110 metres hurdler is the athlete with all the necessary speed, skill etc., but who is also fortunate enough to have a leg length and natural stride that exactly matches the height and spacing of the hurdles. This athlete will not need to 'shuffle' or overstride. It also means that it is not easy for the beginner, who must spend a long preparatory period learning the skills over lower hurdles.

Short athletes and beginners are at less of a disadvantage relative to tall, experienced 400 metres hurdlers where there is more flexibility in the stride requirements, but high-level competition tends to be dominated by those with taller physiques.

110 METRES HURDLES

The 110 metre hurdles event is dealt with first since the specifications for this race are the most demanding on the athlete's skill.

The Start

The reader should refer to the section on sprint starting in Chapter 17, since most of what is said there is relevant to the 110 metres hurdles, though, since the first hurdle comes so near the start, it is important to assume the more upright running posture sooner. Bosen recommends a medium block spacing with the front block about 38—46 cm behind the starting line, and about 40—50 cm between the blocks, though he recognizes that there may be individual variations. Most hurdlers use an eight-stride run to the first hurdle, but some of the longer striding athletes use only seven. Ewen is of the opinion that, at the highest level, 110 metres hurdling requires a 'shuffle step' for the three strides between the barriers, and that it is not logical to stretch out for seven strides only to have to change to a shuffle for the next 27. He considers that the eight-stride approach leads to a smoother transition from the start to rhythm between the barriers.

The foot that the hurdler has on his front block will be his take-off foot for the hurdle if he takes eight strides. Similarly the foot that the hurdler has on his rear block will be his take-off foot for the hurdle if he takes seven strides. An athlete who finds he is the 'wrong way round' and cannot change stride patterns will have to learn to start with the other foot forward.

Bosen suggests that the first three strides out of the blocks should be normal sprinting and that only in the fourth or fifth should the eyes be focussed on the crossbar ahead. Any lengthening or shortening of stride should occur between the fourth and sixth, and the last two should be normal.

Davenport considers the first hurdle to be technically and psychologically the most important of the race, because whatever the athlete does over the first hurdle, there is a good chance that he will do the same throughout the race. 'You must get over the first hurdle and on the ground as soon as possible.'

McInnis advises high hurdlers to 'develop their fastest acceleration and most aggressive start, maximizing all the controlled speed possible to the first take-off'. For most hurdlers the speed at the first take-off is a terminal one and determines their speed for the rest of the race. Top-class hurdlers may have the hurdle technique, strength and speed to accelerate later in the race, but even their ability is limited. The physical presence of a barrier every four strides prevents the hurdler from substantially increasing his speed after the run-up to the first hurdle.

The Clearance

Each hurdler will have his own individual stride pattern, but as an indication of what is usual, Doherty has measured take-off distances of elite 110 metres hurdlers and found a range of 1.75–2.44 metres, with an average of 2.1 metres. Landing distances ranged from 1.22–1.52 metres, with an average of 1.38 metres. The height of the hurdle usually means that the dipped body position is very pronounced, even to the extent that some use the Jack Davis method of dropping the head until the face is parallel to the ground. At the other extreme there are the few (usually tall) who maintain a more erect trunk over the hurdle and rely on superior speed, flexibility and skill to benefit from this more stable position.

Strides between the Hurdles

Bosen gives an example of stride pattern between the hurdles as follows:

Landing distance after first hurdle	1.4 m
First stride	1.55 m
Second stride	2.1 m
Third stride	2 m
Take-off distance to second hurdle	2.09 m

Overleaf

Fig. 21.3. Mark Holtom (Great Britain) just touches the first hurdle in this sequence but clears the second more efficiently.

The hurdler, like the sprinter, must have a good leg drive with the body weight forward, and the key to the speed between the hurdles is the first stride after the landing. Although the measurements of top hurdlers show this to be about 60 cm less than an average sprinting stride, the hurdler must attempt to reach out on this first stride to maintain the rhythm and ensure that over-striding is not necessary to clear the next hurdle. If Ewen's 'shuffle' is used by some hurdlers, it should at least be with an even rhythm.

It was noted by Davenport that the further the hurdler goes in a 110 metres race the closer he gets to each hurdle. This is not because of the increasing speed since Ewen, for example, measured the times between successive landings in Olympic finalists and found them to increase from 1 to 1.1 seconds during the race. A probable explanation is that the athlete's stride is affected by the proximity of his rivals.

Coming off the last hurdle the athlete must concentrate on good sprinting technique right through the finish. A too early lean-in to the tape must be avoided.

Tactics

Although the 110 metres hurdler is not able to employ tactics like the middle distance runner, it is as well for him to study the styles of his close rivals so that he can, for example, stay out of possible trouble from wild swinging arms. He must also be able to maintain his technique, balance and rhythm when under the pressure of rivals on either side matching his speed or even going ahead of him. Similarly he must not 'tighten up' in the bustle of a race where others are banging against hurdles and even knocking them over. If he himself clips a hurdle he must not allow it to break his concentration or relaxation.

Training

Guy Drut, 1976 Olympic champion, says: 'For me, it's all a question of rhythm. In training, I put the hurdles low, between 91.4 and 100 cm. This way, I can practice without tiring and make sure that my hurdle technique is smooth; that I can stay in rhythm and don't lose pace between the hurdles. The teeth-gritting stuff is not for this event.'

Davenport emphasizes that hurdle technique training should be done while the athlete is fresh, and that endurance work and weight training must follow the technique practices. 'When you work on hurdles you should work for one thing and that is perfection.'

'Part' training is possible, and indeed is a must in high hurdling technique sessions. For example, lead leg technique in the upswing and snap-down can be worked on at slow running speeds between the hurdles when five strides are used instead of three. Also the trailing leg action can be isolated if the athlete runs the lead leg by that side of the hurdle, without carrying it over, so that only the trailing leg has to be lifted high over the hurdle.

Technique training should be a progression, starting from the resumption after the post-competitive season rest and building up gradually in hurdle height, number of hurdles in a set and number of sets in a session. The full distance with ten hurdles should not be neglected. Technique should improve with the background of endurance and strength work, which starts by occupying about 80 or 90 per cent of the training time, gradually decreasing as technique time increases until by the beginning of the competitive season endurance and strength training is still important but only takes up about 20 per cent of the time. 'Endurance' for the 110 metres hurdler means running a fast flat 300 metres, though many champions do not run further than 200 metres without a rest. Speed training is mainly over very short distances, between 20 and 60 metres, and from the third or fourth month some hurdle practices should be made from starting blocks, preferably with a gun to simulate competitive conditions.

WOMEN's 100 METRES HURDLES

The specifications for the women's hurdles seem to have been drawn up without a true appreciation of the capabilities of modern-day women athletes, and there has been over-compensation in relation to the men's 110 metres specifications.

The hurdle height and the spacings are considerably less than in the men's event, to such an extent that there are frequent calls for the height to be raised. At present the women's hurdles are 23 cm lower than the men's, whereas the difference in average height of women's and men's finalists in the 1976 Olympics was about 15 cm.

The basic mechanics of the 100 metres are very similar to the men's 110 metres hurdles.

The Start and First Hurdle

The start from the blocks is the same as for the men's hurdles, with the athlete having to focus her eyes on the crossbar after three or four normal sprinting acceleration strides. Although the first hurdle is 72 cm closer than in the men's race it is only the exceptional woman who can use seven strides and even then, as Bosen points out, this has proved less than effective since the seven longer strides require a switch over to a quick three-stride rhythm between hurdles. So eight strides to the first hurdle are the norm (all 16 semi-finalists in the 1976 Olympics used eight strides), with adjustments being made in the fifth and sixth strides. Bosen recommends a shorter eighth stride of approximately 1.6 metres, compared with about 1.85 metres in the seventh, and a take-off distance of about 1.85 metres before the hurdle.

Hurdle Clearance

The hurdle is comparatively low in comparison to the leg length of the average woman hurdler, and there is not the same requirement to exaggerate the lean-in at take-off and to keep very low over the hurdle as in the men's short race. The woman can therefore match her hurdle clearance more closely to the sprinting action, which means that only the leg driving from the ground needs a full extension at the knee. The thigh of the leading leg is brought up to a horizontal position (again moving upwards in a vertical plane), but the lower leg only needs to swing forwards and upwards to a level for safe clearance. A tall woman's knee can be well bent for a quick snap-down over the hurdle, though a short woman may have to use an almost straight knee, approaching that of a man in the 110 metres hurdles. For a good drive away from the hurdle, however, the knee of the leading leg should be unlocked and slightly bent.

Table 21.2. Touchdown Times. (After McFarlane.)

110 Metres Hurdles—Men

Target	H—1	H—2	H—3	H—4	H—5	H—6	H—7	H—8	H—9	H—10	Finish
12.8	2.4	3.4	4.3	5.2	6.2	7.2	8.2	9.2	10.3	11.4	12.8
13.0	2.4	3.4	4.4	5.4	6.4	7.4	8.4	9.4	10.5	11.6	13.0
13.2	2.5	3.5	4.4	5.4	6.4	7.4	8.5	9.6	10.7	11.8	13.2
13.6	2.5	3.6	4.6	5.6	6.6	7.7	8.8	9.9	11.0	12.2	13.6
14.0	2.5	3.6	4.6	5.7	6.8	7.9	9.0	10.1	11.2	12.4	14.0

100 Metres Hurdles—Women

Target	H—1	H—2	H—3	H—4	H—5	H—6	H—7	H—8	H—9	H—10	Finish
11.8	2.2	3.2	4.1	5.0	5.9	6.9	7.9	8.9	9.9	10.9	11.8
12.0	2.3	3.3	4.2	5.1	6.0	7.0	8.0	9.0	10.0	11.1	12.0
12.3	2.3	3.3	4.2	5.1	6.1	7.1	8.1	9.1	10.2	11.3	12.3
12.8	2.4	3.4	4.4	5.4	6.4	7.4	8.4	9.5	10.6	11.7	12.8
13.2	2.4	3.4	4.4	5.5	6.6	7.7	8.8	9.9	11.0	12.1	13.2

The trailing leg action is also less emphasized in the case of a tall woman, who can afford to have the knee and foot of this leg slightly lower than her hip. But it is still important to bring the knee through to a high bent position in front of the body for the first stride away from the hurdle after landing.

Strides between the Hurdles

Bosen gives an example of stride pattern between the women's 100 metres hurdles as follows:

Landing distance after hurdle	1.15 m
First stride	1.55 m
Second stride	2.00 m
Third stride	1.85 m
Take-off distance to second hurdle	1.95 m

Again the athlete should adopt as near a normal sprinting position as possible and concentrate on making the first stride a good length.

Training

Training should be the same as for the men's short hurdles race, though not as much emphasis need be placed on running over lower hurdles.

Women tend to be satisfied running over just a few hurdles at a time in training, but it is essential to run over the full distance in some sessions to ensure that endurance and consistency are built up for race conditions.

MEN'S 400 METRES HURDLES

The 400 metres hurdler is less rigidly bound by the specifications in his stride pattern and hurdle technique than the high hurdler. The hurdles are 15.2 cm lower and more than three times further apart, so some scope exists for different stride patterns. On the other hand the athlete has to negotiate some hurdles while running the two bends, and is subject to considerable fatigue in the second part of the race, when his anaerobic capacity is put severely to the test.

The Start

Although beginners may be better off with a standing start, the serious 400 metres hurdler should learn the crouch start from blocks, preferably setting them like a 200 metres sprinter and coming out fast on the gun to run a straight line on the tangent to the bend. World-class athletes run anything from 20 to 23 strides to the first hurdle. It should be remembered that the take-off foot for the first hurdle will be the one that is placed in the front block when the number of strides is even.

Hurdle Clearance

Because the barriers are lower than those in the high hurdles race the athlete can maintain his speed over them without the necessity for the same vigorous, exaggerated action used in the high hurdles. However, all the other mechanical considerations have to be taken into account. For example, there must be a lean-in to the hurdle at take-off to cancel out the undesirable effects of the angular momentum built up in the lead leg, and to ensure that balance is maintained on landing. The amount of lean-in is less than in the high hurdles because the more upright posture disturbs the movement less, and conserves a precious small amount of energy. The lead leg can be brought up bent at the knee, though some experts still straighten it when having to stretch out to fit in a 'tight' pace. The less flexible hurdler is able to compromise on the extreme position attained by the high hurdler, and can drop the thigh of the trailing leg slightly so that it is not horizontal, but sloping downwards. The price he must pay, however, is a higher centre of mass over the crossbar.

All the same considerations of Newton's third law of motion have to be taken into account, but in addition the 400 metres hurdler has the problem of having to negotiate some hurdles while running the bends. A left leg lead

Overleaf

Fig. 21.4. Grazyna Rabsztyn (Poland), second from the camera, winning the 1979 World Cup 100 metres event from Tatyana Anisimova (USSR), who is nearest the camera.

Overleaf

Fig. 21.5. Ed Moses (USA), 400 metres hurdles world record holder and Olympic champion, taking a hurdle at the second bend during the 1979 World Cup event.

over these hurdles has the advantage that the right leg's eccentric thrust and an exaggerated movement of the right arm across to the left leg helps to maintain the body lean into the centre of the track that is necessary for running the bend. The hurdler should aim to land with his body weight in a sound position close to the inner edge of his lane. The left leg lead over the hurdles on the bends also has the advantage of ensuring that the athlete is not in danger of disqualification as he is in a right leg lead, where his trailing leg may inadvertently move outside the hurdle. On the other hand there are stride pattern considerations which may have to be weighed against the advantages of a left leg lead on the bends.

Stride Patterns

The choice of the number of strides a 400 metres hurdler can use must be made in relation to the length of his normal running stride when running all out for this particular distance, because understriding and overstriding will adversely affect his speed. Le Masurier has calculated the average stride length necessary to cover the distance between hurdles in a given number of strides, after deducting take-off, landing and first stride distances. The author's own estimates are based on measurements of elite hurdlers.

Table 21.3

Number of Strides between Hurdles	Average Stride Length	
	Le Masurier	Payne
13	2.49 m	2.50 m
14	2.31 m	2.32 m
15	2.13 m	2.16 m
16	1.98 m	2.03 m
17	1.85 m	1.9 m

However it must be remembered that the 400 metres hurdler is restricted to a certain whole number of strides between hurdles. If, for example, he can only fit in 15½ normal strides between landing from one hurdle to the take-off for the next, he will either have to stretch out or chop each stride by about 7 cm to achieve 15 or 16 respectively. For reasons given later in this chapter he will probably prefer to overstride slightly, to take fewer strides.

Most people have a 'preferred foot'—for example, when kicking a ball the body is supported on one foot while the preferred foot is swung to kick the ball. Generally (but not always) athletes start from blocks with the preferred foot in the back block so that it can be swung through, and in hurdling the preferred leg is the swinging lead leg. The high hurdler always runs so that he takes full advantage of his preference in the clearance. The 400 metres hurdler, however, is at a distinct disadvantage if he cannot lead equally well with either leg.

If an athlete is unable to lead with either leg when hurdling he will be restricted to an odd number of strides between the hurdles e.g. 13, 15, 17. Now a natural 15-strider may have to alter his pattern later in a race because of fatigue, but if he cannot lead with either leg he only has the option of going to 17 strides, which may cause him to lose even more speed in chopping his stride length. It is much better if he can learn to hurdle with the other leg leading so that he can alter his stride pattern from 15 to 16 when fatigue demands.

Arnold gives a most illuminating example of different stride patterns (not including hurdle clearance):

1. Novice hurdler takes 23 strides to first hurdle = 23 strides
   15 strides to hurdle 5 = 60 strides
   17 strides to hurdle 10 = 85 strides
   20 strides to the finish = 20 strides
   Total 188 strides

2. Expert hurdler takes 21 strides to first hurdle = 21 strides
   13 strides to hurdle 5 = 52 strides
   14 strides to hurdle 9 = 56 strides
   15 strides to hurdle 10 = 15 strides
   18 strides to finish = 18 strides
   Total 162 strides

Assuming that the athletes had the same rate of striding, it is obvious who would win, since the expert takes 26 fewer strides than the novice. The expert achieves this because he is capable of alternating the lead leg, and running with as few as 13 strides between some hurdles.

To take the extreme example:

Edwin Moses has run 20 strides to first hurdle = 20 strides
   13 strides to hurdle 10 = 117 strides
   16 strides to finish = 16 strides
   Total 153 strides

And since Moses himself is working to perfect 12 strides between hurdles it is not inconceivable that as few as 142 strides (not including hurdle clearances) may be a future possibility.

The serious hurdler must train for stride and hurdling perfection, and it is likely to be the athlete who is nearest perfection on the day who wins an important race such as his event in the Olympics. However, it may be that some unfavourable condition exists which causes the hurdler to miss his pre-planned race stride pattern. His training should have prepared for almost any eventuality, and he should be able to fall immediately into another pattern of striding which least affects his speed.

Differentials

The differential between the athlete's 400 metres hurdles time and his time to run 400 metres flat has been estimated at between 2 and 4 seconds by Arnold, who gives a formula for calculating an athlete's potential at 400 metres hurdles from his fastest 200 metres sprint time:

2 x (fastest 200m time + 1 second) + (2-second differential between first and second 200m) + (2-second hurdling differential) = 400m hurdles time.

Table 21.4. Men's 400 Metres Hurdles Statistics — 1968, 1972 and 1976 Olympic Finals. (After Le Masurier.)

Athlete	To H1 Lead Leg	H1	H2	H3	H4	H5	1st 200	H6	H7	H8	H9	H10	H10 to finish	2nd 200	Diff.	Time
Moses USA '76	20(L)	6.0	9.8 13(3.8)	13.5 13(3.7)	17.4 13(3.9)	21.4 13(4.0)	23.1	25.4 13(4.0)	29.6 13(4.2)	33.9 13(4.3)	38.2 13(4.3)	42.6 13(4.4)	5.04	24.54	1.44	47.64
Akii-Bua UGA '72	21(R)	6.1	9.8 13(3.7)	13.6 13(3.8)	17.4 13(3.8)	21.3 13(3.9)	23.0	25.4 14(4.1)	29.5 14(4.1)	33.7 14(4.2)	38.1 14(4.4)	42.6 15(4.5)	5.2	24.8	1.8	47.82
Hemery GB '68	21(L)	6.1	9.8 13(3.8)	13.6 13(3.8)	17.5 13(3.9)	21.5 13(4.0)	23.3	25.4 13(3.9)	29.6 15(4.2)	33.9 15(4.3)	38.3 15(4.4)	42.8 15(4.5)	5.3	24.8	1.5	48.1

Table 21.6. Some Women's 400 Metres Hurdles Statistics — 1978 European Championships

Athlete	Stride Pattern	to H1	H2	H3	H4	H5	H6	H7	H8	H9	H10	H10 to Finish	1st 200 m	2nd 200 m	Diff.	Final Time
Zelencova (168 cm)	24 (L) 17s	6.8	11.3	15.7	20.3	24.9	29.4	34.1	38.9	43.8	48.9	5.99	26.9 (est.)	28.0	1.1	54.89 (W.Rec)
USSR	21 in		(4.5)	(4.4)	(4.6)	(4.6)	(4.5)	(4.7)	(4.8)	(4.9)	(5.1)					
Hollman (178 cm)	23(R) 15 to 7 16 to 9 17 to 10	6.5	10.8	15.2	19.6	24.2	28.8	33.5	38.5	43.6	49.0	6.14	26.2	28.94	2.74	55.14
FGR	29½ in		(4.3)	(4.4)	(4.4)	(4.6)	(4.6)	(4.7)	(5.0)	(5.1)	(5.4)					
Rossley (171 cm)	23 (L) 15 to 5 16 to 7 17 to 10	6.5	10.5	14.8	19.2	23.7	28.6	33.7	38.8	44.0	49.3	6.06	25.7	29.7	4.0	55.36
GDR	21½ in		(4.0)	(4.3)	(4.4)	(4.5)	(4.9)	(5.1)	(5.1)	(5.2)	(5.3)					

After detailed statistical analysis of over 100 athletes, Letzelter thinks that it is inappropriate to give general guiding values for the differential between 400 metres hurdles and 400 metres flat times and to classify them as many eminent authors have done. 'It is not as simple as being able to claim that a differential of 2.5 seconds is good or even very good. It is "average" for running times of 49.0 seconds; it can only be given the value judgement of "good" or "very good" in the case of less proficient hurdlers. All evaluations must be made relative to performance.' Some of these authors had reported differentials of up to 5 seconds, but Arnold must have the last word, for he states that: 'If the differential is higher than 4 seconds, then the hurdler cannot yet be called a hurdler!'

Another important differential is that between the first and second 200 metres of a race. Arnold points out that the 10 hurdles are equidistant, and demand an even tempo, since 'any unevenness is punished'. If the first 200 metres is run too fast, the second will be affected by the resulting extra fatigue which will more than cancel out the time saved in the first half. Arnold goes on to suggest that the first 200 metres should be between 1.5 and 2 seconds faster than the second, and that the winner of a close race is generally the one who slows down least in the second half.

Training

The 400 metres hurdler has to develop three important areas—speed-endurance running, stride consistency between hurdles, and hurdling technique. The last two must not break down when the athlete is fatigued.

During the annual cycle, starting after the post-competitive season rest, the athlete will progress from long steady distance and circuit training to interval work both over hurdles and on the flat. The hurdles can be varied in height and spacings to provide variety—for example, 4 x 1,200 metres in which the hurdles are set at 1 metre every 100 metres.

The last major phase of preparation should be fast runs, mainly over hurdles, with complete recovery between runs. The hurdles should be at normal height and spacings, and runs should build up from simply starting and running over the first hurdle, to runs over the first five hurdles, to runs to the tenth hurdle. Runs must be made to and beyond the hurdles where the stride pattern is to change, and the change must be practised regularly to develop the necessary spatial judgment. At this stage endurance can be maintained and improved by running 100 or 200 metres over normally spaced hurdles, and then continuing on to 600 metres without hurdles.

The 400 metres hurdler must train in all lanes of the track so that he is as able to run the tight-bended inner lane as he is the 'blind' outside lane.

WOMEN'S 400 METRES HURDLES

The 400 metres hurdles for women was only recognized as an official International Amateur Athletic Federation event in 1973, which makes it one of the most recent events to find its way into the track and field athletics programme. It is not surprising, therefore, that it is developing rapidly and will continue to progress faster than other events for the next few years.

In 1980 the differences between the world records at 400 metres hurdles and 400 metres flat for men and women were 3.27 seconds and 5.69 seconds respectively, which is indicative of the scope for further improvement by the women hurdlers.

After careful consideration of many factors such as problems of track markings, existing events, etc., the IAAF set the spacings of the hurdles exactly the same as the men's, but lowered the height from 91.4 cm to 76.2 cm.

The Start

This is described in the section on the men's 400 metres hurdles and is similar for women, except that stride lengths will generally be shorter. Le Masurier gives the following number of strides to the first hurdle:

22 strides for a subsequent 15-stride pattern
22 or 23 strides for a subsequent 16-stride pattern
23 or 24 strides for a subsequent 17-stride pattern

The above values have been shown from experience to allow for a smooth transition in running to and from the first hurdle.

Hurdle Clearance

The mechanics of hurdle clearance have been described in earlier sections, and modified actions have been noted in the lower men's 400 metres hurdles. The women's hurdles in this race are even lower—in fact they are the lowest barriers in the IAAF programme of events—and therefore clearance technique can be modified even further. Stefanovic compared the morphology of male and female semi-finalists in the 400 metres hurdles at the 1978 European Championships and found the following:

	Average Body Height	Variation Coefficient	Hurdle Height as % of Body Height
Male	183.5 cm	2.74%	49.8%
Female	171 cm	2.53%	44.4%

Recognizing that women have shorter legs in relation to body height than men, Stefanovic used data from the general population to adjust the last column and found

	Hurdle Height as a % of Leg Length
Male	103 %
Female	96.6%

He concluded that in crossing hurdles men have to raise their centres of mass higher than women, which means that 'women have some energetic advantages in a 400m hurdles race'.

Stefanovic's figures in fact show that those women semi-finalists could have merely stepped over their hurdles without raising their centres of mass at all! However, in order to clear both legs of the hurdles without excessive dipping of the trunk, the centre of mass will need to be lifted higher than in the flight phase of normal fast running.

The hurdle clearance then will need to be a compromise between the relative desirabilities of maintaining the running posture and not raising the centre of mass too high. Certainly the trunk is much more upright than in the high hurdles, the lead leg is bent at the knee and the trailing leg can be allowed to swing through below the horizontal position. Because of these considerations, take-off and landing positions will be closer to the hurdle, though the lead leg need not be snapped down so quickly as in the high hurdles.

Stride Pattern

McFarlane estimates the average stride length for various stride patterns as follows:

Number of Strides between Hurdles	Stride Length
15	2.10 m
16	1.96 m
17	1.85 m
18	1.64 m

These have been calculated after deducting take-off, landing and first stride distances. The figures seem a little low when compared with those given for the men's race. Not only are women required to take more strides between the hurdles than men, because of their shorter legs, but one would expect that their closer take-off and landing distances to the hurdles would mean that they are striding a slightly greater distance between the hurdles, and therefore average stride lengths (for the same number of strides) would be longer.

A 17-stride pattern seems to be fairly comfortable for the present generation of elite women hurdlers, but as Wubbenhorst predicts, the greatest potential for improvement lies in a 15-step rhythm. Already the taller, stronger and faster women are running 15s for about half the race, changing to 16s for one or two hurdles and then changing again to 17s for the rest of the race.

Training

Training should be based on the outline given in the men's 400 metres hurdles section. Emphasis should be on the so-called 'fatigue' hurdling practice in which the athlete learns to change stride and maintain hurdling form from hurdles 5 to 10. There should be no question about the ability to lead with either leg.

It was noted in Chapter 15 that women are generally inferior to men in spatial awareness and judgment, and it is possible that some women 400 metres hurdlers will have more than the usual problems of judging the distance to the next hurdle, especially when changing stride patterns. It is therefore essential that they experience this situation many times in training, for example by running their intervals over irregularly spaced hurdles.

When applying statistical analysis to the results of over 100 top men and

Overleaf

Fig. 21.6. Marina Makeeva (USSR), 400 metres hurdles ex-world record holder, at the first hurdle.

women 400 metres hurdlers, Letzelter concluded that women are clearly inferior to men, with the men achieving their lead through a 13.7 per cent better flat racing time and by hurdling technique which is more favourable by 33.1 per cent. When viewed in relation to overall performance in the race, 86 per cent of the overall lead of the men depended on 'athletic condition' and 14 per cent on 'motory technique'. Letzelter concludes that at top level the women hurdlers still lie a long way behind the men in condition and in technique. 'An argument against the fundamental [technique] disadvantages in the women athletes is the fact that in coordinative abilities and rhythmical movement the women are in no way inferior; and the argument in favour of inadequate training and competition is the recent rapid improvement in running times of women.'

REFERENCES

ARNOLD, M., '400 Metres Hurdling. Conditioning and planning the race', *Athletics Coach*, Vol. 9,3 September 1975.

ARNOLD, M., '400 metre hurdles—some technical considerations', *Athletics Coach*, Vol. 9,2 June 1975.

BOSEN, K.O., 'The Hurdle Race', *International Track and Field Coaching Encyclopaedia*, ed. F. Wilt and T. Ecker, Parker Publishing Co. Inc, New York, 1970.

COUEDEL, N., 'Guy Drut. 1976 Olympic Hurdle Preparation', *Track and Field Quarterly Review* 78:4, 1978.

DAVENPORT, W., 'High Hurdling', *Track and Field Quarterly Review*, 74:2 1974.

DOHERTY, J.K., *Modern Track and Field*. Prentice Hall, 1963.

DYSON, G., *The Mechanics of Athletics*. University of London Press, 1970.

EWEN, S., 'An evaluation of the 1976 Olympic 110m hurdles', *Technical Bulletin, Ontario Track and Field Association*, V:4 and VI:1, 1977 and 1978.

EWEN, S., 'An evaluation of the 1976 Olympic 100 hurdles', *Technical Bulletin, Ontario Track and Field Association*, V:4 and VI:1, 1977 and 1978.

HAY, J.G., *The Biomechanics of Sports Techniques*. Prentice Hall, 1978.

LE MASURIER, J., 'Some Factors of Performance in the 400 metre hurdles', *Athletics Weekly*, 13 September 1969.

LE MASURIER, J., 'Olympic 400 metres hurdles . . . ', *Track and Field Quarterly Review*, 78:4, 1978.

LE MASURIER, J., 'The First Two Years of Women's 400 Metres Hurdles.' *Proceedings of the Xth Congress of the European Track and Field Coaches Association*, Edinburgh, 3—9 January 1979.

LETZELTER, H. and M., 'The Influence of form and technique on the 400 metres hurdles for men and women', *Proceedings of 10th European Track Coaches' Congress*, ed. F. Dick, 1979.

MCFARLANE, B., 'Touchdown Times', *Track and Field Quarterly Review*, 78:4, 1978.

MCINNIS, A., 'A need to supply "Sprint Sense" to Hurdling', *Technical Bulletin, Ontario Track and Field Coaches' Association*, VII:1, winter 1979.

MARLOW, W., *British National Coach*. Private communication.

STEFANOVIC, D., 'The possibilities for improving the female athlete's performance in the 400m hurdles . . . ' *Proceedings of the Xth Congress of the European Track and Field Coaches' Association*, Edinburgh, 3—9 January 1979.

WUBBENHORST, K., 'The development of the 400 m hurdles event for women in the G.D.R., *Track and Field Quarterly Review*, 78:4, 1978.

22

RELAYS

GENERAL

These are the only true team events in athletics, usually placed at the end of the competition programme to provide an exciting finish to a match. There are world records listed for 4 x 100 metres, 4 x 200 metres, 4 x 400 metres, and 4 x 800 metres for men and women, and 4 x 1,500 metres for men only, but the relays generally incorporated in most athletics meetings are those of 4 x 100 metres and 4 x 400 metres.

In all relay races the baton (a smooth hollow tube 280–300 mm long with a circumference of 120–130 mm) must be passed within the 20 metre take-over zone. In the 4 x 100 metres the runners, other than the first, may start running not more than 10 metres before the beginning of the take-over zone. The first lap and that part of the second lap up to the exit from the first bend in the 4 x 400 metres are run in lanes, after which the competitors are free to take up any position on the track.

4 x 100 METRES RELAY

The logic of which hand each runner uses to receive and carry the baton and the line of run he adopts is based on the principle that the shortest distance around a bend is the inside limit of that bend. The reader is referred to the section on 'Bend Running' page 219 which explains the geometry of track bends.

It is therefore most important that the first and the third runners, who are required because of the track layout to run the bends, do so on the inside of their lane, whereas the second and fourth runners, who run the straights, can keep on a line along the outside of their lane without running any significant extra distance. This means that for maximum efficiency in baton changing the first runner should hug the bend and should carry the baton in his right hand so that he can pass to the second runner's left hand. The second runner keeps to the outside of his lane and passes the baton into the right hand of the third runner, and so on.

The outgoing runner at each of the take-overs must be able to judge when to start running so that he reaches maximum speed just as the incoming runner comes to within comfortable baton-passing distance. In other words the outgoing runner accelerates as the incoming runner closes the distance between them and the pass is made at top sprinting speed without either of them having to slow down.

A modified crouch start is preferable to the less predictable standing start, but the runner must be able to look back comfortably to the check mark and the incoming runner. The decision when to start running is critical, and the outgoing runner must be able to guarantee a consistent start and acceleration every time if training change-overs are to have any meaning in competition. This means that baton-changing practices must be made at full competitive speed so that check marks can be accurately worked out. Any glancing sideways or downwards by the receiver must be resisted.

The actual passing of the baton should be made on the command 'hand' from the incoming runner and should cause as little interruption of the normal arm action of running on the parts of both runners. The incoming runner should bring the baton forward with the normal forward and upwards swing of his arm just as the outgoing runner brings his receiving arm backwards and makes a clear target with his hand. The 'upswing' pass means that less of the baton is available for the next change-over, but is still preferable to the more deliberate 'downswing' pass, which tends to disturb the running action.

Skill Learning

All this may sound simple and relay teams in good-class competitions may make efficient baton passing look easy, but in reality the timing is crucial and the runners must have complete confidence in their own and their team-mates' ability. There is only a fraction of a second when it is possible to make a really efficient change, so it must be done with confidence. Much practice is needed to ensure this.

Composition of a Team

The putting together of a 4 x 100 metres relay team needs careful consideration from the coach and selectors. The first runner needs to be a good starter and bend runner, and the third runner must also be good on bends. The second and third runners cover a little over 120 metres and the fourth has to run about 119 metres, so they should have the endurance to run more than the usual 100 metres sprint. Marlow says that although he prefers all his relay runners to be intelligent, if he is faced with one who is unpredictable, he allocates him to the first leg where at least the decision when to start running is made for him!

In a well-run relay the baton should travel along the centre line of the lane and should cover the total distance faster than the sum of the individuals' 100 metre splits, provided that there is no over-running or slowing down during the baton changes, since with good changes the baton should 'gain' 0.5 metre each time.

4 x 400 METRES RELAY

Unlike the 4 x 100 metres relay the change-over in the 4 x 400 metres is a visual one, because the incoming runner may be contending with the other jostling competitors and/or experiencing fatigue.

Fig. 22.1. Even in a simple two-team race the 4 x 400 metres changeovers can get crowded! Great Britain versus West Germany.

Although it may seem logical at first to use the alternating carrying and receiving hand, as in the 4 x 100 metres relay, in practice the only sensible method is for the first runner to carry the baton in his right hand and pass to the left hand of the second runner, who immediately changes it over to his right hand as he accelerates away. Similar passes are made at the other change-overs.

Overleaf

Fig. 22.2. Doris Maletzki passing to Renate Stecher in the first changeover of East Germany's 4 x 100 metres relay world record run in 1974. Fig. 22.2a shows Stecher's starting position. Fig. 22.2b shows Stecher's start as Maletzki passes the check mark. The sequence reveals a slight over-run in which Stecher somehow receives the top end of the baton.

Moving the baton from the left to the right hand of the outgoing runner as he starts his lap may disturb his running rhythm slightly but he, and every runner, knows that he must do this and so there is less chance of a mix-up when he passes the baton to the next runner. Because each leg is started at the entrance to the first bend, turning to the left to receive the baton gives the advantage that the receiver's peripheral vision is better for him to judge this bend. Another advantage in the left turn to receive the baton is that the runner has his back to the outgoing competitor outside him, which tends to discourage crowding tactics.

Tactics

Tactics need to be carefully worked out before the race in the light of the known abilities of the team and the opposition. For example, advantage may be gained by putting one of the fastest members in the first leg to get the team clear of trouble right from the start. On the other hand, even in such a short run, the leading runner from the second leg onwards is a pace setter, meets the wind resistance full on, and presents a psychological incentive to runners close behind.

The last runner, in particular, must know his opposition well if he is to take the initiative early in his leg and decides to take the lead. He may discourage the following runners with a fast positive move to the front, but then again he may also set the scene for someone behind making a late burst for the tape. For the same reasons the last runner will find himself in an unenviable situation if his own third runner manages to pass to him with only a slight lead over the other teams. In this case the last runner can do little else than either (a) hope that the opposition will draw its own sting by attempting to pass too soon, or (b) run the best 400 metres of which he is capable, bearing in mind that even the stride or two he has on the opposition can be too much for them to gain in a fast lap.

REFERENCE

MARLOW, W. (British Coach). Private communication.

23

HIGH JUMP

The rules for high jumping require the athlete to take off from one foot, and a competitor fails if he either knocks the bar off the supports or touches the ground, including the landing area, beyond the plane of the uprights without first clearing the bar.

Hay has analyzed the height with which an athlete is credited in the high jump as the sum of three separate vertical distances:

1. The height of his centre of mass at the moment he leaves the ground (H_1).
2. The height to which his centre of mass is lifted during the jump (H_2).
3. The difference in height of the bar and the peak height of his centre of mass (H_3). (Note that this is negative if his centre of mass rises above the bar.)

Thus if the jumper in Fig. 23.1 has her centre of mass 1.45 m above the ground at the moment of losing contact with the ground, lifts it a further 0.75 m and then makes it clear the bar by 10 cm, the height of the bar and the height with which she is credited is:

$$H_1 + H_2 + H_3 = 1.45 \text{ m} + 0.75 - 0.10 \text{ m}$$
$$= 2.10 \text{ m}$$

It is clear from this that the best high jumping technique is that which maximizes H_1 and H_2 and minimizes H_3. If this is not possible then the technique should be the one which provides the optimum combination of the three terms. The requirements of technique can then be studied in terms of these three separate heights.

Fig. 23.1. The rise in the centre of mass (x) in high jumping.

Height of centre of mass at end of take-off (H₁)

This height depends on the physique of the jumper and on his posture at this particular instant. Tall, thin jumpers with long legs have higher centres of mass than those with other builds, and this is a major reason why most good high jumpers have this type of physique.

The jumper's technique will also influence H_1 and he will maximize this, if, at the moment of losing contact with the ground, his take-off leg is fully extended, his trunk is upright and his free swinging leg and arms are as high as possible. Sometimes certain aspects of ideal technique have to be sacrificed for other more important principles, and many good flop jumpers do not achieve the high arm lift.

Height through which centre of mass is raised in flight (H₂)

The peak height any object reaches in flight is dependent on the vertical velocity it possesses as flight begins (assuming no aerodynamic forces act), so this velocity is of major importance to the high jumper. Vertical velocity is affected by several considerations:

1. Horizontal motion of the run-up can be converted into vertical motion

if at the final touchdown of the take-off foot the athlete's body is leaning backwards. The checking of this foot starts a rotation of the whole body about the foot, and throughout the rotation up to a vertical body position there exists a vertical component of velocity of the centre of mass.

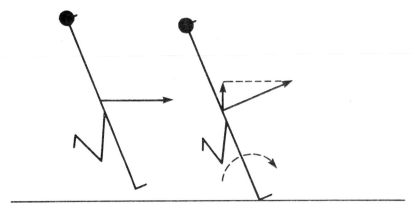

Fig. 23.2. Conversion of horizontal momentum into vertical momentum at take-off. The left-hand diagram shows lean-back during run-up, the right-hand one checking of the foot.

The faster the run-up and the quicker the checking of the take-off foot the greater is the rotation and therefore also the vertical velocity produced. One requirement here is that the take-off leg should not 'give' at the knee and cancel out the rotation, but in practice the high forces caused by the sudden checking do cause a eccentric bending at the knee. However this 'elastic' bending is essential for the next contribution to vertical velocity.

2. The vertical impulse produced during take-off is perhaps the most important contribution to the height credited to the jumper. This is a product of the vertical force on the centre of mass and the time during which it acts (more correctly it is the force—time integral, since the force does not remain constant during take-off). One would think that a longer take-off time would result in a greater vertical velocity at the start of flight, but research evidence (Hay) points to the opposite, and this is confirmed by observation of elite jumpers who have shorter take-off times than average ability jumpers using the same techniques. The better jumpers more than compensate for the shorter times by exerting greater forces during take-off. Part of the reason for this apparent anomaly may be that the eccentric stretching of the knee extensors mentioned in point 1. above is greater in elite jumpers and contributes even more to the forces evoked by the extension of the whole body during take-off. Also contributing to the total vertical impulse are the effects of the rapid upswing of the arms and free leg, whose upward drives are accompanied

by reactions on the ground. If timed correctly they should reach the ends of their swings just as the ground contact is lost, so that maximum momentum is transferred to the whole body.

The height between the centre of mass flight peak and the bar (H_1)

Assuming that a jumper's centre of mass reaches the same peak height and that this is directly above the bar, the bar must be lower for a scissors technique jumper than for a straddler. Hay has produced a table of the theoretical best values of H_3 that can be achieved by an athlete, by measuring the positions of the centre of mass in various poses (author's metrication):

Technique	H_3
Scissors	$- 15$ cm
Western roll	$- 9$ cm
Eastern cut off	$- 6.5$ cm
Back layout	$- 6$ cm
Flop	8.3 cm
Straddle	17.5 cm

In practice it is unlikely that any leading jumper has succeeded in clearing the bar while having his centre of gravity pass below it. However it is clear that, in terms of H_3, the flop and the straddle are much superior to the other techniques, and are virtually the only techniques used by the world's leading high jumpers.

Hay has proposed the use of a front dive roll to maximize H_3, and although several good athletes have used this method in recent years, gains from more efficient bar clearance have been lost in the less efficient take-off.

The choice of techniques, then, seems to be between the flop and the straddle and both have their advantages and disadvantages.

THE FOSBURY FLOP

The Fosbury flop, named after Dick Fosbury, who won the 1968 Olympic title with the technique he has developed, allows more rapid success for the beginner than the straddle and has been largely responsible for the event's increase in popularity in recent years. The flop needs a good landing area for safe landings, and the athlete should ensure that he takes off from in front of the upright nearest his run-up, so that with his horizontal travel he comes down in the middle of the landing area. This take-off position also allows bar clearance to occur about the middle of the bar, where, even in the best makes of crossbar, the sag is the greatest.

As in the straddle method, the run-up for the jump is most important and it should be fast, but controlled, without any hesitations or adjustments. Most floppers use a curved run so that the body comes naturally into the side-on-to-the-bar take-off position. (The take-off foot is further from the bar.) High jump literature contains much controversy about the mechanics involved in the curved run. Contrary to some reports, centrifugal force does not throw the jumper out in a line from the centre of his curved run-up over the bar at take-off. All forces, except gravity, cease to exist the moment contact is lost with the ground, and the athlete's movement is then on a vertical plane at a tangent to the instantaneous circle at the end of take-off. The main purpose of the curved run is to bring the athlete side-on to the bar, but it also aids the lean-away from the bar, since like a cyclist the athlete has to lean towards the centre of the run-up circle to maintain his balance. The movement from the lean-back-and-away position up to the vertical then aids the jumper's rotation about the bar.

Floppers tend to have various types of curved run ranging from pure circular to parabolic to J-shaped. Some of the very best have used J-shaped run-ups, for example five strides in a straight line and five in a curve.

There tend to be two extremes of technique in the flop take-off—the speed take-off and the power take-off—each influencing the type of run-up required. The speed take-off involves a very fast run and a lean-back which is not quite as pronounced as in the 'power' take-off. The greater speed allows less time for the take-off (about 0.13 second) and the athlete tends to run on the front of the foot rather than heel and toe. The power take-off involves a greater lean-back-and-away from the bar, which inevitably slows the run, since it makes the athlete land his feet heel first, certainly during the last few strides. The power take-off is a few hundredths of a second longer in duration, and tends to be used by jumpers with stronger legs than those using the speed take-off. No great difference in height seems to be achieved by jumpers using the two extremes of technique, and indeed the world record has been held by athletes using techniques over the whole range.

The last three to five strides, then, require a stretching out of the legs ahead of the body, sometimes referred to as a 'settling down' of the body, though acceleration should still be the athlete's aim during these last strides.

The last stride tends to be shorter than the few immediately preceding it, with the speed flopper coming up over the take-off foot quickly as the bent free leg is swung past it in a tight movement close to the body. The power or 'force application' (Stones) jumper comes up over the take-off foot slightly more slowly and there is a more pronounced drive off that leg, while the free leg exhibits more of a pendulum swing—some floppers even use a straight free leg swing similar to the straddle technique.

The take-off foot is placed in a line parallel or nearly parallel to the cross-bar. The line through the hips at this stage should be about 45° to the cross-bar, but the shoulders should already be at right-angles to the bar. From this position at the start of the take-off, the swing of the free leg across and close to the body will start making the back turn towards the bar. Although a certain amount of torque is produced during take-off, the athlete should not

Overleaf

Fig. 23.3. The Fosbury flop. Mark Naylor (Great Britain) curving in the approach to a pronounced lean-back for the start of his take-off.

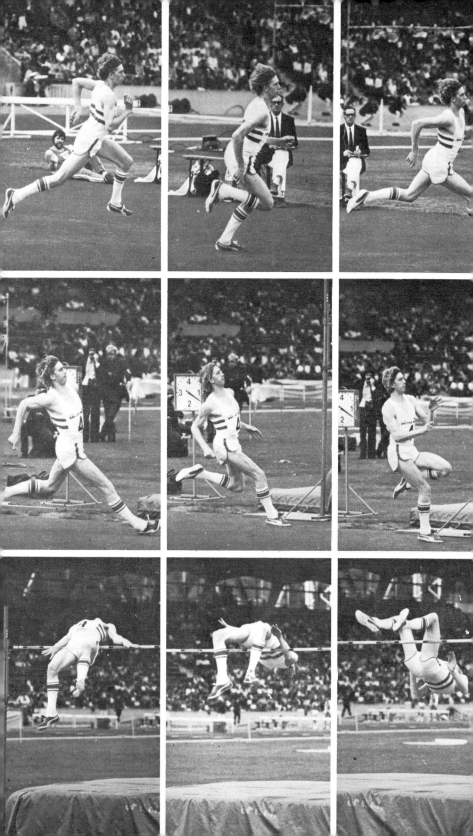

consciously strive for this. Bernie Wagner, who coached Dick Fosbury, warned against twisting of the body prematurely.

Bar clearance is facilitated by the characteristic arching of the back. As soon as his hips have crossed the bar the athlete lifts his head and shoulders upwards. The reaction produced in the lower body to this movement forces the hips downwards and raises the legs, so that the legs clear the bar in a well timed flexing at the hips.

It only remains for the athlete to continue lifting his head and shoulders so that he makes a safe landing on his shoulders and upper back.

THE STRADDLE

Unlike the flop jumper, the straddle jumper runs towards the bar in a straight line, takes off from the foot nearer the bar and clears the bar face downwards. Although he has an even more pronounced lean-back at the start of the take-off, the movement from this up to the vertical position is done purely to lengthen the take-off time and enable greater forces to be evoked from the ground. It does not aid the rotation of the body about the bar as it does in the flop; indeed the rotation up over the take-off foot is mostly in the opposite direction to that required. In order to obtain the rotation into a horizontal layout for crossing the bar, the straddle jumper must sacrifice some of his vertical lift. The energy for rotation must come at the expense of the energy used for raising his body vertically, and although the free swinging leg produces some of this rotation for the layout, much of it comes from an eccentric thrust in a line in front of the centre of mass. Note that the better jumpers stay longer in the air and therefore require less angular momentum for bar clearance.

The run-up should be at an angle between 20° and 40° to the bar, without hesitations, skips or steps outside the normal line of running. As in the flop, the lower body stretches out over the last few strides to provide the lean-back.

The take-off time for the straddle is longer than for the flop (typically 0.18–0.22 second), partly because the run-up is usually slower, but also because the lean-back is so pronounced.

The checking of the body's forward momentum by the take-off foot produces very large forces in that leg, causing it to bend at the knee in an eccentric contraction of the leg extensors. Straddle jumpers must have strong legs to withstand these large forces and then to extend the take-off leg during the latter part of the take-off. The take-off action is a well co-ordinated interplay of take-off leg plant and drive, free leg swing, and both arms lift, all of which

Opposite

Fig. 23.4. Flop bar clearance. Gabrielle Hahn (West Germany) showing a good back bend followed by a flexing of her hips to raise her legs clear of the bar.

Overleaf

Fig. 23.5. Straddle. Rolf Beilschmidt (East Germany) demonstrating the 'power' take-off which has made him one of the world's greatest high jumpers.

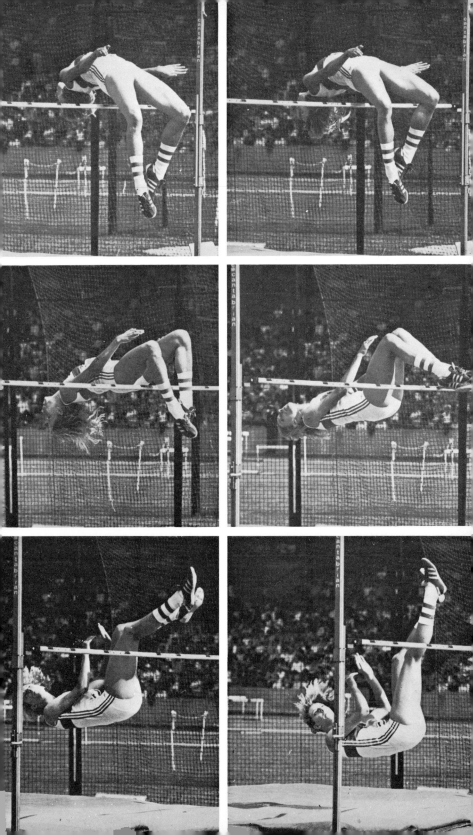

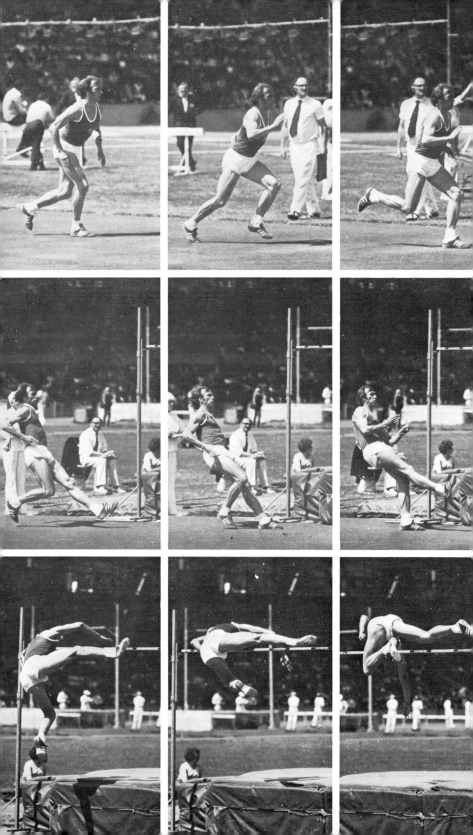

must be directed forward and upward without any conscious effort on the part of the jumper to lean in towards the bar. If the movement is executed correctly the jumper should lose contact with the ground in an extended posture that maximizes the height of his centre of mass at this moment. The angular momentum from the take-off should then be sufficient just to lift him to a horizontal layout as he reaches bar height.

Bar clearance is a controversial subject among high jump experts. Some prefer the jumper to do very little as he rolls and drapes himself around the bar, even to the extent of not kicking or straightening his trailing leg since this extends the length of the body which must clear the bar. Others feel that the jumper should abduct his knees as his body just passes the bar. This tends to lower the trunk but lift the trailing leg. Similarly, diametrically opposed instructions exist concerning the leading arm, especially since high ranking performers have both dropped that arm low over the far side of the bar and thrown it up high behind them. The important thing to remember is that actions in one part of the body in the air must create reactions in the rest of the body, and the path of the centre of mass cannot be changed in flight.

FLOP OR STRADDLE?

The straddle is a difficult technique to learn and needs considerable leg strength. The straight run-up, however, tends to be more consistent and the bar remains well in sight throughout the jump. Although there is more time to create the lift, some of the energy of take-off must be sacrificed to rotational requirements.

The flop is easy to learn, at least in the early stages, and is useful for the fast, explosive type of athlete; it is especially popular with the combined events athlete, who has less time for learning straddle techniques. The flop's take-off produces a rotation similar to that required for bar clearance, so more energy at take-off goes into the vertical lift. Its disadvantages lie in the accuracy required in the run and take-off, combined with the restricted sight of the bar during flight. Failures are also sometimes painful if one lands on the bar in the landing area! The techniques of world record breakers in recent years have alternated between flop and straddle, and counts of jumpers using each method in top competitions do not indicate any preference. Perhaps the best advice to the novice high jumper is that he should try both techniques to discover which is suitable for him.

REFERENCE

HAY, J.G., *The Biomechanics of Sports Techniques*. Prentice Hall, 1978.

24

POLE VAULT

GENERAL

The only rule which effectively limits the technique used in pole vaulting is the one which disqualifies the vaulter who 'after leaving the ground places his lower hand above the upper one or moves the upper hand higher on the pole'. In other words he cannot 'climb' the pole. This means that the height of the upper hand hold on the pole is of great importance, since it cannot be changed during the vault.

As most textbooks on pole vaulting point out, the movement of the athlete and pole is similar to a double pendulum—the athlete's body is one pendulum swinging about his hands, and the athlete and pole form the other pendulum which is inverted like a metronome and swings about the end of the pole in the box. The picture is complicated by the fact that the effective lengths of both pendulums change during the vault. Changes in the vaulter's body posture can alter the rotary inertia of his body about his hands, but at the same time this has an effect on the inverted pendulum. For example, if he bends his knees in order to increase the velocity of his body's upward swing about his hands, the rotary inertia of the pole and athlete turning about the pole end is increased and slows this inverted pendulum's swing. A too hurried upswing of the athlete about his hands may slow the rotation of the pole in the box so much that the vertical position of the pole is never reached and the vaulter 'stalls out'. On the other hand the action of swinging the legs upwards produces a downward force on the hands which tends to bend the pole even more, and this can shorten the effective length of the inverted pendulum.

Unlike the high or long jumper after take-off, the pole vaulter is faced with

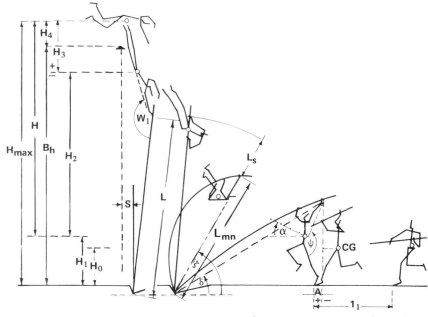

Fig. 24.1. Selected parameters of the pole vault. (Modified from Bergeman/Keller.)

Definition of Parameters

Distances

CG	Centre of gravity.
A	Distance from vertical projection of top hand to the top of the take-off (TO) foot.
1_1	Length of last step.
L_{mn}	Minimum distance from top hand to pole tip in the box. Corresponds to maximum pole bend.
L_s	Distance of shortening as a percentage of grip height L.
L	Grip height from top hand to pole tip.
S	Horizontal distance between vertical projection of crossbar and pole tip in the box.
B_h	Height of crossbar above runway.
H_0	Height of CG at placement of TO foot.
H_1	Height of CG at TO.
H_2	Distance CG raised from TO to pole release.
H_3	Distance CG raised after pole release.
H_4	Distance CG above the crossbar.
H	Total distance CG raised above H_1, the height of the CG at TO.
H_{max}	Total distance CG raised above runway.

Angles

α	Initial 'flight' angle of CG

ψ	Angle formed by top hand, hip and knee *joints at TO.*
δ	Angle formed by a line connecting the top hand with the pole tip and the horizontal at TO.
ζ	Same angle as δ at maximum pole bend.
ω_1	Angle formed by a line connecting the CG with the top hand and the pole at release.

many different possibilities and compromises for the control of his vault. Indeed the pole vaulter has more variables to cope with than any athlete performing in the other events. Also the movement is fairly fast (typically 1.4 seconds in the arm support phase) and does not allow much thinking time. It is the fascination of rarely, if ever, mastering all the variables to produce the perfect vault that motivates pole vaulters to be the most obsessive of all athletes. An attempt will be made here simply to describe these variables.

THE RUN-UP

Most experts agree that the single most important contributory factor to success is the velocity at take-off. The vaulter possesses kinetic energy (KE) by virtue of his running which is equal to $\frac{1}{2} mv^2$ where m is his mass and v is his velocity. If all of this energy can be transformed into potential energy (PE), which is the energy a body possesses by virtue of its height, h, and is equal to mgh where g is the acceleration due to gravity, then:

$$\text{KE (before)} = \text{PE (after)}$$
$$\frac{1}{2} mv^2 = mgh$$
$$\text{Thus h} = \frac{v^2}{2g}$$

Because g is a constant, varying only slightly according to the venue, it can be seen from this simplified view that the height achieved is proportional to the square of the run-up velocity. A small increase in velocity produces a large increase in height. For example, a doubling of velocity produces a quadrupling in height. Thus from an energy standpoint it is important for the athlete to have as high a velocity at take-off as he can control.

A vaulter running at 8 m/second should be able to raise his centre of mass about 3.3 m, according to this reasoning. With his centre of mass already at about 1.2 m above the ground at take-off, and with a contribution from his arms' pull up and push off of about 2 m, this means that the peak height above the ground of his centre of mass would be about 6.5 m.

In reality kinetic energy is not completely coverted into potential energy, since the vaulter still has horizontal kinetic energy to carry him across the bar and some energy is lost in stretching his body at take-off, in the sound energy of pole in the box and in heat energy absorbed by the pole, etc.

In the run-up the vaulter has, of course, to carry his pole, and this not only modifies the arm action of normal running, but, because of the moment of force created by the pole, he must run with a more upright body position to balance it. Solutions such as a vertical carry of the pole in the right arm of a right-handed vaulter have been suggested, but the difficult transition down to the plant seems to have frustrated this idea. Perhaps the best advice is for the vaulter to accustom himself to sprinting with the pole by training at repetition 50 metre runs with it. As in the other jumping events, the pole vaulter must be precise in his run-up so that he can consistently hit the same mark on the runway with his take-off foot. He must use check marks and adjust these for varying track conditions, wind, rain, etc. Run-up distances vary from 30 to 40 metres. He should develop a definite rhythm during the planting movement and preparation for take-off. Some experts recommend a conscious effort at acceleration during these last few strides, with the last stride shorter than the previous two. However, Cramer and Keller have reported world class vaulters who have a shorter second last stride.

POLE PLANT AND TAKE-OFF

Some of the main requirements of the plant and take-off are seen more clearly when considering a vault with the old-fashioned rigid aluminium pole which did not bend appreciably, since certain parameters of the rigid pole have not changed very much with the introduction of the fibreglass pole. It is the angle that the pole makes with the ground at the plant that determines how much of the linear horizontal velocity is converted into the angular momentum of the pole and athlete about the box. Many other variables are involved in the rotation up to the vertical, but it can be seen that in a low plant of the pole the horizontal motion is going to have a smaller component at right angles to the pole than in the case of a high plant where the angle α is large. The angle α will depend upon the height of the vaulter, his body extension at take-off and the height of his hand hold.

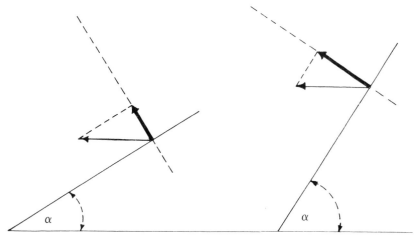

Fig. 24.2. Effect of rigid pole plant angle (α) on the component of run-up momentum at right-angles to pole.

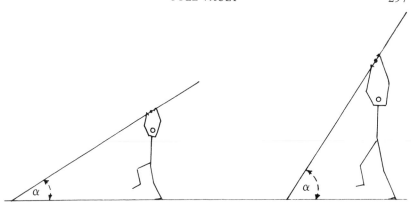

Fig. 24.3. The taller the athlete, the greater is the pole plant angle for the same hand-hold.

In the rigid pole technique the vaulter swings in the 'hang' with his body extended, to reduce the moment of inertia of himself and the pole about the box for as long as possible, to allow the pole to get up to the vertical. His swing-up about his hands has to be done quickly, at the end of a long hang phase. However there is still a limit to his hand hold, above which he will 'stall out' and never reach the vertical. He can then only increase his hand hold by a faster approach run, or change to a fibreglass pole.

The horizontal linear motion at take-off also has a component in a direction along the length of the pole, but with the rigid pole this component is wasted because the pole jars into the box. However this energy is not lost in the case of the fibreglass plant because it is converted into the potential, or elastic, energy of the bending of the pole. If the athlete chooses a fibreglass pole with just the right amount of elasticity to suit his body weight, his speed and his technique, the elastic energy should be returned to him as the momentum which has caused the pole to bend reduces with his upward movement. The straightening of the pole can then precede and aid a well-timed pull and push.

The bending of the pole has other implications besides storing some of the energy of the horizontal run-up. The bend, which is started at the plant by the vaulter's arm actions, means that the effective hand hold on the pole can be higher than in the rigid pole because the angle the end of the pole makes in the box is greater. Looked at another way, for a certain angle of the straight line joining the top hand to the end of the pole in the box, the greater the bend of the pole the greater is the effective hand hold.

Further, because the pole bends at take-off and continues to bend after it, the length of the straight line from the top hand to the end of the pole reduces, making the athlete–pole pendulum shorter and thereby aiding the swing up to the vertical. The higher the hand hold, the easier it is to bend the pole.

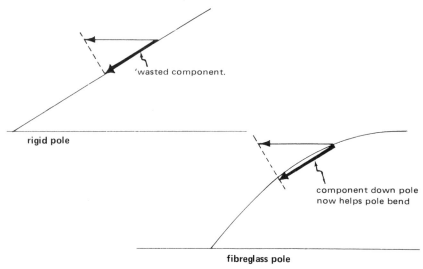

Fig. 24.4. The 'wasted' component of the run-up momentum of the rigid pole is put to good use with the fibreglass pole.

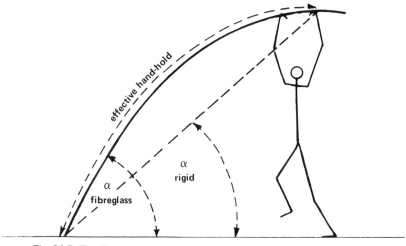

Fig. 24.5. The fibreglass pole enables a higher hand-hold to be achieved and increases α.

Vaulters today are gripping the pole at 4.8 m and higher, though L_{mn}. (see Fig. 24.1) turns out to be around 3.7 m, which is about the height of hand hold that top vaulters used in the days of the rigid pole.

Various lower arm techniques are adopted, and research has not yet provided enough evidence about the forces exerted by this arm. The purpose of applying force with the lower arm is not only to bend the pole but also to

retard the forward swing of the body. The distance between the hands varies
between about 0.4 and 1 m among top vaulters. A wide hand spread is helpful
as far as contribution to pole bend is concerned, but it makes subsequent
movements during the vault more awkward. A hand spread of about 0.5 m is
more usual and, to produce the moment of force for pole bend, the vaulter's
lower arm is tensed, with an elbow angle of about 90°.

With the top arm and body fully extended at take-off, the angle the line
joining the top hand to the pole end makes with the ground is about 30°. At
this instant the toe of the take-off foot is recommended to be directly below
the top hand, though many elite pole vaulters have had the take-off foot
around 0.2 m in front of the vertical projection of the top hand hold.

THE SWING

Gravity produces a changing moment of force, tending to reduce the angular
momentum around the pole end, and the moment of inertia varies according
to the pole bend, so the mechanics from one moment to the next are complex.

In the rigid pole technique the vaulter kept an extended body position, or
'hang', for as long as possible during the swing, not only to reduce the moment
of inertia about the pole end but also to maximize his moment of inertia of
the pendulum about his hands, so that he did not swing prematurely ahead of
his hand hold for an inefficient final pull and push. Since this problem of premature movement ahead of the pole is reduced when using the fibreglass pole,
because it bends away from the vaulter anyway, there is less need for the large
moment of inertia about the hands to keep the body behind the pole. Although
there is still a requirement, but less important, for a small amount of inertia
about the pole end with the fibreglass pole relative to the old rigid pole, a
further complication now exists in the mechanical analysis—the vaulter can
exert a measure of control over the pole bend by the way in which he swings
his legs upwards. It is usual in modern day vaulting to see the complicated
'swing tuck' manoeuvres that are apparent in Fig. 24.6.

The posture changes during this phase can increase the amount of pole
bend that is eventually obtained, since a swinging upwards and forwards of
the legs produces an extra force at the hand hold. Ganslen and Hay have
explained part of this additional force in terms of the centrifugal force of the
swing about the hands, which acts from take-off until the end of the body
tuck, probably being greatest during the so-called 'shortened pendulum' phase.
The shortened pendulum appears to be initiated just before maximum pole
bend, which adds one last additional force to bend the pole. However, this
last force, caused by lifting the legs, need not be explained in terms of centrifugal or centripetal force since any lifting action of the body will evoke a
force at the hands which will tend to bend the pole.

THE POLE EXTENSION

As the forward component of the vaulter's momentum decreases and the
forces due to the swing about his hands and the lifting of his legs expend

themselves, the pole begins to straighten. The potential energy of the pole bend is converted into potential energy of the vaulter above the ground. The vaulter also does work with his body extension and pull on the pole. The vaulter is coached to propel his feet vertically along the pole above his hands while keeping his upper arm straight. The body turns about the long axis as the arms begin to pull when the body is nearly straight and close to the vertical. The centre of mass should be close to the hands, and the legs should be nearly vertically above the hands, if the force due to the pull is not to cause a premature rotation of the body which will bring the legs downwards too soon.

PUSH-OFF AND BAR CLEARANCE

The final push upwards from the hands contributes a small, but valuable, part to the total vault and some control is possible to guide the body over the bar. The rise in height of the centre of mass after the push-off has been estimated at about 0.2 m. It is most important for the vaulter to have adjusted the cross-bar to be vertically aligned with the peak of his trajectory, and for this purpose the rules allow for the uprights to be moved in either direction, but they may not be moved more than 0.6 m from the prolongation of the inside edge of the top of the stop board. Elite vaulters today use nearly all of this allowance, moving the uprights away from the runway, and changes in the rules are being sought to increase this.

The first part of bar clearance is in the body pike position. As the hips clear the bar the vaulter should hyperextend his body, which has the effect of raising both the upper body and legs while dropping the hips. The timing of this 'action and reaction' is important in that it lifts the upper body clear after the peak of the centre of mass trajectory has been reached.

THE VAULTER HIMSELF

Pole vaulters were getting bigger and stronger during the late 1950s in the last years of the rigid pole, but a dramatic change was seen in the physique of top vaulters in the 1960s after the introduction of the fibreglass pole. This was partly the result of the scarcity of good poles suitable for the heavy men who dominated the rigid pole scene, but also because the fibreglass pole suddenly opened up the event to smaller, more agile men. Bitter remarks were made by some old-timers, that the event had become a circus act for acrobats! However, in recent years the event has seen a return of the tall, powerfully built athlete.

Opposite and overleaf
Fig. 24.6. Mike Tully (USA) clearing 5.45 metres with a lot to spare.
Overleaf
Fig. 24.7. Extension at the hips raises the upper part of the body, enabling the final clearance of the bar to be achieved. Note, however, that the legs also rise while the hips are forced downwards.

The taller the vaulter the further he can keep his centre of mass from his hands, making the pole—athlete system about the pole end more effective in the swing to the vertical. However, this emphasizes the delayed hang (or 'elongated swing') and requires much more work from the muscles to produce a quick swing tuck at the end of the hang. The small vaulter, however, has the disadvantage of a shorter distance between his hands and his centre of mass, giving the pole—athlete system about the pole end a larger moment of inertia, though he partly makes up for this by being able to perform the swing-tuck that much more easily.

What is certainly required of the pole vaulter is running speed with the pole. Most experts agree that this is the most important single factor contributing to success.

In the early days of fibreglass technique gymnastic agility was able to outclass sheer upper body strength, but as more and more athletes now have gymnastic agility the importance of good upper body strength is returning. Besides the psychological advantage to be gained from this strength, it also allows the athlete to control the action better and enables him to correct small errors. As Tucker points out, pole vaulting strength should be trained for by performing exercises specific to pole vaulting. Hand stand presses, for example, are preferable to normal weight training presses.

The pole vault competition is generally a long drawn out affair lasting many hours, since among other things each vaulter, before each vault, must carefully adjust the plane of the uprights before walking back to prepare for his attempt.

The pole vaulter therefore needs to have a particular kind of endurance, mental as well as physical, since he will have to wait up to half an hour between attempts. He must develop a well drilled technique so that, even after such a wait, he can look down the runway with confidence at a bar near or at his best performance.

REFERENCES

BERGEMAN, B., 'Contribution of Research to the Pole Vault', *Track and Field Quarterly Review*, 79:1, 1979.

CRAMER, J.L., 'Steve Smith: Technique and Training Profile', *Scholastic Coach*, 45:7, 1976.

GANSLEN, R.V., *Mechanics of the Pole Vault*, Privately published, 1970.

HAY, J.G., 'Pole Vaulting Energy Storage and Pole Bend', *Scholastic Coach*, 35, 1966.

KELLER, P., Reported by Bergeman (see above).

TUCKER, E., 'Polish Pole Vaulting Program', *Track and Field Quarterly Review*, 79:1, 1979.

25

LONG JUMP

The rules of long jumping are very simple—the athlete attempts to jump as far as he can from a 20 cm wide wooden board, set flush with the surface of the runway, into a sandpit whose surface is also level with the runway. A take-off from beyond the board is not permitted. As a valid performance is measured from the pit-side edge of the take-off board to the nearest mark made by the athlete in landing, the athlete should try to take off as close as possible to the pit-side edge and with his feet ahead of the rest of his body, but in such a way that he does not reduce the distance thus achieved by sitting back into the sand.

To the uninitiated the technique also appears simple, but in fact the long jump is a highly skilled event requiring precision in the run-up, concentrated effort in the take-off, and unusual actions in flight. The jumper must be able to accelerate and sprint at top speed over about 40 metres, and hit the take-off position with the correct foot consistently from trial to trial with a precision of just a few centimetres. There can be no last moment adjustment of stride if the maximum jump is to be achieved. During the run-up the athlete gains only the horizontal momentum for the jump, and must add the whole of the vertical component in the very short time available while the take-off foot is in contact with the take-off board. The best jumpers use a hitch kick or running-in-the-air action during flight in order to get the feet to land ahead of the body, but because there is no resistance to this running action it feels completely different from normal track running.

THE RUN-UP

Many coaches point out that 90 per cent of the performance of a long jump is in the run-up, and to a certain extent this is true because there is so little time to influence the jump during the take-off, and in flight the path of the centre of mass of the athlete is unalterable. It is therefore most important for the jumper also to be a good sprinter. In addition to this he must be consistent in stride length, both when accelerating and also when sprinting at top speed.

Although jumping practice from short run-ups is valuable, the athlete must also train for speed and consistency over the full run-up distance. Check marks at various positions down the runway can aid the jumper in his run-up, but he should avoid looking down at them. Check marks may be used but cannot be placed on the actual runway during competition, and since they can easily be displaced anyway in a competition with many entrants, it is best not to become too dependent upon them.

Everything that was said about running in Chapter 17 is relevant to the long jumper, though his running may involve a modification during the last few strides of the run-up. Most top class long jumpers make a conscious attempt to relax without slowing down during this part of the run-up. At the end of the penultimate stride and beginning of the last stride many long jumpers try to sink their hips so that they begin the take-off from a leaning-back, low, powerful position that increases the time—and therefore the impulse—of the drive.

THE TAKE-OFF

During take-off the jumper is in contact with the board for such a short time (typically 0.11 second for an 8 m jump) that CNS feedback has no part to play in this phase. The athlete has to rely on trained reflexes to get the maximum benefit from this drive. There are some great 'natural' long jumpers, but very few reach their full potential without practising the take-off drive. Strength and co-ordination can be developed by weight training and depth jumping, but actual jumping practice is vital too.

As in top speed sprinting, the athlete is in a situation where the ground is moving under him so fast that his legs are unable to extend fast enough other than to enable him to exert a net horizontal force to deal with air resistance. So unless his run-up speed at the board is much less than maximum he will be unable to increase his horizontal velocity at take-off. It turns out that horizontal velocity is actually reduced during the take-off in a competitive jump because of the need to produce a vertical component of velocity for the flight phase.

Haven and Smith, in a study of several 8 metre jumpers including the 1976 Olympic champion, observed a reduction of about 12 per cent from the run-up horizontal velocity after take-off. They defined a 'braking angle' as that between the horizontal and the take-off leg at the moment of first contact with the board, and found this to be around $60°$.

During take-off the athlete concentrates on driving upwards with a full extension of the leg on the board, a high, free knee lift and an exaggerated pumping action of the arms which raises the arms, shoulders and chest. Not only does this attempt to raise the free limbs achieve a high position of the centre of mass at the moment flight begins, but it also produces reaction at the ground that adds to the vertical component of the drive from the take-off leg.

The nature of the take-off is such that the reaction force acts mostly in a line behind the centre of mass, and forward angular momentum is produced in the athlete's body. It is possible to lean backwards and drive in such a way that no rotation is created for flight, and even in the extreme to produce backward rotation during the take-off, but these actions have the effect of reducing the distances jumped.

FLIGHT

As stated above, the long jumper generally produces forward angular momentum in his body during the take-off. In flight, gravity acts through his centre of mass and air resistance is relatively low, so that no moment of force is capable of being exerted to change this angular momentum. The path of his centre of mass during flight is unalterable, so the effect of forward rotation is to bring the feet to the ground prematurely, thus reducing the distance achieved.

The forward rotation can be slowed by means of the 'hang' technique, in which the athlete keeps an extended body position with a large moment of inertia throughout most of the flight. However, a superior method of dealing with the forward rotation, and even producing a net backward rotation, is that of the 'hitch-kick' or 'running-in-the-air' technique. In this method the forward angular momentum of the whole body is transferred to the legs (and to a lesser extent to the arms, if they are also rotated in a forward sense). Since the whole body angular momentum developed during take-off is conserved in flight, any rotation produced in the same sense in the arms and legs must reduce or even reverse the rotation in the rest of the body. Thus the athlete is able to land with his feet cutting the sand well ahead of his body. Linear speed in the run-up is combined by the expert long jumper with angular momentum in the take-off and correct flight actions in exactly the right proportions, so that his feet break the sand as far as possible ahead of the extension of his mass centre flight path without him sitting back into the sand.

The skill of running-in-the-air is not as simple as it may seem. When running normally, the athlete has the kinaesthetic sensations of driving against the ground, but in the long jumping flight movement the feelings are quite different since there is no resistance to the driving leg. Novices tend to waggle their legs ineffectively in the air. It is essential for the transfer of angular momentum to the legs that the backward movement of each leg is made with an extended knee and that the thigh is taken back well beyond the vertical line

Opposite and overleaf

Fig. 25.1. Women's long jump; Sue Reeve (Great Britain) attacking right up to the end of the board.

Overleaf

Fig. 25.2. Daley Thompson (Great Britain) taking off too far before the board but showing excellent form in the hitch-kick during flight.

from the hip. Less of a kinaesthetic problem, but vital nevertheless, is the requirement to bend the leg on its forward travel. Throughout the circling of the legs the hips must be thrust forward in a full extension of the body.

LANDING

As explained above, landing is an important phase of the jump if vital centimetres are not to be lost. 'Jack-knifing', or flexing quickly at the hips just before making contact with the sand allows the flight path of the centre of mass to continue longer and causes the feet to break the sand further ahead than if the body had continued as before in the extended position.

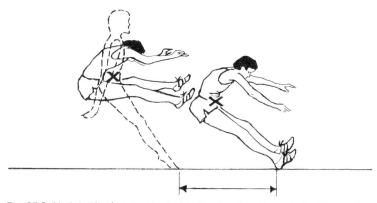

Fig. 25.3. 'Jack-knifing' at the hips just before landing allows the feet to continue further.

In addition to the critical combination of linear speed, angular momentum developed and technique in flight mentioned above, the jumper is further able, depending on the depth and consistency of the sand, to control any tendency to sit back by flexing his legs into the sand so that his hips follow into the same mark made by his feet. Some jumpers twist to the side as the feet hit the resistance deep in the sand, so that the rest of the body is not braked too soon, thus again avoiding sitting back. However there is some doubt about this being a desirable aspect of landing technique.

REFERENCE

HAVEN and SMITH, Private communication with Cooper, J.

26

TRIPLE JUMP

'The hop shall be made so that the competitor lands first upon the same foot as that from which he has taken off; in the step he shall land on the other foot, from which subsequently the jump is performed,' reads IAAF Rule 174—4. The rules allow an unlimited length of runway (minimum 40 metres), and, in addition to the rules defining failures which include those for the long jump, they also specify that: 'If a competitor while jumping touches the ground with the "sleeping" leg it shall be considered a failure'. Simple-sounding rules, but then simple rules quite often define highly technical events—as is the case with the triple jump. Because the objective is to triple jump as far as possible, one may think that an enormous hop is the best way to start the movement off the take-off board. However, even the strongest triple jumpers have to keep this phase under control if the rest is not to suffer.

Presumably because of the strength requirement, the triple jump is a male preserve. However many women athletes use the triple jump as a training exercise for other events, so there is no physiological or anatomical reason why it should not be a competitive event for women. It was suggested in the past that the action might damage the pelvis and affect childbearing but there is no evidence for this. One surmises that the action is 'unfeminine' and there has consequently been no demand for it from women athletes.

Overleaf

Fig. 26.1. Aston Moore (Great Britain) is behind the board at take-off but maintains excellent technique throughout the rest of the movements.

THE RUN-UP

As in long jumping, the run-up has to be fast, relaxed and precise. It must also be consistent, so that the jumper can reproduce run-ups over and over again which bring him to the take-off board without any adjustment to his strides. Markers can be used outside the actual runway, as in long jumping, but only a starting check mark is recommended here.

The actions during the last few strides of the run-up, though similar to those for the long jump, are not quite as pronounced since the vertical lift of the long jump is not needed. In fact there is a much greater requirement to maintain the forward horizontal speed during the triple jump, where even the experts lose about 1 metre per second at each take-off. A definite attempt to drop the hips is made during the last but one stride, and some technicians drop both arms backwards in the last stride in preparation for the 'double arm shift' at take-off.

THE TAKE-OFF AND THE HOP

There are, of course, three take-offs for flight in the triple jump, each of which is important, though precision and control are most important in the first, from the take-off board. The extreme lean back and rotation up over the take-off leg are not so exaggerated as in long jumping, since loss of horizontal momentum has to be minimized, for there are still two phases to follow. Also since balance on landing is a most important consideration, the triple jumper cannot afford to produce much rotation about the transverse horizontal axis.

There is controversy about the use of the double arm shift, which is a strong forward and upward swing of both arms during each take-off (though some jumpers omit the shift from their first take-off), very similar to the double arm action of the take-off made by the straddle high jumper. The reason why the double arm shift is used is that it evokes an extra force from the ground, assisting the take-off. It also provides some angular momentum in the backward direction about the transverse horizontal axis which cancels out some of the undesirable forward rotation that is almost inevitably gained at take-off. On the other hand, the double arm shift is partly contrary to the normal swing of the arms during running, and therefore has a disturbing effect which causes a loss of forward speed.

During the first take-off the triple jumper must discipline himself, usually to the extent of holding back some of his effort, so that the resulting hop has a relatively low trajectory. This is necessary because too much vertical component of momentum at take-off means sacrificing the horizontal component. In addition a high hop generally means that the jumper has to contend with a heavy landing for the step phase, and if his legs are not very strong indeed his step is likely to suffer. A controlled take-off for the hop also means that forward rotation can be kept to manageable proportions.

Most triple jumpers are able to master the technique of a partial hitch-kick in the hop similar to that used by many long jumpers, and here, as in the long jump, it assists in reducing forward rotation so that on landing the leading leg is ahead of the centre of mass and the body leans slightly backwards. The trailing leg should be well behind so that it can contribute a long powerful forward swing in the step take-off.

THE STEP

The step is the weakest of the three phases of the triple jump and is therefore generally also the area in which concentrated technique training produces the most gain. The landing from the hop is crucial in the performance of the step, since a heavy landing may mean that so much energy is absorbed by the take-off leg that there is neither the strength nor the time to perform an adequate take-off for the step.

The athlete then must concentrate considerable effort on the step take-off and attempt to make it as effective as the other phases in terms of distance covered. Many triple jumpers use the double arm shift in this take-off and stretch out the free leg as far as possible in a high bent knee lift. In flight this position is held with a wide angle between the thighs. Landing from the step is usually less of a problem than the landing from the hop. Again the trailing leg should be well behind so that it can contribute a long, powerful forward swing in the jump take-off.

THE JUMP

The third phase of the triple jump is similar to the long jump except that, inevitably, there is less horizontal momentum left after the hop and the step. The better triple jumpers will have lost less momentum, but the jump will nevertheless be a movement with less than maximum sprinting speed at take-off. The double arm shift ensures an efficient take-off. Most triple jumpers are only able to manage a hang technique in the jump phase, but the one-and-a-half hitch-kick will ensure that the feet land well ahead of the rest of the body.

RHYTHM

The timing of the triple jump is critical, and good rhythm is a characteristic of the better jumpers. An uneven rhythm of an excessively long hop, a short step and a 'rescue attempt' ineffectual jump is a beginners' problem. Measurements of the three phases of many elite triple jumpers' actions have been made by various researchers who have calculated optimum ratios. These vary from a 10:7:10 rather poor step contribution to a more even 7:6:7 ratio. In contradiction of what has been said above, some triple jumpers have managed to compete with distinction, using powerful hops in phase ratios that approach 10:8:9. It is when some coaches begin talking in ratios that go into decimals e.g. 10:7.2:8.1, that it becomes obvious that hairs are being split and common sense should be allowed to prevail over scientific measurement. The expert jumper aims to make every phase count, with a controlled hop that allows a step which contributes as much as possible to the whole, while also ensuring a good take-off for a powerful jump. Perhaps a little trading takes place between the phases, so that the step is shorter in distance covered than the other two phases, but this is a result of the biomechanics rather than a conscious decision by the jumper, who strives hard to make the step an equal partner.

Osolin, one of the Soviet Union's leading track authorities, disagrees with the above reasoning, and considers that it is a conservative approach to triple jumping which is holding back progress in the event. He thinks that the hop is the most neglected phase and should be much closer to the athlete's best long jump distance, in fact about 70 cm shorter. Osolin does not think that progress should be retarded by the problem of a higher, further hop over-loading the landing, and recommends flight movements which produce a 70—75° landing angle of the leading leg. The Soviet Union triple jumpers certainly do lead the world and undergo formidable training schedules, even to the extent of jumping while holding dumb bells.

THE JUMPER

The physical characteristics of triple jumpers in the past have been, on average, the same as those of long jumpers slightly below the top echelons of that event who have strong legs and a good sense of timing. Today the really successful triple jumper must have the speed of a sprinter and the explosive power of a long jumper as well as the other attributes.

The unaccustomed eye may see very little difference between one triple jumper's style and another, but there are differences nevertheless, and fashions tend to change after one particular style is used by a successful athete in setting new standards of performance. The main differences in style revolve around the questions of whether to use the double arm shift or not, and whether to spring high, or maintain forward momentum with the so-called 'flat' method. Controversy will continue to exist over which foot to use at the first take-off —the preferred foot, which then ensures that the step take-off also benefits, or the non-preferred foot, which means that only the jump take-off is opti-mized.

The sensible jumper and his coach will assess the style to be used in the light of the athlete's attributes, for example someone with exceptional speed will take advantage of this and use the flat method. Some form of hang or hitch-kick in the jump is preferable to the sail, but this depends very much upon the jump distances of which the athlete is capable, as well as upon his ability or inability to perform an effective hitch-kick.

TRAINING

In addition to the training done by a sprinter and a long jumper the triple jumper must devote much of his training time to 'plyometrics'—the explosive-type, eccentric muscle contraction work of depth jumping. A few examples of this training method are:

1. Jumping from the top of a box (typically 1 metre high) on to one leg, followed by a hop, step and jump.

2. Jumping from the top of a box to the floor, immediately rebounding

from one or both feet to another box, to the floor, to a box, etc.

3. Hopping, or double foot bounding, over low hurdles placed about 2 metres apart.

4. Vertical jumps in rapid sequence while holding dumb bells.

This type of training ensures that the muscles concerned are attempting to contract while they are being stretched by the much larger force of the landing. The tensions in the muscles and tendons are very much greater in this so-called eccentric contraction than in normal concentric contraction, when the muscles actually shorten and draw together the bones on either side of the appropriate joint. In addition the movement is an intense, short-duration one in which the muscles are called upon to exert a very large force in a short time, which is exactly what is required of them in the triple jump take-offs.

In order to increase speed in training the Soviet Union triple jumpers have used a towing apparatus attached to the athlete which is electrically controlled to give a pulling force of $5-10$ kg in the direction of the jump (Osolin).

Very special demands are placed on the triple jumper's central nervous system, which requires a restrained but optimal first take-off followed by two further all-out take-offs, all of which have to be critically timed and balanced. Add to this the requirement of an exact stride pattern in a flat-out run-up, and it can be seen that a well-planned training schedule is essential for the triple jumper.

If it can be said that the art of training is to extend the body to its limits without causing injury, then the triple jumper and his coach are the master craftsmen of athletics. The triple jump subjects the leg muscles, bones, tendons, cartilages and ligaments to forces many times larger than those found in the other events, which increases the possibilities of injury. It is essential to progress gradually so that the athlete's body has plenty of time to toughen up for the demands of the event. Even in each training session the progression should be gradual so that the body is well warmed up and well prepared for the stresses of hard jumping practice. Good shoes, fitted with heel protection cups, help to prevent foot injuries. Jumping must cease at the first sign of a twinge and any injury must be allowed to heal carefully, in its own time, since those that become chronic spell disaster to a triple jumper.

REFERENCES

Austrailian Track and Field Coaches Association Coaching Manual, 1976.

HAY, J.G., *The Biomechanics of Sports Techniques*. Prentice-Hall, 1978.

International Amateur Athletic Federation Handbook, 1979/80.

OSOLIN, N., 'Towards 19 metres', *Modern Athlete and Coach*, July 1978.

PAT TAN ENG YOON, chapter in *International Track and Field Coaching Encyclopaedia*, ed F. Wilt and T. Ecker. Parker Publishing Co. Inc., New York, 1970.

27

ATHLETIC THROWS IN GENERAL

The International Amateur Athletic Federation rules provide for four men's events in the throws—the shot, discus, javelin and hammer. All, except the hammer are also thrown by the ladies (however there appears to be no reason, other than an already crowded programme, why the hammer should not be thrown by women). The specifications, rules and techniques vary enormously from event to event, which is how it should be, because it means that no one athlete can specialize in all events, and many are encouraged to participate. Because of the great differences each event will be looked at separately, but some aspects are common to all the throws and these will be looked at first.

One very important conclusion should be mentioned at the outset: although there are biomechanically preferred methods of throwing, depending on the weight and shape of the implement, these considerations are outweighed by the rules, which in many cases restrict the possible techniques. Some of the rules have been made for reasons of safety, though others seem to have developed arbitrarily in an effort to ensure the standardization of competitions. The rules have to be borne in mind when any new technique is devised.

GENERAL RULES

The shot, discus and hammer are each thrown from a circle into a specified area which is a 40° sector with the same centre, while the javelin is thrown from a runway into a sector of about 29°. The competitor is not allowed to touch the ground outside the circle, or runway, until the implement has landed, and then must leave from the rear half of the circle, or, in the case of the javelin, without crossing the scratch line.

THE MECHANICS OF THROWING

It is sometimes useful in studying a movement in sport to start with the question: 'What is the required result?' and then to work backwards to find the most efficient and rewarding method of achieving that end. In throwing the obvious objective is to achieve maximum horizontal distance, or range. Elementary mechanics shows that the range of a projectile, where height of release and height of landing are the same, is given by the equation:

$$\text{Range} = \frac{(\text{release speed})^2 \times \text{sine of twice the release angle}}{g}$$

where g is the acceleration due to gravity. The important point that emerges is that the range is proportional to the square of the release speed, which means that if the speed is doubled the distance is multiplied by four, if the speed is trebled the distance is multiplied by nine and so on. On the other hand changes in the release angle round about the optimum release angle of 45° (see below) have much smaller effects on the distance achieved. In athletic throwing it is therefore essential that maximum release speed is always aimed at.

In passing it should be pointed out that it is this (velocity)² factor that makes it difficult to compare running events with throwing (or long jumping) events in terms of speed of movement. If a runner doubles his running speed he halves his time to run a race, whereas a thrower (or jumper) doubling his release speed increases his performance by a factor of four.

Although it is not of such vital importance as release speed, the thrower should also attempt to maximize his performance by using the best release angle. Reference to trigonometrical tables shows that the sine of an angle is maximum when the angle is 90°. As the range equation involves the sine of twice the angle, it means that range is at its maximum when the release angle is 45°. However the equation is a simplified one which takes no account of height of release, aerodynamics or the biomechanics of the human body.

Height of Release

This introduces many more terms into our simple equation, but the conclusion is that as height of release is increased so the release angle needs to be reduced to maximize the range. It turns out for example that a 18.3 m shot putter should strive for a release angle of about 41°40′ if he releases his shot from a height of 2.14 m above the ground (Dyson).

Aerodynamics

This aspect further complicates the consideration of the release angle especially in the discus and the javelin, where 'lift' forces can act to oppose the gravity force. In these events the optimum angle can be as little as 30° depending on the conditions (see page 342).

The Biomechanics of the Human Body

These are such that maximum release speeds are achieved more readily when the body forces are directed more in the horizontal direction. You can prove this for yourself by trying to throw a ball at maximum speeds in directions varying from vertically upwards to horizontally forwards. Even this simple unscientific experiment shows that the human body is designed to throw things horizontally rather than vertically. All of this implies that it may be better to sacrifice a few degrees from the optimum angle in order to achieve the maximum release speed in a throw.

METHODS OF THROWING

Research has shown that maximum range in a throw depends upon the method of throwing, the grip which is available and the weight of the object. For one-handed throws with very light weights, the throw with the bent elbow leading is best, for intermediate weights a straight elbow is best, and for heavy weights the bent elbow following is best, the actual weights at the transition points from one method to another depending on the strength and skill of the individual athlete. The athletic implement weights, and the athletes who throw them, fall into the last two categories, but the rules force the javelin into the first and the shot into the third. There are no rule restrictions on the number of hands to be used in discus and hammer, but it turns out that the forces generated in the hammer require a two-handed grip, whereas the discus is light enough to take advantage of the extra radius to be gained from using only one hand.

TIMING A THROW

Theoretically the optimum timing of the body forces in a throw can be described by McCloy's principle, which states that any particular muscle group must be brought into action at the time of maximum velocity and minimum acceleration developed in the implement by the previous muscle group. Earlier or later firing of the muscles concerned results in a lower final release velocity of the implement. This generally means that the stronger and slower muscles of the lower extremities should be used first, and that the weaker but faster muscles of the arm and hand should be used last. However, the ideal situation is not always possible because of other conditions—for example the run-up in the javelin means that the final leg drive does not have the same importance as it does in the shot.

The efficient timing of any particular muscle group during a throw, in addition to being dependent on the earlier history of the movement, is also dependent on body position and balance. If for the moment we can set aside other factors like the strength and speed of the athlete, it is overall timing and balance of the movement that the athlete is primarily concerned with in his skill training. He must learn the timing of the throw through practice, and all the coach's ingenuity is called for in devising training methods which develop this timing, so that in a competitive throw every muscle concerned is used to its effective maximum, with no wastage of energy.

THE GROUND CONTACT

Since an athlete can only exert force to move his body with the implement by pushing against the ground, it is essential for his feet to be in contact with the ground, especially in the early part of the delivery in a throw, when the large muscle groups of the legs and back are driving. However, in the later stages of the delivery it may be less disadvantageous if the feet leave the ground, and a jump into the final delivery may actually aid the technique, for instance by allowing a good follow-through. For example, the force exerted by the body on a shot in this airborne stage is exactly the same as the force exerted by the shot on the body, but, because the mass of a 100 kg male shot putter is about 14 times that of his shot, the acceleration he produces in the shot is 14 times greater than his own acceleration in the opposite direction.

TRANSMISSION OF FORCES

To be really effective in accelerating the implement, the forces of the lower body evoked from the ground through the feet must be transmitted through the rest of the body without any cushioning or absorption of the energy. In shot putting these forces are transmitted through the skeleton to the shot, which is firmly held against the neck under the chin. In the other throws it is essential that the arm, or arms, are kept fully extended and relaxed, so that no cushioning of the large forces is possible through partial contraction of the weaker arm muscles. This is a particularly difficult aspect of throwing to coach, since the coach needs considerable experience to be aware of excess arm tension in his thrower. To make matters worse, the thrower himself is very often unaware of the tension. However the importance of controlled relaxation is evident in the 'ease' of the top-class performer's throwing.

Even when both coach and athlete are aware of the excess tension it is difficult to achieve relaxation, since the balance feels different and strange. Timing of muscle contractions is altered, and a conflict is felt between the call for relaxation of some muscles and the demands of an all-out effort in a throw.

THE TOTAL TIME OF THE THROW

Many factors contribute to the final velocity of the implement, but mechanically it can be said that the final velocity =

$$\frac{\text{Average force} \times \text{time of application}}{\text{mass of the implement}}$$

Assuming that the thrower's skill is such that the average force is already at a reproducible maximum, it follows that the final velocity can be increased by increasing the time for which this force acts. Thus a shot putter turns his back to the direction of the throw and reaches out behind the circle at the start, and in front of the circle at the end, to increase the time and distance over which he applies his forces.

In order to increase the time and distance over which they apply forces to their implements, the discus thrower and hammer thrower hold their implements at arm's length and rotate since:

Instantaneous velocity = radius x angular velocity

The discus thrower is in contact with his discus, and applying force to it, for about 10 metres, and the hammer thrower extends this to around 70 metres in his swings and turns. These rotations, however, introduce problems of centripetal forces, especially for the hammer thrower who must learn a complicated skill to counterbalance them.

CENTRE OF PERCUSSION

This is a mechanical principle in throwing which causes an increase in the velocity of one end of a moving lever when the other end is stopped abruptly. For example if a rod AB is imagined to be moving linearly as shown in Fig. 27.1 it will instantaneously begin to rotate about A if A is stopped. All parts below a certain point, P, will slow down, but all parts above this point, known as the centre of percussion, will speed up. In the uniform rod the point B will move 50 per cent faster than it did before A was stopped. This is a principle which has been used to explain how the throwing implements gain some of their release velocities, though the precise contribution in the various throws has been a matter of some controversy. In the javelin the lever AB represents the whole body seen from the side as the final delivery commences, whereas in the discus the lever AB represents the throwing arm which rotates about a rigid left side as the thrower reaches the front of the circle.

A beginner in a throwing event can sometimes be seen thrusting his hips backwards in the final delivery, and it seems that this is a case of the body instinctively using the 'hinged moment', as this movement is sometimes called, to increase the speed of the implement. However, the beginner uses the principle in this manner in order to salvage the results of poor technique. In the preferred mechanics of a good throw the hips provide the base for the upper body drive, and do not move backwards until the implement is released.

Fig. 27.1. All points above the centre of percussion (P) speed up when the end (A) of a moving rod is stopped.

ANATOMICAL AND PHYSIOLOGICAL REQUIREMENTS OF THROWING

The body types required for shot, discus, hammer and javelin are usually large, average, medium-small and small respectively—but the adjectives refer to giants in each case! However, not all big men and women make good throwers, and not all small men and women should be discouraged from throwing.

All the throws require powerful athletes, where power means strength x velocity. They have to be able to apply large forces quickly, though this requirement is slightly less important for the hammer thrower who has longer time available for the throw. Throwers need to be born strong and powerful, and they must increase these attributes through strength and power training. They also need to work through technique training for the efficient use of speed. In addition stamina is necessary for long training sessions and for long competitions.

More than most other athletes, the thrower needs to be dedicated to and even obsessed with his event, because he meets with more restrictions to his throwing, both in training and competition. These restrictions are caused in part by the safety precautions necessary, and in part by the damage caused to landing areas by shots and hammers.

The throws are not the glamour events of athletics, and since they require more knowledge on the part of spectators to be of interest to them, the motivation of spectator involvement is usually much less than in track events. So the thrower needs special motivation either from within himself, or from his coach. He also faces stress of an unusual kind in a competition, since this generally consists of six separate attempts with periods in between. In each of his trials he is alone in the circle, or on the runway, and in a way detached from his rivals, unlike the race situation in which there is direct confrontation between athletes.

Training too makes very different demands on the thrower. The runner can spend nearly all his training time running, but the thrower must devote much of his training to strength conditioning in a situation which is remote from his throwing. He and his coach have a criticial decision to make about the split between strength and skill training, both in terms of time available and the training load possible. One advantage, however, is that the throwers' training is more variable than the runners', with less tendency towards boredom and staleness.

REFERENCES

DYSON, G., *The Mechanics of Athletics*. University of London Press Ltd, 1962.

28

SHOT

The specifications for the shot demand a smooth-surfaced sphere of metal not softer than brass. It is possible to have a small-diameter shell of steel or brass filled with lead or other material, but shot putters generally prefer the diameter to be large, which allows a better wrist and finger action in the final delivery.

The rules are all-important in any scientific study of shot putting because they restrict the technique to a rather inefficient one-handed method in which the shot must be kept close to the neck throughout the throw. The possible techniques are the mainly linear 'glide' or 'shift' across the circle, and the rotational style. Although both the professional and amateur men's world records have been held by rotational shot putters, the technique has not yet proved significantly better than the linear one, so most throwers keep to the less complicated orthodox style.

MOVEMENT ACROSS THE CIRCLE

After the initial movement across the circle, both the linear and rotational techniques end up in very similar delivery movements, so their advantages and disadvantages must be looked for in this movement across the circle. The aim is to arrive at the start of the final delivery with maximum body-and-implement momentum. The rotational method probably achieves this with a smoother action, but the balance in the turn is critical. For beginners attempting the turn the presence of the stop board can be dangerous. The turn helps to avoid the fault of the body weight moving to the front of the circle too early, but the turn has to be kept much tighter than in a discus throw because of the smaller diameter of the circle.

Since the rules require the shot to be held close to the neck and not to go behind the plane of the shoulders, the only permitted arm movement is a pushing action. It makes sense mechanically to ensure that the stronger muscles of the upper arm are used behind the shot by keeping the elbow high behind the hand. Thus to prevent the elbow dropping ineffectually under the hand during this final pushing action it is important to hold the elbow high away from the body during the preliminary movements.

The preliminary movement across the circle, in addition to providing as much momentum to the body and the shot, must also blend uninterruptedly into the delivery in such a way that balance, body posture and direction of movement are correct for the crucial actions which follow. For example, although the front foot should be grounded fast, the main body weight should still be over the back foot at this stage if the large leg and lower trunk muscles are to be used in the delivery. There should not be a downward sinking of the body and implement through this transition as would occur in a beginner's 'hop', for example, because this would require extra forces to change the direction of the implement into the delivery.

THE DELIVERY

In order for the very large forces of the legs and trunk to be used in the throw, the landing after the movement across the circle must allow the back leg to be under the body. This leg should be bent at the knee and the foot should be turned to point as far as possible in the direction of the throw. Shot putters refer to the 'pre-tensing' of the lower body—from the hips downwards the body is turned towards the front of the circle, while the upper body is held with the shoulders and head turned as far to the rear as possible, the effect being likened to a coiled spring which is capable of rapid unwinding when released.

The timing of the muscle actions in the delivery is as described in Chapter 27, with the large muscles of the legs and trunk firing first, followed by upper body, shoulder arm and wrist movements in succession. The whole body

Overleaf

Fig. 28.2. Aleksandr Baryshnikov (USSR) using the rotational method, with which he set a world record.

Overleaf

Fig. 28.3. Ilona Slupianek (East Germany) winning the 1979 World Cup women's shot event.

should move up over and around the left side which extends at the same time as the right leg drive. When the ground forces in the shot putting delivery are measured on force platforms it is clear that, although the horizontal component of the rear foot force is in the same direction as the throw, the horizontal component of the front force foot is directed backwards against the throw. One reason for this backward drive is immediately obvious, since the thrower would invalidate his throw by continuing out of the front of the circle if he did not apply a braking force to his forward movement. This backward force has also been used in explanations involving the centre of percussion idea mentioned in Chapter 27. It has been suggested that the backward drive at the feet causes an increase in speed of the shot, provided that the body is kept rigid about the left side.

Measurements of throws by top-class athletes indicated that most use release angles of about 38–40°, which suggests that the optimum of around 42°–reduced from 45° because height of release is different from the point of landing–has to be sacrificed in the interests of release speed, as was described in Chapter 27. Coaches generally do not burden their shot putters with achieving optimum angles. If the actual release angle is very different from 40° it is probably because some other point of technique is inadequate.

29

DISCUS

Unlike those for the shot, the rules for discus throwing are almost completely unrestrictive, requiring only that the throw be made within the confines of a 2.5 m diameter circle. Because of its weight and shape specifications the most efficient method is that in which the implement is held in one hand and 'slung' with a straight elbow. Although throwers have at times experimented with 2½ and 2 turns, it seems that there is nothing to be gained from exceeding the usual 1¾ turns.

The body movements (except for the throwing arm) and the forces evoked at the feet in the final delivery, are very similar to those in the shot, as is shown by force platform measurements. This is probably the reason why an expert shot putter is usually also a good discus thrower and vice versa. The requirements of landing with the body weight well back over a bent right leg, which has attempted to turn as far to the front as possible, while the throwing arm and upper body have remained turned in the opposite direction, are exactly the same as in the shot. The main difference between the two deliveries is that most shot putters think of an up-and-over movement of the shot, whereas discus throwers concentrate on a more rotational action of the arm in a plane almost at right-angles to the body. In spite of this difference discus throwers still need to throw around a rigid left side.

Ground contact during the delivery varies in importance to different discus experts. At one time the East German throwers maintained an exaggerated contact with the ground even at the risk of possible back injury which can result from not allowing a free follow-through of the rear leg. This gives a

Overleaf
Fig. 29.1. Mac Williams (USA), 1976 Olympic Champion.

Overleaf

Fig. 29.2. Ingrid Maneke (West Germany) making the most of her excellent flexibility in the women's discus.

firm base for the delivery which then tends to be more consistent from throw to throw. On the other hand many of the so-called rotational throwers build up a great deal of angular velocity (spin) in their turn across the circle, and their momentum carries them through into another rotation after the release. Under these circumstances it is not always possible to ensure ground contact at the feet during the delivery. This is a situation in which the mechanical requirements for good ground contact at the feet during the delivery conflict to a certain extent with the mechanical requirements for great speed of rotation and follow-through.

Working backwards through the throw then, the conditions at the start of the delivery will be very much determined by the initial turn from the rear of the circle, and if, for instance, the body weight is to be over the right foot at the start of the delivery, the movement from the rear of the circle must ensure that the body weight is held back in such a way that this position is achieved. The beginner's usual fault is to drive the body weight too quickly to the front of the circle so that no right leg contribution is possible in the delivery. Generally a turn with the body weight over the left foot at the rear of the circle will correct this.

Taking a simplistic view of the event it is obvious that if the final velocity is to be maximised then great turning speed and a relaxed long arm are essential since instantaneous velocity = radius x angular velocity. However there is angular acceleration during the delivery and for this reason it is necessary for the thrower to apply force to the discus over as long a period as possible—he therefore strives for a 'wind up' or 'separation' with the legs and hips leading the arm and upper body.

DISCUS AERODYNAMICS

The discus is not an aerodynamic shape like an aeroplane's wing but can be angled to the air flow so that it experiences aerodynamic forces to aid the flight. The air flow the discus 'sees' is the resultant of the equal and opposite movement of itself and of the wind which happens to be blowing at the time. If the discus is tilted slightly to this airflow, the air passing over the top surface has further to go than the air passing under the lower surface thus for a discus travelling horizontally from left to right:

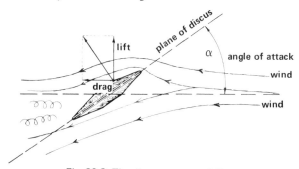

Fig. 29.3. The discus as an aerofoil.

In order to keep up with the adjacent layers of air the flow over the top surface must speed up. An increase in airflow results in a drop in pressure (the Bernoulli effect), and a resultant force then acts as shown by the vector in Fig. 29.3. This force has a vertical component called 'lift' and a horizontal component called 'drag'. See below under 'The Spin of the Discus' for consideration of the resultant force's point of application, which is shown off-centre in Fig. 29.3.

The angle of attack—the angle between the discus plane and the airflow—is an important influence on these aerodynamic forces acting on the discus. As the angle is increased so both lift and drag increase to a point at which turbulence behind the discus causes all lift to be lost and the implement 'stalls'. The optimum ratio of lift to drag has been measured in a wind tunnel and found to be about 10°. However the discus thrower cannot ensure that his discus remains at an angle of 10° to the airflow throughout its flight, because the direction of the airflow relative to the attitude of the discus changes according to the position in the trajectory. If he releases with an angle of attack of 10° this angle will increase as the discus follows the flight parabola, and eventually stalling will occur as shown in Fig. 29.4. This steep fall from the highest point in the implement's trajectory is a common fault in beginners because they attempt to give vertical momentum to the discus by 'scooping' it upwards with a large initial angle of attack.

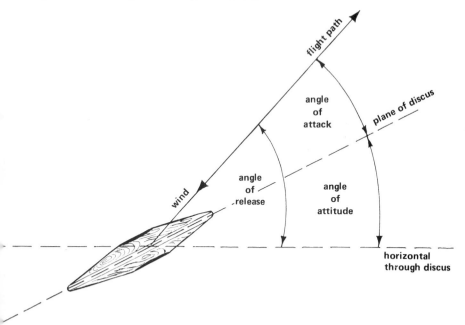

Fig. 29.4. Discus flight angles.

If the attitude of the discus tends to remain stable—as it usually does when given spin—then the thrower has to compromise on the initial angle of attack so that the optimum of 10° is reached about the top of the trajectory.

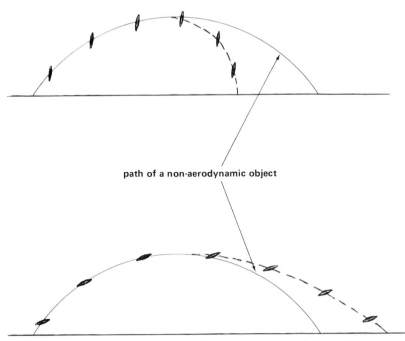

path of a non-aerodynamic object

Fig. 29.5. Effects of flighting the discus. Above, positive angle of attack at the start causes 'stalling'. Below, negative angle of attack at the start causes optimum conditions for the second half of the flight.

Because of the extra lift caused by the well-angled discus, the thrower can afford to reduce the angle of release (angle between the flight path at release and the horizontal) and direct more of his exertions in the horizontal direction.

When there is a wind blowing the situation becomes more complex. A wind blowing towards the thrower will have the effect of increasing the angle of attack during the first half of the trajectory and reducing it in the second half, as well as increasing the relative speed of the discus to the airflow. The experienced athlete adjusts the angle of release and the attitude of the discus to suit the wind conditions. For instance a right-handed thrower can increase his distance thrown by up to 10 metres when a suitable wind blows down the right-hand sector line towards the circle.

THE SPIN OF THE DISCUS

A discus released by a right-handed thrower rotates clockwise when viewed from above and this spin has the effect of both (a) stabilizing the attitude of the discus, and (b) moving the centre of pressure (the point through which the total resultant aerodynamic force acts) away from the geometric centre, which then creates a tendency for the implement to turn about an axis lying on its plane. Points (a) and (b) act in opposition to one another and the predominance of one effect over the other depends on many factors. Any wind has considerable influence on stability and the experienced thrower will know how to control his throw to allow for it. The moment of inertia of the discus will also dictate the amount of rotation about the long axis which occurs in flight. Some makes of discus are constructed with most of the weight in the rims, thus giving them large moments of inertia that make them more stable.

30

HAMMER

GENERAL

The hammer event is quite unlike anything else in the world of sport, and requires very special skills. Just one of its unusual aspects is that the centrifugal force produced in the turns has to be counterbalanced by the thrower's body leaning so far over that his centre of mass no longer lies vertically over his feet, a situation which the balance centres of the brain cannot accept without a great deal of practice.

The event may have had its origins in the ancient military sling, or it may have evolved from the 'wheel feat', a sport dating back some four thousand years, in which a cartwheel (and later the hub plus one spoke) was thrown. The shafted hammer of the Scottish Highland Games is still thrown today, but in track and field athletics the hammer head is connected to the handle by a flexible wire, which complicates the throw even further, since forces can only be transmitted to the hammer head along the length of the wire and not at any angle to the wire. This means that to increase the angular velocity of the turn without 'dragging', and thus reducing the radius of the movement of the hammer head, the thrower has to build up this increase gradually, using multiple swings and turns. Not only are these high-speed turns a difficult skill to acquire but they also cause the human vestibular apparatus (balance mechanism of the inner ear) to produce balance disturbance signals, which again the brain must learn to accept and ignore. So in order to accelerate the hammer up to its maximum release velocity the thrower has to master the subtle timing of small but exact forces throughout a movement lasting some 3–5 seconds, during which his balance is critical and lacking in one of its major control mechanisms.

The usual technique is for the thrower to use two swings around the body with the feet stationary, followed by three or four turns of the whole body culminating in a delivery into the 40° sector landing area.

Usually quoted as the example to illustrate circular motion, the path of the hammer head in an actual throw is far more complicated and moves in a three-dimensional spiral tilted at an angle which varies around 45°. Although the speed of the hammer head and the force in the wire build up to maxima at the moment of release, they do so in an uneven manner since the actual turning forces vary with the double and single foot contact phases. A further complicating factor is that the turning of the body takes place slightly ahead of the turning of the implement. It is in this complexity that we must look for the essential principles.

HAMMER MECHANICS SIMPLIFIED

When analyzing any movement it is helpful to start by making a simple model. In the case of the hammer the old example of a circular motion is a useful beginning. Consider first then a hammer head moving in a circle around a central axis.

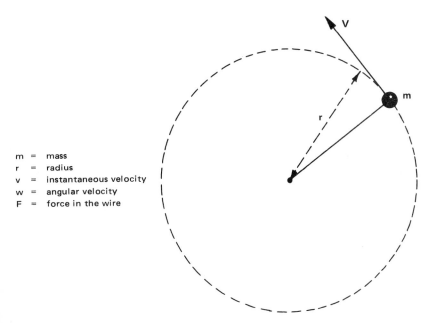

m = mass
r = radius
v = instantaneous velocity
w = angular velocity
F = force in the wire

Fig. 30.1. Simplified rotational mechanics.

Overleaf
Fig. 30.2. The hammer. Karl-Hans Riehm (West Germany) uses the orthodox two swings and three turns in this relaxed and well-balanced throw.

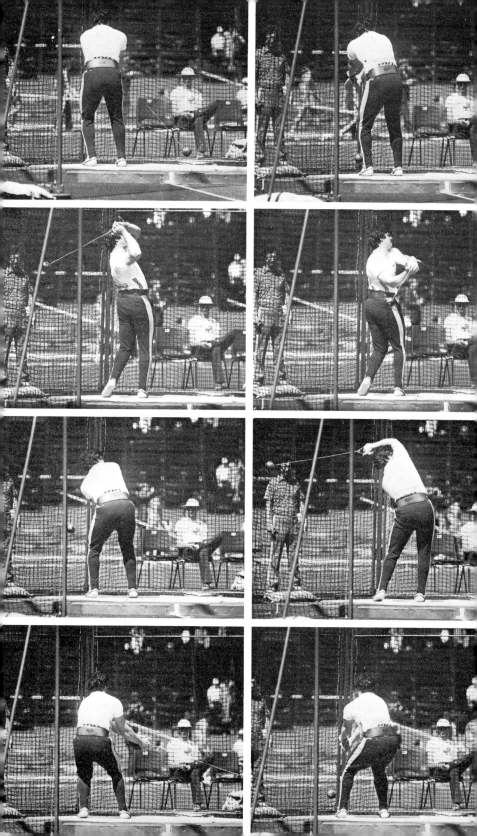

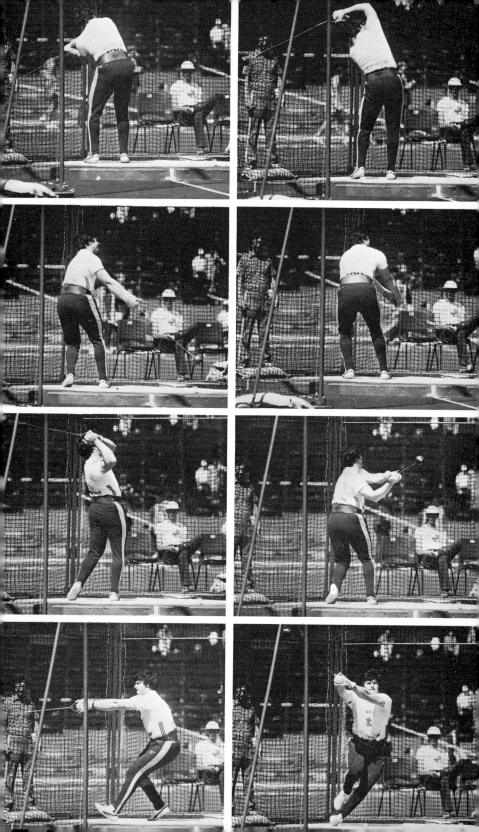

Reference to any text on mechanics of rotation produces several interesting equations:

1. $v = rw$. The thrower aims for maximum release velocity in the throw if he is going to maximize the distance achieved. In other words both w, turning speed, and r, the radius of the path traced out by the head, must be as large as possible. Turning speed comes with repeated practice and the arms and shoulders have to be relaxed to allow a large radius. This requirement goes against the grain for many beginners and indeed for many accomplished throwers—the complete relaxation of arms and shoulders during a movement which calls for all-out effort from the lower body muscles. The relaxation is necessary to ensure as large a radius of turn for the hammer head as possible and also to allow the effective transmission of the forces from the legs through to the hammer head. Any tensing of arm muscles will tend to shorten the radius and, because the arm muscles are not strong enough to withstand the very large forces from the legs during the delivery, a certain amount of cushioning will occur as the arm muscles are stretched eccentrically at this time.

2. $F = \dfrac{mv^2}{r} = mrw^2$. This shows that the centripetal force or tension in the wire required to keep the hammer moving in a circular path even without increasing the instantaneous velocity is very sensitive to turning speeds. (Doubling of the turning speed quadruples the force, while tripling the turning speed multiplies the force by nine.) This centripetal force may be considered a wasted force since it only keeps the hammer head moving in a circle and must be present even when there is no increase in the instantaneous

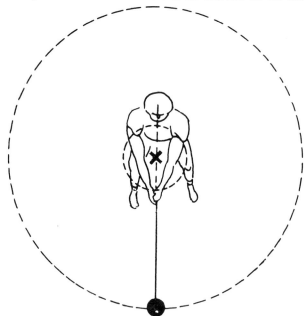

Fig 30.3. The counterbalancing rotation of the thrower.

velocity. (Because the direction of the velocity vector is continuously changing even when the speed remains constant a force must exist.) If the thrower is to control this force in the hammer wire he must counterbalance it exactly with his own body mass. In effect there is a centre of rotation between him and the hammer head and he rotates on one side of it while the head rotates on the other.

The centripetal force keeping him moving in a circle is equal and opposite to the centripetal force keeping the head moving in a larger circle. Because his mass is much larger than the hammer's the axis is closer to him than to the hammer head.

The centripetal force can build up to around 300 kg in a world-class throw, so the athlete needs considerable skill and strength to ensure that he does not lose balance, especially since part of each turn contains a single foot support phase. The counterbalance can produce a situation in which the athlete's centre of mass is not vertically above his base of support, which is a most un-natural condition demanding much skill and confidence on his part. Since the single support is on a right-handed thrower's left foot the point of balance must be shifted to this side if he is to avoid 'falling' on to the right foot.

THE TILT OF THE SPIRAL

The improvement of our hammer model from a pure circular path to that of a spiral introduces a new force necessary to cause the spiralling across the throwing circle, and the tilt away from a horizontal movement means that gravity sometimes slightly increases the tension in the wire and sometimes decreases it, depending on whether the hammer head is moving upwards or downwards respectively.

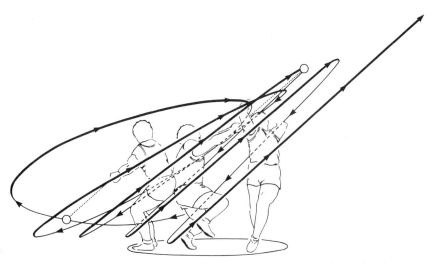

Fig. 30.4. The changing tilt of the hammer plane during Yuri Sedyk's winning throw in the 1976 Olympics.

The plane of the hammer's path needs to be approximately 45° at the delivery for optimum initial flight conditions, so it is fortunate that the swings start the hammer naturally in a tilted plane and not much deliberate effort is required of the thrower to achieve this. Measurements of Olympic finalists on film by one of the authors shows that most achieve a final delivery angle remarkable close to 45°, even though the angles in the preliminary swings may vary by as much as 10° from one thrower to another.

If the plane of the hammer path is at an angle to the horizontal the question must be asked: how is this plane oriented in relation to the thrower? Throwers usually look at this in terms of the 'low point', and much controversy exists over whether this should be on the thrower's right as in older orthodox techniques, or directly in front of him, or even in line with his left foot as in newer techniques advocated by the Russians (Bondarchuk). The advantage of the right-hand side low point is that the 'lead' of the lower body is easier to obtain and maintain, but there is a danger of shortening the radius of the throw by 'dragging' the hammer round on a premature turn of the left shoulder. The advantage of the left-hand side low point is that balance is much easier and the lift in the delivery is more efficient, but it does need great agility to produce the lead of the lower body in the final turn.

LOWER BODY LEAD

An increase in the speed of the hammer head can be achieved by means of 'shortening the radius'. Force has to be used to pull the hammer head towards the centre of rotation if the radius is suddenly reduced, and this causes an increase in the speed. There is probably an element of this in even the best hammer throwers' techniques, but poorer throwers tend to rely heavily on it to the detriment of other requirements—for example, the conflicting requirement to maintain a long radius.

The generally preferred method of increasing the speed of the hammer head during the turns is to make the lower body be ahead in phase of the upper body. This means that the feet, legs and hips attempt to move faster than the rest of the body and the hammer. Provided that the shoulders and arms remain long and relaxed, this rotational acceleration will be transmitted to the hammer head without any cushioning. The main fault encountered in this respect is the thrower's tendency to move the left shoulder into the turn ahead of, or with, the lower body. Usually this is accompanied by bending the right arm and the thrower has the sense of a 'lead', though it is a false one. Correcting the fault starts with the thrower having the thought of a straight right arm uppermost in his mind when throwing.

Keeping the trunk fairly upright on bent knees throughout the throw aids balance and ensures that the thrower is able to add more to the final delivery with a rapid extension of his whole body.

REFERENCES

BONDARCHUK, A., 'Hammer Throwing', *Proceedings of Xth Congress of the European Track and Field Coaches Association*, Edinburgh, January 1979.

31

JAVELIN

Because of its military history, the javelin has always been the subject of attempts to increase the distance it can be thrown. For example, short slings have been connected between the thrower's fingers and small hooks at the grip to increase the release velocity, and the aerodynamic characteristics have been improved to the stage where correct angles of attitude and release for maximum lift in flight are an important part of the thrower's skill. It was not until the mid-1950s that an ingenious Spanish athlete discovered that the best method for distance throwing was to use a discus-style turn while holding the javelin just behind the grip in a pre-soaped or oiled hand. The low-friction hand-hold helped the easy release of the javelin, but this and the rotation made it an unpredictable and dangerous method. The athletics authorities have re-worded the rules and specifications several times to limit aerodynamic improvements, and to prevent the use of slings, hooks and discus-style turns. The javelin and the method of throwing it are now subject to very stringent conditions.

The orthodox style of a linear run-up, a drawing back of the throwing arm followed by a checking of the leading leg and a bent-arm-elbow leading throw is virtually the only method possible, and the thrower must therefore concern himself with a fast controlled run which blends with and adds to the throwing action, resulting in a correctly angled fast delivery. The rules demand that the head of the javelin should land first. Obviously the length of the javelin should travel in the vertical plane of the flight path, since otherwise it would encounter drag forces which would reduce the distance thrown. Although the lift force is not caused by the Bernoulli effect, as it is in the flight of the discus, very similar reasoning applies to the flight requirements for optimum aerodynamic lift. 'Lift' is actually caused by turbulence above the javelin as shown in Fig. 31.1.

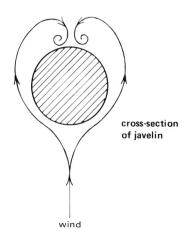

cross-section
of javelin

wind

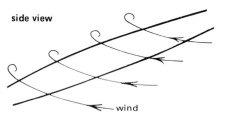

side view

wind

Fig. 31.1. Airflow over a javelin in flight.

This is virtually a type of drag in the vertical direction, opposing the fall caused by gravity, so that optimum conditions are critical if the implement is not to slow too much in the horizontal direction. Javelins are usually designed to have an average centre of pressure behind the centre of gravity, so that they have a tendency to a forward rotation which brings the head down. The centre of pressure can vary in flight in any case, depending on the airflow conditions, but javelins are now designed with varying aerodynamic characteristics so that there is just the correct amount of forward rotation to bring the head down, depending on the distance thrown. For example, a '90 metre' javelin will have its centre of pressure relatively near to its centre of gravity so that rotation of the head downwards is slow, whereas a '60 metre' javelin will be in the air for a shorter time and the turning moment will have to be greater to bring the head down sooner. A poor thrower will probably not throw further with a javelin rated for a good thrower and he will run the risk of an invalid throw unless he exerts a rather wasteful eccentric force during the delivery to increase the forward rotation in flight. Wind tunnel experiments have shown that the optimum lift:drag ratio is obtained from angles of attack around $10°$.

Measurements of throws over 85 metres made by athletes in competition (Terauds) have shown that under fairly normal conditions the mean angle of release was $33°$, with the mean angle of attack a positive $5°$. It is clear, therefore, that the forward rotation of the javelin during flight is sufficient to maintain the angle of attack about the optimum, and that an initial negative angle of attack as in discus throwing is neither necessary nor desirable. The same study showed that release velocities were about 28 metres per second and that the heights of release were about 1.85 metres. The Held 90 metre javelins used in the competition vibrated at 25 oscillations per second and had a surprisingly high spin about the long axis of up to 25 revolutions per second. It is possible that with such large spin velocities javelins may be subjected to significant Magnus effect forces (aerodynamic forces caused by spin) when cross-winds blow. It is unlikely that the correct conditions, i.e. when the benefits of this Magnus lift force exceed the disadvantages of the extra drag forces of a side wind, occur very often. However, the spin will tend to stabilize the javelin's altitude in flight. The oscillation about the axis at right-angles to the javelin, on the other hand, will only be detrimental and its amplitude should be minimized by ensuring a delivery pull along the length of the javelin which must be in the same vertical plane as the flight path.

In order to maximize the release velocity of the javelin the thrower must attempt to extend the distance over which he applies the final delivery forces. He does this by ensuring that at the start of the delivery he is reaching backwards as far as he can without contravening the rule which stipulates that the thrower's back must not be turned to the throwing direction. To obtain the characteristic lean back at this stage the thrower has to reach backwards with the javelin while attempting to accelerate the lower body forwards with large, bounding strides.

The thrower increases the distance of his final delivery pull by also turning his shoulders sideways so that the javelin is carried even further to the rear. Generally the hips are kept in the normal running position during this sideways turning of the shoulders, but some top-class throwers are now allowing their hips to turn with their shoulders to effect an even greater range for the final delivery pull. The sideways turning of the shoulders and the hips produces the characteristic 'cross-step' in the penultimate stride. This should

Overleaf

Fig. 31.2. Miklos Nemeth (Hungary) set a world record to win the 1976 Olympic javelin event. His technique includes a long, powerful pull which starts from a relaxed straight arm.

Overleaf

Fig. 31.3. Tesse Sanderson (Great Britain) throws over a bent left leg in this women's javelin sequence.

occur as a natural consequence of turning the body and is better thought of by the thrower as an acceleration stride rather than as a deliberate cross-step. The final delivery is effected from this exaggerated reaching back position, without any hesitation or loss of speed, by driving the chest through over as rigid a left leg and side as possible. The arm action is delayed and great flexibility of the shoulder girdle is required at this stage to prevent premature forward movement of the javelin. Even when the arm does strike, it is with a flail-type movement in which the elbow leads the javelin. Incorrect timing of the final arm whip can cause injury to the shoulder and elbow because of the large momentum produced.

REFERENCE

TERAUDS, J. 'Computerised Biomechanical Analysis of Javelin Throwers at the 1976 Montreal Olympics'. *Athletics Asia, 7:2,* December 1977.

32

WALKS

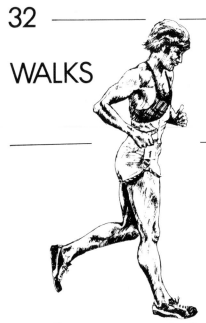

Race walking may appear to be the natural link between ordinary walking and running, and in some respects this is true—with increase in speed, the force—time patterns between foot and ground in the horizontal direction of locomotion and in the vertical direction show progressive increases in their magnitudes as the contact time decreases. However, the horizontal forces at right-angles to the direction of movement do not reveal this tidy progression, because although ordinary walking and running produce only small wasted forces in this direction, race walking shows much the largest peaks which represent a significant amount of energy.

A study of the body movements involved in these activities pinpoints the cause. In normal walking and running the knee of the supporting leg is bent as it passes through the vertical position (i.e. when the centre of mass passes vertically over the foot), but in race walking the knee of this leg is straight in the vertical position. This means that the rest of the body must make compensatory movements to maintain the path of the centre of mass on an efficient line.

We may question a technique that is not completely efficient in terms of energy usage, but in race walking, as in many athletic events, the most efficient method of performing the movement is forbidden by the rules. The logic of these rules is completely justified on philosophical grounds and the reader is referred to the section on 'play' in Chapter 4. The rules define the technique

Overleaf

Fig. 32.1. Roger Mills (Great Britain) maintains very good relaxation and technique in a fast one mile race.

in such a way that race walking does not become a modified run or a Groucho Marx shuffle. Briefly, contact with the ground must be maintained at all times, a heel-and-toe action must be used, and the supporting leg must be straight at the knee as it passes through the vertical position.

Some events exist at the 'shorter' distances of 1 mile, 3,000 metres etc., but it is generally recognized that race walking is an ultra-endurance activity and the more accepted distances raced are 20 kilometres and 50 kilometres. The 20 kilometre event lasts for around 1½ hours and yet some walkers can be heard saying, quite seriously, that the distance is rather too short for them!

Judging a fast walk is an extremely difficult skill, since it is almost impossible to see whether a walker has a foot on the ground at all times or that the knee is straight through the vertical—for it takes only a fraction of a second to pass through this position.

TECHNIQUE

Race walking is not a natural skill in the sense that normal walking and running are, because these latter are the locomotion skills learnt from very early childhood. In some ways this is an advantage because it means that if a good coach is available from the start, the walker can be sure that he will learn good technique and won't have any inbuilt faults to eradicate. However, it also means that race walking technique takes several years to reach a really efficient level, and it is not surprising that walkers tend to have a higher average age than athletes in other events.

As in running, the basic parameters are stride length and stride frequency. When 'sprinting' the walker will be limited by a stride frequency which will not respond much to training once the skill is competent (see Chapter 17). This frequency will depend mainly on his inherited muscle quality. The main area for improvement in sprint walking will be in stride length, a factor which is of obsessive concern to every race walker! In longer races, as in long distance running, there will be a certain amount of compromise depending on stride length, stride frequency and the fatigue experienced by the athlete.

As in most other athletic events, flexibility is an asset and hip mobility especially is an important factor in stride length. This can be proved easily by noting the stride length in normal walking in which the line through the hips is generally kept at right-angles to the direction of walking. If the hip of the forward swinging leg is allowed to twist forward with the leg the stride length is increased considerably. Stride length is also maximized if the feet move along a straight line (see below).

Race walking, of course, involves a rapid leg cadence and if the arms too are to maintain their synchronous swings they have to be bent at the elbows to reduce their moments of inertia, as in running. However, more emphasis is placed on the arm and shoulder action in race walking than in running, because of the need to counterbalance the exaggerated eccentric thrust of the legs and the movements of the hips. But in addition to counterbalancing the leg action they also aid the forward drive with their swinging—the strong upward swing of both arms evokes extra forces from the ground through the driving leg.

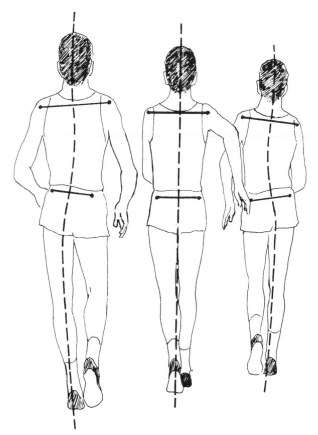

Fig. 32.2. Flexibility of hips and spine allows a smooth flow in race walking.

STYLES OF RACE WALKING

As in other athletic events there are almost as many variations of the technique as there are walkers.

Clawing Action

The leg action includes, in addition to the orthodox drive of the supporting leg once the centre of mass has passed in front of the foot, a 'clawing' action by this foot even while the centre of mass is still behind it. Force platform investigations do not show a positive horizontal drive in this phase even when the athlete is exaggerating the action—there is still a horizontal force opposing the forward motion during the time that the centre of mass is behind the vertical line through the point of application of force by the foot. However, the action does reduce the horizontal braking force during the times that the walker is accelerating generally. And since it makes for a faster movement of the leg, presumably it can increase the overall speed, though this will also raise the rate of energy consumption.

Hyperextension of the Knee

Some walkers have exceptional mobility of the knee joint and are able to exploit this by hyperextending it (extending the joint beyond the straight position of 180° to perhaps 185° or more) during the support phase. Since the judges still regard this as being 'straight at the knee through the vertical position' the walker is able to keep his centre of mass from rising as much as if he had kept his upper and lower legs at 180°. Posner states that this hyperextension, if timed correctly, can aid the 'clawing action' mentioned above.

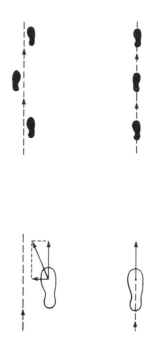

Fig. 32.3. A race walking technique in which the feet are placed on either side of a straight line, as in the left-hand diagrams, tends to produce a wasted sideways component of force. If the feet are moved down a straight line, as in the right-hand diagrams, the action is more efficient.

'Orthodox' European Style

The more usual style in Europe involves relatively little movement of the head and shoulders, with the athlete relying on good hip mobility and a strong arm action to absorb the eccentric thrust of the leg drive. The arms are usually maintained in vertical planes in the direction of the walk and the upper arm is pushed up to a horizontal position behind.

Some successful top-class walkers have used an arm action that sweeps out of the vertical planes across the abdomen, though most experts seem to agree that this is not as efficient.

Mexican Style

Although originally coached by Europeans, the Mexicans have developed a style of their own, and, as they have virtually re-written the record books for walking, their particular style is worthy of careful consideration. Instead of keeping the trunk and head in the rather rigid posture of the Europeans, the Mexicans are much more flamboyant and tend to throw the head, shoulders and trunk around much more. The impression is of a supple, relaxed and care-free movement of the whole upper body which absorbs the eccentric thrust of the legs without the hard driving of the arms practised by the Europeans.

In the Mexican style the feet move along a straight line rather than the two close parallel lines of the European style. As Hopkins explains, this tends to reduce the wasted sideways component of force, which is more apparent when the feet move along parallel lines. The stride length is also slightly longer when walking along the single straight line.

REFERENCES

HOPKINS , J.A., 'The Mexican Race Walkers', *Athletics Coach*, 12:3, 1978.
POSNER, R., Private communication.

Overleaf

Fig. 32.4. The forces evoked at the foot of a race walker, as measured on a force platform. All his body movements combine to produce the forces shown.
Braking occurs while his centre of mass (x) is behind his foot, and propulsion takes place when it is in front.

50 kg

33

COMBINED EVENTS

Multi-discipline events have been included in athletics programmes since the eighth century BC, though originally the five events for men included a run, long jump, discus throw, javelin throw and wrestling. The 10 events with which we are familiar today were practised first in Scandinavia, and the event is now developed in importance for the genuine all-rounders who may not be supreme in any one event but who can maintain a high overall standard. In the early days good sprinter—jumpers tended to be the elite, compensating for their weaker events by expertise in their stronger events. Today it is an event for the decathlon or heptathlon specialist who prepares for it and competes in the event as a whole rather than as a series of separate competitions.

The decathlete or heptathlete needs to be a balanced personality with well-rounded physical development to cope with:

1. *Decathlon* Day 1: 100 metres, long jump, shot, high jump, 400 metres.
   (Men) Day 2: 110 metres hurdles, discus, pole vault, javelin, 1,500 metres.
2. *Heptathlon* Day 1: 100 metres hurdles, shot, high jump, 200 metres.
   (Women) Day 2: Long jump, javelin, 800 metres.

DECATHLON

Day 1 in the decathlon tended to be the higher scoring day in the past because of the sprints and jumps emphasis already mentioned. It was common for the scores on Day 2 to be as much as 20 per cent less, but this has now changed.

No other event lasts for two days, so the physical and psychological demands are great. There is no let-up for the decathlete who must 'fight ten fights'—*Zehnkampf*, as the Germans say. Great concentration is required to make each event as it comes the most important matter in hand, to cut out past events (particularly if they have been disappointing) and to avoid worrying about events yet to come. There are usually only a limited number of opportunities each season to perform the decathlon so the athlete must learn how to handle his competitions well and not waste any opportunities for making a score, even if he, or she in the pentathlon, is tempted to write off certain events because of difficulty or through fatigue.

Though the decathlon is necessarily the most difficult to prepare for and compete in because of its complexity and varied demands on speed, strength and skill, it is also attractive in that it is never boring. Sam Adams of the University of California says that there are various motives for doing the decathlon but whoever chooses the multi-discipline event cannot expect to progress very quickly. Top-class decathletes and pentathletes tend to be older than the average athlete, and it takes about five years of competition before sufficient experience is gained to join the ranks of the elite.

It is interesting that over the two days active competitive participation takes up a total of approximately 8.5 minutes. Howevet, there are also 10 km of distance covered in warm-ups, 300 exercises and drills done, and the athlete's clothes are taken on and off 50 times! (Latridis)

Physique

Top decathletes are generally in the 1.87 m range in height and weigh about 87 kg, though there have been good decathletes as small as 1.74 m and 74 kg and as big as 2.05 m and 95 kg. The strength:weight ratio is very important, with strength and a certain amount of weight being needed for the throws but too much weight being a great disadvantage in the 1,500 metres. Russ Hodge says: 'You want to be as strong and as light as can be.'

Training

Planning the necessary complex training is a long-term process requiring co-operation between athlete and coach, and very individual schedules according to the strengths and weaknesses of the particular athlete. Modern training involves taking the event seriously as a primary event, rather than as secondary to other individual events.

It is important not just to work at the events that one is already good at—a wise maxim for decathlon and pentathlon is: 'Concentrate on weaknesses but do not neglect strengths'. It is important not to be intimidated by one's weak events (Gambetta). Many decathletes rather dread the 400 metres and 1,500 metres, but Jenner actually looked forward to them, which creates a tremendous psychological boost on the last event of each day when the opposition would be flagging.

Gambetta thinks that the key events in the development of a decathlete are the 100 metres, 400 metres, 110 metres hurdles and pole vault. Then he emphasizes specificity of training to balance weak events, to adapt the body through progressive overload, and to allow recovery by a hard/easy cycle of training days.

As in so many events there are three phases in the training year:

1. *Foundation phase:* October–December. Work is done on general strength and endurance.

2. *Preparation or pre-season phase:* January–April. Work is done more on speed and technique.

3. *Competition phase:* May–September. The emphasis is on sharpening, and on quality rather than quantity.

Bergman of West Germany believes that the greatest development is possible in the events of the second day, and that the top decathletes are now tending to make their second day scores as high as their first day scores.

The tendency of many decathletes is to practise the events in order of competition, but the Russians advise training on throws, then jumps, followed by running, since technique should be practised when the body is not too fatigued. The order is really technique and speed first, with strength and jumping in mid-session and endurance at the end of the workout.

Speed, strength and endurance are all important, but so is flexibility. Stewart of Canada encourages heptathletes and decathletes to do a great deal of flexibility training, partly because it is important for injury prevention and also because of the possible improvement in technique. Often in the West athletes decide to become decathletes after trying other events and perhaps finding that they are not quite top class in any one, so they start adding other events. But today, in East Germany and Russia particularly, encouragement is given to young athletes to try the whole range of events early, since it is found that the skills of co-ordination can be acquired by the 12–14 age group who adapt particularly well to training in skill acquisition. When working with youngsters, Kuptschinov builds up through running to hurdling to pole vault and then javelin throw. Kuhn of Russia thinks the hurdles is the key event of both decathlon and heptathlon. Mobility, rhythm and speed are used, which all have good carry-over to other events, and it means a good start to the heptathlon and a good beginning to the second day in the decathlon if the athlete is skilled in hurdling.

Bruce Longden, British National Coach for Combined Events, notes that the greatest difficulty is that of 'buttoning down on the specifics' for a particular athlete, taking account of physique, biomechanics, experience etc. Over a period of years he plans specific loads for specific athletes, aiming towards a specific result. The importance of coaching and planning is emphasized by Russ Hodge, who personally claims that his greatest disadvantage was that he did not have a good coach, indeed any coach, giving him advice in his early days when he needed to learn particular skills. He said that he tended to do too much training, punishing himself for hours every day with too much early morning distance running and not enough recovery spells. He is also a keen advocate of weight training to develop speed in running, with plenty of exercises for the hamstrings as well as the quadriceps.

Mental Preparation

This is well discussed by Kenny Kring of Stanford University, who describes how technically and emotionally charged the event is with its dramatic ups and downs and high energy consumption. It is vital to conserve as much energy as possible and to learn how to relax and wait between events and between jumps and vaults. Repeated, good warm-ups are necessary to get rid of soreness and stiffness, particularly on the second day, and there are the dreads of certain events to cope with. The joyous snowballing effect of doing well in a succession of events can build up, but intensity of concentration is required no matter how well one is scoring. The good multi-event athlete needs preparation that will give confidence.

An analysis of the 1976 US Olympic trialists bore out many of the points already made. They tended to be initially sprinters and jumpers who had then done the specialized work necessary for the decathlon for five or six years, training up to four hours a day. The elite also showed a balance across the 10 events—they had their best events, of course, but did not have the wide variations from event to event of the lower level performers.

HEPTATHLON

The women's heptathlon has had a more mixed history than the men's decathlon, and a variety of events have been tried out in a variety of orders at different times. It was first contested as a pentathlon in the Olympics in 1964 —very much later than the men's début, in 1912. However, in the 1920s there were competitions in the USSR and Germany using versions of triathlon and pentathlon. The 1964 programme used 80 metres hurdles, shot, high jump, long jump and 200 metres, with sprinters and jumpers naturally showing well and competitors coming mainly from specialists in other events. When the 80 metres hurdles was replaced by the 100 metres hurdles the event still suited sprinters and jumpers who showed weakness only in the shot event. In 1969 Prokop of Austria was one of the first true all-rounders who putted well, and indeed by 1977 Wilms, who was primarily a shot putter, held the world record. In 1977 the 800 metres replaced the 200 metres and there was some gain in making it a more all-round test.

As in the development of the men's multi-event, the women competitors now consider themselves to be specialists in the combined event. In Montreal the average age of the first 10 competitors was 26 years, height 1.75 m and weight 69.5 kg so again we find the slightly older and well-built athletes at the top. Time is needed for them to develop physical skills and emotional strengths.

Though the 800 metres runner tends to be smaller and lighter than the all-rounders just described, it was shown that many of the 200 metres pentathletes were able to adapt. Indeed some gained from the change, for instance Jones-Konihowski, who obtained far better points for her 800 metres performances than she could gain in the 200 metres. The 1980 Olympics was the only one to have had the 800 metres pentathlon, because in 1981 the new Heptathlon became the women's multi-event. The West Germans were particularly keen on an Octathlon consisting of 100 metres, discus, long jump and javelin on the first day and 100 metres hurdles, shot, high jump and 800 metres on the second. This was experimented with from 1971, and in 1974 it became an event in the national championships, very popular with both athletes and officials. Despite this well balanced combination of sprints, jumps, throws and endurance the IAAF decided against the Octathlon, and the following Heptathlon was agreed: 100 metres hurdles, shot, high jump, 200 metres on Day 1; and long jump, javelin and 800 metres on Day 2.

The javelin is difficult for many, as over-arm throwing does not come easily to females, but it certainly is a more all-round test than the pentathlon and we are seeing a new group of multi-talented female all-rounders emerging in the eighties.

THE SCORING TABLES

The multi-event scoring tables have caused controversy throughout the histories of the events and it is doubtful that equity will ever be achieved with the statisticians arguing in cold mathematics and the athletes and coaches tending to be too personally involved. Small improvements in some events appear to be better rewarded with greater increments in points than in other events. The 'scientific' approach to be recommended to the multi-event athlete and his or her coach is to make a careful study of the scoring tables as they relate to the athlete's present performances. Depending on the athlete's potential for improvement, the training programme can be designed to produce the greatest returns in points both in the short term and—more importantly—in the long term.

REFERENCES

All references in this chapter in:
Track and Field Quarterly Review, Vol. 79, No. 2, Summer 1979.

CONCLUSION

Is there a science of athletics after all? Is it an art to be practised rather than a science to be discovered? Though there are general principles concerning body function, learning, and response to exercise, every individual is so individual that general principles have to be modified in application to such an extent that they lose that quality of generality that made them anything resembling scientific laws. Sometimes a winning performance goes against the odds, and the efficient engineer of a racing car would despair at the unpredictable response of a human racing model!

This unknown element, this inability to predict completely accurately what the consequences of training, diet, coaching, etc., will be, is what is so intriguing. It will keep coaches, athletes, and scientists involved for ever. The excitement of the unexpected breakthrough will always be there to keep everyone interested and involved. Because athletes are made as well as born, the finding and development of talent is like the discovery of a diamond which must be fashioned carefully into the jewel with all the knowledge of the scientist and all the skill of the artist.

There is room for progress and improvement in the physical and biological sciences relating to athletics, but in the social sciences there are vast fields where it is particularly difficult to put knowledge into practice or even to find the knowledge in the first place. It is difficult to find principles that will apply outside particular situations, times and societies. A totalitarian regime may have the mechanisms to alter social customs and practice but there is no guarantee that their techniques will apply for longer than a generation or two when the historical time is right.

The science of behaviour—psychology—may be the most important area of all. Motives, personality characteristics, emotional involvement—so often these seem to be the mysterious keys to successful performance. The well-prepared body is essential but cannot do much without the well-prepared and determined mind.

The technological revolution of the past fifty years is probably the greatest revolution ever achieved by mankind. Not all people are immediately affected by it directly, just as many people are relatively untouched by advances in medicine, education or sport. But one of the outstanding elements of an 'advanced' society is its rapid acceptance of new inventions such as telephones, radios, T.V.s recorders and micro-processors. In sport we have also to become rapidly adjusted to changing standards—as Dwight Stones said of the 1976 American Olympic Trials, 'It might be necessary to break the world record even to get to the Olympics!'

If the kinds of strides that have been made over the last fifty years are repeated over the next fifty, then we will be in the realms of science fiction where the world is a new and different place because of technological and social changes. A science fiction of athletics similarly requires imagination in the athlete who must believe that fantastic performance can be a possible facet of his or her future, and the index of possibilities can be pointed out by the scientist, writer and coach. Once the incredible is accepted as normal we can progress to future levels of 'impossibility'—if the 7 foot high jump is now very ordinary, what about 8 feet? Today we seem to be living in a climate of change and extremes, sometimes even beyond our wildest dreams of old, just as their superlative performances are often beyond the dreams of the competitors, 'It was even better than I dared to hope' said Bruce Jenner after winning the 1976 Olympic gold for the decathlon.

Who are our modern heroes to be? Where is their individual challenge? Are they to be the scientists to whom we are giving such importance? The bionic man may not just be a T.V. character though the robots in science fiction are only of interest when they 'fail' or when they do not behave as programmed. We would not find science fiction writers so interesting if their stories did not depend on human personality and uncertainty. Our athletes will never be completely mechanistic or technological—that is a contradiction in terms. There is always the human factor, the ghost in the machine, the training robot who persists in being emotional, temperamental, fallible, amazing, heroic—indeed, human. Perfection is the impossible goal, or is it?

INDEX